lone

Venice &
the Veneto

"All you've got to do is decide to go
and the hardest part is over.

So go!"

TONY WHEELER, COFOUNDER – LONELY PLANET

Paula Hardy, Peter Dragicevich, Marc Di Duca

Contents

(left) **Carnevale p20**
Masqueraders party in
the streets.

(above) **Burano p148**
Visit for glass-blowing
and lace-making.

(right) **Piazza San
Marco p57** Witness
glorious architecture.

**Murano, Burano &
the Northern Islands**
p148

Cannaregio
p107

**San Polo &
Santa Croce**
p88

Dorsoduro
p71

San Marco
p48

Castello
p119

**Giudecca, Lido
& the Southern
Islands**
p136

Welcome to Venice & the Veneto

Imagine the audacity of building a city of marble palaces on a lagoon – and that was only the start.

Epic Grandeur

Never was a thoroughfare so aptly named as the Grand Canal, reflecting the glories of Venetian architecture lining its banks. At the end of Venice's signature waterway, the Palazzo Ducale and Basilica di San Marco add double exclamation points. But wait until you see what's hiding in the narrow backstreets: neighbourhood churches lined with Veroneses and priceless marbles, Tiepolo's glimpses of heaven on homeless-shelter ceilings, and a single Titian painting that mysteriously lights up an entire basilica.

Venetian Feasts

Garden islands and lagoon aquaculture yield speciality produce and seafood you won't find elsewhere – all highlighted in inventive Venetian cuisine, with tantalising traces of ancient spice routes. The city knows how to put on a royal spread, as France's King Henry III once found out when faced with 1200 dishes and 200 bonbons. Today such feasts are available in miniature at happy hour, when bars mount lavish spreads of *cicheti* (Venetian tapas). Save room and time for a proper sit-down Venetian meal, with lagoon seafood to match views at canalside bistros and toasts with Veneto's signature bubbly, *prosecco*.

An Artful Lifestyle

Pity the day trippers dropped off at San Marco with a mere three hours to take in Venice. That's about enough time for one long gasp at the show-stopper that is Piazza San Marco, but not nearly enough time to see what else Venice is hiding. Stay longer in this fairy-tale city and you'll discover the pleasures of *la bea vita* (the beautiful life) that only locals know: the wake-up call of gondoliers calling 'Ooooeeeee!', a morning *spritz* in a sunny *campi* (square), lunch in a crowded *bacaro* (bar) with friends and fuschia-pink sunsets that have sent centuries of artists mad.

Defying Convention

Eyeglasses, platform shoes and uncorseted dresses are outlandish Venetian fashions that critics sniffed would never be worn by respectable Europeans. Venetians are used to setting trends, whether it be with controversial artwork in the Punta della Dogana, racy operas at La Fenice or radical new art at the Biennale. On a smaller scale, this unconventional creative streak finds vibrant expression in the showrooms of local artisans where you can find custom-made red-carpet shoes, purses fashioned from silk-screened velvet and glass jewels brighter than semiprecious stones. In a world of cookie-cutter culture, Venice's originality still stands out.

Why I Love Venice

By Paula Hardy, Writer

My love of Venice begins with the lagoon in which it stands. Although often overlooked, this 550-sq-km shallow bowl is as great a marvel of engineering as San Marco's golden domes. Every palace and every person is reflected in its teal-coloured waters creating the mirage-like double image that lends the city its magical quality. Not only has it inspired the extraordinary physical fabric of the city and countless creative and technological inventions, but it also shapes the unconventional and creative spirit of all who reside here. Therein lie possibilities barely imagined in other cities.

For more about our writers, see p249

Top: Venice at sunset

Venice & the Veneto's
Top 10

Basilica di San Marco (p50)

1 Early risers urge you to arrive when morning sunlight bathes millions of *tesserae* (mosaic tiles) with an other-worldly glow, and jaws drop to semi-precious-stone floors. Sunset romantics lobby you to linger in Piazza San Marco until fading sunlight shatters portal mosaics into golden shards, and the Caffè Florian house band strikes up the tango. Yet no matter how you look at it, the basilica is a marvel. Two eyes may seem insufficient to absorb 800 years of architecture and 8500 sq metres of mosaics – Basilica di San Marco will stretch your sense of wonder.

◉ San Marco

Palazzo Ducale (p53)

2 Other cities have government buildings; Venice has the Palazzo Ducale, a monumental propaganda campaign. To reach the halls of power, you must pass the Scala dei Censori (Stairs of the Censors) and Sansovino's staircase lined with 24-carat gold, then wait in a Palladio-designed hall facing Tiepolo's *Venice Receiving Gifts of the Sea from Neptune*. Veronese's *Juno Bestowing her Gifts on Venice* graces the trial chambers of the Consiglio dei Dieci (Council of Ten), Venice's CIA. Upstairs is the Piombi attic-prison, where Casanova was confined in 1756 until his escape.

◉ San Marco

ATLANTIDE PHOTOTRAVEL/CORBIS/VCG/GETTY IMAGES ©

CRIS FOTO/SHUTTERSTOCK ©

Cruising Canals *(p118)*

3 Traffic never seemed so romantic as at sunset in Venice, when smooching echoes under the Ponte dei Sospiri (Bridge of Sighs) from passing gondolas. Venice's morning rush hour may lull you back to sleep with the gentle sounds of footsteps heading to the *vaporetto* (small passenger ferry) and oars slapping canal waters. Road rage is not an issue in a town with no actual roads but over 400 licensed *gondolieri*, who call 'Oooooooeeee!' around blind corners to avoid collisions. Hop on board, or try your hand at the oar with Row Venice.

Tours

Tintoretto's Masterpieces *(p90)*

4 During Venice's darkest days of the Black Death, flashes of genius appeared. Tintoretto's loaded paintbrush streaks across stormy scenes inside the Scuola Grande di San Rocco like a lightning bolt, revealing glimmers of hope in the long shadow of the plague that reduced Venice's population by a third. Angelic rescue squads save lost souls until the very last minute of the master's *Last Judgment* in Chiesa della Madonna dell'Orto – as long as they hold back that teal tidal wave, even a lowly mortal might catch a glimpse of heaven on earth.

San Polo & Santa Croce, Cannaregio

Gallerie dell'Accademia *(p73)*

5 They've been censored and stolen, raised eyebrows and inspired generosity: all the fuss over Venetian paintings becomes clear at the Accademia. The Inquisition did not appreciate Venetian versions of biblical stories – especially Veronese's *Last Supper*, a wild dinner party of drunkards, dwarves, dogs, Turks and Germans alongside apostles. But Napoleon quite enjoyed Venetian paintings, warehousing them here as booty. Wars and floods took their toll, but international donations have restored Sala dell'Albergo's crowning glory: Titian's *Presentation of the Virgin*, where a young Madonna inspires Venetian merchants to help the needy.

Dorsoduro

Opera at Teatro La Fenice (p358)

6 Before the curtain rises, the drama has already begun at La Fenice. Wraps shed in lower-tier boxes reveal jewels, while in top *loggie* (balconies), *loggione* (opera critics) predict which singers will be in good voice, and which understudies may merit promotions. Meanwhile, architecture aficionados debate whether the theatre's faithful reconstruction after its 1996 arson attack was worth €90 million. But when the overture begins, all voices hush. No one wants to miss a note of performances that could match premieres here by Stravinsky, Rossini, Prokofiev and Britten.

☆ *San Marco*

Padua's Scrovegni Chapel (p163)

7 Squint a little at Giotto's 1303–05 Cappella degli Scrovegni frescoes, and you can see the Renaissance coming. Instead of bug-eyed Byzantine saints, Giotto's biblical characters evoke people you'd recognise today: a middle-aged mother (Anne) with a miracle baby (Mary), a new father (Joseph) nodding off while watching his baby boy (Jesus), a slippery schemer (Judas) breezily air-kissing a trusting friend (Jesus). Giotto captures human nature in all its flawed and complex beauty, making a detour to elegant, erudite Padua well worth the effort.

◉ *Day Trips from Venice*

La Biennale di Venezia (p39)

8 When Venice dared the world to show off its modern masterpieces, delegations from Australia to Venezuela accepted the challenge – who turns down an invitation to Venice? Today La Biennale di Venezia is the world's most prestigious creative showcase, featuring art (in odd-numbered years) and architecture (in even-numbered years), and organising the Venice International Film Festival and performing-arts extravaganzas annually. Friendly competition among nationals is obvious in the Giardini's pavilions, which showcase architectural sensibilities ranging from magical thinking (Austro-Hungary) to repurposed industrial cool (Korea). LEFT: "COMMON PLACES, 2017, MARTIN CORDIANO".

⭐ *Entertainment*

Venetian Artisans (p41)

9 In Venice, you're not just in good hands – you're in highly skilled ones. As has been done for centuries, artisans here ply esoteric trades, those that don't involve a computer mouse, such as glass-blowing, paper-marbling and oarlock-carving. Yet while other craft traditions have fossilised into relics of bygone eras, Venetian artisans have kept their creations current. A modern Murano-glass chandelier morphs into an intergalactic octopus, marbled paper turns into must-have handbags, and oarlocks custom-made for rock-and-roll legends are mantelpiece sculptures that upstage any marble bust.

🛍 *Shopping*

Veneto Wines (p171)

10 Toast your arrival in Venice with sprightly *prosecco,* but don't stop there: the Veneto is overflowing with oenological delights. Head north to Valdobbiadene and Conegliano to explore the very home of Venice's best-loved sparkling white, and pit-stop in Bassano del Grappa for a mouthful of fiery grappa. Save space in the cellar for structured whites in Soave, and fall in love with brooding Amarones and rebel Valpolicellas northwest of Verona. For something completely different, sniff, swill and sip at Verona's ViniVeri, Italy's natural-process wine showcase.

🍷 *Drinking & Nightlife*

What's New

Doge's Apartments

New artistic itineraries show off the sumptuously restored Doge's apartments to their best. There's no better view of Piazza San Marco than the one from the Doge's own loggia. (p53)

Scala Contarini del Bovolo

Like an elaborate snail-shell twirling up the exterior of the Contarini Bovolo palace this recently restored grand Gothic staircase peeks in a charming turret with views of San Marco's golden domes. (p59)

Venice Glass Week

For thousands of years Murano's glass masters have wowed the world with their alchemy. Now a new week-long festival aims to showcase their best work and offer visitors an inside peek into previously off-limit furnaces. (p21)

JW Marriott Spa

Occupying the pretty private island of Isola delle Rose, JW Marriott's new Venetian pad has a stunning rooftop spa and pool that's worth a detour. (p195)

Contemporary Gastronomy

Breaking the mould of formal Venetian dining are trailblazing contemporary chefs Enrico Bartolini at Ristorante Glam (p99) and Matteo Tagliapietra at Local (p131). Expect stars to follow.

Casa Burano

Head off the beaten track and claim your own candy-coloured cottage on the fishermen's island of Burano. There are five to choose from and all showcase the work of local artisans. (p196)

Luxury Vintage Shopping

With residents including aristocrats and celebrities, where better to stock up on top-quality vintage clothes than this new luxury vintage outlet from L'Armadio di Coco. (p67)

Venice Halldis Apartments

Out of the shell of Venice's 1930s power station, Halldis has fashioned a selection of well-priced one- to three-bedroom contemporary apartments with views over the Scalzi convent garden. (p192)

Venice Music Gourmet

'If music be the food of love, play on', Duke Orsino opined in *Twelfth Night*. At these well-catered musical evenings you won't have to survive on the music alone. (p134)

Fondaco dei Tedeschi

Venice's most impressive luxury department store now inhabits this 16th-century palace-cum-warehouse converted by Rem Koolhaas' architectural practice OMA. Atop is a spectacular viewing terrace. (p69)

Lagunalonga

Experience the lagoon aboard the luxurious *Linssen yacht Elvira*. With three cabins and multi-week itineraries with knowledgeable captain Francesco you'll see things few others do. (p25)

For more recommendations and reviews, see **lonelyplanet. com/venice**

Need to Know

For more information, see Survival Guide (p237)

Currency
Euro (€)

Language
Italian and Venetian (dialect)

Visas
Not required for EU citizens. Nationals of Australia, Brazil, Canada, Japan, New Zealand and the USA do not need visas for visits of up to 90 days.

Money
ATMs are widely available and credit cards accepted at most hotels, B&Bs and shops. To change money you'll need to present your ID.

Mobile Phones
GSM and tri-band phones can be used in Italy with a local SIM card.

Time
Central European Time (GMT/ UTC plus one hour)

Tourist Information
Vènezia Unica (☑041 24 24; www.veneziaunica.it) runs all tourist information services and offices in Venice. It provides information on sights, itineraries, day trips, transport, special events, shows and temporary exhibitions. Discount passes can be prebooked on its website.

Daily Costs

Budget: Less than €120
➡ Dorm bed: €35–60
➡ Basilica di San Marco: free
➡ *Cicheti* (Venetian tapas) at All'Arco: €5–15
➡ Chorus Pass: €12
➡ *Spritz*: €2.50–4

Midrange: €120–250
➡ B&B: €70–180
➡ Civic Museum Pass: €24
➡ Happy hour in Piazza San Marco: €9–15
➡ Interpreti Veneziani ticket: €27
➡ Dinner at Osteria La Zucca: €35–40

Top End: More than €250
➡ Boutique hotel: €200-plus
➡ Gondola ride: €80
➡ Palazzo Grassi & Punta della Dogana ticket: €18
➡ Dinner at Antiche Carampane: €50–60
➡ La Fenice theatre ticket: from €45

Advance Planning

Two months before Book accommodation for high season and tickets to La Fenice operas, Venice International Film Festival premieres and Biennale openings.

Three weeks before Check special-event calendars at www.unospitedivenezia.it and www.veneziadavivere.com, and reserve boat trips.

One week before Make restaurant reservations for a big night out; skip the queues by booking tickets to major attractions, exhibitions and events online at www.veneziaunica.it.

Useful Websites

Lonely Planet (www.lonely planet.com/venice) Expert travel advice.

Venice Comune (www.comune. venezia.it) City of Venice official site with essential info, including high-water alerts.

Vènezia Unica (www.venezia unica.it) The main tourism portal with information on museums, churches and special events, as well as online ticket-ing for public transport and tourist cards

Venezia da Vivere (www.venezia davivere.com) Music perfor-mances, art openings, nightlife and child-friendly events.

WHEN TO GO

Spring is damp but lovely indoors. Summer is busy: hot and crowded. Autumn offers warm days and lower rates. Winter's chilly but with sociable nights.

Venice

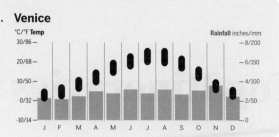

Arriving in Venice

Marco Polo Airport Water shuttles (€15) and water taxis (from €110, or from €25 per person for shared taxis) depart from the airport ferry dock. Buses (one-way €8) run every 30 minutes (5.20am to 12.50am) to Piazzale Roma. A taxi costs €50.

Treviso Airport Buses run to Piazzale Roma (one-way €12, one hour) or Tronchetto (for the monorail to Piazzale Roma). Buses run to Treviso train station for trains to Santa Lucia station. Taxis cost €90.

Piazzale Roma (car parks and bus station) *Vaporetti* (small passenger ferries) to city destinations depart Piazzale Roma docks.

Venezia Santa Lucia train station *Vaporetti* depart from Ferrovia (Station) docks.

Venezia Mestre train station Transfer by train to Venezia Santa Lucia.

Venezia Terminal Passeggeri Docking cruise liners usually shuttle passengers into Venice; otherwise taxis and *vaporetti* leave from the waterfront.

For much more on **arrival** see p238

Getting Around

➡ **Vaporetto** These small passenger ferries are Venice's main public transport. Single rides cost €7.50; for frequent use, get a timed pass for unlimited travel within a set period (1/2/3/7-day passes cost €20/30/40/60). Tickets and passes are available dockside from ACTV ticket booths and ticket vending machines, or from tobacconists.

➡ **Gondola** Daytime rates run to €80 for 40 minutes (six passengers maximum) or €100 for 35 minutes from 7pm to 8am, not including songs (negotiated separately) or tips.

➡ **Traghetto** Locals use this daytime public gondola service (€2) to cross the Grand Canal between bridges.

➡ **Water taxi** Sleek teak boats offer taxi services for €15 plus €2 per minute, plus €5 for pre-booked services and extra for night-time, luggage and large groups. Ensure the meter is working when boarding.

For much more on **getting around** see p241

Sleeping

With many Venetians opening their homes to visitors, you can become a local overnight here. Venice was once known for charmingly decrepit hotels where English poets quietly expired, but new design-literate boutique hotels are spiffing up historic palaces. In peak seasons quality hotels fill up fast. In summer, many people decamp to the Lido where prices are more reasonable and swimming is an option at the end of hot days in the Rialto.

Useful Websites

➡ **Luxrest Venice** (www.luxrest-venice.com) Curated selection of apartments.

➡ **Lonely Planet** (www.lonelyplanet.com/italy/venice/hotels) Expert author reviews, user feedback, booking engine.

➡ **Venice Prestige** (www.veniceprestige.com) The crème de la crème of Venetian apartments to rent in the best locations in town.

➡ **Views on Venice** (www.viewsonvenice.com) Apartments picked for their personality, character and view, of course.

For much more on **sleeping** see p184

Top Itineraries

Day One

San Marco (p48)

 Begin your day in prison on the Secret Itineraries tour of the **Palazzo Ducale**, then break for espresso at the baroque counter of **Grancaffè Quadri** before the Byzantine blitz of golden mosaics inside **Basilica di San Marco**. Browse boutique-lined backstreets to **Museo Fortuny**, the palace fashion house whose goddess-style gowns freed women from corsets.

> **Lunch** Opt for quality surf-and-turf bistro fare at Ai Mercanti (p64).

Dorsoduro (p71)

Pause atop wooden **Ponte dell'Accademia** for **Grand Canal** photo ops, then surrender to timeless drama that no camera can convey inside **Gallerie dell'Accademia**. Wander past **Squero di San Trovaso** to glimpse gondolas under construction, then bask in the reflected glory of Palladio's **Il Redentore** along waterfront **Zattere**. Stop at tiny **Chiesa di San Sebastiano**, packed with Veroneses, then hop between artisan boutiques along Calle Lunga San Barnaba before '*spritz* o'clock' (cocktail hour) in **Campo Santa Margherita**.

> **Dinner** Swoon over lagoon seafood at Enoteca Ai Artisti (p81).

Dorsoduro (p71)

Leap back into the 1700s at nearby **Scuola Grande dei Carmini**, the evocative setting for costumed classical concerts by **Musica in Maschera**. Alternatively, end the night on a saxy note at modern veteran **Venice Jazz Club**.

Day Two

San Polo & Santa Croce (p88)

 Kick off day two with a crash course in lagoon delicacies at the produce-packed **Rialto Market**, side-stepping it to **Drogheria Mascari** for gourmet pantry fillers and regional wines, and to **All'Arco** for a cheeky morning *prosecco*. Boutiques and artisan studios punctuate your way to Campo San Rocco, home to Gothic show-off **I Frari** and its sunny Titian altarpiece. Once admired, slip into **Scuola Grande di San Rocco** for prime-time-drama Tintorettos.

> **Lunch** Market-fresh bites and impeccable wines at vibrant Estro (p79).

Dorsoduro (p71)

Explore the modern art that caused uproars and defined the 20th century at the **Peggy Guggenheim Collection**, and contrast it with works that push contemporary buttons at **Punta della Dogana**. Duck into Baldassare Longhena's domed **Basilica di Santa Maria della Salute** for blushing Titians and legendary curative powers, then cross the **Grand Canal** on Venice's only wooden bridge, Ponte dell'Accademia.

> **Dinner** Superlative Venetian cuisine at Riviera (p80).

San Marco (p48)

 The hottest ticket in town during opera season is at **La Fenice**, but classical-music fans shouldn't miss Vivaldi played with contemporary verve by **Interpreti Veneziani**.

Day Three

Castello (p119)

 Stroll **Riva degli Schiavoni** for views across the lagoon to Palladio's **San Giorgio Maggiore**. See how Carpaccio's sprightly saints light up a room at **Scuola di San Giorgio degli Schiavoni**, then seek out Castello's hidden wonder: **Chiesa di San Francesco della Vigna**. Get stared down by statues atop **Ospedaletto** on your way to Gothic **Zanipolo**, home to 25 marble doges.

> ✗ **Lunch** Graze on homemade pasta in the *campo* outside Didovich (p131).

Cannaregio (p107)

 Dip into pretty, Renaissance **Chiesa Dalmata di Santa Maria dei Miracoli**, a polychrome marble miracle made from Basilica di San Marco's leftovers, before wandering serene *fondamente* (canal banks) past Moorish statues ringing **Campo dei Mori** to reach **Chiesa della Madonna dell'Orto**, the Gothic church Tintoretto pimped with masterpieces. Then tour the Ghetto's **synagogues** until Venice's happiest hours beckon across the bridge at **Timon**.

> ✗ **Dinner** Inventive Venetian cuisine beside the canal at Osteria da Rioba (p114).

Cannaregio (p107)

☾ Take a romantic **gondola** ride through Cannaregio's long canals, seemingly purpose-built to maximise moonlight.

Day Four

Murano, Burano & the Northern Islands (p148)

 Make your lagoon getaway on a *vaporetto* (small passenger ferry) bound for green-and-gold **Torcello** and technicolour **Burano**. Follow the sheep trail to Torcello's Byzantine **Basilica di Santa Maria Assunta**, where the apse's golden Madonna calmly stares down the blue devils opposite. Catch the boat back to Burano to admire extreme home-design colour schemes and handmade lace at **Museo del Merletto**.

> ✗ **Lunch** Sunny Mazzorbo vineyards and inspired cuisine at Venissa (p155).

Murano, Burano & the Northern Islands; Giudecca, Lido & the Southern Islands (p148)

☼ Take in the fiery passions of glass artisans at Murano's legendary *fornaci* (furnaces), and see their finest moments showcased at the fabulously renovated **Museo del Vetro** (Glass Museum). After Murano showrooms close, hop the *vaporetto* to **Giudecca** for some spa-loving at the **Palladio Spa** and unbeatable views of San Marco glittering across glassy waters.

> ✗ **Dinner** Wine and dine with artists and celebrities at Trattoria Altanella (p142).

San Marco (p48)

☾ Celebrate your triumphant tour of the lagoon with a *prosecco* toast and tango across Piazza San Marco at time-warped **Caffè Florian**; repeat these last steps as necessary.

If You Like...

Hidden Gems

Chiesa di San Francesco della Vigna All-star Venetian art showcase and Palladio's first commission. (p126)

Chiesa di Santa Maria dei Miracoli The little neighbourhood church with big Renaissance ideas and priceless marble. (p111)

Basilica di Santa Maria Assunta Lambs bleat encouragement as you traverse the overgrown island of Torcello towards golden glory in apse mosaics. (p150)

Ghetto synagogues Climb to rooftop synagogues on tours run by Museo Ebraico. (p109)

Scala Contarini del Bovolo A secret spiral staircase in an ancient courtyard sets the scene for a clandestine smooch. (p59)

Boats

Arsenale Venice's legendary shipyards built a warship in a day on the world's first assembly line. (p121)

Squero di San Trovaso Watch gondolas being shaped by hand and custom-sized to match the weight and height of the gondolier. (p82)

Le Fórcole di Saverio Pastor Take home Venice's most memorable souvenir: a sculptural walnut oarlock. (p83)

Gilberto Penzo Scale-model gondolas for your bathtub and build-your-own-boat kits from a master artisan. (p105)

Row Venice Learn to row across lagoon waters standing like a gondolier. (p118)

MARCO SECCHI/GETTY IMAGES ©

Frittole, Pasticceria Tonolo (p78)

Backstreet Bars

All'Arco Lip-smacking *cicheti* (Venetians tapas) invented daily with Rialto Market's freshest finds, plus perfect wine pairings – all for the price of a pizza. (p96)

Vino Vero Venice's only *bacaro* (hole-in-the-wall bar) dedicated to biodynamic wines paired with gourmet bar bites. (p115)

El Sbarlefo A pocket-sized bar with tip-top *cicheti*, live weekend music gigs and a great list of spirits and regional wine. (p81)

Cantina Aziende Agricole A tried-and-tested *bacaro* serving well-priced *ombre* (half-glasses of wine) and generously heaped *cicheti*. (p113)

Trattoria e Bacaro Da Fiore Affordable wines and authentic Venetian snacks in the heart of pricey San Marco. (p65)

Fashion

Museo Fortuny Glimpse inside the palatial, radical fashion house that freed women from corsets and innovated bohemian chic. (p58)

Palazzo Mocenigo Find fashion inspiration in a palace packed with Venetian glamour, from bustles and knee breeches to dashing waistcoats. (p94)

Pied à Terre Stock up on candy-coloured velvet and damask gondolier slippers fit for a doge. (p102)

Bottega d'Arte Giuliana Longo Dive into this historic milliner for handcrafted pieces, from Louise Brooks cloches to authentic gondolier hats. (p68)

Declare Bold, contemporary leather bags and accessories from a young-gun duo. (p105)

Sweet Treats

VizioVirtù From edible plague-doctor masks to *vino*-infused pralines, this artisan chocolate maker is terrific-calorific. (p135)

Suso Creamy seasonal gelato, homemade cones and addictive pistachio cream make Suso the best gelateria in town. (p64)

Pasticceria Da Bonifacio Almond *curasan* (croissants), *zaletti* (cornmeal biscuits) and other Venetian treats rich enough to satisfy a doge. (p130)

Panificio Volpe Giovanni A kosher bakery peddling heavenly pastries with the rabbi's blessing. (p113)

Pasticceria Tonolo Flakey apple strudel and mini-profiteroles bursting with hazelnut-chocolate mousse provide energy to take on Titian at I Frari. (p78)

Local Hang-Outs

Lido Beaches When temperatures nudge upwards of 29°C, Venice races to the Lido-bound *vaporetto* (small passenger ferry) to claim sandy beachfront. (p143)

Campo San Giacomo dell'Orio bars Kids tear through the *campo* (square), while parents watch through the bottom of glasses of natural-process *prosecco*. (p99)

Rialto Market Whet your appetite as grandmothers and Michelin chefs drive hard bargains with witty grocers. (p93)

For more top Venice spots, see the following:
→ Eating (p27)
→ Drinking & Nightlife (p33)
→ Entertainment (p37)
→ Shopping (p41)

PLAN YOUR TRIP IF YOU LIKE...

Via Garibaldi Venetian workers heading home always make time for one last *spritz* (prosecco cocktail) in Via Garibaldi bars. (p133)

Murano Linger after the day trippers disperse for soothing glasses of Lugana and Venice's best pizza. (p154)

Curiosities

Museo del Manicomio 'Museum of Madness' is as creepy as it sounds, featuring 'cures' that are happily no longer in use on the island of San Servolo. (p141)

Museo di Storia Naturale di Venezia Dinosaurs, two-headed calves, monstrous Japanese spider crabs and other bizarre scientific specimens brought home by intrepid Venetian explorers – all inside a Turkish fortress. (p95)

Museo d'Arte Orientale The attic of Ca' Pesaro is lined with Japanese samurai gear, thanks to an Italian prince's extravagant 1887–89 Asian shopping binge. (p93)

Fondazione Vedova The future of art galleries? Robots designed by Renzo Piano display Emilio Vedova's abstract canvases, then whisk them back into storage. (p78)

Month by Month

Easter. **Sunny skies and cold nights mean you'll need to pack for every eventuality.**

◉ Arte Laguna Prize

Aimed at promoting contemporary art, this increasingly prestigious two-week art competition (p122) showcases over a hundred large-scale international works in the restored warehouses of the Arsenale.

February

Snow occasionally falls in Venice. Velvet costumes and wine fountains warm February nights, when revellers party like it's 1699 at masked balls.

✶ Carnevale

Masqueraders party in the streets for just over two weeks preceding Shrove Tuesday. Tickets to nightly balls run up to about €800, but there's also many less expensive diversions at Carnevale (www.carnevale.venezia.it).

March

A blissfully quiet period between Carnevale and

April

The winning combination of optimal walking weather and reasonable room rates lasts until Easter.

🍷 Vinitaly

Good spirits abound at Italy's premier expo of wine and spirits (www.vinitaly.com), drawing more than 155,000 visitors to Verona's VeronaFiere pavilions. The four-day expo starts soberly, with expert-guided tastings of rare vintages and Slow Food and wine pairings – but by the final afternoon it's a proper bacchanal.

🏃 Su e Zo Per I Ponti

'Up and Down the Bridges' is a 12km non-competitive

race through Venice (www.suezo.it), with 10,000 to 15,000 participants crossing 43 bridges to raise funds for charity.

✶ Festa di San Marco

Join the celebration of Venice's patron saint on 25 April, when Venetian men carry a *bocolo* (rosebud) in processions through Piazza San Marco, then bestow them on the women they love.

May

As summer edges closer, it's time for headline-grabbing contemporary art.

◉ Biennale di Venezia (Venice Biennale)

Running between May and November, the Biennale (p39) is Venice's largest event, showcasing contemporary art in odd years and architecture in even years. Alongside it there are a host of avant-garde dance, theatre and musical performances.

✶ Festa della Sensa

If Venice loves the sea so much, why don't they get married? Consider it done. Vows have been professed annually since AD 1000 in the Sposalito del Mar (Wedding to the Sea), with celebrations including regattas, outdoor markets and Mass on the Lido. The event takes place on the Feast of the Ascension.

🏃 Vogalonga

A show of endurance, this 32km 'long row' (www. vogalonga.com) starts with over 1500 boats in front of the Palazzo Ducale, loops past Burano and Murano, and ends with cheers at Punta della Dogana. Held in May or June.

July

Fireworks over Giudecca and occasional lightning illuminate balmy summer nights on the lagoon, and performances by jazz greats end sunny days.

☆ Verona's Opera Festival

On balmy summer nights, when 14,000 music lovers fill Verona's Roman Arena for Europe's largest opera festival, which runs to early September.

🎎 Festa del Redentore

Walk on water across the Giudecca Canal to Il Redentore via a bobbing pontoon bridge during this celebration on the third Saturday and Sunday in July. Join the floating picnic along the Zattere, and don't miss the fireworks.

☆ Venice Jazz Festival

International legends bring down the house at La Fenice, while crowd-favourite acts play venues as diverse as the Peggy Guggenheim

Collection and Punta della Dogana. Check the calendar for shows in Vicenza, Verona, Treviso and Bassano del Grappa year-round (www.venetojazz.com).

September

Movie stars bask in flattering autumnal light along Venice Film Festival red carpets and regattas make the most of optimal weather on the lagoon.

☆ Venice International Film Festival

The only thing hotter than Lido beaches this time of year is the red carpet at this star-studded event (www.labiennale.org), running for 11 days from late August or early September.

◉ Venice Glass Week

A week-long festival (www. theveniceglassweek.com) celebrating over a thousand years of alchemy and artisanship with special exhibitions, workshops and seminars. Guided tours at usually off-limits Murano furnaces are a highlight.

🎎 Regata Storica

Never mind who's winning, check out the gear: Regata Storica (www.regatastoricavenezia.it) sees 16th-century costumes and eight-oared gondolas re-enact the Venice arrival of the Queen of Cyprus. A floating parade is followed by four races, where kids and adult rowers compete.

🎎 Riviera Fiorita

Relive the glory days of 1627 along the Brenta river with a flotilla of antique boats, baroque costume parades

at Villa Widmann Rezzoni-co Foscari and Villa Pisani Nazionale, and historically correct country fairs. It's usually held the second Sunday in September.

October

High season ends, festival crowds disperse and hotel rates come back down to earth.

🎎 Festa del Mosto

A genuine country fair on 'garden isle' Sant'Erasmo (www.veneziaunica.it), held on the first Sunday in October. The wine-grape harvest is celebrated with a parade, farmers market, gourmet food stalls, live music and free-flowing *vino*.

🏃 Venice Marathon

On the fourth Sunday in October, 8000 runners work up a sweat over 42km of spectacular scenery, dashing along the Brenta river before heading into Venice and crossing the Grand Canal (www.venicemarathon.it).

November

Venice gives thanks for its miraculous survival before kicking off another year of revelry on 1 January.

🎎 Festa della Madonna della Salute

If you'd survived plague and Austrian invasion, you'd throw a party (http://events. veneziaunica.it) too. Every 21 November since the 17th century, Venetians have crossed a pontoon bridge across the Grand Canal to light a candle in thanks at Santa Maria della Salute and splurge on sweets.

With Kids

Adults think Venice is for them; kids know better. This is where fairy tales come to life, prisoners escape through the roof of a palace, Murano glass-blowers breathe life into pocket-sized sea dragons, and spellbound Pescaria fish balance on their tails.

Attractions

Make an early-morning run down the Grand Canal for cheeky hot chocolates at Caffè Florian (p65); the cafe's fairy-tale interiors are plucked straight out of a giant storybook. Slip into Palazzo Mocenigo (p94) to explore the Cinderella fashions of the past, then roam the secret attic-prisons of the Palazzo Ducale (p53). View giant samurai swords at the Museo d'Arte Orientale in Ca' Pesaro (p93), or the massive sea monsters and dinosaurs at the Museo di Storia Naturale (p95). Grab your sailor hat and shout out 'Ship Ahoy!' at the Museo Storico Navale (p130), jam-packed enough cannons to make any pirate nervous.

Tours for Families

Friend in Venice

History and culture dished up by your **Friend in Venice** (☎338 919 6695; www. friendinvenice.com; 2-/4-hr tours €120/200),

Nadia, with engaging anecdotes and quotidian details perfect for kids aged seven and up.

Monica Cesarato

Ghost tours (www.monicacesarato.com; tours €35) packed with tales of grisly murders, plague, drownings and beheadings are delivered with Monica's mesmerising Marco Polo storytelling skills, and will hook kids aged seven to 14.

Context Travel

Scholarly tours for the curious minded, Context Travel (p26) will have you lion hunting round town, investigating Venetian life and exploring the secrets and science of the lagoon with a marine biologist. For kids aged five to 12, plus separate tours for teens.

Outdoor Activities

Beaches & Picnics

Lido beaches and lagoon picnics on Torcello, Mazzorbo and Le Vignole give the whole family some reinvigorating downtime.

Boating, Kayaking & Surfing

Glide across teal-blue waters to desert islands with Terra e Acqua (p25); kayak down canals and across the open lagoon with Venice Kayak (p157); or hit the Lido beaches at Surf Club Venezia (p118).

Photography Walks

Teens will love Venice Photo Tour (p67) with Marco Secchi, especially when his professional tips make their Instagram shots the envy of all their social media friends and followers.

Island Biking

Team up on tandem bikes for leisurely Lido itineraries, or strike out on two-wheeled nature excursions on the garden island of Le Vignole.

Hands-On Learning

Rowing & Sailing

Kids tall and strong enough to hold an oar can learn to row like *gondolieri* do with Row Venice (p118). Alternatively, sign up for a week of lagoon sailing with Vento di Venezia (p154), with courses for budding sailors aged seven to 13 as well as for older teenagers.

Arts & Crafts

Kids inspired by watching Venetian artists and artisans at work can make their own Carnevale masks at Ca' Macana (p83), and even build their own gondolas with scale-model kits from Gilberto Penzo (p105). Ideal for kids aged seven and up.

Pasta Making

Spend the morning eyeing up sci-fi-like lagoon creatures at the Rialto Market (p93), then head to the Acquolina Cooking School (p145) to learn the art of making pasta and, more importantly, tiramisu. Suitable for teens.

Learning the Lingo

Ordering gelato is an essential skill, so give your kids a head start with a fun, engaging morning language session at the Venice Italian School (p104). For kids aged five and up.

Food

When feet and spirits begin to drag, there's pizza and pasta galore to pick them back up. For an impromptu tea party, settle in with freshly baked brownies and other sweet treats at Rosa Salva (p133) and La Serra dei Giardini (p124). Unless your kids are super adventurous, navigating *cicheti* (Venetian tapas) may be hard. The best compromise is to opt for restaurants that serve full menus as well as *cicheti*. The Lido is the land of pizza lovers and ice-cream shops. Other popular take-away options good for a cheap, quick feed include Antico Forno (p97), Bar alla Toletta (p79), Cip Ciap (p131), Didovich (p131) and Osteria al Duomo (p154). The last of these has a lovely outdoor dining area. That done, challenge your budding gastronomes to try fig and walnut ice-cream at Gelato di Natura (p96).

Given the expense of eating out, many families find that opting for a self-catering apartment is a life-saver. Not only does it offer the flexibility of having your own

kitchen, but the experience of shopping at the Rialto or the city's floating produce barges is a memorable cultural experience. Views on Venice (p189) have a good selection of family-friendly apartments to choose from.

Kid Hang-Outs

Campo San Giacomo dell'Orio

Marathon games of tag in this *campo* (square; p113) probably started around the time its namesake medieval church was built. These days the square is dotted with bar tables where parents can keep an eye on kids, *prosecco* in hand.

Giardini Pubblici & Parco delle Rimembranze

Parents are wowed by the sweeping lagoon views and backdrop of Biennale pavilions, but kids know they've found paradise when they spot the swings, slides and sandlots of Venice's best park playgrounds (p124).

The Lido

The breezy summer vibe and bike-loving culture of the Lido (p141) is a winner with kids wanting to retreat from the stony Rialto to play ball on the beach and pedal madly down the *lungomare* (seafront promenade).

For Free

Despite its centuries-old reputation as a playground for Europe's elite, some of Venice's finest moments are freebies, from glittering glimpses of heaven in Basilica di San Marco to soothing vespers at the healing Basilica di Santa Maria della Salute.

Historical Sites

Some of the most pivotal sites in Venetian history have free entry: the Rialto Market (p93), where an empire sprang up around fishmongers; Basilica di Santa Maria della Salute (p76), the domed church built as thanks for Venice's salvation from plague; and Basilica di San Marco (p50), the apotheosis of Venice's millennium of brilliant self-invention. The Basilica di Santa Maria della Salute also offers free afternoon organ vespers.

Arts & Architecture

While entry to the main art and architecture Biennale shows and Venice Film Festival premieres isn't free, many citywide dance, music, cinema and ancillary arts programs are. Art lovers will appreciate the superb (and often free) shows at Palazzo Franchetti (p59). Commercial art galleries and Murano glass showrooms are yours to enjoy at no cost, and state-run museums such as the Gallerie dell'Accademia (p73) and Ca' d'Oro (p111) are gratis on the first Sunday of the month. Then there is Venice's spectacular architecture. Take in Grand Canal *palazzi* (mansions) for the price of a *vaporetto* (small passenger ferry) ticket, or discover hidden gems like the Scala Contarini del Bovolo on a San Marco walking tour (p62).

Island Getaways

A timed *vaporetto* ticket lets you do laps of the lagoon without paying extra. The Lido (p141) offers six free-access beaches, a miniature version of Venice at Malamocco, a superb Tuesday produce market (p143) and free summer concerts. Giudecca comes with mesmerising views, galleries, a 14th-century church and the Fortuny showroom (p144). Visit the haunting cemetery isle of San Michele (p151) on your way to Murano, where you can glimpse glass-makers at work and spot dragon's bones among the Byzantine mosaics of San Donato (p151). Take a photography expedition to colourful Burano and while you're there, spot masterpieces inside Chiesa di San Martino (p152). For welcome stretches of green, hop off at Torcello, Mazzorbo, Sant'Erasmo and Le Vignole.

Discount Passes

Access some of Venice's finest masterpieces in 16 churches with a Chorus Pass (p244). It costs €12 (for a total saving of €35), and includes such spectacular sights as I Frari, Chiesa di Santa Maria dei Miracoli, Chiesa di San Sebastiano and Chiesa della Madonna dell'Orto.

For €20 the San Marco Pack (p244) covers the Palazzo Ducale, Museo Correr, Museo Archeologico Nazionale and Biblioteca Nazionale Marciana. Or get even more history for your money: for €4 extra, buy the Civic Museum Pass (p244), which grants access to an extra seven museums.

Try the cheap thrill of standing on the *traghetto* (public gondola) as you cross the Grand Canal (€2 per ride). Or ride the length of the Grand Canal on *vaporetto* 1 in the early morning for a spectacular architectural tour for the price of a ferry ticket (€7.50).

Tours

To get to know Venice from the inside out, first you have to see the lagoon city as Venetians have for a millennium – by water – then dive into the calli (lanes) and ascend secret staircases for glimpses of Venetian life behind the scenes and above the fray.

Gondolas

Tours on Water

The following outings offer maritime adventures down canals and out on the lagoon. Reserve ahead, bring sunscreen and check weather forecasts, as trips are subject to climatic conditions.

Rowing

Find your footing on the lagoon as Olympic-trained rowing coach Jane Caporal and her team of rowers at Row Venice (p118) show you how to propel a handcrafted Venetian *batellina coda di gambero* (shrimp-tailed boat) standing up. The outfit also offers night lessons and a combined rowing and *cicheti* (Venetian tapas) bar-hop.

Kayaking & Paddling

Venice Kayak (p157) offers a highly unique way to experience La Serenissima's waterways and quieter islands. Group and private tours are offered, including half- and full-days. Swimming skills and some prior paddling experience is required. Beginners are able to join a more experienced paddler in a two-person kayak.

Also open to confident paddlers over the age of 14 are stand-up paddleboard tours with art historian and paddler Eliana Argine of SUP in Venice (p118). The two-hour tour weaves through the quieter canals of Castello and Cannaregio and out on the lagoon.

Sailing

Eolo Cruises (www.cruisingvenice.com; per person €350-450 for 4-6 people) sails the lagoon on a double-masted 1946 fishing *bragozzo* (flat-bottomed fishing boat) for one- to eight-day trips (€350 to €450 per person for four to six people), including on-board cooking workshops.

Boating

Ecofriendly Terra e Acqua (☏347 4205004; www.veneziainbarca.it; day trips from €400) offers wild rides to the outer edges of the lagoon. Itineraries can cover abandoned plague-quarantine islands, fishing and birdwatching hot spots, and the islands Burano and Torcello. Lunch is served on board its motorised *bragozzo* or at a local trattoria.

GOZZOLI/SHUTTERSTOCK ©

Lagunalonga (☑380 305 30 78; www.lagunalonga.com; 6-person cruises from €2430; ☉mid-Mar-Oct) explores hidden corners of the lagoon with raconteur, documentary maker and all-round lagoon expert Francesco Calzolaio as host. Itineraries range from leisurely single day cruises to seven-day adventures aboard its luxurious three-double-bedroom Linssen yacht.

Tours on Land

Tours of Major Sights

Many major sights offer guided tours, especially the 10 civic museums (www.visitmuve.it), which include the Palazzo Ducale, Museo Correr, Ca' Rezzonico, Ca' Pesaro, Museo del Vetro, Museo del Merletto, Palazzo Mocenigo, Palazzo Fortuny, Casa di Carlo Goldoni and Museo di Storia Naturale di Venezia. The cost is €100 for groups between four and 25 people and they need to be booked in advance online.

The only way to visit the Torre dell'Orologio (p57), Venice's clock tower, and the Fondazione Giorgio Cini (p139) is by pre-arranged tour. Between September and October free tours of the Basilica di San Marco (p50) are offered by the diocese every Saturday morning at 11.30am. Alternatively, **Walks of Italy** (☑069 480 4888; www.walksofitaly.com/venice-tours; tours per person €56-137) offer excellent tours of the basilica, including an after-hours evening tour (from €77). Expert guided tours (€143) of La Fenice (p37) are also possible for groups of up to 11 people.

Tourist offices can set you up with authorised tour guides and can book various tours through accredited providers.

Walking Tours

Venicescapes (☑041 850 57 42; www.venicescapes.org; 4-6hr tour incl book 2 adults US$280-310, additional adult US$60, under 18yr US$30), a nonprofit historical society, runs intriguing walking tours with themes such as 'A City of Nations', exploring multiethnic Venice through the ages. Proceeds support ongoing Venetian historical research.

Walks of Italy offers a select number of top-quality tours of the Palazzo Ducale,

Basilica di San Marco and the Rialto Market. Likewise, **Walks Inside Venice** (☑041 524 17 06; www.walksinsidevenice.com; 3-4hr tours €270-400, lagoon tour €780; 👪) has a spirited team that helps you explore the city's major monuments and backstreets. Similarly good tours, and well-priced, are those run by L'Altra Venezia (p248).

Cultural Tours

International franchise **Context Travel** (☑800 691 60 36; www.contexttravel.com; group tours €315-409) offers a fantastic range of Venetian 'seminars' with knowledgeable docents and specialists. Groups are no larger than six people, and subjects range from politics to art, history and ecology. Other insightful cultural tours are offered by Venetian native Luisella Romeo at **See Venice** (☑349 084 8303; www.seevenice.it; tours per hour €75). She covers all the grand-slam sights as well as off-the-beaten-path itineraries which expand visitors experience of the city.

For those with an artful eye, consider Getty-photographer Marco Secchi's snap-happy Venice Photo Tour (p67), which takes you around hidden corners of the city and offers instruction in the finer points of Venetian light and photography.

Food Tours

Venice Urban Adventures (p101) and Monica Cesarato (p22) offer year-round *cicheti* (Venetian tapas) tours, covering five or six backstreet *bacari* (hole-in-the-wall bars) on a local-guided Venetian bar crawl.

Cicheti (Venetian tapas)

 **Eating**

The visual blitz that is Venice tends to leave visitors weak-kneed and grasping for the nearest panino *(sandwich). But there's more to La Serenissima than simple carb-loading. For centuries Venice has gone beyond the call of dietary duty, and lavished visitors with inventive feasts. Now it's your turn to devour addictive* cicheti *(Venetian tapas) and a lagoon's worth of succulent seafood.*

Venetian Cuisine

'Local food' is the latest foodie credo, but it's nothing new in Venice. Surrounded by garden islands and a seafood-rich lagoon, Venice dishes up local specialities that never make it to the mainland, because they're served fresh the same day in Venetian *bacari* (hole-in-the-wall bars) and *osterie* (casual eateries). A strong sea breeze wafts over the kitchens of the lagoon city, with the occasional meaty dish from the Veneto mainland and traditional, local options of rice and polenta in addition to classic Italian pastas and gnocchi. But side dishes of Veneto vegetables often steal the show, and early risers will notice

Venetians risking faceplants in canals to grab *violetti di Sant'Erasmo* (tender purple baby artichokes), *radicchio trevisano* (ruffled red bitter chicory) and prized Bassano del Grappa white asparagus from produce-laden barges.

Cross-cultural fusion fare is old news here, dating back to Marco Polo's heyday. Thirteenth-century Venetian cookbooks include recipes for fish with galangal, saffron and ginger; a tradition that still inspires dishes at nosh spots like Bistrot de Venise (p65) and Osteria Trefanti (p97). Don't be surprised if some Venetian dishes taste vaguely Turkish or Greek rather than strictly Italian, reflecting Venice's preferred trading partners for

NEED TO KNOW

Prices

With some notable exceptions in Venice – *cicheti* (Venetian tapaos), sandwiches, pizza and gelato – a meal typically consists of two courses, a glass of house wine, and *pane e coperto* (bread and cover charge). Meal prices are defined as follows:

€	less than €25
€€	€25 to €45
€€€	more than €45

Opening Hours

Cafe-bars generally open from 7am to 8pm, although some stay open later and morph into drinking hang-outs. Restaurant kitchens are generally open from noon to 2.30pm or 3pm at lunch and from 7pm to 10pm or 11pm at dinner.

Reservations

Call ahead to book a table at restaurants and *osterie* (casual eateries) whenever possible, especially for lunch in high season. You may get a table when you walk in off the street, but some restaurants buy ingredients according to how many bookings they've got – and when the food runs low, they stop seating. *Cicheti* (bar snacks) are a handy alternative.

Pane e Coperto

'Bread and cover' charges range from €1.50 to €6 for sit-down meals at most restaurants.

Service Charges

Service may be included in *pane e coperto* (especially at basic *osterie*) or added onto the bill (at upscale bistros and for large parties). Read the fine print before you leave an additional tip.

over a millennium. Spice-route flavours from the Mediterranean and beyond can be savoured in signature Venetian recipes such as *sarde in saor,* traditionally made with sardines in a tangy onion marinade with pine nuts and sultanas.

Exceptional ingredients from other parts of Italy sneak into Venetian cuisine, such as Tuscan steaks, white truffles from Alba, aromatic Amalfi lemons and Sicilian pistachios and blood oranges. Just don't ask for pesto: the garlicky basil spread hails from Genoa, Venice's chief trade-route rival for 300 years, and some Venetians still hold culinary grudges.

Cicheti

Cicheti are some of the best culinary finds in Italy, served at lunch and from around 6pm to 8pm with sensational Veneto wines by the glass. *Cicheti* range from basic bar snacks (spicy meatballs, fresh tomato and basil bruschetta) to highly inventive small plates: think white Bassano asparagus and plump lagoon shrimp wrapped in pancetta at All'Arco (p96); pungent gorgonzola paired with spicy *peperoncino* (chilli) jam at Dai Zemei (p96); wild boar salami at Vino Vero (p115); or fragrant, bite-sized bread rolls crammed with tuna, chicory and horseradish at Al Mercà (p99).

Prices start at €1 for tasty meatballs and range from €3 to €6 for gourmet fantasias with fancy ingredients, typically devoured standing up or perched atop stools at the bar. Filling *cicheti* such as *crostini, panini* and *tramezzini* (sandwiches on soft bread, often with mayo-based condiments) cost €1.50 to €6. Nightly *cicheti* spreads could easily pass as dinner.

Peckish? Venice's *cicheti* hot spots include the following:

Cannaregio Along Fondamenta degli Ormesini and off Strada Nova.

San Polo & Santa Croce Around the Rialto Market and Ruga Ravano.

Castello Via Garibaldi and Calle Lunga Santa Maria Formosa.

San Marco Around Campo San Bartolomeo, Campo Santo Stefano and Campo della Guerra.

The Menu

Even in unpretentious Venetian *osterie* and *bacari*, most dishes cost a couple of euros more than they might elsewhere in Italy – not a bad mark-up, considering all that fresh seafood and produce brought in by boat. *Cicheti* are fresh alternatives to fast food worth planning your day around, but you'll also want to treat yourself to a leisurely sit-down meal while you're in town. If you stick to tourist menus you're bound to be disappointed, but adventurous diners who order seasonal specialities are richly rewarded, and often spend less, too.

PIATTI (COURSES)

No one expects you to soldier through multiple courses plus antipasti and dessert, but we wouldn't blame you for trying either, given the many tempting *piatti* on the local menu. Consider your à la carte options:

Antipasti (appetisers) vary from lightly fried *moeche* (tiny soft-shell crabs) and lagoon-fresh *crudi* (Venetian sushi) such as sweet mantis prawns, to old-school *baccala mantecato* (whipped salted cod with olive oil) and traditional platters of cheeses and rustic cured meats.

Primi (first courses) usually include the classic Italian pasta or risotto; one Venetian speciality pasta you might try is *bigoli*, a thick wholewheat pasta, often served *in salsa* (with salted anchovies, Chioggia onions and black pepper). Equally loved are *pasta e fagioli*, a soupy concoction of pasta and borlotti beans, and *risi e bisi*, a risotto-like classic made with peas, pancetta and parmesan. Many Venetian restaurants have adopted a hearty Verona speciality: gnocchi. Another regional option is polenta, white or yellow cornmeal formed into a cake and grilled, or served semisoft and steaming hot. As the Venetian saying goes, '*Xe non xe pan, xe poenta*' (If there's no bread, there's still polenta).

Secondi (second or main courses) are usually seafood or meat dishes. Adventurous eaters will appreciate a traditional Venetian *secondo* of *trippa* (tripe) or *fegato alla veneziana* (calf's liver lightly pan-roasted in strips with browned onion and a splash of red wine). If you're not an offal fan, you can find standard cuts of *manzo* (beef), *agnello* (lamb) and *vitello* (veal) on most menus. Committed carnivores might also try carpaccio, a dish of finely sliced raw beef served with a sauce of crushed tomato, cream, mustard and Worcestershire sauce dreamed up by Harry's Bar (p65) and named for the Venetian painter Vittore Carpaccio, famous for his liberal use of blood-red paint. Popular surf options include *fritto misto*, a golden mix of fried fish and seafood, sometimes accompanied by tempura-style seasonal vegetables.

Contorni (vegetable dishes) are more substantial offerings of *verdure* (vegetables). For vegetarians, this may be the first place to look on a menu – and meat-eaters may want to check them out too, since *secondi* don't always come with a vegetable side dish. Go with whatever's fresh and seasonal.

Dolci (desserts) are often *fatti in casa* (house-made) in Venice, especially Veneto-invented tiramisu, Vienna-influenced *bigne* (cream puffs) and strudel, and safffron-scented Burano *esse* (S-shaped cookies). Otherwise, gelaterie (ice-cream shops) offer tempting options for €1.50 to €5.

DAILY SPECIALS

Here's one foolproof way to distinguish a serious Venetian *osteria* from an imposter: lasagne, spaghetti Bolognese and pizza are not Venetian specialities, and when all three appear on a menu, avoid what is essentially a tourist trap. Look instead for places where there's no menu at all, or one hastily scrawled on a chalkboard or laser-printed in Italian only, preferably with typos. This is a sign that your chef reinvents the menu daily, according to what looked best that morning at the market.

Although fish and seafood are increasingly imported, many Venetian restaurant owners pride themselves on using only fresh, local ingredients, even if that means getting up at the crack of dawn to get to the Pescaria (Fish Market). Lagoon tides and changing seasons on the nearby garden island of Sant'Erasmo bring a year-round bounty to Venetian tables at the Rialto Market.

Beware any menu dotted with asterisks, indicating that several items are *surgelati* (frozen) – seafood flown in from afar is likely to be unsustainable, and indigestible besides.

DRINKS

No Venetian feast would be complete without at least one *ombra* (glass of wine) – and that includes lunch. Fishmongers at the Pescaria get a head start on landlubbers, celebrating the day's haul at 9am by popping a cork on some *prosecco* (sparkling white wine), the Veneto's beloved bubbly. By noon, you already have some catching up to do: start working your way methodically through the extensive seafood menu of tender octopus salad, black squid-ink risotto, and *granseola* (spider crab), paired with appropriate *ombre*.

Many Venetian dishes are designed with local wines specifically in mind to round out the flavours – especially delicate lagoon seafood, whose texture may be changed by the powerful acidity of lemon juice. Some *enoteche* (wine bars) and *osterie* (casual eateries) have wine selections that run into the hundreds of labels, so don't be shy about soliciting suggestions from your server or bartender.

Of course, no meal is complete without a glass of the Veneto's own fire water –

grappa. Far from the rocket fuel you may be accustomed to, respected distilleries such as Bassano del Grappa's Poli produce sophisticated versions that are equally smooth and nuanced.

Vegetarians & Vegans

Even in a city known for seafood, vegetarians need not despair: with a little advance savvy, vegetarian visitors in Venice can enjoy an even wider range of food choices than they might at home. Island-grown produce is a point of pride for many Venetian restaurants, and *primi* (first courses) such as polenta, pasta and risotto *contorni* (vegetable dishes) make the most of such local specialities as asparagus, artichokes, radicchio and *bruscandoli* (wild hops). Venetian *contorni* include grilled local vegetables and salads, and *cicheti* (bar snacks) showcase marinated vegetables and Veneto cheeses.

There are eateries that serve a good range of meat-free dishes at all price points. Meat-free and cheese-free pizza is widely available, and gelaterie offer milk-free *sorbetto* (sorbet) and gelato with *latte di soia* (soy milk). Self-catering is always an option for vegans and others with restricted diets, but if you call ahead, specific dietary restrictions can usually be accommodated at restaurants and *osterie*.

Self-Catering

Picnicking isn't allowed in most *campi* (squares) – Venice tries to keep a lid on its clean-up duties, since all refuse needs to be taken out by barge – but you can assemble quite a feast to enjoy at your B&B, rental apartment or hotel. For lunch with sweeping lagoon views, pack a picnic and head to the Lido beaches, the Biennale gardens or the northern lagoon islands of Mazzorbo, Torcello, Le Vignole and Sant'Erasmo.

FARMERS MARKETS

The Rialto Market (p93) offers superb local produce and lagoon seafood at the centuries-old Pescaria (p93). Second only to it is the Lido's Tuesday food market, Mercato Settimanale del Lido (p143). For produce that floats, make a beeline for the produce barge on the Rio di Sant'Anna at the end of Via Garibaldi in Castello, or the one pulled up alongside Campo San Barnaba in Dorsoduro, near Ponte dei Pugni.

GROCERIES

The area around the Rialto Market has gourmet delis and speciality shops. Close to Piazzale Roma is **Coop** (Map p273; ☑041 296 06 21; Fondamenta di Santa Chiara 506a, Santa Croce; ☺8.30am-9pm; 🚊Piazzale Roma), an agricultural cooperative grocery with a good deli section. You'll find other branches throughout the city, including at Campo San Giacomo dell'Orio. The small supermarket chain Rizzo (p113) stocks sandwiches at its deli counters.

Cooking Courses

If all that produce and tradition inspires the chef within, consider signing up for a Venetian cooking course. **Acquolina Cooking School** (www.acquolina.com; half-/full-day courses €170/290) runs four- and eight-hour courses, the latter option including a morning trip to the Rialto Market. It also offers multiday courses, including accommodation. Local market trawls are also on the menu at **Cook in Venice** (www.cookinvenice.com; tours €35-60, courses €185-225), whose one- and three-day cooking courses include gluten- and lactose-free nosh on request.

Mealtimes

Restaurants and bars are generally closed one day each week, usually Sunday or Monday. If your stomach growls between official mealtimes, cafes and bars generally open from 7am to 8pm and serve snacks all day.

Prima colazione (breakfast) is eaten between 7am and 10am. Venetians rarely eat a sit-down breakfast, but instead bolt down a cappuccino with a *brioche* (sweet bread) or other type of pastry (generically known as *pastine*) at a coffee bar before heading to work.

Pranzo (lunch) is served from noon to 2.30pm. Traditionally, lunch is the main meal of the day, and some shops and businesses close for two or three hours to accommodate it. Relax and enjoy a proper sit-down lunch, and you may be satisfied with *cicheti* (bar snacks) for dinner.

Cena (dinner) is served between 7pm and 10.30pm. Opening hours vary, but many places begin filling up by 7.30pm and few take orders after 10.30pm.

Dining Etiquette

With thousands of visitors trooping though Venice daily demanding to be fed, service can be slow, harried or indifferent. By showing an interest in what Venice brings to the table, you'll get more attentive service, better advice and a more memorable meal. You'll win over your server and the chef with these four gestures that prove your mettle as *una buona forchetta* ('a good fork', or good eater):

Ignore the menu. Solicit your server's advice about seasonal treats and house specials, pick two options that sound interesting, and ask your server to recommend one over the other. When that's done, snap the menu shut and say, '*Allora, facciamo cosi, per favore!*' (Well then, let's do that, please!) You have just won over your server, and flattered the chef – promising omens for a memorable meal to come.

Drink well. Bottled water is entirely optional; *acqua del rubinetto* (tap water) is perfectly potable and highly recommended as an environment-saving measure. But fine meals call for wine, often available by the glass or half-bottle. Never mind that you don't recognise the label: the best small-production local wineries don't advertise or export (even to other parts of Italy), because their yield is snapped up by Venetian *osterie* (casual eateries) and *enoteche* (wine bars).

Try primi without condiments. Your server's relief and delight will be obvious. Venetian seafood risotto and pasta are rich and flavourful enough without being smothered in Parmesan or hot sauce.

Enjoy lagoon seafood. No one expects you to order an appetiser or *secondo,* but if you do, the tests of any Venetian chef are seasonal seafood antipasti and *frittura* (seafood fry). Try yours *senza limone* (without lemon) first: Venetians believe the subtle flavours of lagoon seafood are best complemented by salt, pepper and subtle trade-route spices like star anise. Instead, try washing down seafood with citrusy Veneto white wines that highlight instead of overwhelm briny flavours.

Gourmet Hot Spots

Bad advice has circulated for decades about how it's impossible to eat well and economically in Venice, which has misinformed day trippers clinging defensively to congealed, reheated pizza slices in San Marco. Little do they realise that for the same price a bridge away, they could be dining on *crostini* (open-face sandwiches) topped with scampi and grilled baby artichoke, or tuna tartare with wild strawberries and balsamic re-

duction. Luckily for you, there's still room at the bar to score the best *cicheti,* and reservations are almost always available at phenomenal eateries – especially at dinner, after the day trippers depart.

To find the best Venetian food, dodge restaurants immediately around San Marco, near the train station and along main thoroughfares. Instead, aim your fork at these gourmet trails and outstanding island eateries:

Cannaregio Along Fondamenta Savorgnan, Fondamenta della Sensa and Calle Larga Doge Priulli.

San Polo & Santa Croce Around the Rialto Market.

Castello Around Campo Bandiera e Moro and Zanipolo.

San Marco Along Calle delle Botteghe, Calle Spezier and Frezzeria.

Dorsoduro Along Calle Lunga San Barnaba, Calle della Toletta and Calle Crosera.

Giudecca Along Fondamenta delle Zitelle.

Northern Islands Locanda Cipriani (p156) on Torcello, Gatto Nero (p155) on Burano, Venissa (p154) on Mazzorbo and Acquastanca (p154) on Murano.

Eating by Neighbourhood

➡ **San Marco** (p64) *Panini* (sandwiches), *cicheti* (Venetian tapas) and high-end, traditional restaurants.

➡ **Dorsoduro** (p78) Snug bistros, *campo* (square)-side bar bites and cheap-and-easy pizza by the slice.

➡ **San Polo & Santa Croce** (p108) Market-inspired cuisine, creative *cicheti,* pizza and vegetarian fare.

➡ **Cannaregio** (p113) Traditional *cicheti,* authentic *osterie* (casual eateries) and canalside dining.

➡ **Castello** (p111) Daring, creative cuisine; pizza; and bargain *cicheti.*

➡ **Giudecca, Lido & the Southern Islands** (p107) Traditional seafood and waterfront dining.

➡ **Murano, Burano & the Northern Islands** (p154) Just-caught lagoon seafood and garden dining.

PLAN YOUR TRIP EATING

Lonely Planet's Top Choices

Ristorante Quadri (p64) Michelin-starred cuisine in opulent surroundings overlooking San Marco.

Antiche Carampane (p98) Elegant, traditional dining in one of the oldest restaurants in Venice.

All'Arco (p96) *Panini* (sandwiches) are decoys for day trippers; stick around and let Venice's *cicheti maestri* ply you with market-fresh *fantasie*.

Locanda Cipriani (p156) The Cipriani family's rustic retreat, where soulful flavours are yours by a crackling fire or beneath a scented pergola.

Riviera (p80) The finest Venetian seafood enjoyed with picture-perfect sunsets.

Trattoria Corte Sconta (p132) Superlative surf antipasti, inspired pasta dishes, and subtle modern subversion.

Best by Budget

€

All'Arco (p96) Stand-up gourmet bites made with prime Rialto produce.

Snack Bar Ai Nomboli (p96) Inspired *panini* (sandwiches) made with the finest-quality ingredients.

Pasticceria Tonolo (p78) The best pastry shop in Venice with an eye-watering array of cakes.

€€

Acquastanca (p154) Contemporary regional flavours in a reformed Murano bakery.

Estro (p79) Homemade charcuterie, gourmet *cicheti* and highly creative Venetian cooking.

CoVino (p131) Inventive dishes based on Slow Food–accredited produce.

Osteria Trefanti (p97) Intimate, pared-back elegance meets blue-ribbon produce, textures and arresting wines.

€€€

Ristorante Quadri (p64) Complex cooking delicately executed by the Michelin-starred Alajmos.

Bistrot de Venise (p65) Historical flavours showcasing Venice's trade routes cuisine.

Riviera (p80) Seafood is the star of the show at this stylish waterside restaurant.

Trattoria Corte Sconta (p132) Unexpected ingredients turn tired classics into revamped revelations.

Best by Cuisine

Classic Venetian

Antiche Carampane (p98) Excellent *crudi* (raw seafood) and moreish *fritto misto* (fried seafood) in Venice's former red-light corner.

Trattoria Altanella (p142) Fresh, succulent seafood on the island of Giudecca.

Da Codroma (p79) Thoroughly authentic Venetian dishes accredited by Slow Food.

Inventive Venetian

Venissa (p155) Graze on the island landscape in lagoon-inspired dishes by rising culinary talents.

Ristorante Glam (p99) A modern take on Venetian classics from a Michelin-starred chef.

CoVino (p131) A pocket-sized showcase for Slow Food produce cooked with modern soul.

Best for Cicheti

All'Arco (p96) Market-fresh morsels and zingy *prosecco* (sparkling white wine) close to the Rialto Market.

Vino Vero (p115) Inventive *cicheti* (bar snacks) accompanied by natural-process wines.

Dai Zemei (p96) Unexpected, creative concoctions from food- and *vino*-obsessed twins.

Osteria Al Squero (p81) Classic and lesser-seen *cicheti* opposite a gondola workshop.

Best Waterfront Dining

Trattoria Altanella (p142) Wine, dine and sigh on a balcony that hovers right over the water.

Riviera (p80) Perfectly positioned on the Zattere for hot-pink sunsets and romance.

La Palanca (p142) Panoramic waterfront dining at mere-mortal prices.

Trattoria al Gatto Nero (p155) Canalside seafood with crayon-coloured Burano backdrop.

Best for Vegetarians

Bistrot de Venise (p65) Fine-dining establishment with an excellent vegetarian menu.

Osteria La Zucca (p98) Market-driven menus in a snug, canalside bolt-hole.

Frary's (p98) Pan-Mediterranean and Middle Eastern flavours in the shadow of a Gothic giant.

Aperol spritz (*prosecco* cocktail)

Drinking & Nightlife

When the siren sounds for acqua alta (high tide), Venetians close up shop and head home to put up their flood barriers – then pull on their boots and head right back out again. Why let floods disrupt a toast? It's not just a turn of phrase: come hell or high water, Venetians will find a way to have a good time.

Happy Hour(s)

The happiest hour (or two) in Venice begins around 6pm at booze and *cicheti* (Venetian tapas) *bacari* (hole-in-the-wall bars). If you're prompt, you might beat the crowds to the bar for *un'ombra* (a 'shade'; a small glass of wine), which can go for as little as €0.60 at cupboard-sized Bacareto Da Lele (p101). Heading in early also means grabbing *cicheti* while they're fresh. *Osterie* (taverns) and *enoteche* (wine bars) are also renowned for their *vino*-friendly bites.

Giro d'Ombra

An authentic Venetian *giro d'ombra* (pub crawl) begins around the Pescaria by 9am, drinking *prosecco* (sparkling white wine) with fishermen toasting a hard day's work that began at 3am. For layabouts, Venice offers a second-chance *giro d'ombra* with *cicheti* at *bacari* ringing the Rialto Market around noon. Afterwards, it's a long four-hour dry spell until the next *giro d'ombra* begins in buzzing spots around Campo Santa Margherita in Dorsoduro, Fondamenta degli Ormesini in Cannaregio, Campo Maria Formosa in Castello, and the warren of *calli* (lanes) around Campo San Bartolomeo and Campo Manin in San Marco.

NEED TO KNOW

Opening Hours

Cafe-bars generally open from 7am to 8pm, although some stay open later and morph into drinking hang-outs. Pubs and wine bars are mostly shut by 1am to 2am.

Noise Regulations

Keep it down to a dull roar after 10pm: sound travels in Venice, and worse than a police bust for noise infractions is a scolding from a Venetian *nonna* (grandmother).

What to Order

No rules seem to apply to drinking in Venice. No mixing spirits and wine? Venice's classic cocktails suggest otherwise; try a *spritz*, made with *prosecco*, soda water and bittersweet Aperol, bitter Campari or herbaceous Cynar. Price is not an indicator of quality – you can pay €2.50 for a respectable *spritz*, or live to regret that €16 bellini tomorrow (ouch). If you're not pleased with your drink, leave it and move on to the next *bacaro*. Don't be shy about asking fellow drinkers what they recommend; happy hour is a highly sociable affair.

LOCAL FAVOURITES

Prosecco The crisp, sparkling white that's the life of any Venetian party, from nonvintage to DOCG Conegliano Prosecco Superiore. Persistent bubbles and straw-yellow hues.

Spritz A stiff drink at an easy price, this *prosecco* cocktail is a cross-generational hit with students and pensioners at bars across Venice – except at *enoteche* (wine bars).

Soave A well-balanced white wine made with Veneto Garganega grapes, ideal with seafood in refreshing young versions or as a conversation piece in complex Classico versions.

Amarone The Titian of wines: a profound, voluptuous red blended from Valpolicella Corvina grapes. Complex and costly (€6 to €18 per glass), but utterly captivating while it lasts.

Ribolla Gialla A weighty white with all the right curves from Friuli-Venezia Giulia, this wine gets more voluptuous with age; irresistible with buttery fish, gnocchi and cheese.

Valpolicella A versatile grape that's come into its own with a bright young DOC namesake red wine more food-friendly than Amarone; a structured, aged version called DOG Valpolicella Ripasso; and DOCG sweet late-harvest Recioto della Valpolicella.

Lugana A mineral-rich, well-structured white from Trebbiano grapes grown at the border of Veneto and Lombardy; a favourite with gastronomes.

Refosco dal Peduncolo Rosso Intense and brooding, a Goth rocker that hits the right notes. This order is guaranteed to raise your sommelier's eyebrow, and probably your bill.

Raboso One of Italy's top reds at full maturity, rich in tannins, packed with flavour and with a bouquet of spicy cherries. Perfect with aged cheeses, game and grilled red meats.

Morgana beer A worthy Venetian craft beer from the owners of La Cantina (p116): unpasteurised, unfiltered and undeniably appealing on hot summer days.

Cafes

To line your stomach with coffee and pastry before your next *giro d'ombra* (pub crawl),

---

VENETO: WHERE DRINKING COMES NATURALLY

Detour through the Veneto's glorious wine country for a day, and you'll see why the region is setting Italy's trend for natural-process wines – an umbrella term describing wines made with organic, biodynamic, natural-fermentation and other unconventional methods. With speciality grapes thriving on the Veneto's unspoilt volcanic hills, who needs pesticides, additives and industrial processing? Instead, growing numbers of Veneto vintners are doing what comes naturally, and experimenting with low-intervention, natural-process approaches.

Taste their results for yourself at **ViniVeri** (www.viniveri.net), the natural-process wine showcase held in Verona every April, or sample outstanding natural-process wines year-round at **Vino Vero** (p115), **Cantina Aziende Agricole** (p113) and **Al Prosecco** (p99). *Salute* – here's to your health, and the Veneto's, too.

check out Venice's legendary cafe-bars, and skip milky cappuccino for a stronger *macchiatone* (espresso with a 'big stain' of hot milk). For local flavour, try the Torrefazione Cannaregio (p115) *noxea:* coffee beans roasted with hazelnuts. House-roasted speciality blends are also the order of the day at Caffè del Doge (p101).

Historic baroque cafes around Piazza San Marco like Caffè Florian (p65) and Grancaffè Quadri (p65) serve coffee and hot chocolate with live orchestras – though your heart might beat a different rhythm once you get the bill. Hint: Caffè Lavena (p66) offers a €1 espresso at the counter.

Enoteche

Request *qualcosa di particolare* (something interesting), and your sommelier will accept the challenge to reach behind the bar for one of Veneto's obscure varietals or innovative wines. Even ordinary varietals take on extraordinary characteristics in growing areas that range from marshy to mountainous.

Speciality *enoteche* (wine bars) like Vino Vero (p115), Estro (p79), Al Prosecco (p99), El Sbarlefo (p81) and La Cantina (p116) uphold Venice's time-honoured tradition of selling good stuff by the glass, so you can discover new favourites without committing to a bottle.

To dive deeper into Veneto wines, sign up for a tasting session with Venetian Vine (p115), join a *cicheti* crawl led by Monica Cesarato from Cook in Venice (p30), or request a *vino*-versed guide on a *cicheti* rowing tour with Row Venice (p118).

DOC Versus IGT

In Italy, the official DOC *(denominazione d'origine controllata)* and elite DOCG (DOC *garantita* – guaranteed) designations are usually assurances of top-notch *vino*.

Taste the DOCG wines that put the Veneto on the world wine-tasting map at select wineries in Valdobbiadene and Conegliano *(prosecco),* Soave (Soave Superiore and Recioto di Soave) and Valpolicella (Amarone and Valpolicella).

Yet, successful as its wines are, the Veneto also bucks the DOC/DOCG system. Many of the region's small-production wineries can't be bothered with such external validation as they may already sell out to Venetian *osterie* (casual eateries) and *enoteche* (wine bars). As a result, some top producers prefer the IGT *(indicazione geografica tipica)* designation, which guarantees grapes typical of the region but leaves winemakers room to experiment with nontraditional blends and methods, such as natural-yeast fermentation.

Drinking & Nightlife by Neighbourhood

➡ **San Marco** (p65) High-end cocktails and DOC wines with DJs.

➡ **Dorsoduro** (p81) Bargain booze, buzzing *osterie* (taverns) and rivers of *spritz* (*prosecco* cocktail).

➡ **San Polo & Santa Croce** (p112) Inspired *ombre* (wine by the glass) and *cicheti* at historic *bacari.*

➡ **Cannaregio** (p110) Happy-hour sun spots on southern-facing canal banks.

➡ **Castello** (p115) Drink like a sailor at local *bacari,* or join *artistes* for pre-Biennale cocktails.

➡ **Giudecca, Lido & the Southern Islands** (p108) Fall film festivals, summer beach clubs and year-round happy hours.

➡ **Murano, Burano & the Northern Islands** (p154) A quiet drink with a local crowd.

Lonely Planet's Top Choices

Vino Vero (p115) Superlative wines from small and biodynamic producers, top-notch *cicheti* (bar snacks) and an effortlessly cool vibe.

Al Prosecco (p99) Organic grapes, wild-yeast fermentation, biodynamic methods: with Italy's finest natural-process wines, toasts come naturally.

Al Mercà (p99) Intriguing DOC regional wines, cheeses and small bites enjoyed by the Grand Canal docks.

Cantinone Già Schiavi (p81) Tiny bottles of beer and outsized neighbourhood personalities keep this historic canalside joint hopping.

Timon (p115) Canalside tables, *crostini* (open-face sandwiches), carafes of good house wine and occasional live music: idyllic.

Best Happy-Hour Hang-Outs

Al Mercà (p99) Delectable DOC *vino,* bargain bar bites and alfresco conviviality beside Venice's best-loved market.

Timon (p115) Swill and swoon on a moored vessel with savvy local dreamers.

Cantinone Già Schiavi (p81) Appetite-piquing *cicheti* and a mixed local crowd by a Dorsoduro canal.

El Chioschetto (p81) Front-row seats on the Zattere and endless supply of *spritz* (*prosecco* cocktail).

Il Caffè Rosso (p82) Cheap drinks and eclectic regulars define this Campo San Margherita veteran.

Bacareto Da Lele (p101) Filthy-cheap *ombre*, petite *panini* (sandwiches) and crowds of loyal locals.

Best for Wine

Vino Vero (p115) Natural, biodynamic and boutique drops in a standout Cannaregio wine bar.

Estro (p79) Has 500 personally chosen wines, plus handpicked cheeses, *salumi* (cured meats) and produce-driven menus.

Ai Pugni (p81) Nightly canalside crowds and a long, interesting, ever-changing choice of *vino* by the glass.

Cantina Aziende Agricole (p113) Get indecisive over 150 wines from renowned local producers.

Enoteca Mascareta (p133) Inspired wines by the glass, including the owner's very own organic *prosecco*.

Best for Beer

Birre da Tutto il Mondo o Quasi (p116) Venice's top beer bar keeps punters purring with over 100 brews.

La Cantina (p116) House-brand beer Gaston is a winner with sud-loving locals.

Il Santo Bevitore (p115) Trappist ales, seasonal stouts and chat-igniting football matches on the TV.

Birraria La Corte (p98) Sud sessions overlooking San Polo's sweeping namesake *campo*.

Best Signature Cocktails

Harry's Bar (p65) The driest classic in town is Harry's gin-heavy martini (no olive).

Locanda Cipriani (p156) Harry's famous white-peach bellini tastes even better at Cipriani's island retreat.

Bar Longhi (p65) Drink top-class cocktails like the orange martini in a jewel-like interior.

Bar Terrazza Danieli (p133) Apricot and orange moonlight with gin and grenadine in the Danieli.

Best for Coffee & Tea

Caffè Florian (p65) An 18th-century time-warp in show-off Piazza San Marco.

Torrefazione Cannaregio (p115) A veteran coffee roaster famed for its hazelnut-laced espresso.

Caffè del Doge (p101) A serious selection of world coffees, including the rare kopi luwak.

Fujiyama (p82) Soothing teas and a tranquil vibe.

Best Wine-Tasting Destinations

Vinitaly (p20) Italy's premier wine expo turns Verona into a mecca for professional oenophiles.

ViniVeri (p34) Verona's alternative wine show, dedicated to natural-process drops.

La Strada del Prosecco (p171) The Veneto's revered epicentre of *prosecco* production.

Soave (p182) Medieval walls and crisp, vibrant whites await east of Verona.

Valpolicella (p182) Northwest of Verona, the celebrated home of coveted red Amarone.

Roman Arena (p175), Verona

Entertainment

After the fall of Venice's shipping empire, the curtain rose on the city's music scene. A magnet for classical-music fans for four centuries, Venice continues to fill its palaces with the sounds of arias, cantatas and freestyle sax. Outside, the city's waterways lure with the promise of aquatic thrills, from stand-up rowing to historic regattas.

Opera

Venice is the home of modern opera and the legendary, incendiary La Fenice (p57). One of the world's top opera houses since its founding in 1792, it was here that Giuseppe Verdi premiered *Rigoletto* and *La Traviata*. But the music doesn't stop when La Fenice takes its summer break: opera divas from around the world perform under the stars from June to early September at Verona's **Roman Arena** ([⌕]045 800 32 04; Piazza Brà; adult/reduced €10/7.50; [⊙]8.30am-7.30pm Tue-Sun, from 1.30pm Mon), Italy's top summer opera festival.

Today you can see opera as Venetians did centuries ago, inside a whimsical pleasure-palace music room at Palazetto Bru Zane (p114), in Grand Canal palace salons with Musica a Palazzo (p66), among heavenly frescoes at Scuola Grande di San Giovanni Evangelista (p107) and in period costume at Scuola Grande dei Carmini (p77).

Classical Music

Venice is the place to hear baroque music in its original and intended venues, with notes soaring to Sebastiano Ricci–frescoed ceilings at Palazetto Bru Zane (p37), sweeping

NEED TO KNOW

Opening Hours

Event start times vary, with doors at evening concerts typically opening from 7pm to 8.30pm. Due to noise regulations in this small city with big echoes, live-music venues are limited, and shows typically end by 11pm.

Advance Tickets

Shows regularly sell out in summer, so purchase tickets online at the venue website, www.veneziaunica.it or www.musicinvenice.com. Tickets may also be available at the venue box office, or from Vènezia Unica information offices, located off San Marco, at the train station and on Piazzale Roma.

Events Calendar

For schedules of upcoming performances, Venetian discographies and online ticket sales, see www.musicinvenice.com. For upcoming openings, concerts, performances and other cultural events, check listings at www.veneziadavivere.com (mostly in Italian), and www.venezianews.it and www.turismovenezia.it.

Cover Charge

Entry is often free at bars, but the cover runs from €10 to €25 for shows in established venues; pay in advance or at the door.

Free Shows

In summer, don't miss Venice Jazz Festival outdoor events, plus free beach concerts on the Lido and on Lido di Jesolo. Year-round in good weather, you might luck into outdoor happy-hour shows around Campo San Giacomo dell'Orio and Fondamenta degli Ormesini.

through the salons at Palazzo Querini Stampalia and reverberating through La Pietà (p110), the original Vivaldi venue. Between opera seasons, summer symphonies are performed by **La Fenice's Philharmonic Orchestra** (www.filarmonica-fenice.it) at the opera house or affiliated Teatro Malibran (p111).

Ever-changing classical and jazz concerts are also held in the atmospheric Palazzo Contarini della Porta di Ferro by Venice Music Gourmet (p134). While Interpreti Veneziani (p67) plays Vivaldi and other baroque classics in a deconsecrated church.

Music becomes a religious experience surrounded by Venetian art masterpieces during organ vespers at Basilica di Santa Maria della Salute (p76) and occasional sacred music concerts at other Venetian churches.

Jazz, Rock & Pop

July's Venice Jazz Festival showcases international stars like Keith Jarrett, Cassandra Wilson and Jack Savoretti in iconic venues throughout the city, including La Fenice and the Peggy Guggenheim Collection. Its organising body, **VenetoJazz** (www.venetojazz.com), delivers year-round concerts in numerous towns across the Veneto, including Padua and Bassano del Grappa. Year-round tributes to Miles Davis, Chet Baker and Charles Mingus await at Venice's only dedicated jazz venue, Venice Jazz Club (p82).

A handful of bars sporadically host live music acts, usually rock, reggae, folk and *leggera* (pop). For all-ages alt-rock and punk, check events at Laboratorio Occupato Morion (p134). Bars with regular musical interludes include Paradiso Perduto (p116), Timon (p115), El Sbarlefo (p115), Bacarando (p66) and Il Santo Bevitore (p115). But don't expect to roll in late and still catch the show: according to local noise regulations, bars are expected to end concerts at 11pm.

Summer concerts are held on beaches on the Lido and on Lido di Jesolo – check the local press in July and August.

Theatre & Dance

Although dance performances are staged year-round in Venice, they are especially prolific during the Venice Biennale's International Festival of Contemporary Dance, usually held the first two weeks in June. Ballet performances are usually staged at Teatro Goldoni (p67), which also delivers contemporary theatre and Shakespeare, usually in Italian.

Cinema

International star power and Italian fashion storm Lido red carpets during the Venice International Film Festival, where films are shown in their original language. Year-round, catch films (sometimes subtitled) and blockbusters (usually dubbed) at Multisala Rossini (p67), a three-screen

LA BIENNALE DI VENEZIA

Europe's premier arts showcase since 1895 is something of a misnomer: the **La Biennale di Venezia** (www.labiennale.org; Giardini della Biennale; mid-May–Nov) is actually held every year, but the spotlight alternates between art (odd-numbered years, eg 2019, 2021, 2023) and architecture (even-numbered years, eg 2018, 2020, 2022). The summer art biennial is the biggest draw, with over 300,000 visitors viewing contemporary-art showcases in 30 national pavilions in the Giardini, with additional exhibitions in venues across town. The architecture biennial fills the vast boat sheds of the Arsenale with avant-garde conceptual structures and is a great opportunity to see the usually closed complex.

But the Biennale doesn't stop there. The city-backed organisation also organises an International Festival of Contemporary Dance, not to mention the iconic Venice International Film Festival. Running parallel to the Venice Biennale is a growing number of fringe arts events, offering opportunities to see hidden corners of the city usually off-access to the public. Check La Biennale di Venezia website for upcoming event listings, venues and tickets.

venue with digital sound in the heart of San Marco. La Casa del Cinema (p102) in Santa Croce is where the film archive is located and where you'll often find art-house and independent films being screened. Check **Venice Comune** (www.comune.venezia.it) for upcoming movie-screening schedules.

Sports & Activities

Despite the abundant art, Venice is a city that requires you to engage with it on a physical level. For a start, there are no cars so even getting around requires sturdy walking legs or awesome rowing prowess. The lack of greenery may confuse you, but Venetian's see the lagoon as their natural refuge and at weekends you'll find them out there, striking yoga poses along canals, jogging over bridges, boating and, in summer, basking on Lido beaches.

CYCLING

Though cycling is banned in central Venice, the Lido is a prime stretch of waterfront cycling turf, with tandem bicycle rentals available. Another good option is Sant'Erasmo, where Il Lato Azzurro (p196) rents bikes and offers suggestions for a soothing, tranquil exploration of Venice's famed food-bowl isle.

JOGGING

Jogging is increasingly popular in Venice, with favourite running spots including the Giardini, the Zattere, and along Castello's *fondamente* (canal banks) from Sant'Elena to the Riva degli Schiavoni. In October, sure-footed runners attempt the mad dash

from the Brenta riverbanks to San Marco in the Venice Marathon (p21).

WATER SPORTS

Sailing is a year-round passion, with classes available at the Isola di Certosa. The island is also home to Venice Kayak (p157), which runs kayaking tours of the Venetian lagoon. Paddleboard standing up with SUP in Venice (p118), or learn to row standing up *(voga alla veneta)* at Row Venice (p118), run by regatta champ Jane Caporal. The city's world-renowned regattas run from spring's ambitious 32km Vogalonga (p152) through autumn's costumed Regata Storica (p21). For a summertime swim, hit the beaches on the Lido or Lido di Jesolo.

Entertainment by Neighbourhood

➡ **San Marco** (p66) Opera, classical music, dance, theatre, cinema, DJs.

➡ **Dorsoduro** (p82) Jazz.

➡ **San Polo & Santa Croce** (p114) Cinema, outdoor theatre, live-music nights.

➡ **Cannaregio** (p111) Dance, live-music nights, cinema, casino.

➡ **Castello** (p116) Classical music, dance, live-music nights.

➡ **Giudecca, Lido & the Southern Islands** (p109) Cinema and DJ-fuelled beach parties on the Lido.

➡ **Murano, Burano & the Northern Islands** (p108) DJs and clubs on Lido di Jesolo.

Lonely Planet's Top Choices

La Biennale di Venezia (p39) Europe's signature art and architecture biennials draw international crowds, while musicians and dancers perform in summer showcases.

Teatro La Fenice (p58) Divas hit new highs in this sumptuous, legendary theatre for under 1000 lucky ticket-holders.

Palazzeto Bru Zane (p37) World-class classical music amid heavenly frescoes.

Venice International Film Festival (p21) A paparazzi-packed spectacle of silver-screen royalty and international premieres.

Verona's Roman Arena (p37) Larger-than-life tenors rock the Roman amphitheatre June to early September, rousing choruses of *'Bravo!'* from 30,000 fans.

Best Modern Music Events

Venice Jazz Festival (p21) A-list names play theatres, palaces and galleries.

La Biennale di Venezia (p39) A jam-packed program of new works, including numerous world premieres.

Laboratori Occupato Morion (p38) A radical backdrop for rocking regional bands.

Venice Music Gourmet (p134) Intimate classical and jazz concerts accompanied by a multicourse dinner.

Fondazione Giorgio Cini (p139) Occasionally serves up top-notch, modern world music at the Teatro Verde.

Best for Opera

Teatro La Fenice (p58) Top-tier productions in one of Italy's grandest theatres.

Verona's Roman Arena (p37) Summertime arias in an ancient Roman stadium.

Musica a Palazzo (p37) Historic compositions sung in sumptuous palace surrounds.

Scuola Grande di San Giovanni Evangelista (p37) Sopranos belt out baroque where flagellants once flogged.

Scuola Grande dei Carmini (p77) Costumed opera in a jewel-box former hostel.

Best for Classical Music

Palazzetto Bru Zane (p37) Renowned musicians and lesser-played compositions in the presence of cheeky cherubs.

Teatro La Fenice (p58) A robust program of grand symphonies and choral concerts.

Teatro Malibran (p38) Intimate-chamber music concerts in a 17th-century theatre.

Best for Theatre & Dance

La Biennale di Venezia (p39) Envelope-pushing moves at an international dance fest.

Teatro Goldoni (p38) Mighty classics in the city's starring theatre.

Teatro Junghans (p144) Thought-provoking work from Venice's acting academy.

Best for Cinema

Venice International Film Festival (p21) Red-carpet premieres and Hollywood royalty on the Lido.

Multisala Rossini (p38) Venice's largest cinema screens the odd original-language film.

Circuito Cinema Giorgione Movie d'Essai (p117) Two screens playing film-fest favourites, classics and kid-friendly animations.

Best Live-Music Nights

Laboratorio Occupato Morion (p38) World music, hip hop and folk-rock orchestras shake up Venice.

Paradiso Perduto (p38) Jazz, salsa and the odd legend in an arty, old-school tavern.

Venice Jazz Club (p38) Jazz great tributes and sultry Latin rhythms.

Il Santo Bevitore (p38) Occasional pop, blues and funk in a beer-lover's paradise.

Best Outdoor Activities

Row Venice (p39) Learn to row standing up (*voga alla veneta*), just like a *gondolieri*.

JW Marriott Venice (p195) Take the weight off tired sea legs at this rooftop spa and pool.

Venice Kayak (p39) Explore Venice's network of canals under your own steam.

Lido (p141) Cycle, sunbathe and swim at Venice's barrier island beaches.

Venice Photo Tour (p67) Discover the beauty of Venice on walks with a Getty photographer.

Shopping

Beyond the world-famous museums and architecture is Venice's best-kept secret: the shopping. No illustrious shopping career is complete without trolling Venice for one-of-a-kind, artisan-made finds. All those souvenir tees and kitschy masks are nothing more than the decoys for the amateurs. Dig deeper and you'll stumble across the prized stuff – genuine, local and nothing short of inspiring.

Artisan Specialities

Your Venice souvenirs may be hard to describe back home without sounding like you're bragging. 'It's an original', you'll say, 'and I met the artisan'. Venice has kept its artisan traditions alive and vital for centuries, especially glass, paper, textiles and woodworking.

STUDIO VISITS

For your travelling companions who aren't sold on shopping, here's a convincing argument: in Venice, it really is an educational experience. In backstreet artisans' studios, you can watch ancient techniques used to make strikingly modern *carta memorizzata* (marbled-paper) travel journals (from €12) and Murano glass waterfalls worn as necklaces (from €35). Studios cluster together, so to find unique pieces, just wander key artisan areas: San Polo around Calle Seconda dei Saoneri; Santa Croce around Campo Santa Maria Mater Domini; San Marco along Frezzeria and Calle de la Botteghe; Dorsoduro around the Peggy Guggenheim Collection; and Murano.

Glass showrooms and shelves of fragile handicrafts may be labelled *'non toccare'* (don't touch) – instead of chancing breakage, just ask to see any piece. The person who shows it to you may be the artisan who made it, so don't be shy about saying *'complimenti!'* (my compliments!) on impressive pieces.

Venetian Shopping Highlights

Italian style earns its international reputation for impeccable proportions, eye-catching details, luxe textures and vibrant colours –

but Venice goes one step further, with eclectic fashion statements, highly creative artisanal accessories, limited-edition sunglasses and no shortage of prized and intriguing antiques.

CLOTHING

Venice has the standard Italian designer brands you can find back home, from Armani to Zegna, along Larga XXII Marzo and Marzaria in San Marco – but for original fashion and better value, venture into Venice's backstreets. The chances of a colleague back home showing up to the office party in the same Venetia Studium (p68) goddess dress, hand-printed Fiorella Gallery (p68) smoking jacket or Arnoldo & Battois (p70) sculpted silk frock are infinitesimal. Then there are the Japanese-inspired tube scarves at Anatema (p105), driven by the same whimsical flair that sees vintage fabrics reborn as contemporary threads at Cannaregio's L'Armadio di Coco Vintage Lab (p117).

ACCESSORIES

Don't call Venetian artisans designers: their highly skilled handicrafts can't be mass produced, and stand out in a globalised fashion crowd. Paris' latest 'it' bags seem uninspired compared to the hand-stamped leather satchels bearing the Lion of St Mark that you'll find at Murra (p103), or 'beaded' necklaces made from hand-painted, quilled paper at Paperoowl (p102).

Indeed, the choice of Venetian-made objects are as eclectic as they are irresistible: hand-beaten copper and silver bracelets that look like lagoon ripples from Bottega Orafa

NEED TO KNOW

Opening Hours

Shops generally open around 10am to 1pm and 3.30pm to 7pm Monday to Saturday. A growing number of shops in tourist areas stay open 10am to 7pm daily, while shops off the main thoroughfares may remain closed on Monday morning. Most Murano glass showrooms close by 6pm. Many shops close for major Italian holidays, and for all or part of August.

Shipping

Never mind arbitrary airline luggage limits: most home decor and Murano glass showrooms offer shipping services at reasonable costs, especially within Europe. On new merchandise, customs duties may apply in your home country – check before you buy.

Taxes

Visitors from outside the EU may be entitled to VAT sales tax refunds on major purchases (p247).

ABC (p105), hand-sewn Venetian slippers at Pied à Terre (p102), even world-renowned *forcole* (gondola oarlocks) from Saverio Pastor (p83). Add cascading, hand-blown glass bead necklaces from Marina e Susanna Sent (p156) and custom-fit shoes from Daniela Ghezzo (p68) and there really is no point of comparison.

EYEWEAR

Centuries before geek chic, the first eyeglasses known to Europe were worn in the Veneto c 1348, and Venetian opticians have been hand-grinding lenses and stylish frames ever since. Bring your prescription to San Marco's Ottica Carraro (p69) or San Polo's Ottica Vascellari (p105), or snap up a replica of Peggy Guggenheim's outrageous frames at the Peggy Guggenheim Museum Shop (p84) in Dorsoduro.

ANTIQUES

Venice's penchant for conjuring up the past goes beyond Byzantine domes and baroque salons. The city is a giant attic of rare, well-worn trinkets and treasures, from 19th-century postcards and lithographs to centuries-old leather-bound books. Dorsoduro is a good place to start your antiques hunt, whether you're looking for vintage lighting at L'Angolo del Passato (p85), turn-of-the-century Venetian prints, erotic literature or baroque card games at Segni nel Tempo (p85), or fin de siècle miniatures and repurposed earrings at Antiquariato Claudia Canestrelli (p83). Italian design fiends lust after 20th-century glassware at San Polo's Campiello Ca' Zen (p105), whose inventory includes cult-status Venini items. San Polo is also home to **Scriba** (Map p270; ☑041 523 67 28; Campo dei Frari 3030, San Polo; ⊙10am-6pm; ⊠San Tomà), where contemporary art is sold alongside old maps. More vintage cartography awaits at Cannaregio's Antichità al Ghetto (p118), whose beautifully curated collection includes Jewish liturgical objects, damask and 18th-century cameos. Across in Castello lies Ballarin (p135), its eclectic, well-priced booty spanning everything from long-forgotten toys to elegant prints and hand-painted glassware. Last but not least is San Marco's Mercatino dell'Antiquariato (p69), a much-loved antiques flea market held several weekends a year in Campo San Maurizio. Head in early for the best finds, among them vintage Campari posters, Venetian postcards, Murano glassware and delicate Burano lace.

Shopping by Neighbourhood

→ San Marco (p67) Art galleries, international designers and high-end artisan showcases.

→ Dorsoduro (p83) Antique shops and fashion-forward boutiques.

→ San Polo & Santa Croce (p115) Artisan studios: glass, paper, fashion, gondolas.

→ Cannaregio (p112) High-street retail and artisan bargains.

→ Castello (p117) Cutting-edge artisans and quirky curios.

→ Giudecca, Lido & the Southern Islands (p109) Heritage textiles, paper-made design and sculptural knits.

→ Murano, Burano & the Northern Islands (p104) Handmade lace and the world's finest art glass.

Lonely Planet's Top Choices

ElleElle (p156) Murano art glass balancing modernity and tradition.

Ca' Macana (p83) Elaborate Carnevale masks made by a master artisan.

Marina e Susanna Sent Studio (p156) Minimalist Murano glass jewellery with vivid colours and architectural impact.

Oh My Blue (p102) Striking contemporary jewellery and accessories curated with a Venetian eye.

Chiarastella Cattana (p68) Locally loomed linens in history-inspired modern designs.

Best Venetian Souvenirs

Gilberto Penzo (p105) Scale-model gondolas.

I Vetri a Lume di Amadi (p105) Glass mosquitoes.

Pied à Terre (p102) *Furlane* (gondolier shoes).

Gianni Basso (p117) Calling cards with the lion of San Marco.

Paolo Brandolisio (p134) Miniature *forcole* (carved gondola oarlocks).

Best Venetian Home Decor

Fortuny Tessuti Artistici (p144) Luxury, handmade textiles from an Italian style icon.

Bevilacqua Fabrics (p69) Purveyors of the world's finest brocades, damask and tassles.

Chiarastella Cattana (p68) Sophisticated linens to restyle your *palazzo*.

Caigo da Mar (p69) Dramatic homewares for seasoned individualists.

Madera (p83) Forward-thinking objects, from chopping blocks to floor lamps.

Danghyra (p84) One-of-a-kind ceramics merging elegance and whimsy.

Best Venetian Fashion

L'Armadio di Coco Luxury Vintage (p67) Vintage couture fashions at affordable prices.

Venetia Studium (p68) Delphos tunic dresses and hand-stamped silk-velvet purses.

Venetian Dreams (p69) Lagoon-inspired necklaces made with antique seed beads.

Fiorella Gallery (p68) Head-turning couture for style rebels.

Acqua Marea (p84) Stylish rubber boots so sartorialists can navigate high tide.

Emilio Ceccato (p105) The official supplier of gondolier gear.

Best Jewellery

Marina e Susanna Sent (p83) Striking, contemporary wearables good enough for MoMA.

Sigfrido Cipolato (p68) Arresting, detailed pieces bursting with imagination and intrigue.

Oh My Blue (p102) Cutting-edge creations from local and foreign designers.

Trina Tygrett (p84) Contemporary jewellery mixing glass beads and semi-precious stones.

Leonardo (p118) Exclusive glass jewellery from revered Murano artisans.

Best Antiques

Ballarin (p135) A treasure chest packed with period furniture, lamps, glass and more.

Antiquariato Claudia Canestrelli (p83) A curiosity cabinet of prints, miniatures and repurposed antique earrings.

Antichità al Ghetto (p118) A nostalgic mix of Venetian maps, art and jewellery.

Campiello Ca' Zen (p105) Paintings, furniture and coveted glassware from cult names.

Segni nel Tempo (p85) A burst of rare books, prints and historic oddities.

Best Leather Goods

Daniela Ghezzo (p68) Custom-made shoes created with rare leather and seasoned style.

Balducci Borse (p117) Shoes and bags from a master leather craftsman.

Declare (p105) Hip bags and accessories in striking tones.

Kalimala (p134) Natural tanning and top-shelf leather underlines goods for men and women.

Murra (p103) Embossed journals and leather satchels hand-stamped with the Lion of St Mark.

Best Gifts for Gourmands

Drogheria Mascari (p104) Must-have pantry fillers and coveted wines.

VizioVirtù (p135) Artisan chocolates in unexpected flavours.

Atelier Alessandro Merlin (p134) Talking-point ceramics for a provocative cup of coffee.

THEJJPEN/ISTOCK EDITORIAL/GETTY IMAGES ©

Explore Venice & the Veneto

VENICE'S
TOP SIGHTS

Neighbourhoods at a Glance

❶ San Marco p48

So many world-class attractions are packed into San Marco some visitors never leave – and others are loath to visit, fearing crowds. But why deny yourself the pleasures of two of the world's most famous buildings, Basilica di San Marco and Palazzo Ducale, not to mention the wonderful Museo Correr and Venice's famous

jewel-box opera house La Fenice? But don't stop there. The backstreets are packed with galleries, boutiques and *enoteche* (wine bars).

❷ Dorsoduro p71

Dorsoduro covers prime Grand Canal waterfront with Ca' Rezzonico's gilded splendour, the Peggy Guggenheim Collection's modern edge, Gallerie dell'Accademia's Renaissance beauties and Punta della Dogana's ambitious

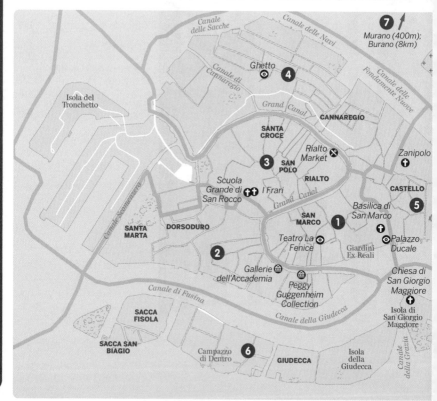

installation art. The neighbourhood lazes days away on the sun-drenched Zattere, and convenes in Campo Santa Margherita for *spritz* (*prosecco* cocktails) and flirtation.

❸ San Polo & Santa Croce p88

Heavenly devotion and earthly delights co-exist in San Polo and Santa Croce, where divine art rubs up against the ancient red-light district, now home to artisan workshops and *osterie* (taverns). Don't miss fraternal-twin masterpieces: Titian's glowing Madonna at I Frari and turbulent Tintorettos at Scuola Grande di San Rocco. Quirky museums fill Grand Canal *palazzo* (mansions), while island-grown produce fills Rialto Market.

❹ Cannaregio p107

Anyone could adore Venice on looks alone, but in Cannaregio you'll fall for its personal-ity. A few streets over from bustling Strada Nova, footsteps echo along moody Fondamenta de la Misericordia, and there's not a T-shirt kiosk in sight. Between the art-filled Chiesa della Madonna dell'Orto, the Renaissance miracle of Chiesa di Santa Maria dei Miracoli and the tiny island Ghetto, a living monument to the outsized contributions of Venice's Jewish community, are some of Venice's top casual eateries and *cicheti* bars.

❺ Castello p119

The vast crenellated walls of the Arsenale still dominate Venice's largest district, but where it was once the secret preserve of highly skilled artisans feeding Venice's naval war machine, it's now thrown open to alternating throngs of art and architecture fans during the famous Biennale. The Riva degli Schiavoni is Venice's prime waterfront promenade, but step back into the maze of lanes and you'll still find washing lines strung between buildings and little cafes on sunny squares.

❻ Giudecca, Lido & the Southern Islands p136

The most evocative of Venice's southern islands are tiny specks capped with monasteries such as San Servolo, San Lazzaro degli Armeni and (especially) San Giorgio Maggiore, its gracious Palladio church forming the essential backdrop for dreamy lagoon views. The much larger crescent of Giudecca has its own Palladian masterpieces and is a fascinating mash-up of luxury hotels, workaday apartments, the remnants of industry and a still-functioning women's prison. Lido is Venice's 12km beach escape, its A-list film festival a hangover from its days as one of Europe's most glamorous resorts.

❼ Murano, Burano & the Northern Islands p148

Venetian life had its origins in the northern reaches of the lagoon, and when things get too frantic in the city proper, these ancient island settlements remain the best escape. Serious shoppers head to Murano for one-of-a-kind glass art. Others prefer to head to the islands of Burano and Mazzorbo for extended seafood feasts, or to Torcello for glimpses of heaven in the golden mosaics.

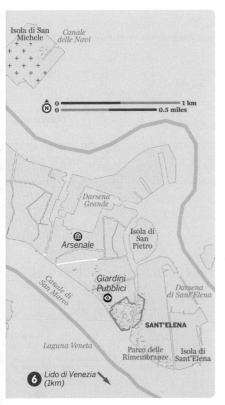

San Marco

Neighbourhood Top Five

❶ Basilica di San Marco (p50) Joining the chorus of gasps rippling through the crowd as you enter Venice's magnificent cathedral, looking up to discover angels dancing across 8500 sq metres of glittering golden mosaics.

❷ Palazzo Ducale (p53) Discovering over-the-top state rooms, dark secrets, dingy prisons and blockbuster exhibitions behind the rosy facade.

❸ La Fenice (p37) Shouting *'Brava!'* for encore performances from one of the boxes at Venice's jewel-box opera house.

❹ Museo Correr (p57) Adopting a philosopher painted by Veronese or Tintoretto as your personal mentor at the Biblioteca Nazionale Marciana.

❺ Caffè Florian (p65) Tangoing across Piazza San Marco at sunset to the tune of the orchestra.

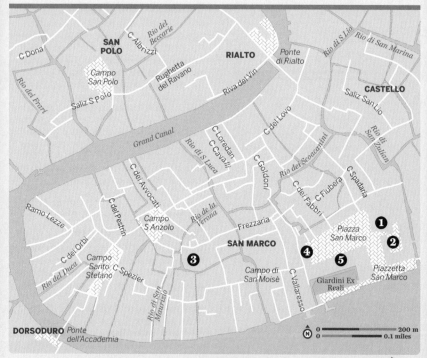

For more detail of this area see Map p266 and p267 ➡

Explore: San Marco

The neighbourhood of San Marco is Venice's oldest and most famous. Everything started here in the 9th century, when Doge Partecipazio founded the modern settlement of Venice in the vicinity of the Rialto Bridge. Venice's fairy-tale golden basilica followed shortly after, built to house the bones of St Mark the Evangelist.

With the palace, prisons, government offices, mint and library crowding around the basilica, Piazza San Marco was the fulcrum of Venetian power and it still attracts throngs of visitors today. You could spend days here, so start early and choose one big sight a day. Just as in the past, your path from Campo San Moisè to Campo Santo Stefano is lined with purveyors of dazzling luxury goods. The throngs only thin out when narrow *calli* (lanes) disgorge them into sunny *campi* (squares) faced by the lavishly decorated churches of Santa Maria del Giglio, San Maurizio and Santo Stefano).

In the evening, the red carpets and gilt boxes of La Fenice and Teatro Goldoni beckon music and theatre enthusiasts. Alternatively, take a pew on the Gritti terrace for sunset views over Salute or dive down canyon-like *calli* near the Rialto for welcoming trattorias and endless glasses of *vino*.

Local Life

➡ **Attend church** Venice's famous churches are far from museum pieces; attend Sunday Mass and you'll see locals keeping their age-old traditions alive.

➡ **Cheap eats** In this touristy neighbourhood, locals can be found propping up the counter at Rosa Salva (p64), Marchini Time (p64) and Rosticceria Gislon (p64).

➡ **Drinking dens** Locals hide out at unassuming bars like Bacarando (p66), Enoteca al Volto (p66) and Teamo (p66).

Getting There & Away

➡ **Vaporetto** San Marco has six vaporetto stops (Rialto, Sant'Angelo, San Samuele, Giglio, San Marco Vallaresso and San Marco Giardinetti) served by Line 1. The faster line 2 stops at Rialto, San Samuele and San Marco Giardinetti. Line 10 stops at San Marco Giardinetti.

➡ **Traghetto** A gondola ferry crosses the Grand Canal from Santa Maria del Giglio.

➡ **Walking** Look out for yellow signs pointing the way to Rialto and San Marco. It's often quicker to walk.

Lonely Planet's Top Tip

The Palazzo Ducale and Museo Correr are combined on one ticket, but if you upgrade to a Museums Pass you gain access to another seven civic museums (including Murano's Glass Museum, Burano's Lace Museum and the wonderful Ca' Rezzonico *palazzo*) for only €5 extra.

✕ Best Places to Eat

➡ Ristorante Quadri (p64)
➡ Bistrot de Venise (p65)
➡ Ai Mercanti (p64)
➡ Marchini Time (p64)
➡ Suso (p64)

For reviews, see p64.➡

🍷 Best Places to Drink

➡ Caffè Florian (p65)
➡ Bar Longhi (p65)
➡ Harry's Bar (p65)
➡ Grancaffè Quadri (p65)
➡ Osteria all'Alba (p66)

For reviews, see p65.➡

◉ Best Interior Decor

➡ Museo Correr (p57)
➡ Palazzo Ducale (p53)
➡ Museo Fortuny (p58)
➡ Negozio Olivetti (p63)
➡ Palazzo Grassi (p59)

For reviews, see p50.➡

 TOP SIGHT
BASILICA DI SAN MARCO

In a city packed with architectural wonders, none beats St Mark's for sheer spectacle and bombastic exuberance. In AD 828, wily Venetian merchants allegedly smuggled St Mark's corpse out of Egypt in a barrel of pork fat to avoid inspection by Muslim authorities. Venice built a basilica around its stolen saint in keeping with its own sense of supreme self-importance.

Construction

Church authorities in Rome took a dim view of Venice's tendency to glorify itself and God in the same breath, but the city defiantly created a private chapel for their doge that outshone Venice's official cathedral (the Basilica di San Pietro in Castello) in every conceivable way. After the original St Mark's was burned down during an uprising, Venice rebuilt the basilica two more times (mislaying and rediscovering the saint's body along the way). The current incarnation was completed in 1094, reflecting the city's cosmopolitan image, with Byzantine domes, a Greek cross layout and walls clad in marbles looted from Syria, Egypt and Palestine. Unbelievably, St Mark's only replaced St Peter's as Venice's cathedral in 1807, after the fall of the republic.

Facade

The front of St Mark's ripples and crests like a wave, its five niched portals capped with shimmering mosaics and frothy stonework arches. It's especially resplendent just before sunset, when the sun's dying rays set the golden mosaics ablaze. Grand entrances are made through the central portal, under an ornate triple arch featuring Egyptian pur-

DON'T MISS

➡ Pala d'Oro
➡ Dome of Genesis
➡ Loggia dei Cavalli
➡ Ascension Cupola
➡ St Mark's sarcophagus

PRACTICALITIES

➡ St Mark's Basilica
➡ Map p266, H4
➡ ☎041 270 83 11
➡ www.basilicasanmarco.it
➡ Piazza San Marco
➡ admission free
➡ ⏰9.45am-5pm Mon-Sat, 2-5pm Sun summer, to 4pm Sun winter
➡ 🚤San Marco

ple porphyry columns and intricate 13th- to 14th-century stone reliefs. The oldest mosaic on the facade, dating from 1270, is in the lunette above the far-left portal, depicting St Mark's stolen body arriving at the basilica. The theme is echoed in three of the other lunettes, including the 1660 mosaics above the second portal from the right, showing turbaned officials recoiling from the hamper of pork fat containing the sainted corpse.

Dome Mosaics

Blinking is natural upon your first glimpse of the basilica's 8500 sq metres of glittering mosaics, many made with 24-carat gold leaf fused onto the back of the glass to represent divine light. Just inside the narthex (vestibule) glitter the basilica's oldest mosaics, **Apostles with the Madonna**, standing sentry by the main door for more than 950 years. The atrium's medieval **Dome of Genesis** depicts the separation of sky and water with surprisingly abstract motifs, anticipating modern art by 650 years.

Inside the church proper, three golden domes vie for your attention. The images are intended to be read from the altar end to the entry, so the **Cupola of the Prophets** shimmers above the main altar, while the **Last Judgment** is depicted in the vault above the entrance (and best seen from the museum). The dome nearest the door is the **Pentecost Cupola**, showing the Holy Spirit represented by a dove shooting tongues of flame onto the heads of the surrounding saints. In the central 13th-century **Ascension Cupola**, angels swirl around the central figure of Christ hovering among the stars. Scenes from St Mark's life unfold around the main altar, which houses the saint's simple stone **sarcophagus**.

Pala d'Oro

Tucked behind the main **altar** (admission €2), this stupendous golden screen is studded with 2000 emeralds, amethysts, sapphires, rubies, pearls and other gemstones. But the most priceless treasures here are biblical figures in vibrant cloisonné, begun in Constantinople in AD 976 and elaborated by Venetian goldsmiths in 1209. The enamelled saints have wild, unkempt beards and wide eyes fixed on Jesus, who glances sideways at a studious St Mark as Mary throws up her hands in wonder – an understandable reaction to such a captivating scene. Look closely to spot touches of Venetian whimsy: falcon-hunting scenes in medallions along the bottom, and the by-now-familiar scene of St Mark's body smuggled out of Egypt on the right.

FOUR TETRARCHS

Set into a corner of the church's southern wall, near the entrance to the Palazzo Ducale, is a highly significant ancient Roman statue looted from Constantinople. Carved out of purple porphyry, it depicts Diocletian (ironically, a great persecutor of the Christians) and his three co-emperors of the short-lived Tetrachy (AD 293–313).

Those simply wishing to pray or attend Mass can enter from the Porta dei Fiori, on the north side of the church. Attending evening vespers, a sung service held before the main evening Mass, allows you to enter the basilica after hours, when the tour groups are long gone. Everyone is welcome, as long as they sit quietly and behave respectfully.

BASILICA DI SAN MARCO

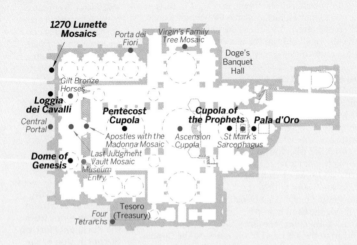

Museum

Accessed by a narrow staircase leading up from the basilica's atrium, the **Museo di San Marco** (🕒9.45am-4.45pm; adult/reduced €5/2.5) transports visitors to the level of the church's rear mosaics and out onto the **Loggia dei Cavalli**, the terrace above the main facade. The four magnificent bronze horses positioned here are actually reproductions of the precious 2nd-century originals, plundered from Constantinople's hippodrome, displayed inside.

Architecture buffs will revel in the beautifully rendered drawings and scale models of the basilica. In the displays of 13th- to 16th-century mosaic fragments, the Prophet Abraham is all ears and raised eyebrows, as though scandalised by Venetian gossip. Positioned above an interior balcony, Salviati's restored 1542–52 mosaic of the **Virgin's family tree** shows Mary's ancestors perched on branches, alternately chatting and ignoring one another, as families do. A corridor leads into a section of the Palazzo Ducale containing the **doge's banquet hall**, where dignitaries wined and dined among lithe stucco figures of *Music*, *Poetry* and *Peace*.

Treasury

Holy bones and booty from the Crusades fill the **Tesoro** (admission €3), including a 4th-century rock-crystal lamp, a 10th-century rock-crystal ewer with winged feet made for Fatimid Caliph al-'Aziz-bi-llah, and an exquisite enamelled 10th-century Byzantine chalice. Don't miss the bejewelled 12th-century Archangel Michael icon, featuring tiny, feisty enamelled saints that look ready to break free of their golden setting and mount a miniature attack on evil. In a separate room, velvet-padded boxes preserve the remains of sainted doges alongside the usual assortment of credulity-challenging relics: St Roch's femur, the arm St George used to slay the dragon and even a lock of the Madonna's hair.

TOP SIGHT
PALAZZO DUCALE

Don't be fooled by its genteel Gothic elegance: behind that lacy, pink-and-white-patterned facade, the doge's palace shows serious muscle and a steely will to survive. The seat of Venice's government for over seven centuries, this powerhouse stood the test of storms, crashes and conspiracies – only to be outwitted by Casanova, the notorious seducer who escaped from the attic prison.

Exterior

The Doge's official residence probably moved to this site in the 10th century, although the current complex only started to take shape in around 1340. In 1424, the wing facing Piazzetta San Marco was added and the palace assumed its final form, give or take a few big fires and refurbishments. The first-floor **loggia** fronting the square may seem like a fanciful flourish, but it served a solemn purpose: death sentences were read between the darker coloured ninth and 10th columns from the left. Abutting the Basilica, Zane and Bartolomeo Bon's 1443 **Porta della Carta** (Paper Door) was an elegant point of entry and public bulletin board for government decrees.

Courtyard

Entering through the colonnaded courtyard you'll spot Sansovino's statues of *Apollo* and *Neptune* flanking Antonio Rizzo's **Scala dei Giganti** (Giants' Staircase). Recent restorations have preserved charming cherubim propping up the pillars, though slippery incised-marble steps remain off-limits. Just off the courtyard in the wing facing the square is the **Museo dell'Opera**, displaying a collection of stone columns and capitals from older incarnations of the building.

DON'T MISS

➡ Sala del Maggior Consiglio (Grand Council Chamber)

➡ Sala dello Scudo (Shield Room)

➡ Scala d'Oro (Golden Staircase)

➡ Anticollegio (Council Antechamber)

➡ Scala dei Giganti (Giant's Staircase)

PRACTICALITIES

➡ Ducal Palace

➡ Map p266, H5

➡ ☏041 271 59 11

➡ www.palazzoducale.visitmuve.it

➡ Piazzetta San Marco 1

➡ adult/reduced incl Museo Correr €19/12, or with Museum Pass

➡ ⏰8.30am-7pm Apr-Oct, to 5.30pm Nov-Mar

➡ 🚤San Zaccaria

THE MISSING DOGE

A frieze along the top of the Sala del Maggior Consiglio depicts the first 76 doges of Venice, but note the black space: Doge Marin Falier would have appeared there had he not lost his head for treason in 1355.

On the terrace of the loggia level look for the face of a grimacing man with his mouth agape. This *bocca di leoni* (lion's mouth) was a postbox for secret accusations. These slanders reported any number of unholy acts from cursing and tax avoidance (forgivable) to Freemasonry (punishable by death). The notes, which had to be signed by two accusers, were then investigated by Venice's dreaded security service, led by the Council of Ten.

The Main Circuit

A standard entry ticket takes you on a circuit through main state and institutional rooms of the palace as well as the armoury and prisons.

Level Two

From the loggia level, head to the top of Sansovino's 24-carat gilt stuccowork **Scala d'Oro** (Golden Staircase) and emerge into rooms covered with gorgeous propaganda. In Palladio-designed **Sala delle Quattro Porte** (Hall of the Four Doors), ambassadors awaited ducal audiences under a lavish display of Venice's virtues by Giovanni Cambi, whose over-the-top stuccowork earns him the nickname Bombarda. Other convincing shows of Venetian superiority include Titian's 1576 *Doge Antonio Grimani Kneeling Before Faith* and Tiepolo's 1740s *Venice Receiving Gifts of the Sea from Neptune*.

Delegations waited in the **Anticollegio** (Council Antechamber), where Tintoretto drew parallels between Roman gods and Venetian government: *Mercury and the Three Graces* reward Venice's industriousness with beauty, and *Minerva Dismissing Mars* is a Venetian triumph of savvy over brute force. The recently restored ceiling is Veronese's 1577 *Venice Distributing Honours,* while on the walls is a vivid reminder of diplomatic behaviour to avoid: Veronese's *Rape of Europe*.

Few were granted an audience in the Palladio-designed **Collegio** (Council Chamber), where Veronese's 1575–78 *Virtues of the Republic* ceiling shows Venice as a bewitching blonde waving her sceptre like a wand over Justice and Peace. Father-son team Jacopo and Domenico Tintoretto attempt similar flattery, showing Venice keeping company with Apollo, Mars and Mercury in their *Triumph of Venice* ceiling for the **Sala del Senato** (Senate Chamber).

Government cover-ups were never so appealing as in the **Sala Consiglio dei Dieci** (Chamber of the Council of Ten), where Venice's star chamber plotted under Veronese's *Juno Bestowing her Gifts on Venice,* a glowing goddess strewing gold ducats. Over the slot where anonymous treason accusations were slipped into the **Sala della Bussola** (Compass Room) is his *St Mark in Glory* ceiling. The route then leads through the weapon-adorned **Armoury**.

Level One

After exiting the Armoury, stairs lead down to the chambers of the **Quarantia Civil Vecchia** (Council of Forty), a kind of court, split into sections dealing with criminal matters, civil disputes concerning Venetians and civil disputes pertaining to Venice's other territories.

PALAZZO DUCALE

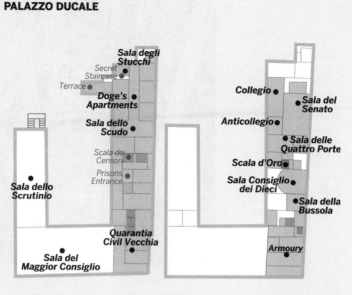

Level 1

Level 2

Next up is the grandest room of all: the cavernous 1419 **Sala del Maggior Consiglio** (Grand Council Chamber). The doge's throne once stood in front of the staggering 22m-by-7m *Paradise* backdrop (by Tintoretto's son, Domenico) that's more politically correct than pretty: heaven is crammed with 500 prominent Venetians, including Tintoretto patrons. Veronese's political posturing is more elegant in his oval *Apotheosis of Venice* ceiling, where gods marvel at Venice's coronation by angels, with dignitaries and Venetian blondes rubbernecking from the balcony below.

This room opens out onto the only slightly less vast **Sala dello Scrutinio** (Ballot Room), a former library which was subsequently used for elections of the doge and the various councils of state. From here the route backtracks and passes through more rooms relating to the Quarantia Civil Vecchia, before entering the prisons.

Prisons & Loggia Level

Follow the path of condemned prisoners across the Ponte dei Sospiri (p63) to Venice's 16th-century **Priggione Nove** (New Prisons). Dank cells covered with graffitied protestations of innocence are spread over three floors, with a central courtyard. After crossing back over the bridge, the route descends to the loggia level and through the rooms of the **censors**, **state advocates** and **naval captains**.

Doge's Apartments

The doge's suite of private rooms take up a large chunk of the 1st floor above the loggia. This space is now used for temporary art exhibitions, which are ticketed separately (around €10 extra). The doge lived like a caged lion in his gilded suite in the palace, which he could not leave without permission. Still, consider the real estate: a terrace garden with private entry to the basilica, and a dozen salons with splendidly restored marble fireplaces carved by Tullio and Antonio Lombardo. The most intriguing room is the **Sala dello Scudo** (Shield Room), covered with world

DEATH OF A DOGE

On the death of the doge, the Council announced: 'With much displeasure we have heard of the death of the most serene prince, a man of such goodness and piety; however, we shall make another.' The signet ring, symbol of his power, was then slipped from his finger and broken in half. The doge's family had three days to vacate the palace and remove all their furniture. Three Inquisitors were also appointed to scrutinise the doge's past office and, if necessary, punish his heirs for any fraud or wrongdoing.

Easily the most over-rated architectural feature in Venice, the Ponte dei Sospiri, which links the palace with the prisons, was popularised by the famous British libertine Lord Byron (1788–1824), who mentioned it in one of his poems. Condemned prisoners were said to sigh as they passed through the enclosed bridge and caught their last glimpse of the beauty of the lagoon. Now the sighs are mainly from people trying to dodge the snapping masses as they attempt to cross the neighbouring bridges.

Interior ceiling, Palazzo Ducale

maps that reveal the extent of Venetian power (and the limits of its cartographers) c 1483 and 1762. The New World map places California near *Terra Incognita d'Antropofagi* (Unknown Land of the Maneaters), aka Canada, where Cuzco is apparently located. Once you realise that the maps don't necessarily have north at the top, it's easy to make sense of them.

Secret Itineraries Tour

Further rooms can be visited on a fascinating 75-minute guided **tour** (☏041 4273 0892; adult/reduced €20/14; ⊘in English 9.55am, 10.45am & 11.35am, in Italian 9.30am & 11.10am, in French 10.20am & noon). It takes in the damp ground-floor cells known as **Pozzi** (wells) and then heads up into the cramped **Council of Ten Secret Headquarters**. Beyond this ominous office suite, the vast **Chancellery** is lined with drawers of top-secret files, including reports by Venice's far-reaching spy network, accusations by Venetians against their neighbours, and judgements copied in triplicate by clerks. The accused might be led to the windowless **Torture Chamber**, where confessions were sometimes extracted from prisoners dangling from a rope. Upstairs lie the **Piombi** (Leads), the attic prison cells where Casanova was condemned to five years' confinement in 1756 for corrupting nuns and the more serious charge of spreading Freemasonry. Casanova made an ingenious escape through the roof, then convinced a guard he was an official locked into the palace overnight.

SIGHTS

BASILICA DI SAN MARCO   CATHEDRAL
See p50.

PALAZZO DUCALE   MUSEUM
See p53.

PIAZZA SAN MARCO   PIAZZA
Map p266 (🚤San Marco) This grand showpiece square beautifully encapsulates the splendour of Venice's past and its tourist-fuelled present. Flanked by the arcaded **Procuratie Vecchie** and **Procuratie Nuove**, and two of the city's top sights – Basilica di San Marco (p50) and Museo Correr (p57) – it's filled for much of the day with tourists, their guides and pigeons.

CAMPANILE   TOWER
Map p266 (Bell Tower; www.basilicasanmarco. it; Piazza San Marco; adult/reduced €8/4; ⊘8.30am-9.30pm summer, 9.30am-5.30pm winter, last entry 45min prior; 🚤San Marco) The basilica's 99m-tall bell tower has been rebuilt twice since its initial construction in AD 888. Galileo Galilei tested his telescope here in 1609, but modern-day visitors head to the top for 360-degree lagoon views and close encounters with the Marangona, the booming bronze bell that originally signalled the start and end of the working day for the craftsmen *(marangoni)* at the Arsenale shipyards. Today it rings twice a day, at noon and midnight.

The tower's distinctive profile was the brainchild of Bartolomeo Bon, whose 16th-century design was initially criticised for being ungainly. However, when the tower suddenly collapsed in 1902, the Venetians painstakingly rebuilt it exactly as it was, brick by brick.

Sansovino's classical marble loggia at the base of the Campanile is decidedly mythical, showcasing bronzes of pagan deities Minerva, Apollo and Mercury, plus Peace.

TORRE DELL'OROLOGIO   LANDMARK
Map p266 (Clock Tower; ☑041 4273 0892; www. museiciviciveneziani.it; Piazza San Marco; adult/reduced €12/7; ⊘tours by appointment; 🚤San Marco) The two hardest-working men in Venice stand duty on a rooftop around the clock, and wear no pants. No need to file workers' complaints: the 'Do Mori' (Two

---

⊙ TOP SIGHT
MUSEO CORRER

Napoleon knocked down an ancient church to build his royal digs over Piazza San Marco. However, he lost Venice to Austrian emperor Franz Joseph before completing the construction. The Austrians loved luxury and Empress Sissi's suite showcases her 19th-century penchant for luxe curtains and silk-swathed walls – shocking, considering the poverty of Venice's citizenry at the time.

Napoleon's wing links the 16th-century **Procuratie Vecchie** on the northern side of the square to the **Procuratie Nuove** on the south. The latter, described by Palladio as the most sumptuous palace ever built, is incorporated into the museum. It includes the **Biblioteca Nazionale Marciana**, a library designed by Jacopo Sansovino in the 16th century and covered with frescoes by Veronese, Titian and Tintoretto. Adjoining it is the collection of the **Museo Archeologico Nazionale**, showcasing ancient sculpture and cameos. Look out for Jacopo di Barbari's minutely detailed woodblock perspective view of Venice and Antonio Canova's 1776 statues of star-crossed lovers *Orpheus and Eurydice*.

Upstairs is a large collection of mainly religious masterpieces spanning four centuries.

DON'T MISS
➡ Biblioteca Nazionale Marciana
➡ Empress Sissi's suite
➡ Bellini's bright-eyed saints (room 36)

PRACTICALITIES
➡ Map p266, F5
➡ ☑041 240 52 11
➡ www.correr.visit muve.it
➡ Piazza San Marco 52
➡ adult/reduced incl Palazzo Ducale €19/12, or with Museum Pass
➡ ⊘10am-7pm Apr-Oct, to 5pm Nov-Mar
➡ 🚤San Marco

Moors) exposed to the elements atop the Torre dell'Orologio are made of bronze, and their bell-hammering mechanism runs like, well, clockwork. Below the Moors, Venice's gold-leafed, 15th-century timepiece tracks lunar phases. Visits are by guided tour; bookings essential.

The clock had one hitch: the clockworks required constant upkeep by a live-in clock-watcher and his family until 1998. After a nine-year renovation, the clock's works are now in independent working order – 132-stroke chimes keep time in tune, moving barrels indicate minutes and hour on the world's first digital clock face (c 1753), and wooden statues of the three kings and angel emerge from side panels annually on Epiphany and the Feast of the Ascension. Tours climb steep four-storey spiral staircases past the clockworks to the roof terrace, for giddy, close-up views of the Moors in action.

Children must be over six years of age to climb the tower and the steep climb is not recommended for pregnant women and those suffering from vertigo or claustrophobia.

MUSEO FORTUNY   MUSEUM

Map p266 (☑041 52 00 995; www.fortuny.visitmuve.it; Campo San Beneto 3958; adult/reduced €12/10; ☉10am-6pm Wed-Mon; ⬤Sant'Angelo) Find design inspiration at the palatial home-studio of art-nouveau designer Mariano Fortuny y Madrazo (1871–1949), whose shockingly uncorseted Delphi goddess frocks set the standard for bohemian chic. First-floor salon walls are eclectic mood boards: Fortuny fashions and Isfahan tapestries, family portraits and artfully peeling plaster. Interesting temporary exhibitions spread from the basement to the attic, the best of which use the general ambience of grand decay to great effect.

If these salons inspire design schemes, visit Fortuny Tessuti Artistici (p144) in Giudecca, where textiles are still hand-printed according to Fortuny's top-secret methods.

CHIESA DI SANTO STEFANO   CHURCH

Map p266 (☑041 522 50 61; www.chorusvenezia.org; Campo Santo Stefano; museum €4, or with Chorus Pass; ☉10.30am-4.30pm Mon-Sat; ⬤Sant'Angelo) **FREE** The free-standing bell tower, visible from the square behind,

---

⊙ TOP SIGHT
TEATRO LA FENICE

Once its dominion over the high seas ended, Venice discovered the power of high Cs, hiring San Marco choirmaster Claudio Monteverdi, the father of modern opera, and opening La Fenice (The Phoenix) in 1792. Rossini, Donizetti and Bellini staged operas here, making La Fenice the envy of Europe – until it went up in flames in 1836.

Venice without opera was unthinkable, and within a year the opera house was rebuilt. Verdi premiered *Rigoletto* and *La Traviata* at La Fenice, and international greats Stravinsky, Prokofiev and Britten composed for the house. But La Fenice was again reduced to ashes in 1996; two electricians, found guilty of arson, were apparently behind on repairs. A €90-million replica of the 19th-century opera house reopened in late 2003 (though some critics had lobbied for Gae Aulenti's avant-garde design), and the reprise performance of *La Traviata* was a sensation.

From January to July and September to October, opera season is in full swing. If you can't attend a performance, which is highly recommended, it's possible to explore the theatre with an audio guide. Check also for chamber-music concerts staged at La Fenice's sister venue, **Teatro Malibran** (p116).

DON'T MISS

➡ Opera season
➡ *Intermezzo* (intermission) at the baroque bar
➡ Summer symphonies

PRACTICALITIES

➡ Map p266, D5
➡ ☑041 78 66 72
➡ www.teatrolafenice.it
➡ Campo San Fantin 1977
➡ restricted view from €30
➡ ⬤Giglio

leans disconcertingly, but this brick Gothic church has stood tall since the 13th century. Credit for shipshape splendour goes to Bartolomeo Bon for the marble entry portal and to Venetian shipbuilders, who constructed the vast wooden *carena di nave* (ship's keel) ceiling that resembles an upturned Noah's Ark.

It's well worth visiting the sacristy museum to see three extraordinary and brooding 1575–80 Tintorettos: *The Last Supper,* with a ghostly dog begging for bread; the gathering gloom of *The Agony in the Garden;* and the mostly black, surprisingly modern, *Washing of the Feet.* There's also a small cloister.

PALAZZO GRASSI   GALLERY

Map p266 (☑041 200 10 57; www.palazzograssi. it; Campo San Samuele 3231; adult/reduced incl Punta della Dogana €18/15; ☉10am-7pm Wed-Mon mid-Apr–Nov; ☒San Samuele) Grand Canal gondola riders gasp at first glimpse of massive sculptures by contemporary artists docked in front of Giorgio Masari's neoclassical palace (built 1748–72). French billionaire François Pinault's provocative art collection overflows Palazzo Grassi, while clever curation and shameless artstar namedropping are the hallmarks of rotating temporary exhibits. Still, despite the artistic glamour, Tadao Ando's creatively repurposed interior architecture steals the show.

Postmodern architect Gae Aulenti peeled back rococo decor to highlight Masari's muscular classicism in 1985–86, and minimalist master Ando added stage-set drama in 2003–05 with ethereal backlit scrims and strategic spotlighting. Ando's design directs attention to contemporary art, without detracting from baroque ceiling frescoes. Don't miss the cafe overlooking the Grand Canal, with interiors redesigned by contemporary artists with each new show.

Next door, the **Teatrino** occupies a space that once served as the palace's garden before it was converted into a theatre. Here, once again, Ando has worked his magic, transforming the interior into a curvaceous, 220-seat, concrete auditorium which now hosts concerts, conferences and film projections.

PALAZZO FRANCHETTI   PALACE

Map p266 (Istituto Veneto di Scienze Lettere ed Arti; ☑041 240 77 11; www.palazzofranchetti.it;

Campo Santo Stefano 2842; ☉10am-6pm Mon-Fri; ☒Accademia) This 16th-century *palazzo* passed through the hands of various Venetian families before Archduke Frederik of Austria snapped it up and set about modernising it. The Comte de Chambord (aka King Henry V of France in exile) continued the work, while the Franchetti family, who lived here after independence, restored its Gothic fairy-tale look and introduced a fantastical art nouveau staircase dripping with dragons. It's now used for arts exhibitions, although the works have to compete with showstopping Murano chandeliers.

SCALA CONTARINI DEL BOVOLO   NOTABLE BUILDING

Map p266 (☑041 309 66 05; www.scalacon tarinidelbovolo.com; Calle Contarini del Bovolo 4299; adult/reduced €7/6; ☉10am-6pm; ☒Sant'Angelo) Under the republic, only the church and state were permitted to erect towers, as they could conceivably be used for military purposes. In around 1400 the Contarini family, eager to show off their wealth and power, cheekily built this nontower instead. Combining Venetian Gothic, Byzantine and Renaissance elements, this romantic 'staircase' looks even higher than its 26m due to the simple trick of decreasing the height of the arches as it rises.

There's a wonderful view from the **belvedere** at the top, gazing over the rooftops to San Marco. Admission includes entry to the **Tintoretto Room** gallery on the second landing.

CHIESA DI SANTA MARIA DEL GIGLIO   CHURCH

Map p266 (Santa Maria Zobenigo; www.chorus venezia.org; Campo di Santa Maria del Giglio; €3, or with Chorus Pass; ☉10.30am-4.30pm Mon-Sat; ☒Giglio) Founded in the 9th century but almost completely rebuilt in the late 17th, this church is distinguished by a series of six relief maps on its facade featuring Rome and five cities which were Venetian possessions at the time: Padua, the Croatian cities of Zadar and Split, and the Greek cities of Heraklion and Corfu. Inside are some intriguing masterpieces.

Two canvases by Tintoretto, each featuring two of the four evangelists, flank the organ. There's a small treasury in the Molin Chapel, although the real gem is Peter Paul Rubens' bare-breasted *Madonna & Child with St John,* featuring a characteristically chubby baby Jesus.

Grand Canal

A WATER TOUR

The 3.5km route of vaporetto (passenger ferry) No 1, which passes some 50 palazzi (mansions), six churches and scene-stealing backdrops featured in four James Bond films, is public transport at its most glamorous.

The Grand Canal starts with controversy: **1 Ponte di Calatrava** a luminous glass-and-steel bridge that cost triple the original €4 million estimate. Ahead are castle-like **2 Fondaco dei Turchi**, the historic Turkish trading-house; Renaissance **3 Palazzo Vendramin**, housing the city's casino; and double-arcaded **4 Ca' Pesaro**. Don't miss **5 Ca' d'Oro**, a 1430 filigree Gothic marvel.

Points of Venetian pride include the **6 Pescaria**, built in 1907 on the site where fishmongers have been slinging lagoon crab for 600 years, and neighbouring **7 Rialto Market** stalls, overflowing with island-grown produce. Cost overruns for 1592 **8 Ponte di Rialto** rival Calatrava's, but its marble splendour stands the test of time.

The next two canal bends could cause architectural whiplash, with Sanmicheli-designed Renaissance **9 Palazzo Grimani** and Mauro Codussi's **10 Palazzo Corner-Spinelli** followed by Giorgio Masari-designed **11 Palazzo Grassi** and Baldassare Longhena's baroque jewel box, **12 Ca' Rezzonico**.

Wooden **13 Ponte dell'Accademia** was built in 1930 as a temporary bridge, but the beloved landmark remains. Stone lions flank the **14 Peggy Guggenheim Collection**, where the American heiress collected ideas, lovers and art. You can't miss the dramatic dome of Longhena's **15 Chiesa di Santa Maria della Salute** or **16 Punta della Dogana**, Venice's triangular customs warehouse reinvented as a contemporary art showcase. The Grand Canal's grand finale is pink Gothic **17 Palazzo Ducale** and its adjoining **18 Ponte dei Sospiri**.

Palazzo Grassi
French magnate François Pinault scandalised Paris when he relocated his contemporary art collection here, to be displayed in galleries designed by Gae Aulenti and Tadao Ando.

Ca' Rezzonico
See how Venice lived in baroque splendour at this 18th-century art museum with Tiepolo ceilings, silk-swagged boudoirs and even an in-house pharmacy.

13 Ponte dell'Accademia

14 Peggy Guggenheim Collection

Chiesa di Santa Maria delle Salute

Punta della Dogana
Minimalist architect Tadao Ando creatively repurposed abandoned warehouses as galleries, which now host contemporary art installations from François Pinault's collection.

Fondaco dei Turchi
Recognisable by its double colonnade, watchtowers, and dugout canoe parked at the Museo di Storia Naturale's ground-floor loggia.

Ponte di Calatrava
With its starkly streamlined fish-fin shape, the 2008 bridge was the first to be built over the Grand Canal in 75 years.

Ca' d'Oro
Behind the triple Gothic arcades are priceless masterpieces: Titians looted by Napoleon, a rare Mantegna and semiprecious stone mosaic floors.

②

③ Palazzo Vendramin

④

⑤

⑥ Pescaria

⑦ Rialto Market

⑩

Palazzo Corner-Spinelli

Palazzo Grimani

⑨

⑧ Ponte di Rialto

Ponte dei Sospiri

⑱

Palazzo Ducale ⑰

Ponte di Rialto
Antonio da Ponte beat out Palladio for the commission of this bridge, but construction costs spiralled to 250,000 Venetian ducats – about €19 million today.

Ca' Pesaro
Originally designed by Baldassare Longhena, this palazzo was bequeathed to the city in 1898 to house the Galleria d'Arte Moderna and Museo d'Arte Orientale.

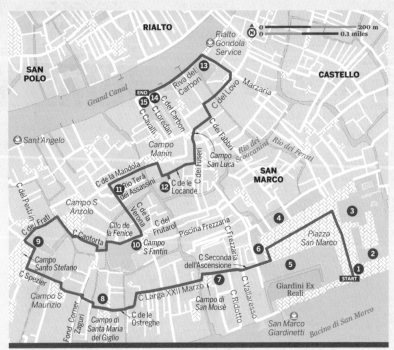

Neighbourhood Walk
San Marco Highlights

START PIAZZETTA SAN MARCO
END CA' LOREDAN & CA' FARSETTI
LENGTH 2KM; ONE HOUR

Venetians still hurry past the granite **❶ Columns of San Marco**, site of public executions for centuries. Past the **❷ Palazzo Ducale** (p53) is the **❸ Basilica di San Marco** (p50) flanked by Mauro Codussi's 16th-century **❹ Procuratie Vecchie** and Scamozzi-designed and Longhena-completed **❺ Procuratie Nuove**. Today the Museo Correr occupies the Procuratie Nuove and **❻ Ala Napoleonica**, the palace Napoleon brazenly razed San Geminiano church to build.

Cut through the arcade and follow Venice's ritziest shopping strip, Calle Larga XXII Marzo, past **❼ Chiesa di San Moisè** towards baroque **❽ Chiesa di Santa Maria del Giglio** (p59) covered with peculiar city maps. Further west, Bartolomeo Bon's marble Gothic portals grace the red brick **❾ Chiesa di Santo Stefano** (p58), while

next door its leaning bell tower looks like it's had one *spritz* too many.

Turn right down Calle Caotorta to reach Venice's **❿ La Fenice** (p37). Take canyon-like Calle de la Verona into the shadows and continue on to **⓫ Calle dei Assassini**. Corpses were so frequently found here that in 1128, Venice banned the full beards assassins wore as disguises. Just off Campo Manin you can duck into the romantic courtyard flanking the **⓬ Scala Contarini del Bovolo** (p59).

Continue on, turn left onto Calle dei Fuseri, cut through Campo San Luca and wind your way to the Grand Canal. To the left is Sansovino-designed **⓭ Palazzo Dolfin-Manin** (1547), where the last doge, Ludovico Manin, died in seclusion in 1802. Further along are conjoined **⓮ Ca' Loredan** and **⓯ Ca' Farsetti**, home to Venice's city hall; George Clooney and Amal Alamuddin were married here in 2014. On the side facing Calle del Carbon look for a plaque honouring Elena Lucrezia Cornaro Piscopia, the first woman to earn a Padua University PhD, in 1678.

Admiral Antonio Barbaro commissioned Giuseppe Sardi to undertake the reconstruction of the church for the glory of the Virgin, Venice, and of course himself – his statue gets prime facade placement and the cities featured are all places where he served. This self-glorifying architectural audacity enraged 19th-century architectural critic John Ruskin, who called it a 'manifestation of insolent atheism'.

PONTE DEI SOSPIRI
BRIDGE

Map p266 (Bridge of Sighs; ⛴San Zaccaria) One of Venice's most photographed sights, the Bridge of Sighs connects the Palazzo Ducale to the 16th-century Priggione Nove (New Prisons). Its improbable popularity is due to British libertine Lord Byron (1788–1824), who mentioned it in one of his poems. Condemned prisoners were said to sigh as they passed through the enclosed bridge and glimpsed the beauty of the lagoon. Now the sighs are mainly from people trying to dodge the snapping masses as they attempt to cross the neighbouring bridges.

NEGOZIO OLIVETTI
ARCHITECTURE

Map p266 (Olivetti Store; ☎041 522 83 87; www.negozioliveitti.it; Piazza San Marco 101; adult/reduced €6/3; ◎10.30am-5.30pm Tue-Sun; ⛴San Marco) Like a revolver pulled from a petticoat, ultramodern Negozio Olivetti was an outright provocation when it first appeared under the frilly arcades of the Procuratie Vecchie in 1958. High-tech pioneer Olivetti commissioned Venetian architect Carlo Scarpa to transform a narrow, dim souvenir shop into a showcase for its sleek typewriters and 'computing machines' (several 1948–54 models are displayed).

CHIESA DI SAN MOISÈ
CHURCH

Map p266 (☎041 528 58 40; Campo di San Moisè; ◎9.30am-12.30pm & 3.30-6.30pm Mon-Sat, 9.30-11am & 2.30-6.30pm Sun; ⛴San Marco) FREE Icing flourishes of carved stone across the 1660s facade make this church, dedicated to Moses, appear positively lickable, although 19th-century architecture critic John Ruskin found its wedding-cake appearance indigestible. From an engineering perspective, Ruskin had a point: several statues had to be removed in the 19th century to prevent the facade from collapsing under their combined weight.

The remaining statuary by Flemish sculptor Heinrich Meyring (aka Merengo in Italian) includes scant devotional works but a sycophantic number of tributes to church patrons. Among the scene-stealing works inside are Tintoretto's *Washing of the Feet*, in the chapel to the left of the altar, and Palma il Giovane's *The Supper*, facing it.

CHIESA DI SAN ZULIAN
CHURCH

Map p266 (☎041 523 53 83; Campo San Zulian 604; ◎9am-6.30pm; ⛴Rialto) FREE Founded in 829, San Zulian got a Sansovino makeover funded by physician Tomasso Rangone, who made his fortune by selling syphilis cures and secrets to living past 100 (he died at 84). The doctor is immortalised in bronze over the portal, holding sarsaparilla – his VD 'miracle cure'. Inside, beneath a painted ceiling, are works by Palma il Giovane and Veronese's *Dead Christ and Saints*.

CHIESA DI SAN SALVADOR
CHURCH

Map p266 (☎041 523 67 17; www.chiesasansalvador.it; Campo San Salvador 4835; ◎9am-noon & 4-6.30pm Mon-Sat; ⛴Rialto) FREE A dream made real, San Salvador was conceived in the 7th century when Jesus appeared to a sleeping Bishop Magnus and pointed out the exact spot on a lagoon map where he should build a church. There was, however, a minor technical glitch: the city of Venice didn't exist yet, and the area was mostly mud banks. But Bishop Magnus had faith that once the church was built the parishioners would follow – and today this church perched on a bustling *campo* (square) proves his point.

CHIESA DI SAN VIDAL
CHURCH

Map p266 (www.interpretiveneziani.com; Campo di San Vidal 2862; ◎9am-6pm; ⛴Accademia) FREE Built by Doge Vitale Falier in the 11th century, Chiesa di San Vidal got a 1706-14 Palladian facelift to commemorate Doge Francesco Morosoni's victory over Turkish foes. Inside is *St Vitale on Horseback and Saints* by Vittore Carpaccio, featuring his signature traffic-light red and miniaturist's attention to detail. The deconsecrated church now houses a collection of historic musical instruments and serves as a concert venue for Interpreti Veneziani (p67).

PONTE DELL'ACCADEMIA
BRIDGE

Map p266 (btwn Campo di San Vidal & Campo della Carità; ⛴Accademia) The wooden Ponte dell'Accademia was built in 1933 as a temporary replacement for an 1854 iron bridge, but this span, arched like a cat's back, remains a beloved landmark. Engineer Eugenio Miozzi's notable works include the Lido Casino, but none has lasted like this elegant little footbridge – and recent structural improvements have preserved it for decades to come.

✕ EATING

★MARCHINI TIME — BAKERY €

Map p266 (☎041 241 30 87; www.marchinitime. it; Campo San Luca 4589; items €1.20-3.50; ⊙7.30am-8.30pm; ⑤Rialto) Elbow your way through the morning crush to bag a warm croissant filled with runny apricot jam or melting Nutella. Everything here is freshly baked, which is why the crowd hangs around as croissants give way to foccacia, *pizette* (mini pizzas) and generously stuffed *panini*.

★SUSO — GELATO €

Map p266 (☎348 564 65 45; www.gelatovenezia. it; Calle de la Bissa 5453; scoops €1.60; ⊙10am-midnight; ⑤Rialto) 🍦 Indulge in gelato as rich as a doge, in original seasonal flavours like marscapone cream with fig sauce and walnuts. All Suso's gelati are locally made and free of artificial colours; gluten-free cones are available.

DRINKS WITH A VIEW
···

Enjoy a coffee or *spritz* (*prosecco* cocktail) with superlative views at these great bars:

Bar Longhi The Gritti's jewel-box bar is hung with priceless artworks and has a Grand Canal terrace fringed with flowers.

Caffé dell'Art (p57) The cafe of Museo Correr offers frescoed rooms and 1st-floor views of Basilica di San Marco.

L'Ombra del Leoni (p66) The Biennale's Grand Canal terrace offers a triple-whammy view of the Salute, Dogana and San Giorgio Maggiore.

Grancaffè Quadri Quadri's glamorous baroque bar has been serving *aperitivi* since 1638 in a prime position on Piazza San Marco.

ROSTICCERIA GISLON — VENETIAN, DELI €

Map p266 (☎0415 22 35 69; Calle de la Bissa 5424; meals €15-25; ⊙9am-9.30pm Tue-Sun, to 3.30pm Mon; ⑤Rialto) Serving San Marco workers since the 1930s, this no-frills *rosticceria* (roast-meat specialist) has an ultramarine canteen counter downstairs and a small eat-in restaurant upstairs. Hot to trot you'll find *arancini* (rice balls), deep-fried mozzarella balls, croquettes and fish fry-ups. No one said it was going to be healthy!

Those with more time might indulge in surprisingly good seafood risottos, grilled cuttlefish and, of course, the perennially popular roast chicken.

ROSA SALVA — BAKERY €

Map p266 (☎041 522 79 34; www.rosasalva.it; Mercerie 5020; items €1.30-7.50; ⊙8am-8pm; ⑤Rialto) With just-baked strudel and reliable cappuccino, Rosa Salva has provided Venetians with fresh reasons to roll out of bed for over a century. Cheerfully efficient women working the spotless counter supply gale-force espresso and turbo-loaded pistachio profiteroles to power you across 30 more bridges.

★AI MERCANTI — ITALIAN €€

Map p266 (☎041 523 82 69; www.aimercanti.it; Corte Coppo 4346a; meals €34-38; ⊙11.30am-3pm & 7-10pm Tue-Sat, 7-11pm Mon; ⑤Rialto) With its pumpkin-coloured walls, gleaming golden fixtures and jet-black tables and chairs, Ai Mercanti effortlessly conjures up a romantic mood. No wonder dates whisper over glasses of wine from the vast selection before tucking into modern bistro-style dishes. Although there's a focus on seafood and secondary cuts of meat, there are some wonderful vegetarian options as well.

OSTERIA DA CARLA — VENETIAN €€

Map p266 (☎041 523 78 55; www.osteriadacarla.it; Corte Contarina 1535a; meals €43-48; ⊙8.30am-11pm Mon-Sat; ⑤San Marco) Diners in the know duck into this hidden courtyard, less than 100m from Piazza San Marco, to snack on *cicheti* (Venetian tapas) at the counter or to sit down to a romantic meal. The surroundings are at once modern and ancient, with exposed brick and interesting art.

★RISTORANTE QUADRI — MODERN ITALIAN €€€

Map p266 (☎041 522 21 05; www.alajmo.it; Piazza San Marco 121; meals €110-138; ⊙12.30-2.30pm & 7.30-10.30pm Tue-Sun; ⑤San Marco) When it comes to Venetian glamour, nothing beats this historic Michelin-starred restaurant overlooking Piazza San Marco. A small swarm of servers greets you as you're shown to your table in a room decked out with silk damask, gilt, painted beams and Murano chandeliers. Dishes are precise and delicious, deftly incorporating Venetian touches into an inventive modern Italian menu.

★BISTROT DE VENISE
VENETIAN €€€

Map p266 (☑041 523 66 51; www.bistrotde venise.com; Calle dei Fabbri 4685; meals €47-78; ☺noon-3pm & 7pm-midnight; ✔; ⚲Rialto) Indulge in some culinary time travel at this fine-dining bistro where they've revived the recipes of Renaissance chef Bartolomeo Scappi. Dine like a doge in the red-and-gilt dining room on braised duck with wild apple and onion pudding, or enjoy the Jewish recipe of goose, raisin and pine-nut pasta. Even the desserts are beguilingly exotic.

TRATTORIA DA FIORE
VENETIAN €€€

Map p266 (☑041 523 53 10; www.dafiore.it; Calle de le Botteghe 3461; meals €46-62; ☺12.30-2.30pm & 7.30-10.30pm; ⚲San Samuele) Rustic-chic decor sets the scene for excellent Venetian dishes composed of carefully selected seasonal ingredients from small Veneto producers. The restaurant is justly famous for its seafood dishes. Next door, the bar's *cicheti* counter serves tasty snacks at more democratic prices.

TRATTORIA VINI DA ARTURO
ITALIAN €€€

Map p266 (☑041 528 69 74; Calle dei Assassini 3656; meals €71-81; ☺noon-3.30pm & 6.30-11pm Mon-Sat; ✚; ⚲Sant'Angelo) For over 40 years this corridor-sized restaurant has dispensed charm and simple meals, with the same owner, same chef and same maître d'. Your host will happily trot out irrefutable proof that Nicole Kidman actually eats and that producer Joel Silver managed to escape *The Matrix* for steak here. Atmosphere aside, the prices are astronomical for what is offered.

⬛ DRINKING & NIGHTLIFE

★BAR LONGHI
COCKTAIL BAR

Map p266 (☑041 79 47 81; www.hotelgrittipalace venice.com; Campo di Santa Maria del Giglio 2467;

☺11am-1am; ⚲Giglio) The Gritti's beautiful Bar Longhi may be hellishly expensive, but if you consider the room – with its Fortuny fabrics, intarsia marble bar, 18th-century mirrors and million-dollar Piero Longhi paintings – its signature orange martini (the work of art that it is) starts to seem reasonable. In summer you'll have to choose between the twinkling interior and a spectacular Grand Canal terrace.

★CAFFÈ FLORIAN
CAFE

Map p266 (☑041 520 56 41; www.caffeflorian. com; Piazza San Marco 57; ☺9am-11pm; ⚲San Marco) The oldest still-operating cafe in Europe and one of the first to welcome women, Florian maintains rituals (if not prices) established in 1720: besuited waiters serve cappuccino on silver trays, lovers canoodle in plush banquettes and the orchestra strikes up as the sunset illuminates San Marco's mosaics. Piazza seating during concerts costs €6 extra, but dreamy-eyed romantics hardly notice.

★GRANCAFFÈ QUADRI
CAFE

Map p266 (☑041 522 21 05; www.alajmo.it; Piazza San Marco 121; ☺9am-midnight; ⚲San Marco) Powdered wigs seem appropriate inside this baroque bar-cafe, serving happy hours since 1638. During Carnevale, costumed Quadri revellers party like it's 1699 – despite prices shooting up to €15 a *spritz*. Grab a seat on the piazza to watch the best show in town: the sunset sparking the basilica's golden mosaics ablaze.

★HARRY'S BAR
BAR

Map p266 (☑041 528 57 77; www.harrysbarvene zia.com; Calle Vallaresso 1323; ☺10.30am-11pm; ⚲San Marco) Aspiring auteurs hold court at tables well scuffed by Ernest Hemingway, Charlie Chaplin, Truman Capote and Orson Welles, enjoying the signature €22 bellini (Giuseppe Cipriani's original 1948 recipe: white peach juice and *prosecco*) with a side of reflected glory.

CAFFÈ BRASILIA
WINE BAR

Map p266 (☑041 523 99 18; Calle dei Assassini 3658; ☺7am-2am Mon-Sat, from 11am Sun; ⚲Sant'Angelo) There's a pub-like quality to this friendly little back-lane bar – a rarity in ritzy San Marco. It's the main haunt of a local football team comprised of off-duty lawyers, hence the trophy cabinet.

TARNOWSKA'S AMERICAN BAR BAR

Map p266 (☎041 520 83 33; www.hotelala.it; Campo di Santa Maria del Giglio 2494; ⏰5pm-1am Tue-Sun; ☣Giglio) Decked out in primary colours and comfy leather couches, the bar of the Hotel Ala takes its name from a countess convicted of a particularly sordid 1907 murder which took place in this very hotel, involving no less than three of her lovers. Read all about it while sipping cocktails and listening to bad American soft rock.

BLACK-JACK WINE BAR

Map p266 (Campo San Luca 4267b; ⏰7.30am-9pm; ☣Rialto) Charming staff dispense delicious *cicheti* from a central horseshoe-shaped bar in this upmarket little place in the main shopping precinct. It's a great place for a snack and a tipple on your way to La Fenice or Teatro Goldoni; you could easily make a meal of it.

BÀCARO JAZZ BAR

Map p266 (Salizada del Fontego dei Tedeschi 5546; ⏰noon-2am; ☣Rialto) A bar with a ceiling completely covered with bras could hardly be accused of being classy, but if you're after a change from sedate *cicheti* bars, this loud and unashamedly trashy place is usually packed to its quirkily decorated rafters on the weekends.

L'OMBRA DEL LEONI BAR

Map p266 (☎041 521 87 11; Calle Ridotto 1364a; ⏰9am-midnight summer, to 9pm winter; ☣San Marco) Lucky Biennale workers have Grand Canal views from their upstairs offices in Ca' Giustinian, but you too can enjoy the *palazzo's* peerless waterside position in the downstairs cafe-restaurant. Try to nab a seat on the outdoor terrace – it's the perfect spot to watch the gondolas come and go, with basilicas as the backdrop.

OSTERIA ALL'ALBA WINE BAR

Map p266 (Ramo del Fontego dei Tedeschi 5370; ⏰4pm-midnight; ☣Rialto) That roar behind the Rialto means the DJ's funk set is kicking in at All'Alba. Squeeze inside to order salami sandwiches and DOC Veneto wines, and check out walls festooned with vintage LPs and effusive thanks scrawled in 12 languages.

CAFFÈ LAVENA CAFE

Map p266 (☎041 522 40 70; www.lavena.it; Piazza San Marco 133/134; ⏰9.30am-11pm; ☣San Marco) Opera composer Richard Wagner had the right idea: when Venice leaves you weak in the knees, get a pick-me-up at Lavena. An espresso at Lavena's mirrored bar is a baroque bargain – never mind the politically incorrect antique 'Moor's head' chandeliers. Spring for piazza seating to savor *caffè corretto* (coffee 'corrected' with liquor) accompanied by Lavena's nimble violinists.

ENOTECA AL VOLTO WINE BAR

Map p266 (☎041 522 89 45; Calle Cavalli 4081; ⏰10am-3pm & 6-11pm; ☣Rialto) Join the crowd working its way through the vast selection of *cicheti* in this historic wood-panelled bar that feels like the inside of a ship's hold. Lining the ceiling above the golden glow of the brass bar lanterns are hundreds of wine labels from just some of the bottles of regional wines that are cracked open every night.

CAFFÈ CENTRALE COCKTAIL BAR

Map p266 (☎041 887 66 42; www.caffecentralev enezia.com; Piscina de Frezzaria 1659b; ⏰7pm-1am; ☣San Marco) You might spot a celebrity or two lurking on the black-leather sofas under Centrale's moody Murano chandeliers. Meals are pricey and canalside VIP tables chilly, but this slick modern bar draws La Fenice post-opera crowds with signature *spritz* cocktails, midnight snacks, chill-out DJ sets and occasional live jazz.

TEAMO WINE BAR

Map p266 (☎041 528 37 87; www.teamowinebar. com; Rio Terà de la Mandola 3795; ⏰8.30am-10.30pm Fri-Wed; ☣Sant'Angelo) By day it's more of a cafe, but in the evening the little tables fill up with a mixed crowd, drinking wine and snacking on massive platters of *salumi* (cured meats) and cheese.

BACARANDO BAR

Map p266 (☎041 523 82 80; www.bacarando. com; Corte dell'Orso 5495; ⏰10.30am-midnight; ☣Rialto) If you've managed to find this wood-panelled bar in the warren of streets off San Bartolomeo, toast yourself with a cocktail and order a plate of heaped *cicheti*. Thanks to its divey vibe and a lively program of cultural events and live music, it's popular with a hip young crowd.

☆ ENTERTAINMENT

MUSICA A PALAZZO OPERA

Map p266 (☎340 971 72 72; www.musicapalazzo. com; Palazzo Barbarigo Minotto, Fondamenta

SEEING VENICE WITH AN ARTIST'S EYE

Wandering through sun-drenched *campi* (squares) and over glassy canals, it's easy to see why Venice has inspired an endless stream of artists. From Veronese, Tiepolo and Canaletto, to Turner and Monet, each tried to capture the elusive quality of the city's light-filled beauty and unique colour palette, and many of their efforts are crammed in the museums, *palazzi* (mansions) and galleries of San Marco. Why not join them and try your hand at painting or photographing the city light with experts?

Painting Venice (☎340 544 52 27; www.paintingvenice.com; Cannaregio; 2hr private lessons €100, 2-day workshops €280) Sign up for a session with professionally trained and practising artists Caroline, Sebastien and Katrin and you'll strike out into tranquil *campi* in the tradition of classic Venetian *vedutisti* (outdoor artists). Beginners learn the basic concepts of painting 'en plein air', while those with more advanced skills receive tailor-made tuition. It's a great way to slow down and really appreciate the colour and composition of each view. Lessons are offered in English, Italian, French and German.

Venice Photo Tour (☎041 963 73 74; www.venicephototour.com; 2-/3-/6-hr walking tours for up to 4 people €210/300/600) Throughout San Marco you'll find yourself tripping over smart-phone-toting tourists. Everyone, it seems, wants to capture the perfect Venetian scene. Getty photojournalist Marco Secchi will show you how during an in-depth tutorial exploring the secret corners of the city. In particular, you'll learn how to capture the nuances of light and how to frame that masterpiece for the mantlepiece. He can work with all types of camera, tailor tours to personal interests and arrange photography tours of the lagoon.

Duodo o Barbarigo 2504; ticket incl beverage €85; ⊙from 8pm; ☒Giglio) Hang onto your *prosecco* and brace for impact: in historic salons, the soprano's high notes imperil glassware, and thundering baritones reverberate through inlaid floors. During performances of opera from Verdi or Rossini, the drama progresses from receiving-room overtures to parlour duets overlooking the Grand Canal, followed by second acts in the Tiepolo-ceilinged dining room and bedroom grand finales.

INTERPRETI VENEZIANI CLASSICAL MUSIC
Map p266 (☎041 277 05 61; www.interpretiven eziani.com; Chiesa San Vidal, Campo San Vidal 2862; adult/reduced €29/24; ⊙performances 8.30pm; ☒Accademia) Hard-core classical fans might baulk at the idea of Vivaldi being played night after night for decades, but it truly is a fitting soundtrack to this city of intrigue. You'll never listen to *The Four Seasons* again without hearing summer storms erupting over the lagoon, or snow-muffled footsteps hurrying over footbridges in winter's-night intrigues.

TEATRO GOLDONI THEATRE
Map p266 (☎041 240 20 14; www.teatrostabi leveneto.it; Calle del Teatro 4650b; ☒Rialto) Named after the city's great playwright,

Venice's main theatre has an impressive dramatic range that runs from Goldoni's comedy to Shakespearean tragedy (mostly in Italian), plus ballets and concerts. Don't be fooled by the huge 20th-century bronze doors: this venerable theatre dates from 1622, and the jewel-box interior seats just 800.

MULTISALA ROSSINI CINEMA
Map p266 (☎041 241 72 74; Salizada de la Chiesa o del Teatro 3997a; adult/reduced €7.50/7; ⊙shows Tue-Sun; 🖶; ☒Sant'Angelo) Film buffs who miss the proverbial boat to the annual Venice Film Festival on the Lido, rejoice: award-winning films and blockbusters screen year-round at the city's cinema. Some films are screened in the original language, but most are dubbed in Italian.

🛍 SHOPPING

★**L'ARMADIO DI COCO**
LUXURY VINTAGE VINTAGE
Map p266 (☎041 241 32 14; www.larmadiod icoco.it; Campo di Santa Maria del Giglio 2516a; ⊙10.30am-7.30pm; ☒Giglio) Jam-packed with pre-loved designer treasures from yesteryear, this tiny shop is the place to

come for classic Chanel dresses, exquisite cashmere coats and limited-edition Gucci shoulder bags.

CHIARASTELLA CATTANA   HOMEWARES

Map p266 (☑041 522 43 69; www.chiarastellacat tana.com; Salizada San Samuele 3216; ☺11am-1pm & 3-7pm Mon-Sat; ⚓San Samuele) Transform any home into a thoroughly modern *palazzo* with these locally woven, strikingly original Venetian linens. Whimsical cushions feature chubby purple rhinoceroses and grumpy scarlet elephants straight out of Pietro Longhi paintings, and hand-tasselled jacquard hand towels will dry your royal guests in style. Decorators and design aficionados should save an afternoon to consider dizzying woven-to-order napkin and curtain options here.

L'ISOLA   GLASS

Map p266 (☑041 523 19 73; www.lisola.com; Calle de la Botteghe 2970; ☺10.30am-7.30pm; ⚓San Samuele) Backlit chalices and spotlit vases emit an other-worldly glow at this shrine to Murano modernist glass master Carlo Moretti. Strict shapes contain freeform swirls of orange and red, and glasses etched with fish-scale patterns add wit and a wink to high-minded modernism. Prices for signature water glasses start at €105.

ARCOBALENO   ARTS & CRAFTS

Map p266 (☑041 241 20 71; Calle de le Botteghe 3457; ☺10am-6pm; ⚓Sant'Angelo) After seeing umpteen Venetian masterpieces, anyone's fingers will start twitching for a paintbrush. Arcobaleno provides the raw materials, with shelves fully stocked with jars of all the essential pigments: Titian red, Tiepolo sky-blue, Veronese rose, Bellini peach and Tintoretto teal. It also sells leather aprons, raw incense and interesting brass knick-knacks.

BOTTEGA D'ARTE GIULIANA LONGO   HATS

Map p266 (☑041 522 64 54; www.giulianalongo. com; Calle del Lovo 4813; ☺10am-7pm Mon-Sat; ⚓Rialto) Giuliana's shop is the dream hatcupboard of any true sartorialist. Styles range from hand-woven Montecristi panama hats to a fuchsia felt number that looks like a doge's cap for Peggy Guggenheim. Giuliana is here most days, polishing leather aviator hats or affixing a broad band to a *baretero,* the wide-brimmed gondolier's hat best worn with a rakish tilt (from €65).

SIGFRIDO CIPOLATO   JEWELLERY

Map p266 (☑041 522 84 37; www.sigfridocipo lato.com; Calle de la Mandola 3717a; ☺11am-8pm Mon-Sat; ⚓Sant'Angelo) Booty worthy of pirates is displayed in the fishbowl-size window display: a constellation of diamonds in star settings on a ring, a tiny enamelled green snake sinking its fangs into a pearl, and diamond drop earrings that end in enamelled gold skulls. Though they look like heirlooms, these small wonders were made on the premises by master jeweller Sigfrido.

FIORELLA GALLERY   FASHION & ACCESSORIES

Map p266 (☑041 520 92 28; www.fiorellagallery. com; Campo Santo Stefano 2806a; ☺9.30am-1.30pm & 3.30-7pm Tue-Sat, 3-7pm Mon; ⚓Accademia) Fiorella's been pioneering rebel couture since 1968 but you'll need a rockstar budget to afford one of her silk-velvet smoking jackets in louche lavender and oxblood, printed by hand with skulls, peacocks or a Fiorella signature: wide-eyed rats. Hours are approximate; as the sign says, 'I open some time'.

ATELIER SEGALIN DI DANIELA GHEZZO   SHOES

Map p266 (☑041 522 21 15; www.danielaghezzo. it; Calle dei Fuseri 4365; ☺10am-1pm & 3-7pm Mon-Fri, 10am-1pm Sat; ⚓San Marco) A gold chain pulled across this historic atelier doorway means Daniela is already consulting with a client, discussing rare leathers while taking foot measurements. Each pair is custom-made, so you'll never see your emerald ostrich-leather boots on another diva, or your dimpled manta-ray brogues on a rival mogul. Expect to pay around €1000 and wait six weeks for delivery.

VENETIA STUDIUM   FASHION & ACCESSORIES

Map p266 (☑041 523 69 53; www.venetia studium.com; Calle de le Ostreghe 2427; ☺10am-7.30pm; ⚓Giglio) Get that 'just got in from Monaco for my art opening' look beloved of bohemians who marry well. The high-drama Delphos tunic dresses make anyone look like a high-maintenance modern dancer or heiress (Isadora Duncan and Peggy Guggenheim were both fans), and the hand-stamped silk-velvet bags are more arty than ostentatious.

SV LAB   FASHION & ACCESSORIES

Map p266 (☑041 522 05 95; www.svlab.it; Campo San Maurizio 2663; ☺11am-6.30pm; ⚓Giglio) SV

Lab sells deadly cool men's and women's apparel with a rock-and-roll sensibility but with a patrician's eye to quality. The silk and cashmere jackets are particularly beautiful, but you might need access to a patrician's wallet as well.

GALLERIA LA SALIZADA PHOTOGRAPHY
Map p266 (☏041 241 07 23; www.lasalizada.it; Calle de la Botteghe 3448; ◷3.30-7.30pm Mon, 10am-1pm & 3.30-7.30pm Tue-Sat; ⛴Sant'Angelo) This interesting store showcases rare vintage prints of Venice from the Fratelli Alinari photographic archives alongside the work of current photographers. Smaller prints are surprisingly affordable and make for wonderful keepsakes.

BEVILACQUA FABRICS DESIGN
Map p266 (☏041 241 06 62; www.bevilacquatesuti.com; Campo di Santa Maria del Giglio 2520; ◷10am-7pm; ⛴Giglio) TV dens become grand salons with Venetian swagger at Bevilacqua, purveyor of fine silk-velvet brocades, damasks and tassels to Venice's baroque palaces and Italy's swankiest modern apartments. Master artisans still weave the fabrics in Venice on 18th-century wooden looms, and the front-room display here is just a sample of their artistry; ask about custom cushions and upholstery.

MERCATINO DELL'ANTIQUARIATO MARKET
Map p266 (www.mercatinocamposanmaurizio.it; Campo San Maurizio; ⛴Giglio) A much-loved antiques flea market held several weekends a year in Campo San Maurizio; check the website for dates. Head in early for the best finds, among them vintage Campari posters, Venetian postcards, Murano glassware and delicate Burano lace.

MATERIALMENTE DESIGN
Map p266 (☏041 528 68 81; www.materialmentevenezia.com; Mercerie San Salvador 4850; ◷10.30am-7pm Mon-Sat; ⛴Rialto) Prolific sibling artisans Maddelena Venier and Alessandro Salvadori pack their tiny boutique with whimsical creations such as wire fish-skeleton chandeliers, whale mobiles and interesting jewellery.

VENETIAN DREAMS FASHION & ACCESSORIES
Map p266 (☏041 523 02 92; www.venetiandreams.altervista.org; Calle de la Mandola 3805a; ◷11am-6.30pm Wed-Mon; ⛴Sant'Angelo) High fashion meets *acqua alta* in Marisa Convento's aquatic accessories. La Fenice divas demand her freshwater-pearl-encrusted velvet handbags, while Biennale artistes snap up octopus-tentacle glass-bead necklaces. Between customers, Marisa can be glimpsed at her desk, painstakingly weaving coral-branch collars from antique Murano *conterie* (seed beads). To wow Carnevale crowds, ask about custom costume orders.

OTTICA CARRARO FASHION & ACCESSORIES
Map p266 (☏041 520 42 58; www.otticacarraro.it; Calle de la Mandola 3706; ◷9.30am-1pm & 3-7.30pm Mon-Sat; ⛴Sant'Angelo) Lost your sunglasses on the Lido? Never fear: Ottica Carraro can make you a custom pair within 24 hours, including the eye exam. The store has its own limited-edition 'Venice' line, ranging from cat-eye shades perfect for facing paparazzi to chunky wood-grain frames that could get you mistaken for an art critic at the Biennale.

FONDACO DEI TEDESCHI DEPARTMENT STORE
Map p266 (www.dfs.com; Calle del Fontego dei Tedeschi 5350; ◷10am-8pm; ⛴Rialto) Occupying one of the Grand Canal's most imposing buildings, a 16th-century German trading house, this branch of the DFS chain is worth visiting whether you're in the market for a handbag with a four-digit price tag or not. Four floors of colonnaded galleries rise up to line the vast central void, leading to sublime views from the rooftop.

DECLARE FASHION & ACCESSORIES
Map p266 (☏041 522 55 59; www.dclr.it; Calle de la Mandola 3801; ◷10.30am-7.30pm; ⛴Sant'Angelo) Expect to fall in lust with these richly hued, contemporary leather-goods. Made by artisans using full-grain Tuscan leather, these coveted, butter-soft creations include origami-inspired wallets, slinky clutch purses and totes, as well as effortlessly stylish duffle and messenger bags. You'll find a second branch in San Polo (p105).

CAIGO DA MAR HOMEWARES
Map p266 (☏041 243 32 38; www.caigodamar.com; Calle de le Botteghe 3131; ◷11am-1pm & 4-7pm Mon-Sat; ⛴San Samuele) Venetian pirates once headed to Constantinople for all their interior-decoration needs, but today they'd need look no further than Caigo da Mar. This tiny treasure trove brims with dramatic black Murano glass candelabras

and a designer booty of Fornasetti cushions, plus enough octopus-shaped lamps and nautilus-shell dishes to make any living room look like the lost city of Atlantis.

ARNOLDO & BATTOIS FASHION & ACCESSORIES
Map p266 (☑041 528 59 44; www.arnoldoebattois.com; Calle dei Fuseri 4271; ☺10am-1pm & 3.30-7pm Mon-Thu & Sat; ⓢRialto) Handbags become heirlooms in the hands of Venetian designers Massimiliano Battois and Silvano Arnoldo, whose handcrafted clutches come in bold turquoise and magenta leather with baroque closures in laser-cut wood. Artfully draped emerald and graphite silk dresses complete the look for Biennale openings.

PAGINE E CUOIO FASHION & ACCESSORIES
Map p266 (☑041 528 65 55; Calle del Frutarol 1845; ☺9.30am-7pm Mon-Sat; ⓢGiglio) The lion of San Marco looks fashionably fierce embossed upon a turquoise billfold by leather artisan Davide Desanzuane. Unexpected colours update Venetian heraldry for the 21st century on Davide's tablet cases, smartphone carriers and business-card holders – and since they're all one of a kind, they make singular fashion statements.

CAMUFFO GLASS
Map p266 (Calle de le Acque 4992; ☺10am-5pm Mon-Sat; ⓢRialto) Kids, entomologists and glass collectors seek out Signor Camuffo in this cabinet of miniature natural wonders. Expect to find him wielding a blowtorch as he fuses metallic foils and molten glass into shimmering wings for the city's finest lampworked glass beetles and dragonflies. Between bugs, he'll chat about his work and sell you strands of Murano glass beads.

ESPERIENZE GLASS, FASHION
Map p266 (☑041 521 29 45; www.esperienzevenezia.com; Calle dei Specchieri 473b; ☺10am-noon & 3-7pm; ⓢSan Marco) When an Italian minimalist falls in love with a Murano glass-blower, the result is spare, spirited glass jewellery. Esperienze is a collaborative effort for husband-wife team Graziano and Sara: he breathes life into her designs, including matte-glass teardrop pendants and cracked-ice earrings. They also stock a range of women's clothing.

CHARTA BOOKS
Map p266 (☑041 522 98 01; www.chartaonline.com; Calle dei Fabbri 831; ☺10am-12.30pm & 4-7.30pm; ⓢSan Marco) Even pulp fiction becomes high art at Charta, where favourite books are custom-bound in bespoke covers. Customised titles run into the hundreds of euros.

Dorsoduro

Neighbourhood Top Five

❶ Gallerie dell'Accademia (p73) Getting a crash course in Venetian painting at the Accademia, a former convent now positively blushing with masterpieces of glowing colours, censored subjects, prime-time drama and breathless elegance.

❷ Peggy Guggenheim Collection (p75) Viewing Picasso, Pollock, Giacometti and Kapoor at the former Grand Canal pad of an American heiress.

❸ Ca' Rezzonico (p76) Waltzing through baroque palace boudoirs filled with social graces.

❹ Punta della Dogana (p78) Absorbing fearless contemporary art and boldly repurposed architecture.

❺ Basilica di Santa Maria della Salute (p76) Testing the curative powers of Longhena's mystical marbles and finding hidden Titian wonders.

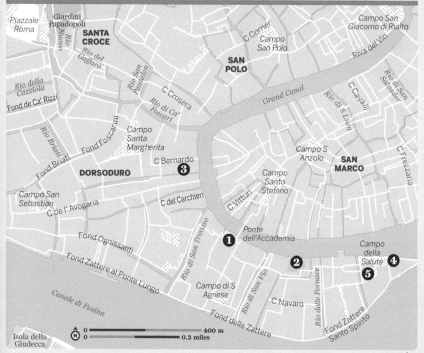

For more detail of this area see Map p276 ➡

Lonely Planet's Top Tip

If you're mad about modern art consider signing up for the Guggenheim's annual Open Pass (€39 per person), which gives you free access to the Venice museum, reduced admission for guests, a discount on the audio guide and in the museum cafe, and free entrance to 10 other major modern art museums in Italy. The Young Pass (€19 per person) offers the same benefits for those under the age of 26.

✖ Best Places to Eat

➡ Riviera (p80)

➡ Estro (p79)

➡ Enoteca Ai Artisti (p81)

➡ Da Codroma (p79)

For reviews, see p78.➡

🍷 Best Places to Drink

➡ Cantinone Giá Schiavi (p81)

➡ El Sbarlefo (p81)

➡ Ai Pugni (p81)

➡ El Chioschetto (p81)

For reviews, see p81.➡

👁 Best Venetian Views

➡ *Feast in the House of Levi*, Gallerie dell'Accademia (p73)

➡ Grand Canal alongside *Angel of the City*, Peggy Guggenheim Collection (p75)

For reviews, see p73.➡

Explore: Dorsoduro

Sites in Dorsoduro are spread out: museums flank the Grand Canal on the eastern side, bars and eateries rustle around Campo Santa Margherita and Campo San Barnaba to the northwest. Start with masterpieces at Gallerie dell'Accademia, then recover with canalside *prosecco* (sparkling white) at Cantinone Giá Schiavi. Revived, see how Pollock splatter-paintings make a splash at the Peggy Guggenheim Collection.

Steal a glance at haunted Ca' Dario on your way to Basilica di Santa Maria della Salute and cutting-edge Punta della Dogana. Alternatively, head northwest from the Guggenheim to mingle with Venetian socialites of yore at Ca' Rezzonico. Either way, refocus with a post-museum sunset stroll and *spritz* (*prosecco* cocktail) along the Zattere.

In the evening dine on regional nosh at Riviera, Estro or Ristorante La Bitta, after which you can join the party in Campo Santa Margherita. Just don't be late for your concert at Scuola Grande dei Carmini or the first set at Venice Jazz Club.

Local Life

➡**Spritz o'clock** When the clock strikes *spritz* (six) o'clock, join the neighbourhood's hedonists in Campo Santa Margherita, Venice's nightlife hub.

➡**Antique and avant-garde** Rummage through relics from Venice's past at Antiquariato Claudia Canestrelli (p83) and L'Angolo del Passato (p85), then fast-forward to cutting-edge Venetian style at Marina e Susanna Sent (p83), Danghyra (p84) and PerlaMadreDesign (p84).

➡**Rush-hour detour** Dodge pedestrian traffic in peak season and take the Zattere instead to bask in the late-afternoon sun.

➡**Musical interludes** Choose your scene: costume-drama arias at Scuola Grande dei Carmini (p83) or swinging tributes at Venice Jazz Club (p82).

Getting There & Away

➡**Vaporetto** Grand Canal 1, 2 and N lines stop at Accademia; line 1 also calls at Ca' Rezzonico and Salute. Lines 5.1, 5.2, 6 and the N (night) stop at the Zattere and/or San Basilio.

➡**Traghetto** The San Marco *traghetto* (ferry) connects Santa Maria del Giglio, around 500m west of Piazza San Marco, to Salute (San Gregorio stop), saving you a 40-minute walk.

TOP SIGHT
GALLERIE DELL'ACCADEMIA

Hardly academic, these galleries contain more murderous intrigue, forbidden romance and shameless politicking than the most outrageous Venetian parties. The former Santa Maria della Carità convent complex maintained its serene composure for centuries, but ever since Napoleon installed his haul of Venetian art trophies in 1807, there's been nonstop visual drama inside these walls.

The grand gallery you enter upstairs features vivid early works that show Venice's precocious flair for colour and drama. Case in point: Jacobello Alberegno's late 14th-century *Apocalypse* (Room 1) shows the whore of Babylon riding a hydra, babbling rivers of blood from her mouth. In the same room but at the opposite end of the emotional spectrum is Paolo Veneziano's *Coronation of Mary* (1553–59), where Jesus bestows the crown on his mother with a gentle pat on the head to the tune of an angelic orchestra.

The arrival of UFOs seems imminent in the eerie, glowing skies of Carpaccio's lively *Crucifixion and Glorification of the Ten Thousand Martyrs of Mount Ararat* (Room 2). But Giovanni Bellini's *Pala di San Giobbe* shows hope on the horizon, in the form of a sweet-faced Madonna and Child emerging from a dark niche as angels play their instruments. The martyrs surrounding them include St Roch and St Sebastian, suggesting that this luminous, uplifting work dates from the dark days of Venice's second plague in 1478.

Lock eyes with fascinating strangers across portrait-filled Room 4. Hans Memling captures youthful stubble and angst with the exacting detail of a miniaturist in *Portrait of a Young Man*, while Giorgione's sad-eyed *La Vecchia* (Old Woman) points to herself as the words 'with time' unfurl by her arm. Trumping them both, however, is Giovanni Bellini's sublime *Madonna and Child between St Catherine and Mary Magdalene*.

DON'T MISS

- ➡ Veronese's *Feast in the House of Levi*
- ➡ Tintoretto's *Creation of the Animals*
- ➡ Giorgione's *The Storm*
- ➡ Bellini's *Miracle of the True Cross*
- ➡ Carpaccio's St Ursula Cycle

PRACTICALITIES

- ➡ Map p276, F5
- ➡ ✆041 520 03 45
- ➡ www.gallerie accademia.org
- ➡ Campo della Carità 1050
- ➡ adult/reduced €12/6, 1st Sun of month free
- ➡ ⏰8.15am-2pm Mon, to 7.15pm Tue-Sun
- ➡ 🛥Accademia

DORSODURO GALLERIE DELL'ACCADEMIA

Rooms 6–11

Venice's Renaissance awaits in Room 6, where you'll find Titian and Tintoretto. The latter's *Creation of the Animals* is a fantastical bestiary suggesting God put forth his best efforts inventing Venetian seafood (no argument here).

In Room 10, Tintoretto's *St Mark Rescues a Saracen* (1562) is an action-packed blockbuster, with fearless Venetian merchants and a muscular saint rescuing a turbaned sailor. In the same room, Titian's 1576 *Pietà* was possibly finished posthumously by Palma il Giovane, but notice the smears of paint Titian applied with his hands and the column-base self-portrait, foreshadowing Titian's own funeral monument.

Artistic triumph over censorship underlines Paolo Veronese's monumental *Feast in the House of Levi,* originally called *Last Supper* until Inquisition leaders condemned him for showing dogs, drunkards, dwarves, Muslims and Reformation-minded Germans cavorting with Apostles. He refused to change a thing, besides the title, and Venice stood by this act of defiance against Rome. Follow the exchanges among the characters, and you'll concede that not one Turkish trader, clumsy server or bright-eyed lapdog could have been painted over without losing an essential piece of the Venetian puzzle.

TOP TIPS

There's free admission to the gallery on the first Sunday of each month. To skip ahead of the queues in high season, book tickets in advance online (booking fee €1.50). Queues tend to be shorter in the afternoon; last entry is 45 minutes before closing, but a proper visit takes at least 1½ hours. The audio guide (€6) is mostly descriptive and largely unnecessary. Bags larger than 20x30x15cm need to be stored in the lockers, which require a refundable €1 coin.

The Accademia represents Venice's single most important art collection – and the work of several of its finest architects. Bartolomeo Bon completed the spare, Gothic-edged Santa Maria della Carità facade in 1448. A century later in 1561, Palladio took a classical approach to the Convento dei Canonici Lateranensi, which was absorbed into the Accademia. From 1949 to 1954, modernist Carlo Scarpa chose a minimalist approach to restorations, taking care not to upset the delicate symmetries achieved between architects over the centuries.

As you enter Room 11, you may feel observed by the gossipy Venetian socialites hanging over balconies in 1743–45 lunettes by Tiepolo. These ceiling details originally hung in the Scalzi Church, and were salvaged after 1915 Austrian bombings. Here you'll also find the rich hues and refreshing wit of Bernardo Strozzi's *Feast in the House of Simon*. In it, a mischievous cat seems intent on stealing the spotlight from a parable-recounting Christ and his perturbed host, Simon.

Rooms 12–24

Rooms 12 to 19 are occasionally used for temporary exhibitions, though it's in Room 12 that you'll find Giambattista Piazzetta's saucy, fate-tempting socialite in *Fortune Teller*. Yet even her lure is no match for the glorious works gracing Room 20. Among them is Gentile Bellini's *Miracle of the True Cross,* thronged with cosmopolitan merchant crowds. The artist's late 15th-century *Procession in St Mark's Square* offers an intriguing view of Venice's most famous square before its 16th-century makeover, while the former wooden version of the city's most famous bridge appears in Vittore Carpaccio's *The Miracle of the Reliquary of the Cross at Rialto Bridge.* Room 21 is no less extraordinary, home to Carpaccio's St Ursula Cycle, a series of nine paintings documenting the saint's ill-fated life. One can only imagine Carpaccio's smug sense of satisfaction from beyond the grave, with his paintings now hung in the former premises of the Scuola Grande Santa Maria della Carità, which snubbed him more than once when commissioning work.

The original convent **chapel** (Room 23) is a show-stopper fronted by a Bellini altarpiece. Sharing the space is Giorgione's *La Tempesta* (The Storm). Art historians still debate the meaning of the mysterious nursing mother and soldier with a bolt of summer lightning: is this an expulsion from Eden, an allegory for alchemy, or a reference to Venice conquering Padua in the War of Cambria?

Ornamental splendours were reserved for the Scuola della Carità's boardroom, the **Sala dell'Albergo**. Board meetings would not have been boring here, under a lavishly carved ceiling surrounded by Antonio Vivarini's 1441–50 masterpiece, filled with fluffy-bearded saints keeping an eye on proceedings.

Titian closes the Accademia with his touching *Presentation of the Virgin* (1534–39). Here, a young, tiny Madonna trudges up an intimidating staircase while a distinctly Venetian crowd of onlookers point at her – yet few of the velvet- and pearl-clad merchants offer alms to the destitute mother, or even feed the begging dog.

TOP SIGHT
PEGGY GUGGENHEIM COLLECTION

After tragically losing her father on the *Titanic*, heiress Peggy Guggenheim befriended Dadaists, dodged Nazis and changed art history at her palatial home on the Grand Canal. Peggy's Palazzo Venier dei Leoni is a showcase for surrealism, futurism and abstract expressionism by some 200 breakthrough modern artists, including Peggy's ex-husband Max Ernst and Jackson Pollock (among her many rumoured lovers).

Collection

Peggy collected according to her own convictions rather than for prestige or style, so her collection includes inspired folk art and lesser-known artists alongside Kandinsky, Picasso, Magritte, Man Ray, Rothko, Mondrian, Joseph Cornell and Dalí. Major modernists also contributed custom interior decor, including the Calder silver bedstead hanging in the former bedroom. In the corners of the main galleries, you'll find photos of the rooms as they appeared when Peggy lived here, in fabulously eccentric style.

For this champion of modern art who'd witnessed the dangers of censorship and party-line dictates, serious artwork deserved to be seen and judged on its merits. The Jewish American collector narrowly escaped Paris two days before the Nazis marched into the city, and arrived in Venice in 1948 to find the city's historically buoyant spirits broken by war. More than a mere taste-maker, Peggy became a spirited advocate for contemporary Italian art, which had largely gone out of favour with the rise of Mussolini and the partisan politics of WWII.

Peggy sparked renewed interest in postwar Italian art and resurrected the reputation of key Italian Futurists, whose dynamic style had been co-opted to make Fascism more visually palatable. Her support led to reappraisals of Umberto Boccioni, Giorgio Morandi, Giacomo Balla, Giuseppe Capogrossi and Giorgio de Chirico, and aided Venice's own Emilio Vedova and Giuseppe Santomaso. Never afraid to make a splash, Peggy gave passing gondoliers an eyeful on her Grand Canal quay: Marino Marini's *Angel of the City* (1948), a bronze male nude on horseback, is visibly excited by the possibilities on the horizon.

Garden & Pavilion

The Palazzo Venier dei Leoni was never finished, but that didn't stop Peggy from filling every available space indoors and out with art. Wander past bronzes by Moore, Giacometti and Brancusci, Yoko Ono's *Wish Tree,* and intriguing granite creations by Anish Kapoor and Isamu Noguchi in the **sculpture garden**. The city of Venice granted Peggy an honorary dispensation to be buried beneath the Giacometti sculptures and alongside her dearly departed lapdogs in 1979. Through the gardens is a **pavilion** housing a sunny cafe, a bookshop, bathrooms, and temporary exhibits highlighting underappreciated modernist rebels. Around the corner from the museum, on Fondamenta Venier dei Leoni, is a larger museum shop (p84), selling art books in several languages and replicas of Peggy's signature glasses – winged, like the lion of San Marco.

DON'T MISS

- ➡ Rotating permanent collection
- ➡ Calder silver bedstead
- ➡ *Angel of the City*
- ➡ Sculpture garden
- ➡ Temporary pavilion shows

PRACTICALITIES

- ➡ Map p276, G5
- ➡ 🗊 041 240 54 11
- ➡ www.guggenheim-venice.it
- ➡ Palazzo Venier dei Leoni 704
- ➡ adult/reduced €15/9
- ➡ ⏱10am-6pm Wed-Mon
- ➡ 🚤Accademia

DORSODURO PEGGY GUGGENHEIM COLLECTION

SIGHTS

GALLERIE DELL'ACCADEMIA GALLERY
See p73.

**PEGGY GUGGENHEIM
COLLECTION** MUSEUM
See p75.

**BASILICA DI SANTA
MARIA DELLA SALUTE** BASILICA
Map p276 (La Salute; www.basilicasalutevenezia.
it; Campo della Salute 1b; basilica free, sacristy
adult/reduced €4/2; ☉basilica 9.30am-noon
& 3-5.30pm, sacristry 10am-noon & 3-5pm
Mon-Sat, 3-5pm Sun; ⑤Salute) Guarding the
entrance to the Grand Canal, this 17th-
century domed church was commissioned
by Venice's plague survivors as thanks for
their salvation. Baldassare Longhena's uplifting design is an engineering feat that
defies simple logic; in fact, the church is
said to have mystical curative properties.
Titian eluded the plague until age 94, leaving 12 key paintings in the basilica's art-
slung sacristy.

Longhena's marvel makes good on an official appeal by the Venetian Senate directly
to the Madonna in 1630, after 80,000 Venetians had been killed by plague brought in
by a carpenter working on Venice's quarantine island, the Lazzaretto Vecchio. The
Senate promised the Madonna a church in
exchange for her intervention on behalf of
Venice – no expense or effort spared. Before
'La Salute' could even be started, at least
100,000 pylons had to be driven deep into
the *barene* (mudbanks) to shore up the tip
of Dorsoduro.

The Madonna provided essential inspiration, but La Salute draws its structural
strength from a range of architectural and
spiritual traditions. Architectural scholars
note striking similarities between Longhena's unusual domed octagon structure and
both Greco-Roman goddess temples and
Jewish Kabbalah diagrams. The lines of the
building ingeniously converge beneath the
dome to form a vortex on the inlaid marble
floors, and the black dot at the centre is said
to radiate healing energy.

The sacristy is a wonder within a wonder, its glorious collection of Titian masterpieces including a vivid self-portrait in the
guise of St Matthew and his earliest known
work, *Saint Mark on the Throne* (1510). Sa-

◉ TOP SIGHT
CA'REZZONICO

Baroque dreams come true at Baldassare Longhena's
Grand Canal palace. Giambattista Tiepolo's **Throne
Room ceiling** is a masterpiece of elegant social climb-
ing, showing gorgeous Merit ascending to the Temple
of Glory clutching the Golden Book of Venetian nobles'
names – including Tiepolo's patrons, the Rezzonico
family.

In the **Pietro Longhi Salon**, sweeping Grand Canal
views are upstaged by the artist's winsome satires of
society antics observed by disapproving lapdogs. **Sala
Rosalba Carriera** features Carriera's wry, unvarnished
pastel portraits of socialites who aren't conventionally
pretty but look like they'd be the life of any party. Giandomenico Tiepolo's swinging court jesters and preening
parrots add cheeky humour to the reassembled **Zianigo
Villa frescoes**.

On the top floor, don't miss Emma Ciardi's moody
Venice canal views in the Vedutisti Gallery (Gallery Nine),
and an **antique pharmacy** with 183 majolica ceramic
jars of 18th-century remedies.

DON'T MISS
→ Tiepolo's *trompe
l'œil* ceilings
→ Pietro Longhi Salon

PRACTICALITIES
→ Museum of the 18th
Century
→ Map p276, E3
→ ☏041 241 01 00
→ www.visitmuve.it
→ Fondamenta
Rezzonico 3136
→ adult/reduced
€10/7.50
→ ☉10am-6pm Wed-
Mon summer, to 5pm
winter
→ ⑤Ca' Rezzonico

lute's most charming allegory for Venice's miraculous survival from plague is Palma Il Giovane's painting of Jonah emerging from the mouth of the whale, where the survivor stomps down the sea creature's tongue like an action hero walking the red carpet. Life in a time of plague is a miracle worth celebrating in Tintoretto's upbeat 1561 *Wedding Feast of Cana,* featuring a Venetian throng of multi-culti musicians, busy wine pourers, and Tintoretto himself in the pink, gently schooling a young, thin-bearded Paolo Veronese.

PALAZZO CINI GALLERY

Map p276 (☎041 220 12 15; www.palazzocini.it; Campo San Vio 864; adult/reduced €10/8; ⏲11am-7pm Wed-Mon mid-Apr–mid-Nov; Accademia) This elegant 16th-century Gothic *palazzo* was the former home of industrialist and philanthropist Vittorio Cini, who filled it with first-class Renaissance paintings, period furnishings, ceramics and Murano glass. Wonderful paintings by lesser known Renaissance lights such as Filippo Lippi, Piero di Cosimo and Dosso Dossi festoon the walls, their glowing brilliance even more impactful in these intimate, domestic spaces.

SCUOLA GRANDE DEI CARMINI HISTORIC BUILDING

Map p276 (☎041 528 94 20; www.scuolagrandecarmini.it; Campo Santa Margherita 2617; adult/reduced €5/4; ⏲11am-5pm; Ca' Rezzonico) Eighteenth-century backpackers must have thought they'd died and gone to heaven at Scuola Grande dei Carmini, with its lavish interiors by Giambattista Tiepolo and Baldassare Longhena. The gold-leafed, Longhena-designed stucco stairwayheads up towards Tiepolo's nine-panel ceiling of a rosy *Virgin in Glory.* The adjoining hostel room is bedecked in *boiserie* (wood carving).

This *scuola* (confraternity) was the first formed by women in the 13th century. It was also Venice's first known order of Battuti (Flagellants), who practiced self-mortification with a wooden rod – a practice since discredited. The Carmini continued to extend hospitality to destitute and wayward travellers from the 13th century right through to the time of Napoleon's occupation of Venice. Sadly, cots are no longer available in this jewel-box building, but evening concerts (p83) are held here, and members of the Carmini continue to organise charitable works to this day.

CHIESA DI SAN SEBASTIANO CHURCH

Map p276 (www.chorusvenezia.org; Campo San Sebastiano 1687; €3, with Chorus Pass free; ⏲10.30am-4.30pm Mon-Sat; San Basilio) Antonio Scarpignano's relatively austere 1508–48 facade creates a sense of false modesty at this neighbourhood church. Currently undergoing restoration, the interior is adorned with floor-to-ceiling masterpieces by Paolo Veronese, executed over three decades. According to popular local legend, Veronese found sanctuary at San Sebastiano in 1555 after fleeing murder charges in Verona, and his works in this church deliver lavish thanks to the parish and an especially brilliant poke in the eye of his accusers.

Veronese's virtuosity is everywhere here, from the horses rearing on the coffered ceiling to organ doors covered with his *Presentation of the Virgin.* In Veronese's *Martyrdom of Saint Sebastian* near the altar, the bound saint defiantly stares down his tormentors amid a Venetian crowd of socialites, turbaned traders and Veronese's signature frisky spaniel. St Sebastian was the fearless patron saint of Venice's plague victims, and Veronese suggests that, although sticks and stones may break his bones, Venetian gossip couldn't kill him.

Pay respects to Veronese, who chose to be buried here underneath his masterpieces – his memorial plaque is to the right of the organ – but don't miss Titian's *San Nicolò* (1563) to the right of the entry. Peek into the sacristy to glimpse Veronese's glowing *Coronation of the Virgin* (1555) on the ceiling.

CHIESA DEI GESUATI CHURCH

Map p276 (Church of Santa Maria del Rosario; www.chorusvenezia.org; Fondamenta delle Zattere 918; €3, with Chorus Pass free; ⏲10.30am-4.30pm Mon-Sat; Zattere) The fact that Tiepolo's ceiling frescoes (1737–39) star St Dominic is hardly surprising given that this baroque church – designed by Giorgio Massari and completed in 1735 – was built for the Dominicans. Overwhelming grief grips Mary in Tintoretto's sombre 1565 *Crucifixion,* a painting subsequently restored by Giambattista Piazzetta. Altogether lighter is Sebastiano Ricci's *Saints Peter and Thomas with Pope Pius V* (1730–33), complete with comical cherubim performing celestial tumbling routines.

FONDAZIONE VEDOVA GALLERY

Map p276 (Magazzini del Sale; ☑041 522 66 26; www.fondazionevedova.org; Fondamenta delle Zattere 266; adult/reduced €8/6; ⊙exhibitions 10.30am-6pm Wed-Mon; ☑Zattere) A retrofit designed by Pritzker Prize–winning architect Renzo Piano transformed Venice's historic salt warehouses into Fondazione Vedova art galleries, commemorating pioneering Venetian abstract painter Emilio Vedova. Shows here are often literally moving and rotating: powered by renewable energy sources, 10 robotic arms designed by Vedova and Piano move major modern artworks in and out of storage slots.

✖ EATING

★PASTICCERIA TONOLO PASTRIES €

Map p276 (☑041 532 72 09; Calle dei Preti 3764; pastries €1-4; ⊙7.45am-8pm Tue-Sat, 8am-1pm Sun, closed Sun Jul; ☑Ca' Rezzonico) Long, skinny Tonolo is the stuff of local legend, a fact confirmed by the never-ending queue of customers. Ditch packaged B&B croissants for flaky *apfelstrudel* (apple pastry), velvety *bignè al zabaione* (marsala cream pastry) and oozing *pain au chocolat* (chocolate croissants). Devour one at the bar with a bracing espresso, then bag another for the road.

PANE, VINO E SAN DANIELE ITALIAN €

Map p276 (☑041 5237456; www.panevinoesandaniele.net; Calle Lunga San Barnaba 2861; meals €15-30; ⊙9am-11pm Thu-Tue; ☑Ca' Rezzonico) Artists can't claim they're starving any more after a meal in this wood-beamed trattoria, a favourite of art students and professors alike. Settle in to generous plates of gnocchi with truffle cheese, Veneto game such as roast rabbit and duck, lavish appetisers featuring the namesake San Daniele cured ham, and Friulian house wines made by the Fantinel family owners.

ORIENT EXPERIENCE II MIDDLE EASTERN €

Map p276 (☑041 520 02 17; Campo Santa Margherita 2920; meals €12-18; ⊙11.30am-11pm; ☑Ca' Rezzonico) Despite its dialogue with the East, Venice lacks good ethnic eateries, but this

---

◉ TOP SIGHT
PUNTA DELLA DOGANA

Fortuna, the weather vane atop the Dogana, swung Venice's way in 2005, when bureaucratic hassles in Paris convinced François Pinault to showcase his art collection in Venice's abandoned customs warehouses.

Built by Giuseppe Benoni in 1677 to ensure that no ship entered the Grand Canal without paying duties, the warehouses reopened in 2009 after a striking reinvention by Tadao Ando. Inside, the Japanese architect stripped back centuries of alterations, returning the interior to red brick and wooden beams. Within this space, Ando added his own contemporary vision, cutting windows in Benoni's water gates to reveal views of passing ships, adding floating concrete staircases in honour of Venetian modernist Carlo Scarpa, and erecting his trademark polished concrete panels.

The end result is a conscious and dramatic juxtaposition of the old and the new, one that simultaneously pays due to the city's seafaring history and its changing architecture, and one which provides a suitable scale and mood for Pinault's rotating exhibitions of ambitious, large-scale contemporary artworks from some of the world's most prolific and provocative creative minds.

DON'T MISS

➜ Fortuna
➜ Tadao Ando interiors
➜ Rotating art installations

PRACTICALITIES

➜ Map p276, H5
➜ ☑041 271 90 39
➜ www.palazzograssi.it
➜ Fondamente della Dogana alla Salute 2
➜ adult/reduced €15/10, incl Palazzo Grassi €18/15
➜ ⊙10am-7pm Wed-Mon Apr-Nov
➜ ☑Salute

LOCAL KNOWLEDGE

GRAND CANAL GHOSTS

Grand Canal palaces rank among the world's most desirable real estate, and multi-coloured marble Gothic marvel **Ca' Dario** (Map p276; Ramo Ca' Dario 352; ⊘closed to public; ⬛Salute) casts a mesmerising reflection painted by no less than Claude Monet – but there's a catch. Starting with the daughter of its original 15th-century owner, Giovanni Dario, an unusual number of Ca' Dario occupants have met untimely deaths. According to local legend, the palace is associated with at least seven deaths; gossips claim this effectively dissuaded Woody Allen from buying it in the 1990s.

The former manager of the Who, Kit Lambert, moved out after complaining of being hounded by the palace's ghosts, and was found dead shortly after in 1981. One week after renting the place for a holiday in 2002, the Who's bass player, John Entwistle, died of a heart attack.

---

wildly popular deli aims to set that straight. Run by Ahmed, it dishes up colourful bowls of Afghan, Iranian, Turkish and Maghrebi cuisine to hungry students, curious Venetians and adventurous travellers. Round it all off with a delicious cup of cardamom coffee and some pistachio baklava.

GELATERIA IL DOGE   GELATERIA €
Map p276 (✆389 1288965; www.gelateriaildoge. com; Campo Santa Margherita 3058a; scoops from €1.50; ⊘8am-midnight summer, to 11pm winter; 🐾; ⬛Ca' Rezzonico) This venerable gelateria in Campo Santa Margherita is usually mobbed in summer thanks to its extensive range of gluten- and fat-free gelato. Among the 23 flavours you'll find its signature Crema di Doge (candied orange and chocolate confection), ginger and lemon, chocolate and black cherry, and a refreshing range of Sicilian-style *granita* (sorbet).

BAR ALLA TOLETTA   SANDWICHES €
Map p276 (✆041 520 01 96; Calle la Toletta 1192; sandwiches €1.60-5; ⊘7am-8pm; 🖋🐾; ⬛Ca' Rezzonico) Midway through museum crawls from Accademia to Ca' Rezzonico, Bar Toletta satisfies starving artists with lip-smacking, grilled-to-order *panini* (sandwiches), including *prosciutto crudo* (cured ham), rocket and mozzarella, and daily vegetarian options. *Tramezzini* (triangular stacked sandwiches) are tasty too – Bar Toletta goes easy on mayonnaise in favour of more flavourful toppings like olive tapenade. Get yours to go, or grab a seat for around a €1 more.

★**ESTRO**   VENETIAN, WINE BAR €€
Map p276 (✆041 476 49 14; www.estrovenezia. com; Calle dei Preti 3778; meals €35; ⊘11am-

midnight Wed-Mon; ❄; ⬛San Tomà) Estro is anything you want it to be: wine bar, *aperitivo* pit stop, or sit-down degustation restaurant. The 500 wines – all of them naturally processed – are chosen by young-gun owners Alberto and Dario, whose passion for quality extends to the grub, from *cicheti* (Venetian tapas) topped with house-made *porchetta* (roast pork) to roasted guinea fowl and a succulent burger dripping with Asiago cheese.

DA CODROMA   VENETIAN €€
Map p276 (✆041 524 67 89; www.osteriada codroma.it; Fondamenta Briati 2540; meals €30-35; ⊘10am-4pm & 6-11.30pm Tue-Sat; ⬛San Basilio) In a city plagued by high prices and indifferent eating experiences, da Codroma wears its Slow Food badge of approval with pride. Chef Nicola faithfully maintains Venetian traditions here, serving up boiled baby octopi with a spritz of lemon and buckwheat *bigoli* pasta with anchovy sauce. It's a local favourite thanks to the quiet location and democratic prices.

OSTERIA AI DO FARAI   VENETIAN €€
Map p276 (✆041 277 03 69; Calle del Cappeller 3278; meals €25-35; ⊘noon-2.30pm & 7-10.30pm Mon-Sat; ⬛Ca' Rezzonico) Venetian regulars pack this wood-panelled room, hung with nautical photographs and illustrations. The house mixed antipasto is a succulent prologue to dishes like pasta with shellfish and sweet prawns; herb-laced, grilled *orata* (bream); and Venetian *bis di saor sarde, scampi e sogliole* (sardines and prawns in tangy Venetian *saor* marinade). Service is leisurely; bide your time with a Negroni *aperitivo*.

WORTH A DETOUR

CHIESA DI SAN NICOLÒ DEI MENDICOLI

Other churches in town might be grander, but none is more quintessentially Venetian than **Chiesa di San Nicolò dei Mendicoli** (☏041 528 45 65; Campo San Nicolò 1907; ☷10am-noon & 3-5.30pm Mon-Sat, 9am-noon Sun; ☷San Basilio). This striking brick Veneto-Gothic church dedicated to serving the poor hasn't changed much since the 12th century, when its cloisters functioned as a women's refuge and its portico sheltered *mendicoli* (beggars). The tiny, picturesque *campo* (square) out front is Venice in miniature, surrounded on three sides by canals and featuring a pylon bearing the winged lion of St Mark – one of the few in Venice to escape target practice by Napoleon's troops.

Dim interiors are illuminated by an 18th-century golden arcade and a profusion of clerestory paintings, including Palma Il Giovane's masterpiece *Resurrection*. In the painting, onlookers cower in terror and awe as Jesus leaps from his tomb in a blaze of golden light. The right-hand chapel is a typically Venetian response to persistent orders from Rome to limit music in Venetian churches: Madonna in glory, thoroughly enjoying a concert by angels on flutes, lutes and violins. The parish's seafaring livelihood is honoured in Leonardo Corona's 16th-century ceiling panel *San Nicolo Guiding Sailors Through a Storm,* which shows the saint as a beacon guiding sailors rowing furiously through a storm.

Film buffs might recognise church interiors from the 1973 Julie Christie thriller *Don't Look Now* as the church Donald Sutherland was assigned to restore. Although the movie cast Venice in a spooky light, the publicity apparently helped San Nicolò: the British Venice in Peril Fund underwrote extensive church renovations, completed in 1977.

RISTORANTE LA BITTA
RISTORANTE €€

Map p276 (☏041 523 05 31; Calle Lunga San Barnaba 2753a; meals €35-40; ☷6.30-11pm Mon-Sat; ☷Ca' Rezzonico) Recalling a cosy, woody bistro, La Bitta keeps punters purring with hearty rustic fare made using the freshest ingredients – no fish, just meat and seasonal veggies. Scan the daily menu for mouthwatering options like tagliatelle with artichoke thistle and gorgonzola or juicy pork *salsiccette* (small sausages) served with *verze* (local cabbage) and warming polenta. Reservations essential. Cash only.

AL VECIO MARANGON
VENETIAN €€

Map p276 (☏041 523 57 68; Calle Toletta 1210; meals €30; ☷noon-10.30pm Mon-Sat; ☷Ca' Rezzonico) It may sit on a backstreet, but snug Al Vecio Marangon is one of Dorsoduro's worst-kept secrets. Head in early or book ahead for one of the handful of tables, then tackle the *piatto di cicchetti misti,* a generous tasting plate of succulent morsels like *baccala mantecato* (whipped codfish and olive oil), warming *polpette* (meatballs) and grilled seasonal vegetables.

RISTOTECA ONIGA
VENETIAN €€

Map p276 (☏041 522 44 10; www.oniga.it; Campo San Barnaba 2852; meals €19-35; ☷noon-2.30pm & 7-10.30pm, closed Tue Feb; ☏; ☷Ca' Rezzonico) ✿ Oniga serves exemplary *sarde in saor* (sardines in onion marinade), seasonal pastas and the odd Hungarian classic like goulash (a nod to former chef Annika Major), often made with organic ingredients. Oenophiles will appreciate the selection of wines, handy for toasting the set lunch menu (€19). Grab a sunny spot in the *campo,* or get cosy in a wood-panelled corner.

AI QUATTRO FERI
VENETIAN €€

Map p276 (☏041 520 69 78; Calle Lunga San Barnaba 2754a; meals €35; ☷12.30-2.30pm & 7-10.30pm Mon-Sat; ☷Ca' Rezzonico) Adorned with artworks by some well-known creative fans, this honest, good-humoured *osteria* (casual tavern) is well known for its simple, classic seafood dishes like al dente *spaghetti con seppie* (with cuttlefish), grilled *orata* (sea bream) and tender calamari. Post-meal coffees are made using a traditional Italian percolator for that homely, old-school feeling. No credit cards.

★RIVIERA
VENETIAN €€€

Map p276 (☏041 522 76 21; www.ristorante riviera.it; Fondamenta Zattere al Ponte Lungo 1473; meals €70-85; ☷12.30-3pm & 7-10.30pm

Fri-Tue; ⬛Zattere) Seafood connoisseurs concur that dining at GP Cremonini's restaurant is a Venetian highlight. A former rock musician, GP now focuses his considerable talents on delivering perfectly balanced octopus stew, feather-light gnocchi with lagoon crab, and risotto with langoustine and hop shoots. The setting, overlooking the Giudecca Canal, is similarly spectacular, encompassing views of Venetian domes backed by hot pink sunsets.

For serious gourmands, the seven-course tasting menu (€105 per person) with wine pairings (€50 per person) is an unmissable experience.

ENOTECA AI ARTISTI ITALIAN €€€

Map p276 (🖉041 523 89 44; www.enotecaartisti. com; Fondamenta della Toletta 1169a; meals €45; ☺noon-3pm & 7-10pm Mon-Sat; ⬛Ca' Rezzonico) Indulgent cheeses, exceptional *nero di seppia* (cuttlefish ink) pasta, and tender *tagliata* (sliced steak) drizzled with aged balsamic vinegar atop arugula are paired with exceptional wines by the glass by your gracious oenophile hosts. Sidewalk tables for two make great people-watching, but book ahead for indoor tables for groups; space is limited. Note: only turf (no surf) dishes on Monday.

🍷 DRINKING & 🍸 NIGHTLIFE

★CANTINONE GIÀ SCHIAVI BAR

Map p276 (🖉041 523 95 77; www.cantina schiavi.com; Fondamenta Nani 992; ☺8.30am-8.30pm Mon-Sat; ⬛Zattere) Regulars gamely pass along orders to timid newcomers, who might otherwise miss out on smoked swordfish *cicheti* (bar snacks) with top-notch house Soave, or *pallottoline* (mini-bottles of beer) with generous *sopressa* (soft salami) *panini*. Chaos cheerfully prevails at this legendary canalside spot, where Accademia art historians rub shoulders with San Trovaso gondola builders without spilling a drop.

EL SBARLEFO BAR

Map p276 (🖉041 524 66 50; www.elsbarlefo.it; Calle San Pantalon 3757; ☺10am-midnight; ⬛San Tomà) If you're looking to escape the raucous student scene on Campo Santa Margherita, head to this grown-up bar with its chic industrial look, sophisticated rock and blues soundtrack, and live music at weekends. Aside from the long list of regional wines, there's a serious selection of spirits here. Accompany with plates of high-brow *cicheti* such as swordfish wrapped in robiola cheese.

OSTERIA ALLA BIFORA BAR

Map p276 (🖉041 523 61 19; Campo Santa Margherita 2930; ☺noon-3pm & 5pm-2am Wed-Mon; ⬛Ca' Rezzonico) Other bars around this *campo* cater to *spritz*-pounding students, but this chandelier-lit medieval wine cave sets the scene for gentle flirting over a big-hearted Veneto merlot. Cured-meat platters are carved to order on that Ferrari-red meat slicer behind the bar, but there are place-mats to doodle on and new-found friends aplenty at communal tables.

AI PUGNI BAR

Map p276 (🖉041 523 98 31; Ponte dei Pugni 2859; ☺8.30am-1am Mon-Sat, 10.30am-1am Sun; ⬛Ca' Rezzonico) Centuries ago, brawls on the bridge out the front inevitably ended in the canal, but now Venetians settle differences with one of over 50 wines by the glass at this ever-packed bar, pimped with recycled Magnum-bottle lamps and wine-crate tables. The latest drops are listed on the blackboard, with *aperitivo*-friendly nibbles including *polpette* (meatballs) and cured local meats on bread.

Cash only for bills under €25.

EL CHIOSCHETTO BAR

Map p276 (🖉348 3968466; Fondamente della Zattere al Ponte Lungo 1406a; ☺8.30am-2am Mar-Nov; ⬛Zattere) There's really no better place to park yourself for *aperitivo* than at this pint-sized kiosk on the Zattere overlooking the Giudecca Canal. Even on frosty spring evenings the tables fill up with a mixed crowd downing cocktails and *spritzes* and watching the spectacular Venetian sunset. In summer, on Wednesday and Saturday evenings, there's even live music.

If you're feeling peckish, it serves a good selection of *piadini* (sandwiches) and salads.

OSTERIA AL SQUERO BAR

Map p276 (🖉335 6007513; Fondamenta Nani 943-944; ☺11am-11.30pm Thu-Tue, 4-9.30pm Wed; 📶; ⬛Zattere) After a stroll along the Zattere, retreat to this snug local drinking hole, right opposite the city's oldest functioning gondola workshop. Wines are

DORSODURO DRINKING & NIGHTLIFE

LOCAL KNOWLEDGE

SQUERO DI SAN TROVASO

The **wood-brick cabin** (Map p276; Campo San Trovaso 1097; ⊛Zattere) along Rio di San Trovaso may look like a stray ski chalet, but it's one of Venice's handful of working *squeri* (shipyards), complete with refinished gondolas drying in the yard. When the door's open, you can peek inside in exchange for a donation left in the basket by the door. To avoid startling gondola-builders working with sharp tools, no flash photography is allowed.

well priced and the crostini delicious and imaginative, with combos like artichoke with blue cheese, ricotta and mascarpone. On your own? Lose yourself in one of Al Squero's collection of well-worn books on Venice.

CAFFÈ BAR AI ARTISTI
BAR

Map p276 (☎393 9680135; Campo San Barnaba 2771; ⊗7am-midnight Mon-Fri, 8am-midnight Sat, 9am-midnight Sun; ⊛Ca' Rezzonico) The cast of characters who sweep into this tiny cafe throughout the day seem borrowed from Pietro Longhi's paintings at neighbouring Ca' Rezzonico. Bartenders aren't the least bit fazed by dashing caped strangers swilling double espresso, spaniels tucked under-arm jealously eying the pastries, and Ca' Macana shoppers requesting straws to sip DOC *prosecco* through long-nosed plague doctor masks.

BAKARÒ
BAR

Map p276 (Calle della Chiesa 3665; ⊗10am-1am; ⊛Ca' Rezzonico) *'Permesso!'* (Pardon!) is the chorus inside this hip, pocket-sized *bacaro* (bar), where the crowd spills onto the sidewalk and tries not to spill drinks in the process. Below a tangle of filament bulbs is the tiny wooden bar, peddling respectable *cicheti* and around 45 wines by the glass, most of which are organic or from smaller producers.

IL CAFFÈ ROSSO
CAFE

Map p276 (☎041 528 79 98; www.cafferosso. it; Campo Santa Margherita 2963; ⊗7am-1am Mon-Sat; ⊛; ⊛Ca' Rezzonico) Affectionately known as *Il Rosso,* this red-fronted cafe has been at the centre of the bar scene on Campo Santa Margherita since the late

1800s. It's at its best in the early evening, when locals snap up the sunny piazza seating to sip on inexpensive *spritzes.*

IMAGINA CAFÉ
BAR

Map p276 (☎041 241 06 25; www.imaginacafe. it; Rio Terà Canal 3126; ⊗7am-9pm Sun-Thu, to 1am Fri & Sat; ⊛; ⊛Ca' Rezzonico) Running the show at modern, upbeat Imagina are affable Stefano and Domenico, busy brewing top-notch espresso, pouring quaffable wines, and serving fresh, tasty salads, focaccias and cakes. Monthly exhibitions showcase local artists, while the free wi-fi makes it a handy, comfy spot to kick back and check on all those Instagram likes.

CAFÉ NOIR
COCKTAIL BAR

Map p276 (☎041 528 09 56; Calle dei Preti 3805; ⊗11am-2am Mon-Sat, 9am-7.30pm Sun; ⊛; ⊛San Tomà) Laid-back Noir will leave you full and satisfied for less than €7 with its long list of cocktails, wines, beers and even Guinness. To accompany the beverages is an extensive list of jaw-busting *panini* and *piadine* (from €4). Herbivores aren't over-looked, with flesh-free combos like aubergine, zucchini, rucola, salad and cheese. No wonder it's a solid favourite with the budget-conscious university crowd.

FUJIYAMA
TEAHOUSE

Map p276 (Tea Room Beatrice; ☎041 724 10 42; Calle Lunga San Barnaba 2727a; ⊗11am-7.45pm Mon-Fri, 2-7.45pm Sat; ⊛Ca' Rezzonico) After long museum days, Fujiyama offers a relaxing alternative to espresso bolted at a bar. Rainy days call for pots of organic genmaicha tea and comforting brownies, while sunshine brings iced drinks and salty pistachios to the garden patio. Gossip is a given in this discreet spot with Venice's best eavesdropping (overhead: 'But I'm old enough to be your grandmother...')

☆ ENTERTAINMENT

VENICE JAZZ CLUB
LIVE MUSIC

Map p276 (☎041 523 20 56; www.venicejazzclub. com; Ponte dei Pugni 3102; admission incl 1st drink €20; ⊗doors 7pm, set begins 9pm, closed Thu & Sun; ⊛Ca' Rezzonico) Jazz is alive and swinging in Dorsoduro, where the resident Venice Jazz Club Quartet pays regular respects to Miles Davis and John Coltrane, as well as heating up with Latin and bossa nova beats on Tuesday and Friday. Arrive by 8pm to pounce on complimentary cold-cut platters. The venue closes for all of August and much of January.

🛍 SHOPPING

★ PAOLO OLBI   ARTS & CRAFTS
Map p276 (☑041 523 76 55; http://olbi.atspace.com; Calle Foscari 3253a; ⊙10.30am-12.40pm & 3.30-7.30pm Mon-Sat, 11.30am-12.40pm & 4-7.30pm Sun; 🚊Ca' Rezzonico) Thoughts worth committing to paper deserve Paolo Olbi's keepsake books, albums and stationery, whose fans include Hollywood actors and NYC mayors (ask to see the guestbook). Ordinary journals can't compare to Olbi originals, handmade with heavyweight paper and bound with exquisite leather bindings. The €1 watercolour postcards of Venice make for beautiful, bargain souvenirs.

★ MARINA E SUSANNA SENT   GLASS
Map p276 (☑041 520 81 36; www.marinaesusannasent.com; Campo San Vio 669; ⊙10am-1pm & 1.30-6.30pm; 🚊Accademia) Wearable waterfalls and soap-bubble necklaces are Venice style signatures, thanks to the Murano-born Sent sisters. Defying centuries-old beliefs that women can't handle molten glass, their minimalist art-glass statement jewellery is featured in museum stores worldwide, from Palazzo Grassi to MoMA. See new collections at this store, their flagship Murano studio, or the San Marco branch.

CA' MACANA   ARTS & CRAFTS
Map p276 (☑041 277 61 42; www.camacana.com; Calle de le Botteghe 3172; ⊙10am-7.30pm Sun-Fri, to 8pm Sat; 🚊Ca' Rezzonico) Glimpse the talents behind the Venetian Carnevale masks that impressed Stanley Kubrick so much he ordered several for his final film *Eyes Wide Shut*. Choose your papier-mâché persona from the selection of coquettish courtesan's eye-shades, chequered Casanova disguises and long-nosed plague doctor masks – or invent your own at Ca' Macana's mask-making workshops (one-hour per person €49, two-hour per person from €80).

MADERA   ACCESSORIES, HOMEWARES
Map p276 (☑041 522 41 81; www.shopmaderavenezia.it; Campo San Barnaba 2762; ⊙10am-1pm & 3.30-7.30pm Tue-Sat; 🚊Ca' Rezzonico) Restyle your life at this modern design showcase, which stocks a sharply curated selection of Italian and international jewellery, accessories, homewares and gifts. The emphasis is on handmade and harder-to-find objects, whether it's sculptural chopping blocks and necklaces, or geometric serving trays and bags.

ANTIQUARIATO CLAUDIA CANESTRELLI   ANTIQUES
Map p276 (☑340 5776089; Campiello Barbaro 364a; ⊙11am-1pm & 3-5pm Mon & Wed-Sat, 11am-1pm Tue; 🚊Salute) Hand-coloured lithographs of fanciful lagoon fish, 19th-century miniatures of cats dressed as generals, and vintage cufflinks make for charming souvenirs of Venice's past in this walk-in curio cabinet. Collector-artisan Claudia Canestrelli brings back bygone elegance with her repurposed antique earrings, including free-form baroque pearls dangling from gilded bronze cats.

LE FÓRCOLE DI SAVERIO PASTOR   ARTS & CRAFTS
Map p276 (☑041 522 56 99; www.forcole.com; Fondamenta Soranzo detta Fornace 341; ⊙8.30am-12.30pm & 2.30-6pm Mon-Sat; 🚊Salute) Only one thing in the world actually moves like Jagger: Mick Jagger's bespoke *fórcola*, hand-carved by Saverio Pastor. Each forked wooden gondola oarlock is individually designed to match a gondolier's height, weight and movement, so the gondola doesn't rock too hard when the gondolier hits a groove. Pastor's miniature *fórcole*

SOIREES AT THE SCUOLA

Music and dancing in a religious institution? Rome tried to forbid it for centuries, but the Venetian tradition continues today at the Scuola Grande dei Carmini with **Musica in Maschera** (Musical Masquerade; Map p276; ☑041 528 76 67; www.musicainmaschera.it; tickets €22-85; ⊙9pm Mar-Dec; 🚊Accademia), concerts performed in 1700s costume with opera singers and a ballet corps. Tickets are available downstairs at the Scuola (p77).

twist elegantly, striking an easy balance on gondolas and mantelpieces alike.

SIGNOR BLUM
TOYS

Map p276 (📍041 522 63 67; Campo San Barnaba 2840; ⏰9.45am-1.30pm & 2.15-7.15pm Mon-Sat; 🚤Ca' Rezzonico) Kids may have to drag adults away from the 2-D wooden puzzles of the Rialto bridge and grinning wooden duckies before these clever handmade toys induce acute cases of nostalgia. Calderesque mobiles made of colourful carved gondola prows would seem equally at home in an arty foyer and a nursery. And did we mention the Venice-themed clocks?

TRINA TYGRETT
JEWELLERY

Map p276 (📍041 523 94 26; Calle del Bastion 188; ⏰11am-7pm Mon-Sat; 🚤Salute) American transplant Trina Tygrett studied glassmaking at the Academy of Fine Arts and subsequently married into a Murano glass family. This solid foundation shows in her original jewellery which mixes semi-precious stones, gold, fabric and glasswork in a refreshing contemporary style. Her work has even caught the eye of organisations like the V&A and Fondation Maeght, with whom she has collaborated.

ACQUA MAREA
SHOES

Map p276 (📍329 1264533; Calle San Pantalon 3750; ⏰noon-7pm Mon-Fri; 🚤San Tomà) Question: how do you maintain a *bella figura* (good impression) when high tides are sloshing around your ankles? The answer is Martina Ranaldo's delightful rubber boot store, where you can find Wellingtons in lemon yellow and floral prints, ingenious two-tone rubber spats, Meduse ankle boots with coloured soles and comfortable non-leather walking shoes from Cammina Leggero, certified by PETA.

BRUNO
BOOKS

Map p276 (📍041 523 03 79; www.b-r-u-n-o.it; Calle Lunga San Barnaba 2729; ⏰3-7pm Mon, 10am-1pm & 3-7pm Tue-Fri; 🚤Ca' Rezzonico) One of the most innovative and vibrant art and design bookshops in Venice is Bruno. It's creativity is stoked by the graphic design studio and editorial consultancy behind it, which is headed by Andrea Codolo and Giacomo Covacich. They not only produce beautiful one-off editions, but also host special presentations and book launches with interesting contemporary writers and artists.

PEGGY GUGGENHEIM MUSEUM SHOP
ARTS & CRAFTS

Map p276 (📍041 240 54 22; www.guggenheim-venice.it; Fondamente Venier 710; ⏰10am-6pm Wed-Mon; 🚇; 🚤Accademia) This bright, enticing museum shop is stuffed with brilliant things designed to get your creative juices flowing. Books on art and art history aside, there are artful bags, Oybo's funny odd-socks, Moro glasses and playful contemporary jewellery from Cristina Brampti. There's also a super selection of art supplies, notebooks and sketch pads.

PERLAMADREDESIGN
GLASS

Map p276 (📍340 8449112; www.perlamadre design.com; Calle de le Boteghe 3182; ⏰10am-1pm & 3.30-6.30pm Tue-Sat; 🚤Ca' Rezzonico) Chances are you'll find glass-maker Patrizia Iacovazzi (known as Simona to her friends) at her work table, turning glass into striking, elegant wearables, from necklaces and bracelets, to earrings and cufflinks. Patrizia was born in Puglia, and the vibrant hues of her creations echo the rich, sun-drenched hues of southern Italy. With its frost-like finish and intriguing dual tones, the Sommerso range is especially irresistible.

PAPUNI ART
JEWELLERY

Map p276 (📍041 241 04 34; www.papuniart.it; Ponte dei Pugni 2834a; ⏰11am-7pm Mon & Thu-Sat, 3-7pm Tue & Wed; 🚤Ca' Rezzonico) Handmade industrial chic isn't what you'd expect to find across the footbridge from baroque Ca' Rezzonico, but Ninfa Salerno's clients delight in the unexpected. The Venetian artisan gives staid pearl strands a sense of humour with bouncy black rubber, weaves fuchsia rubber discs into glowing UFO necklaces, and embeds Murano glass beads in rubber daisy cocktail rings.

DANGHYRA
CERAMICS

Map p276 (📍041 522 41 95; www.danghyra.com; Calle de le Botteghe 3220; ⏰10am-1pm & 3-7pm Tue-Sun; 🚤Ca' Rezzonico) Spare white bisque cups seem perfect for a Zen tea ceremony, but look inside – that iridescent lilac glaze is pure Carnevale. Danghyra's striking ceramics are hand-thrown in Venice with a magic touch: her platinum-glazed bowls make the simplest pasta dish appear fit for a modern doge.

L'ANGOLO DEL PASSATO
GLASS

Map p276 (📍347 1586638; Campiello dei Squelini 3276; ⏰3.30-7pm Mon, 9.30am-12.30pm & 3.30-

7pm Tue-Sat; ⚇Ca' Rezzonico) The 19th century bumps into the 21st in this hidden corner showcase of rare Murano glass, ranging from spun-gold chandeliers beloved by royal decorators to sultry smoked-glass sconces that serve Hollywood stars better than Botox. Contemporary creations line the shelves, from geometric-patterned vases to bold, Dalí-esque drinking glasses.

SEGNI NEL TEMPO   BOOKS
Map p276 (☑041 72 29 09; www.segnineltempo. it; Calle Lunga San Barnaba 2856; ☺9.30am-1.30pm & 2-7.30pm; ⚇Ca' Rezzonico) Not so much a bookshop as a tiny time machine, where cramped shelves might reveal a 16th-century edition of Giovanni Pontano's *De Prudentia* or a *History of Oxford* dating from 1676. Most titles are in Italian, with a good selection of Venetian history books. Bound beauties aside, you'll also find vintage prints of the city and the odd curiosity – perhaps an 18th-century card game of seduction.

Secrets of the Calli

Yellow signs point the way to major sights, but the secret to any Venetian adventure is: *ignore them*. That *calle* (backstreet) behind the thoroughfare leads to a world of artisan studios, backstreet *bacari* (bars) and hidden *campi* (squares).

Campo San Polo to San Giacomo dell'Orio

Take Calle del Scalater past a couple of artisan studios to hidden Campiello Sant'Agostin for draught beer and dramatic glass jewellery; cross the bridge to join happy hour and tag games alongside medieval San Giacomo dell'Orio.

Campo Bandiera e Moro to Campo San Giovanni e Paolo

Head north of Riva degli Schiavoni through neighbourly Campo Bandiera and along studio-lined Salizada San Antonin. Then zigzag up narrow *fondamente* and *calli* to emerge on Barbaria de le Tole, where bars flank the route to sundowners in the shadow of stunning Zanipolo.

1. Statue, Campo dei Mori (p113) **2.** Campo San Barnaba, Dorsoduro (p71) **3.** Rialto Market (p93)

Rialto Market to Museo di Storia Naturale

Gather picnic supplies at Rialto Market, then *campo*-hop from nearby Campo delle Beccarie through sunny Campo San Cassian to artisan studio–dotted Campo Santa Maria Domini; then follow wiggling, sometimes shoulder-width *calli* to Museo di Storia Naturale for your garden picnic.

Chiesa della Madonna dell'Orto to the Ghetto

Cannaregio calm restores overloaded senses as you pass sculptures flanking Campo dei Mori, stroll the sunny Fondamente della Misericordia and Ormesini, and reach bridges leading into the historic Ghetto.

Chiesa di San Sebastiano to I Frari

Follow bargain *osterie* (taverns) along Calle Lunga San Barnaba to its bustling namesake *campo*, where Calle delle Botteghe leads past antiques, shawls, jewellery and contemporary glassware to Titian's masterpiece.

San Polo & Santa Croce

Neighbourhood Top Five

1 **Scuola Grande di San Rocco** (p90) Seeing lightning strike indoors at this lavish museum, where Tintoretto's streaky brush-work illuminated hope in a time of plague, death and despair.

2 **I Frari** (p92) Watching Titian's red-hot Madonna light up the room inside Gothic glory.

3 **Rialto Market** (p93) Working up a serious appetite over lagoon surf and turf at this gut-rumbling, produce-bursting market.

4 **Museo di Storia Naturale di Venezia** (p95) Following the trail of intrepid Venetian explorers through a world of natural wonders and oddities.

5 **Palazzo Mocenigo** (p94) Posing like a Venetian at this tres-chic aristocratic pad turned ode to centuries of fashion, furnishings and exotic fragrances.

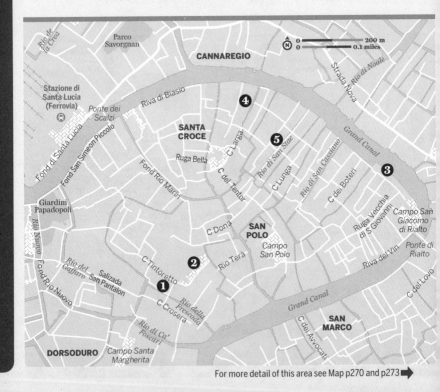

For more detail of this area see Map p270 and p273 ➤

Explore: San Polo & Santa Croce

So this is how Venice lives when it's not busy entertaining. These twin *sestieri* (districts) are a warren of winding lanes, in which you can easily lose yourself for hours browsing artisan studios and neighbourhood churches, before emerging in sunny *campi* (squares) where kids tear round on tricycles and adults sip *prosecco* (sparkling white wine) at ring-side bars.

Start the morning among masterpieces at the Scuola Grande di San Rocco, then bask in the glow of Titian's Madonna at I Frari. Shop backstreet galleries and artisan studios all the way to the Rialto Market. Stop at All'Arco for *cicheti* (Venetian tapas) before breezing through elegant salons of fashion and scents at Palazzo Mocenigo. Alternatively, zip through millennia of natural history at the epic Museo di Storia Naturale di Venezia.

Next, swing by medieval San Giacomo dell'Orio for happy hour at Al Prosecco. Appetite-piqued, wander Venice's former red-light district to celebrated Antiche Carampane for dinner.

Local Life

➜**Market mornings** Gently elbow fastidious chefs and *nonne* (grandmothers) on your quest for the morning's finest produce at the Rialto Market (p93).

➜**Bacaro-hopping** Ringing the Rialto are *bacari* (bars) offering inventive Venetian bites with top-notch *ombre* (half-glasses of wine) at All'Arco (p96), Osteria alla Ciurma (p101), Al Mercà (p99) and Do Mori (p99).

➜**Artisan studios** Despite skyrocketing rents, local artisans continue to design handmade treasures at Gilberto Penzo (p105), Veneziastampa (p103), Bottega Orafa ABC (p105) and Paperoowl (p102).

➜**Musical accompaniment** Take in lesser-known compositions inside a frescoed pleasure palace at Palazzetto Bru Zane (p102), opera at the Scuola Grande di San Giovanni Evangelista (p102), or a sonata at the Scuola Grande di San Rocco (p90).

Getting There & Away

➜**Vaporetto** Most *vaporetti* call at Piazzale Roma or Ferrovia at the northwestern corner of Santa Croce. For Santa Croce sights, San Stae, served by lines 1 and N (night), is most convenient. Lines 1 and N also service Rialto-Mercato and San Tomà, which is handy for I Frari and the Scuola Grande di San Rocco.

➜**Traghetto** The San Tomà *traghetto* (ferry) nips across the Grand Canal to San Marco.

Lonely Planet's Top Tip

Many of Venice's best restaurants, artisan studios and *bacari* (bars) are in the backstreets of San Polo and Santa Croce – if you can find them. This is the easiest area in which to get lost, so allow extra time if you have dinner reservations or a powerful thirst. If totally lost, follow the flow of foot traffic toward yellow Rialto or Ferrovia signs or red-and-white Scuola Grande di San Rocco signs, or head to central Campo San Polo.

✖ Best Places to Eat

➜ All'Arco (p96)

➜ Antiche Carampane (p98)

➜ Osteria Trefanti (p97)

➜ Ristorante Glam (p99)

➜ Osteria La Zucca (p98)

For reviews, see p96.➡

☕ Best Places to Drink

➜ Al Prosecco (p99)

➜ Al Mercà (p99)

➜ Bacareto Da Lele (p101)

➜ Cantina Do Spade (p99)

➜ Vineria all'Amarone (p99)

For reviews, see p99.➡

🔒 Best Artisan Finds

➜ Paperoowl (p102)

➜ Oh My Blue (p102)

➜ Pied à Terre (p102)

➜ Veneziastampa (p103)

➜ Gmeiner (p102)

For reviews, see p102.➡

TOP SIGHT
SCUOLA GRANDE DI SAN ROCCO

You'll swear the paint is still fresh on the 50 action-packed Tintorettos completed between 1575 and 1587 for the Scuola Grande di San Rocco, dedicated to the patron saint of the plague-stricken. While the 1575–77 plague claimed one-third of Venice's residents, Tintoretto painted nail-biting scenes of looming despair and last-minute redemption, illuminating a survivor's struggle with breathtaking urgency.

Assembly Hall

Downstairs in the assembly hall, Tintoretto steals the scene with the story of the Virgin Mary, starting on the left wall with *Annunciation,* where the angel sneaks up on Mary at her sewing table through a broken door. Tintoretto shows a light touch in *Presentation at the Temple,* where the infant Mary is steadied on her feet by a cheerleading cherub.

Tintoretto's Virgin cycle ends with *Ascension* opposite; it's a dark and cataclysmic work, compared with Titian's glowing version at I Frari.

Sala Grande Superiore

Take the grand **Scarpagnino staircase** to the Sala Grande Superiore, where you may be seized with a powerful instinct to duck, given all the action in the **Old Testament ceiling scenes** – you can almost hear the swoop overhead as a winged angel dives to nourish the ailing prophet in *Elijah Fed by an Angel.* Grab a mirror to avoid the otherwise inevitable neck strain as you follow dramatic, superheroic gestures through these ceiling panels. Mercy from

DON'T MISS

- ➡ *Ascension*
- ➡ Scarpagnino staircase
- ➡ *Elijah Fed by an Angel*
- ➡ New Testament wall scenes
- ➡ Francesco Pianta's sculpture of Tintoretto
- ➡ *St Roch in Glory* ceiling

PRACTICALITIES

- ➡ Map p270, A6
- ➡ ☎ 041 523 48 64
- ➡ www.scuolagrande sanrocco.it
- ➡ Campo San Rocco 3052, San Polo
- ➡ adult/reduced €10/8
- ➡ ⏱9.30am-5.30pm
- ➡ ⛴San Tomà

above is a recurring theme, with Daniel's salvation by angels, the miraculous fall of manna in the desert, and Elisha distributing bread to the hungry.

Tintoretto's **New Testament wall scenes** read like a modern graphic novel, with eerie lightning-bolt illumination striking his protagonists against the backdrop of the Black Death. Scenes from Christ's life aren't in chronological order: birth and baptism are followed by resurrection. The drama builds as background characters disappear into increasingly dark canvases, until an X-shaped black void looms at the centre of *Agony in the Garden*.

When Tintoretto painted these works, Venice's outlook was grim indeed: the plague had just taken 50,000 Venetians, including Titian, and the cure for the bubonic plague would not be discovered for centuries yet. By focusing his talents on dynamic lines instead of Titianesque colour, Tintoretto creates a shockingly modern parable for epidemics through the ages. A portrait of the artist with his paintbrushes is captured in Francesco Pianta's 17th-century carved-wood **sculpture**, third from the right beneath Tintoretto's New Testament masterpieces. Titian's own work – along with paintings by Giorgione and Tiepolo – is also on show here, on the handful of easels dotting the space.

Tesoro

Through a side door in the Sala Superiore, climb to the landing to see unexpected multicultural marvels in the Tesoro, including 13th-century lustreware from Iran and a 1720–27 chinoiserie tea set. Upstairs, pass through heavy bolted doors to see the jewel of San Rocco: an enchanting candlestick made from a branch of coral.

Sala Albergo

The New Testament cycle ends with the *Crucifixion* in the Sala Albergo, where things suddenly begin to look up – literally. Every Venetian artist who'd survived the plague wanted the commission to paint this building, so Tintoretto cheated a little. Instead of producing sketches like his rival Paolo Veronese, he painted this magnificent *tondo* (ceiling panel) and dedicated it to the saint, knowing that such a gift couldn't be refused, or matched by other artists.

The Sala Albergo is crowned by Tintoretto's restored *St Roch in Glory*, surrounded by representations of the four seasons and the saving graces of Felicity, Generosity, Faith and Hope. The angels are panting from their efforts at salvation, and feeble Hope is propped up on one elbow – still reeling from the tragedy of the Black Death, but miraculously alive.

AN INTERFAITH EFFORT AGAINST THE PLAGUE

While the Black Death ravaged the rest of Europe, Venice mounted an interfaith effort against it. The city dedicated a church and *scuola* (religious confraternity) to San Rocco, where Venetians could pray for deliverance from the disease while also consulting resident Jewish and Muslim doctors about preventative measures. Venice established the world's first quarantine, with inspections and 40-day waiting periods for incoming ships at the Lazzaretto Nuovo. Venice's forward-thinking, inclusive approach created artistic masterpieces that provide comfort to the afflicted and bereaved to this day, and set a public-health standard that has saved countless lives down the centuries.

Scarpagnino's uplifting, proto-baroque facade sees veined marble frame windows and doors, figures leaning out from atop the capitals, and flowering garlands adorning pillars as welcome signs of life post-plague. Bartolomeo Bon began the *scuola* in 1517, and at least three other architects were called in to finish the work by 1588.

TOP SIGHT
I FRARI

As you've no doubt heard, there's a Titian – make that *the* Titian – altarpiece at I Frari. But the 14th-century Italian-brick Gothic basilica is itself a towering achievement, with intricate marquetry choir stalls, a rare Bellini, and an eerie Longhena funeral monument. While Canova's white-marble tomb seems permanently moonlit, Titian's *Assunta* seems to shed its own sunlight.

Assunta

Visitors are inexorably drawn to the front of this cavernous Gothic church by a petite altarpiece that seems to glow from within. This is Titian's 1518 *Assunta* (Ascension), capturing the split second the radiant Madonna reaches heavenward, finds her footing on a cloud, and escapes this mortal coil in a dramatic swirl of Titian-red robes. According to local lore, one glimpse of the Madonna's wrist slipping from her cloak has led many monks to recant their vows over the centuries.

Both inside and outside the painting, onlookers gasp and point at the glorious, glowing sight. Titian outdid himself here, upstaging his own 1526 **Pesaro altarpiece** – a dreamlike composite family portrait of the Holy Family with the Venetian Pesaro family.

Other Masterpieces

As though this weren't quite enough artistic achievement for one church or planet, there's puzzlework marquetry worthy of MC Escher in the **coro** (choir stalls), Bellini's achingly sweet and startlingly 3-D *Madonna with Child* triptych in the **sacristy**, and Bartolomeo Vivarini's *St Mark Enthroned,* showing the fluffy-bearded saint serenaded by an angelic orchestra in the **Capella Corner**.

In the middle of the nave, Baldassare Longhena's **Doge Pesaro funereal monument** is hoisted by four burly, black-marble figures bursting from ragged white clothes like Invincible Hulks. Bringing up the rear are disconsolate mourners dabbing at their eyes with the hems of their cloaks on Canova's marble **pyramid mausoleum**, originally intended as a monument to Titian. The great painter was lost to the plague at the age of 90 in 1576, but legend has it that, in light of his contributions here, Venice's strict rules of quarantine were bent to allow Titian's burial near his masterpiece.

Architecture

Built of modest brick rather than stone for the Franciscans in the 14th and 15th centuries, the Frari has none of the flying buttresses, pinnacles and gargoyles typical of international Gothic – but its vaulted ceilings and broad, triple-nave, Latin-cross floor plan give this basilica a grandeur befitting the masterpieces it contains.

The facade facing the canal has delicate scalloping under the roofline, contrasting red-and-white mouldings around windows and arches, and a repeating circle motif of *oculi* (porthole windows) around a high rosette window. The tall bell tower has managed to remain upright since 1386 – a rare feat, given the shifting *barene* (shoals) of Venice.

DON'T MISS

→ Titian's *Assunta*
→ Titian's Pesaro altarpiece
→ Coro
→ Bellini's *Madonna with Child*
→ Vivarini's *St Mark Enthroned*
→ Canova's pyramid mausoleum

PRACTICALITIES

→ Basilica di Santa Maria Gloriosa dei Frari
→ Map p270, B6
→ ☏ 041 272 86 18
→ www.basilicadeifrari.it
→ Campo dei Frari 3072, San Polo
→ adult/reduced €3/1.50
→ ☉ 9am-6pm Mon-Sat, 1-6pm Sun
→ 🚊 San Tomà

SIGHTS

SCUOLA GRANDE DI SAN ROCCO MUSEUM
See p90.

I FRARI CHURCH
See p92.

CA' PESARO MUSEUM
Map p270 (Galleria Internazionale d'Arte Moderna e Museo d'Arte Orientale; ☑041 72 11 27; www.visitmuve.it; Fondamenta di Ca' Pesaro 2070, Santa Croce; adult/reduced €14/11.50; ☉10am-6pm Tue-Sun summer, to 5pm winter; ⛴San Stae) Like a Carnevale costume built for two, the stately exterior of this Baldassare Longhena–designed 1710 *palazzo* hides two intriguing museums: **Galleria Internazionale d'Arte Moderna** and **Museo d'Arte Orientale**. While the former includes art showcased at the Venice Biennale, the latter holds treasures from Prince Enrico di Borbone's epic 1887–89 souvenir-shopping spree across Asia. Competing with the artworks are Ca'Pesaro's fabulous painted ceilings, which hint at the power and prestige of the Pesaro clan.

The Galleria Internazionale d'Arte Moderna spans numerous art movements of the 19th and 20th centuries, including the Macchiaioli, Expressionists and Surrealists. The 1961 De Lisi bequest added Kandinskys and Morandis to the modernist mix of de Chiricos, Mirós and Moores, plus radical abstracts by postwar Venetian artists Giuseppe Santomaso and Emilio Vedova. Later more treasures accrued from the 1990 Wildt-Scheiwiller bequest, including de Wildt's extraordinary sculptures *Silent Man* (1899) and *Vir Temporis Acti* (1921). Other collection highlights include Lino Selvatico's startlingly modern 19th-century portraits, Medrado Rosso's melting wax-work busts, Armando Pizzinato's timely and troubling *A Ghost is Haunting Europe* (1950), and Leoncillo's forceful, neo-Cubist *Woman Partisan,* rendered in vividly coloured majolica.

Climb the creaky attic stairs of the Museo d'Arte Orientale past a phalanx of samurai warriors guarding a princely collection of Asian travel mementos. Prince Enrico di Borbone reached Japan when Edo art was discounted in favour of modern Meiji, and Edo-era netsukes, screens and a

SAN POLO & SANTA CROCE SIGHTS

◉ TOP SIGHT
RIALTO MARKET

Restaurants worldwide are catching on to a secret that this market has loudly touted for 700 years: food tastes better when it's seasonal and local. Before there was a bridge at the Rialto or palaces along the Grand Canal, there was a **Pescaria** and a **produce market**. So loyal are locals to their market that talk of opening a larger, more convenient mainland fish market was swiftly crushed.

Pescaria fishmongers call out today's catch, from glistening mountains of *moscardini* (baby octopus) to tiny *moeche* (soft-shell crabs). Sustainable fishing practices are not a new idea here; marble plaques show regulations set centuries ago for the minimum allowable sizes for lagoon fish. Seafood tagged 'Nostrana' is locally sourced.

Veneto *verdure* (vegetables) intrigue with their other-worldly forms, among them Sant'Erasmo *castraure* (baby artichokes), white Bassano asparagus and *radicchio trevisano*. In the winter, look out for prized *rosa di Gorizia*, a rose-shaped chicory specimen, often eaten raw with honey, vinegar and pancetta in its native region Friuli Venezia Giulia.

DON'T MISS
➡ The Pescaria (fish market)
➡ Chanted boasts about local produce at bargain prices
➡ Veneto speciality produce
➡ Cheeses at **Casa del Parmigiano** (p103)
➡ Seasonal fruit

PRACTICALITIES
➡ Map p270, G3
➡ ☑041 296 06 58
➡ San Polo
➡ ☉7am-2pm
➡ ⛴Rialto-Mercato

TOUR THE ULTIMATE WALK-IN WARDROBE

Fashion alert: by prior reservation, Palazzo Mocenigo now opens its secret attic storeroom for fascinating tours through fashion history. Costume historians lead up to 12 people into the ultimate walk-in closet, and open cupboards to reveal 1700s cleavage-revealing, nude-coloured silk gowns, men's 1600s embroidered peacock frock-coats with exaggerated hips, and other daring fashions too delicate for permanent display. Reserve ahead for tours in Italian and English (groups of up to eight people €100).

lacquerware palanquin are standouts in his collection of 30,000 objets d'art. Around three-quarters of the collection is Japanese; the remaining quarter includes a small collection of 12th- to 15th-century Islamic ceramic and an intricately carved Chinese chess set from the 18th century.

At the very top of the *palazzo*, temporary exhibitions are held showcasing modernist and contemporary masters such as Cy Twombly, William Merritt Chase and David Hockney. Entry is included in the ticket price.

PONTE DI RIALTO   BRIDGE

Map p270 (⚓Rialto-Mercato) A superb feat of engineering, Antonio da Ponte's 1592 Istrian stone span took three years and 250,000 gold ducats to construct. Adorned with stone reliefs depicting St Mark, St Theodore and the Annunciation, the bridge crosses the Grand Canal at its narrowest point, connecting the neighbourhoods of San Polo and San Marco. Interestingly, it was da Ponte's own nephew, Antonio Contino, who designed the city's other iconic bridge, the Ponte dei Sospiri (Bridge of Sighs).

When crowds of shutterbugs clear out around sunset, the bridge's southern side offers a romantic view of black gondolas pulling up to golden Grand Canal *palazzi*.

CHIESA DI SAN ROCCO   CHURCH

Map p270 (📌041 523 48 64; Campo San Rocco 3053, San Polo; ⊙9.30am-1pm & 2.30-5.30pm; ⚓San Tomà) **FREE** Originally built between 1489 and 1508, Bartolomeo Bon's creation received a baroque facelift in 1765–71,

which included a grand portal flanked by Giovanni Marchiori statues. Bon's rose window was moved to the side of the church, near the architect's original side door. Inside the church's Sala dell'Albergo are a couple of comparatively quiet Tintorettos, including *San Rocco Healing the Animals*.

PALAZZO MOCENIGO   MUSEUM

Map p270 (📌041 72 17 98, tour reservations 041 270 03 70; www.visitmuve.it; Salizada di San Stae 1992, Santa Croce; adult/reduced €8/5.50; ⊙10am-5pm Tue-Sun Apr-Oct, to 4pm Nov-Mar; ⚓San Stae) Venice received a dazzling addition to its property portfolio in 1945 when Count Alvise Nicolò Mocenigo bequeathed his family's 17th-century *palazzo* to the city. While the ground floor hosts temporary exhibitions, the *piano nobile* (main floor) is where you'll find a dashing collection of historic fashion, from duchess *andrienne* (hip-extending dresses) to exquisitely embroidered silk waistcoats. Adding to the glamour and intrigue is an exhibition dedicated to the art of fragrance – an ode to Venice's 16th-century status as Europe's capital of perfume.

Palazzo Mocenigo's opulent, chandelier-graced rooms look pretty much as they did at 18th-century A-list parties. Yet, even when flirting shamelessly under Jacopo Guarana's *Allegory of Nuptial Bliss* (1787) ceiling in the Green Living Room, wise guests minded their tongues. The Mocenigos reported philosopher and sometime house guest Giordano Bruno for heresy to the Inquisition; the betrayed philosopher was subsequently tortured and burned at the stake in Rome.

SCUOLA GRANDE DI SAN
GIOVANNI EVANGELISTA   HISTORIC BUILDING

Map p270 (📌041718234; www.scuolasangiovanni. it; Campiello della Scuola 2454, San Polo; scuola & church adult/reduced €8/6; ⊙9.30am-2pm & 2.30-5.30pm; ⚓San Tomà) Flagellants founded this confraternity in 1261, and it served as social club to the Council of Ten, Venice's dreaded secret service. Political power had obvious perks: Pietro Lombardo's 1481 triumphal entry arch, a Codussi-designed staircase, and a 1729 1st-floor meeting hall designed by Giorgio Massari and decorated by Giandomenico Tiepolo, who was obliged to finish contracts signed by his father.

Bellini and Titian turned out world-class works for the *scuola* that have since been moved to the Gallerie dell'Accademia – but

Palma Il Giovane's works still illuminate the Sala d'Albergo, and Pietro Longhi's wriggling baby Jesus is magnetic in *Adoration of the Wise Men.* The confraternity was suppressed by Napoleon, and today the *scuola* hosts conferences and concerts (p102), opening to the public when not in use for events.

Across the street, the deconsecrated **Chiesa di San Giovanni Evangelista** houses a Tintoretto *Crucifixion,* and the adjoining private chapel, founded by the Badoer family in 970, features Pietro Vecchia's painting of St John the Evangelist holding a pen, eagerly awaiting dictation from God.

FONDAZIONE PRADA
MUSEUM

Map p270 (Ca' Corner; ☑041 810 91 61; www. fondazioneprada.org; Calle de Ca' Corner 2215, Santa Croce; admission varies; ☺hours vary; ⏹San Stae) This stately Grand Canal palace – designed by Domenico Rossi and completed in 1728 – has been commandeered by Fondazione Prada who are renovating the palace. In between restoration work, Ca' Corner della Regina is the setting for slick temporary exhibitions that explore the art and avant-garde that shape contemporary visual sensibilities. Frescoes on the *piano nobile* (main floor) of the *palazzo* depict Caterina Cornaro, Queen of Cyprus, born in a Gothic building on this very site in 1454.

If there isn't an exhibition scheduled, groups of six people or more can visit the palace free of charge between noon and 6pm on Friday. Bookings are required a week in advance. In addition, the palace is open on all major feast days.

MUSEO DI STORIA NATURALE DI VENEZIA
MUSEUM

Map p270 (Fondaco dei Turchi, Museum of Natural History; ☑041 275 02 06; www.visitmuve.it; Salizada del Fontego dei Turchi 1730, Santa Croce; adult/reduced €8/5.50; ☺10am-6pm Tue-Sun Jun-Oct, 9am-5pm Tue-Fri, 10am-6pm Sat & Sun Nov-May; ⏹San Stae) Never mind the doge: insatiable curiosity rules Venice, and inside the Museo di Storia Naturale it runs wild. The adventure begins upstairs with dinosaurs and prehistoric crocodiles, then dashes through evolution to Venice's great age of exploration, when adventurers like Marco Polo fetched peculiar specimens from distant lands.

Out-stare the only complete ouransaurus skeleton found to date, a macabre menagerie of colonial trophies and a 19th-century *wunderkammer* (cabinet of curiosities) housing a pair of two-headed calves. Although the museum's grand finale downstairs is comparatively anti-climatic – a fish tank of Venetian coastal specimens bubbling for attention – it does offer you a close-up glimpse of the enormous dugout canoe moored at the water door.

Alongside the exit staircase you'll notice marble heraldic symbols of kissing doves and knotted-tail dogs, dating from the building's history as a ducal palace and international trading house. The dukes of Ferrara had the run of this 12th-century mansion until they were elbowed aside in 1621 to make room for Venice's most important trading partner: Turkey.

Known as the Fondaco dei Turchi (Turkish Trading House), the building remained rented out to the Turks until 1858. Afterwards, a disastrous renovation indulged 19th-century architectural fancies, including odd crenellations that made the gracious Gothic building resemble a prison. Luckily, the renovation spared the courtyard and charming back garden, which is open during museum hours and ideal for picnics.

CHIESA DI SAN GIACOMO DELL'ORIO
CHURCH

Map p270 (www.chorusvenezia.org; Campo San Giacomo dell'Orio 1457, Santa Croce; €3, with Chorus Pass free; ☺10.30am-4.30pm Mon-Sat; ⏹Riva de Biasio) La Serenissima seems as serene as ever inside the cool gloom of this Romanesque church, founded in the 9th to 10th centuries and completed in Latin-cross form by 1225 with chapels bubbling along the edges. Notable 14th- to 18th-century artworks include luminous **sacristy paintings** by Palma Il Giovane, a rare Lorenzo Lotto *Madonna with Child and Saints,* and an exceptional Veronese crucifix.

Don't miss Gaetano Zompini's macabre *Miracle of the Virgin,* which shows a rabble-rouser rudely interrupting the Virgin's funeral procession, only to have his hands miraculously fall off when he touches her coffin. Architectural quirks include decorative pillars, a 14th-century *carena di nave* (ship's keel) ceiling and a Lombard pulpit perched atop a 6th-century Byzantine green-marble column.

CASA DI CARLO GOLDONI   MUSEUM

Map p270 (☑041 275 93 25; www.visitmuve.it;
Calle dei Nomboli 2794, San Polo; adult/reduced
€5/3.50, with Museum Pass free; ☺10am-5pm
Thu-Tue summer, to 4pm winter; ☒San Tomà)
Venetian playwright Carlo Goldoni (1707–
93) mastered second and third acts: he was
a doctor's apprentice before switching to
law, which proved handy when an *opera
buffa* (comic opera) didn't sell. But as the
1st-floor display at his birthplace explains,
Goldoni had the last laugh with his social
satires. The real highlight here is an 18th-
century puppet theatre.

CHIESA DI SAN STAE   CHURCH

Map p270 (www.chorusvenezia.org; Campo San
Stae 1981, Santa Croce; €3, with Chorus Pass
free; ☺1.45-4.30pm Mon-Sat; ☒San Stae)
English painter William Turner painted
San Stae obsessively, capturing early-
morning Grand Canal mists swirling
around the angels gracing its Palladian
facade. The church was founded in 966
but finished in 1709, and though the interiors are surprisingly sparse for a baroque edifice, Giambattista Tiepolo's *The
Martyrdom of St Bartholomew* and Sebastiano Ricci's *The Liberation of St Peter*
are grace notes.

IL GOBBO   MONUMENT

Map p270 (San Polo; ☒Rialto-Mercato) Rubbed
for luck for centuries, the 1541 statue *Il
Gobbo* (The Hunchback) is now protected
by an iron railing. *Il Gobbo* served as a po-
dium for official proclamations and punishments: those guilty of misdemeanours were
forced to run a gauntlet of jeering citizens
from Piazza San Marco to the Rialto. The
minute they touched *Il Gobbo,* their punishment was complete.

CHIESA DI SAN POLO   CHURCH

Map p270 (www.chorusvenezia.org; Campo San
Polo 2118, San Polo; €3, with Chorus Pass free;
☺10.30am-4.30pm Mon-Sat; ☒San Tomà)
Travellers pass this modest 9th-century
Byzantine brick church without guessing
that major dramas unfold inside. Under
the *carena di nave* (ship's keel) ceiling,
Tintoretto's *Last Supper* shows apostles
alarmed by Jesus' announcement that one
of them will betray him. Giandomenico
Tiepolo's *Stations of the Cross* sacristy cycle shows onlookers tormenting Jesus, who
leaps triumphantly from his tomb in the
ceiling panel.

EATING

★ALL'ARCO   VENETIAN €

Map p270 (☑041 520 56 66; Calle dell'Ochialer
436, San Polo; cicheti from €2; ☺8am-2.30pm
Mon, Tue & Sat, to 7pm Wed-Fri summer, 8am-
2.30pm Mon-Sat winter; ☒Rialto-Mercato)
Search out this authentic neighbourhood
osteria (casual tavern) for the best *cicheti*
in town. Armed with ingredients from
the nearby Rialto Market, father-son team
Francesco and Matteo serve miniature
masterpieces such as *cannocchia* (mantis
shrimp) with pumpkin and roe, and *otrega
crudo* (raw butterfish) with mint-and-olive-
oil marinade. Even with copious *prosecco,*
hardly any meal here tops €20.

★DAI ZEMEI   VENETIAN €

Map p270 (☑041 520 85 96; www.ostariadaize-
mei.it; Ruga Vecchia San Giovanni 1045, San
Polo; cicheti from €1.50; ☺8.30am-8.30pm Mon-
Sat, 9am-7pm Sun; ☒San Silvestro) Running
this closet-sized *cicheti* counter are *zemei*
(twins) Franco and Giovanni, who serve
loyal regulars small meals with plenty of
imagination: gorgonzola lavished with *peperoncino* (chilli) marmalade, duck breast
drizzled with truffle oil, or chicory paired
with leek and marinated anchovies. A gourmet bargain for inspired bites and impeccable wines – try a crisp *nosiola* or invigorat-
ing *prosecco* brut.

GELATO DI NATURA   GELATO €

Map p270 (☑340 2867178; www.gelatodinatura.
com; Calle Larga 1628, Santa Croce; 1 scoop
€1.50; ☒; ☒Riva di Biasio, San Stae) Along with
a dozen other things, Marco Polo is said to
have introduced ice cream to Venice after
his odyssey to China. At this gelato shop the
experimentation continues with vegan versions of your favourite flavours, Japanese
rice cakes and the creamiest, small-batch
gelato incorporating DOP and IGT accredited local ingredients such as Bronte pistachios, Piedmontese hazelnuts and Amalfi
lemons.

SNACK BAR AI NOMBOLI   SANDWICHES €

Map p270 (☑041 523 09 95; Rio Terà dei Nomboli
271c, San Polo; sandwiches €2, panini €6; ☺7am-
9pm Mon-Fri, to 3pm Sat; ☒; ☒San Tomà) This
snappy Venetian comeback to McDonald's
is never short of local professors, labourers
and clued-in out-of-towners. Crusty rolls
are packed with local cheeses, fresh greens,
roast vegetables, salami, prosciutto and

roast beef, and served at an antique marble lunch counter. Beyond standard mayo, condiments range from spicy mustard to wild nettle sauce and fig salsa. Cheap, filling and scrumptious.

ACQUA E MAIS
STREET FOOD €

Map p270 (𝒥041 296 05 30; www.acquaemais. com; Campiello dei Meloni 1411-12, San Polo; cones €3.50-7; ⊘9.30am-8pm; 🚊San Silvestro) Ignore the proliferating pizza stalls and head to Acqua e Mais where you'll find authentic Venetian street food wrapped in a *scartosso* (paper cone). The delectable treats include cones of fried mixed fish, squid and shrimps or a selection of vegetables from the Rialto Market. To accompany add a dollop of creamed cod, some fried polenta fingers and a glass of *prosecco*.

AL PONTE STORTO
VENETIAN €

Map p270 (𝒥041 528 21 44; www.alpontestorto. com; Calle del Ponte Storto 1278, San Polo; cicheti from €1, meals €33; ⊘10am-3pm & 6-10pm Tue-Sun; 🛜; 🚊San Silvestro) Once an anarchist clubhouse, intimate, art-slung 'At The Crooked Bridge' serves up scrumptious *cicheti,* whether it's radicchio, pancetta and Brie quiche or their famed *polpette* (meatballs). For a more substantial feed, plonk yourself down at a table and tuck into house favourites like *pappardelle con scampi e radicchio* (pasta with prawns and chicory). In the warmer months, request one of the two canalside tables.

SACRO E PROFANO
ITALIAN €

Map p270 (𝒥041 523 79 24; Ramo Terzo del Parangon 502, San Polo; meals €15-25; ⊘11.30am-3pm & 6.30-midnight Mon-Tue & Thu-Sat; 🚊Rialto-Mercato) Musicians, artists and philosophising regulars make this hideaway under the Rialto exceptionally good for eavesdropping – but once that handmade gnocchi or spaghetti *alla búsara* (Venetian prawn sauce) arrives, all talk is reduced to satisfied murmurs. The place is run by a Venetian ska-band leader, which explains the trumpets on the wall and the upbeat, arty scene.

PASTICCERIA RIZZARDINI
PASTRIES €

Map p270 (𝒥041 522 38 35; Campiello dei Meloni 1415, San Polo; pastries €1.30-4; ⊘7am-8pm Mon & Wed-Sat, 7.30am-8pm Sun; 🚊San Silvestro) 'From 1742' boasts this corner bakery, whose reputation for *krapfen* (cream puffs), strudel and doughnuts has survived many

an *acqua alta* – record flood levels are marked by the door. Stop by any time for reliable espresso, *spritz (prosecco* cocktails) and *pallone di Casanova* (Casanova's balls) biscuits – but act fast if you want that last slice of tiramisu.

OSTERIA MOCENIGO
VENETIAN €

Map p270 (𝒥041 523 17 03; www.osteriamocenigo. it; Salizada San Stae 1919, Santa Croce; meals €25; ⊘noon-3pm & 7-10.30pm; 🛜🍴; 🚊San Stae) Times and dining habits have changed since doges strained waistcoat buttons at neighbouring Palazzo Mocenigo: warm, homely Osteria Mocenigo offers casual lunches and dinners of dishes like ravioli with radicchio and whitefish, and grilled meats. A single dish here makes a satisfying meal with Veneto wine by the glass.

ANTICO FORNO
PIZZA €

Map p270 (𝒥041 520 41 10; Ruga Rialto 973, San Polo; pizza slices from €2.50; ⊘11.30am-10pm Mon-Sat; 🛜; 🚊San Silvestro) The counter at this hole-in-the-wall take-away is a sea of oven-fresh pizza perfection of both the thin- and thick-crust varieties. Join the queue for staples like margherita or more imaginative pairings such as fresh ricotta with spinach and tomato. Two slices make for a cheap and satisfying lunch on the go.

★OSTERIA TREFANTI
VENETIAN €€

Map p270 (𝒥041 520 17 89; www.osteriatrefanti. it; Fondamenta Garzotti 888, Santa Croce; meals €40; ⊘noon-2.30pm & 7-10.30pm Tue-Sun; 🛜; 🚊Riva de Biasio) 🌿 La Serenissima's spice trade lives on at simple, elegant Trefanti, where a dish of marinated prawns, hazelnuts, berries and caramel might get an intriguing kick from garam masala. Furnished with old pews and recycled copper lamps, it's the domain of the competent Sam Metcalfe and Umberto Slongo, whose passion for quality extends to a small, beautifully curated selection of local and organic wines.

The space is small and deservedly popular, so book ahead, especially later in the week.

ANTICA BESSETA
VENETIAN €€

Map p270 (𝒥041 72 16 87; www.anticabesseta. it; Salizada de Cà Zusto 1395, Santa Croce; meals €35; ⊘6.30-10pm Mon, Wed & Thu, noon-2pm & 6.30-10.30pm Fri-Sun; 🛜; 🚊Riva de Biasio) Wood panelling and fresh flowers set the scene at this veteran trattoria, known for giving contemporary verve to regional classics. The *delizie di pesce dell'Adriatico* – a tasting plate which might see seared scallops served with a brandy and asparagus salsa – makes for a stimulating prologue to dishes like almond-crusted turbot with artichokes and cherry tomatoes.

Dapper owner Gigi Cassan is a trained sommelier, a fact reflected in the inspired wine list.

OSTERIA LA ZUCCA   MODERN ITALIAN €€

Map p270 (☑041 524 15 70; www.lazucca.it; Calle del Tentor 1762, Santa Croce; meals €35-40; ⌚12.30-2.30pm & 7-10.30pm Mon-Sat; ⊿; ⛴San Stae) With its menu of seasonal vegetarian creations and classic meat dishes, this cosy, woody restaurant consistently hits the mark. Herbs and spices are used to great effect in dishes such as cinnamon-tinged pumpkin flan and chicken curry with yoghurt, lentils and rice. The small interior can get toasty, so reserve canalside seats in summer.

IL REFOLO   PIZZA, ITALIAN €€

Map p270 (☑041 524 00 16; Campiello del Piovan 1459, Santa Croce; pizzas €15, meals €35; ⌚7-11pm Tue, noon-2.30pm & 7-11pm Wed-Sun; 👪; ⛴Riva di Biasio, San Stae) With outdoor tables occupying the *campo* in front of San Giacomo dell'Orio, this is a sunny spot from which to watch gondolas drift by. The food, too, is relaxed and unfussy with a menu offering a range of pizzas, pasta and light seafood dishes. Owned by the Martin family of Michelin-starred Da Fiore; expect top-quality ingredients and standout flavours.

FRARY'S   MIDDLE EASTERN €€

Map p270 (☑041 72 00 50; www.frarys.it; Fondamenta dei Frari 2559, San Polo; 2-course weekday lunch €12, meals €25; ⌚11.30am-3pm & 6-10.30pm; 🛜⊿; ⛴San Tomà) Spice things up at Frary's, a bohemian-spirited bolt-hole serving Middle Eastern classics. The antipasto platter might pair Greek *hortopita* (filo pastry stuffed with cheese and vegetables) with Kurdish *kubbe* (fried rice ball stuffed with spiced ground meat), while the fragrant mains include classic moussaka and spicy Jordanian rice dish *maglu'ba*. The menu includes vegan and gluten-free options. If she's 'in the zone', owner Federica might even read your future in the bottom of your coffee cup.

RISTORANTE RIBOT   VENETIAN €€

Map p273 (☑041 524 24 86; www.ristoranteribot.com; Fondamenta Minotto 160, Santa Croce; meals €32; ⌚noon-2.30pm & 7-10.30pm Mon-Fri, 7-10.30pm Sat; ⛴Piazzale Roma) White linen on the tables, cookbooks on the shelves, and the day's menu written on a single sheet of paper – friendly Ribot is a sound bet for a fresh, flavoursome regional feed. Dishes span surf and turf, from a simple, well-balanced *impepata di cozze* (mussels with pepper and white wine) to a remarkably delicate *fegato alla veneziana* (Venetian-style calves liver).

There's courtyard seating in the summer months, and a well-stocked cellar with around 500 wines.

MURO SAN STAE   PIZZA, ITALIAN €€

Map p270 (☑041 524 16 28; www.murovenezia.com; Campiello dello Spezier 2048, Santa Croce; pizzas €7-15, meals €35; ⌚noon-3pm & 7-10.30pm; ⛴San Stae) Contemporary and relaxed, versatile Muro plays the role of both restaurant and pizzeria. Tuck into inventive pizzas and seasonal salads, or linger over fresh, flavour-packed dishes like *zuppa di pesce* (fish soup). Carnivores are especially well catered for, with no shortage of grilled meats and a succulent tartare to boot.

BIRRARIA LA CORTE   PIZZA €€

Map p270 (☑041 275 05 70; www.birrarialacorte.it; Campo San Polo 2168, San Polo; pizzas €7-14, meals €35; ⌚10am-midnight Apr-Oct, 10am-3pm & 6pm-midnight Nov-Mar; 🛜; ⛴San Tomà) This one-time bull stable became a brewery in the 19th century to keep Venice's Austrian occupiers occupied, and beer and beef remain reliable bets. There's also pizza and much coveted piazza-side seating.

⭐ANTICHE CARAMPANE   VENETIAN €€€

Map p270 (☑041 524 01 65; www.antichecarampane.com; Rio Terà delle Carampane 1911, San Polo; meals €50; ⌚12.45-2.30pm & 7.30-10.30pm Tue-Sat; ⛴San Stae) Hidden in the once-shady lanes behind Ponte delle Tette, this culinary indulgence is a trick to find. Once you do, say goodbye to soggy lasagne and hello to a market-driven menu of silky *crudi* (raw fish/seafood), surprisingly light *fritto misto* (fried seafood) and *caramote* prawn salad with seasonal vegetables. Never short of a smart, convivial crowd, it's a good idea to book ahead.

RISTORANTE GLAM
VENETIAN €€€

Map p270 (Palazzo Venart; ☑041 523 56 76; www.enricobartolini.net/i-ristoranti/glam; Calle Tron 1961, Santa Croce; tasting menu €90-110; ☺12.30-2.30pm & 7.30-10.30pm; ⬆San Stae) Step out of your water taxi into the canalside garden of Enrico Bartolini's new Venetian restaurant in the Venart Hotel. Italy's youngest Michelin-starred chef, Bartolini offers a tasting menu focused on local ingredients, pepping up Veneto favourites with unusual spices that would once have graced the tables of this trade-route city. Sommelier Adele Furno supplies the equally excellent wine selection.

TRATTORIA DA IGNAZIO
VENETIAN, SEAFOOD €€€

Map p270 (☑041 523 48 52; www.trattoriada ignazio.com; Calle dei Saoneri 2749, San Polo; meals €45-50; ☺noon-3pm & 7-10pm Sun-Fri; ⬆San Tomà) Dapper white-jacketed waiters serve pristine grilled lagoon fish, fresh pasta and desserts made in-house ('of course') with a proud flourish, on tables bedecked with yellow linen. On cloudy days, homemade crab pasta with a bright Lugana white wine make a fine substitute for sunshine. On sunny days and warm nights, the neighbourhood converges beneath the garden's grape arbour.

At lunch time there are three more affordable three-course menus between €18 and €20.

🍷⚱ DRINKING & NIGHTLIFE

★AL PROSECCO
WINE BAR

Map p270 (☑041 524 02 22; www.alprosecco. com; Campo San Giacomo dell'Orio 1503, Santa Croce; ☺10am-8pm Mon-Fri, to 5pm Sat Nov-Mar, to 10.30pm Apr-Oct; ⬆San Stae) ✐ The urge to toast sunsets in Venice's loveliest *campo* is only natural – and so is the wine at Al Prosecco. This forward-thinking bar specialises in *vini naturi* (natural-process wines) – organic, biodynamic, wild-yeast fermented – from enlightened Italian winemakers like Cinque Campi and Azienda Agricola Barichel. So order a glass of unfiltered 'cloudy' *prosecco* and toast to the good things in life.

★AL MERCÀ
WINE BAR

Map p270 (☑346 8340660; Campo Cesare Battisti 213, San Polo; ☺10am-2.30pm & 6-8pm Mon-Thu, to 9.30pm Fri & Sat; ⬆Rialto-Mercato) Discerning drinkers throng to this cupboardsized counter on a Rialto Market square to sip on top-notch *prosecco* and DOC wines by the glass (from €3). Edibles usually include meatballs and mini *panini* (€1.50), proudly made using super-fresh ingredients.

BASEGÒ
BAR

Map p270 (☑041 850 02 99; www.basego.it; Campo San Tomá, San Polo; ☺9am-11pm; ⬆San Tomà) Focusing on three essential ingredients – good food, good wine and good music – newly opened Basegò has rapidly formed a dedicated group of drinkers. Indulge in a *cicheti* feast of lagoon seafood, Norcia prosciutto, smoked tuna and Lombard cheeses, and on Friday night enjoy live music from the likes of Alessia Obino and Simone Massaron.

DO MORI
WINE BAR

Map p270 (☑041 522 54 01; Sotoportego dei do Mori 429, San Polo; ☺8am-2.30pm & 5-7.30pm Mon-Sat, to 2pm Wed; ⬆Rialto-Mercato) You'll feel like you've stepped into a Rembrandt painting at venerable Do Mori, a dark, rustic bar with roots in the 15th century. Under gleaming, gargantuan copper pots, nostalgists will swirl one of around 40 wines by the glass, or slurp *prosecco* from oldschool champagne saucers. Peckish? Bar bites include pickled onions with anchovies, succulent *polpette* (meatballs) and slices of pecorino.

CANTINA DO SPADE
BAR

Map p270 (☑041 521 05 83; www.cantinado spade.com; Calle delle Do Spade 860, San Polo; ☺10am-3pm & 6-10pm; 🎤; ⬆Rialto-Mercato) Famously mentioned in Casanova's memoirs, cosy, brick-lined 'Two Spades' continues to keep Venice in good spirits with its bargain Tri-Veneto wines and young, laidback management. Come early for marketfresh *fritture* (batter-fried seafood) or linger longer with satisfying, sit-down dishes like *bigoli in salsa* (pasta in anchovy and onion sauce).

VINERIA ALL'AMARONE
BAR, OSTERIA

Map p270 (☑041 523 11 84; www.allamarone. com; Calle degli Sbianchesini 1131, San Polo; meals €35; ☺10am-11.45pm Thu-Tue; ⬆San

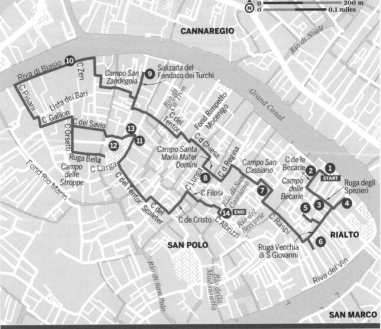

🏃 Neighbourhood Walk
Venice Gourmet Crawl

START RIALTO MARKET
END ANTICHE CARAMPANE
LENGTH 2.9KM, TWO HOURS

A trip through gourmet history starts where great Venetian meals have begun for centuries: the **1 Rialto Market** (p93). Make sure to pop by the **2 Pescaria** (p93), where fishmongers artfully arrange the day's catch atop hillocks of ice.

Around the corner, glimpse the trade-route treasures that made Venice's fortune at **3 Drogheria Mascari** (p104), where fragrant spices mix it with local condiments and fine wines. Make a quick detour to historic deli **4 Casa del Parmigiano** (p103). Appetite piqued, duck into **5 All'Arco** (p96) for *cicheti* – ask for *una fantasia* (a fantasy), and father-son chefs Francesco and Matteo will invent a dish with ingredients you just saw at the market.

Stop for an aromatic espresso at specialist coffee peddler **6 Caffè del Doge**, then wander northwest to **7 Cárte** (p106) to browse recipe albums in marble paper, and then over a couple of bridges until you smell the ink drying on letterpress menus (also sold blank for swanky dinner parties) at **8 Veneziastampa** (p103).

Learn the scientific names of the lagoon creatures at the **9 Museo di Storia Naturale di Venezia** (p95). Walk a sunny stretch of Grand Canal along **10 Riva de Biasio**, allegedly named for 16th-century butcher Biagio (Biasio) Cargnio, whose sausages contained a special ingredient: children. When found out, Biasio was drawn and quartered.

Thankfully, there are no questionable ingredients in the organic gelato at **11 Gelato di Natura** (p96). Grab a scoop and take a pew in **12 Campo San Giacomo dell'Orio**. Once you're done, make a beeline for the best bar on the *campo*, **13 Al Prosecco** (p99), where natural-process *prosecco* awaits – just don't be late for dinner at much-loved **14 Antiche Carampane** (p98).

Silvestro) The warm wood-pannelled interior and huge selection of Veneto wines by the glass are just part of the popularity of this friendly bar-cum-restaurant. Other reasons to stop by are generous *cicheti* platters, belly-warming plates of gnocchi and braised beef in red wine, and wine-tasting flights (€27 to €43), including the heady, heavy Amarone's after which the bar takes its name.

OSTERIA ALLA CIURMA   BAR

Map p270 (Calle Galeazza 406, San Polo; ⊙9am-3pm & 5.30-8.30pm Mon-Sat; 🚊Rialto-Mercato) This old Rialto storeroom has been converted into a drinking den with a mast holding up the bar and a crew of regulars who come here for a €0.90 glass of house wine and *cicheti* (€1.50) piled high with *baccalà mantecato*. Other top-notch nibbles include courgette flowers stuffed with mozzarella and anchovies and huge plates of marinated seafood, salami or cheese (platters €28).

BACARETO DA LELE   BAR

Map p273 (Campo dei Tolentini 183, Santa Croce; ⊙6am-8pm Mon-Fri, to 2pm Sat; 🚊Piazzale Roma) Pocket-sized Da Lele is never short of students and workers, stopping for a cheap, stand-up *ombra* (from €0.60) on their way to and from the train station. Scan the blackboard for the day's wines and pair them with bite-sized *panini* (€1), stuffed with freshly shaved cured meats and combos like pancetta and artichoke. The place closes for much of August.

BARCOLLO   BAR

Map p270 (📞041 522 81 58; Campo Cesare Battista 219, San Polo; ⊙8.30am-2.30am Tue-Fri, to 3am Sat, 10.30am-2.30am Sun, 5pm-2.30am Mon; 🛜; 🚊Rialto-Mercato) Its name might mean stagger, but there's more to Barcollo than heady cocktail sessions and Friday night DJ sets. Just steps away from the Rialto Market, the cafe-bar makes for a handy daytime pit stop, with everything from OJ and coffee to brioche and *arancini* (rice balls). Come evening and the €1 house wine ensures the party crowd spills out onto the *campo*.

CAFFÈ DEL DOGE   CAFE

Map p270 (📞041 522 77 87; www.caffedeldoge. com; Calle dei Cinque 609, San Polo; ⊙7am-7pm; 🚊San Silvestro) Sniff your way to the affa-

GUIDED BAR CRAWLS

Why eat and drink alone? To help visitors navigate Venice's vast *cicheti* (bar snacks) repertoire and confusing backstreets, **Venice Urban Adventures** (📞348 980 85 66; www. veniceurbanadventures.com; tours €36-180; ⊙tours 11.30am & 5.30pm Mon-Sat) offers tours of happy-hour hot spots led by knowledgeable, enthusiastic, English-speaking local foodies. Tours cost €80 per person (with up to 12 participants), covering *ombre* (wine by the glass) and *cicheti* in five (yes, five) *bacari* (hole-in-the-wall bars) and a tipsy Rialto gondola crossing (weather permitting). Departure points vary seasonally; consult the website.

ble Doge, where dedicated drinkers slurp their way through the menu of speciality imported coffees from Ethiopia to Guatemala, all roasted on the premises. If you're feel especially inspired, you can even pick up a coffee percolator. Add a block of chocolate and you have yourself the perfect pick-me-up.

CAFFÈ DEI FRARI   BAR

Map p270 (📞041 476 73 05; www.ilmercante venezia.com; Fondamenta dei Frari 2564, San Polo; ⊙9am-5pm & 6pm-1am Tue-Sun, 9am-5pm Mon; 🚊San Tomà) Take your (admittedly expensive) espresso with a heaping of history at this century-old carved wooden bar, or recover from the sensory overload of I Frari with *cicheti* and a rather good cocktail at the dinky indoor cafe downstairs or on the Liberty-style wrought-iron balcony upstairs. At weekends there's even the chance of some live music.

OSTERIA DA FILO   BAR

Map p270 (Hosteria alla Poppa; 📞041 524 65 54; www.facebook.com/osteriadafilo; Calle delle Oche 1539, Santa Croce; ⊙4-11pm Mon-Fri, 11am-11pm Sat & Sun; 🛜; 🚊Riva de Biasio) A living room where drinks are served, this *osteria* comes complete with creaky sofas, free wi-fi, abandoned novels and the occasional live-music gig. Service is brusque, but drinks are cheap and the Mediterranean tapas tasty.

SAN POLO & SANTA CROCE DRINKING & NIGHTLIFE

⭐ ENTERTAINMENT

★PALAZZETTO BRU ZANE   CLASSICAL MUSIC

Map p270 (Centre du Musique Romantique Française; ☏041 521 10 05; www.bru-zane.com; Palazzetto Bru Zane 2368, San Polo; adult/reduced €15/5; ☉box office 2.30-5.30pm Mon-Fri, closed late Jul–mid-Aug; ⓢSan Tomà) Pleasure palaces don't get more romantic than Palazzetto Bru Zane on concert nights, when exquisite harmonies tickle Sebastiano Ricci angels tumbling across stucco-frosted ceilings. Multi-year restorations returned the 1695–97 Casino Zane's 100-seat music room to its original function, attracting world-class musicians to enjoy its acoustics from late September to mid-May.

Free guided tours of the building run on Thursday (in Italian/French/English at 2.30pm/3pm/3.30pm), with the added offer of discounted €12 concert tickets.

SCUOLA GRANDE DI SAN GIOVANNI EVANGELISTA   OPERA

Map p270 (☏041 426 65 59; www.scuolasangiovanni.it; Campiello della Scuola 2454, San Polo; adult/reduced from €20/5; ⓢSan Tomà) Drama comes with the scenery when Italian opera favourites – Puccini's *Tosca,* Verdi's *La Traviata,* Rossini's *Il Barbiere di Seviglia* – are performed in the lavish hall where Venice's secretive Council of Ten socialised. Stage sets can't compare to the scuola (p94): sweep up Mauro Codussi's 15th-century staircase into Giorgio Massari's 1729 hall, and take your seat amid Giandomenico Tiepolo paintings.

LA CASA DEL CINEMA   CINEMA

Map p270 (Videoteca Pasinetti; ☏041 274 71 40; www.comune.venezia.it/cinema; Salizada San Stae 1990, Santa Croce; annual membership adult/reduced €35/25; ☉9am-1pm & 3-10pm Mon-Fri; ⓢSan Stae) Venice's public film archive shows art films in a modern 50-seat, wood-beamed screening room inside Palazzo Mocenigo (p94). Original-language classics are shown Monday and Thursday, while first-run independent films are screened on Friday; check online for pre-release previews and revivals with introductions by directors, actors and scholars.

🛍 SHOPPING

GMEINER   SHOES

Map p270 (☏338 8962189; www.gabrielegmeiner.com; Campiello del Sol 951, San Polo; ☉by appointment 9am-1pm & 3-7pm Mon-Fri; ⓢRialto-Mercato) Paris, London, Venice: Gabriele Gmeiner honed her shoemaking craft at Hermès and John Lobb, and today jet-setters fly to Venice just for her ultra-sleek Oxfords with hidden 'bent' seams and minutely hand-stiched brogues, made to measure for men and women (around €3000, including hand-carved wooden last).

★OH MY BLUE   JEWELLERY, HANDICRAFTS

Map p270 (☏041 243 57 41; www.ohmyblue.it; Campo San Tomà 2865, San Polo; ☉11am-1pm & 2.30-7.30pm; ⓢSan Tomà) In her white-on-white gallery, switched-on Elena Rizzi showcases edgy, show-stopping jewellery, accessories and decorative objects from both local and international talent like Elena Camilla Bertellotti, Ana Hagopian and Yoko Takirai. Expect anything from quartz rings and paper necklaces to sculptural bags and ceramics.

PAPEROOWL   ARTS & CRAFTS

Map p270 (☏041 476 19 74; www.paperoowl.com; Calle Seconda del Cristo 2155a, San Polo; ☉10.30am-6pm Mon-Fri; ⓢSan Silvestro) Stefania Giannici's nimble fingers have been practising origami since she was four years old. Now a master of her craft, she folds, prints, rolls and weaves an extraordinary array of paper artworks, ranging from Japanese-style decorative panels to paper wind chimes, *kuzudama* flower balls and chic necklaces that look like Murano glass beads but cost a fraction of the price.

PIED À TERRE   SHOES

Map p270 (☏041 528 55 13; www.piedaterre-venice.com; Sotoportego degli Oresi 60, San Polo; ☉10am-12.30pm & 2.30-7.30pm; ⓢRialto-Mercato) Pied à Terre's colourful *furlane* (Venetian slippers) are handcrafted with recycled bicycle tyre treads, ideal for finding your footing on a gondola. Choose from velvet, brocade or raw silk in vibrant shades of lemon and ruby, with optional piping. Don't see your size? Shoes can be custom-made and shipped.

ATTOMBRI   GLASS, JEWELLERY

Map p270 (☏041 521 25 24; www.attombri.com; Sottoportico degli Orefici 65, San Polo; ☉10am-

THE OTHER RIALTO MARKET

No one remembers the original name of **Ponte delle Tette** (Map p270; ⬛San Silvestro), known since the 15th century as 'Tits Bridge'. Back in those days, shadowy porticoes around this bridge sheltered a designated red-light zone where neighbourhood prostitutes were encouraged to display their wares in windows instead of taking their marketing campaigns to the streets in their platform shoes. Between clients, the most ambitious working girls might be found studying: for educated conversation, *cortigiane* (courtesans) might charge 60 times the going rates for basic services from average prostitutes.

Church authorities and French dignitaries repeatedly professed dismay at Venice's lax attitudes towards prostitution, but Venice's idea of a crackdown was to prevent women prostitutes from luring clients by cross-dressing (aka false advertising) and to ban prostitutes from riding in two-oared boats – lucky that gondolas only require one oar. Fees were set by the state and posted in Rialto brothels (soap cost extra), and the rates of high-end *cortigiane* were published in catalogues extolling their various merits. The height of platform shoes was limited to a staggering 30cm by sumptuary laws intended to distinguish socialites from *cortigiane,* with little success.

1pm & 2.30-7pm Mon-Sat; ⬛Rialto-Mercato) With a clientele ranging from Hollywood stars to New York socialites, Stefano and Daniele Attombri's contemporary glass jewellery embraces art deco, Japanese and ethnic elements for universal appeal. Combining antique and modern Venetian beads with unique blown-glass cameos and sculptural shapes formed by wire frames in silver, copper and anti-allergic alloys this is statement jewellery at its best.

DAMOCLE EDIZIONI
BOOKS

Map p270 (☑346 8345720; www.edizioni damocle.com; Calle Perdon 1311, San Polo; ⊘10am-1pm & 3-7pm Mon-Fri, 10am-1pm Sat; ⬛San Silvestro) Pocket-sized Damocle is both a bookshop and publisher, translating literary greats like Oscar Wilde and Luigi Pirandello, as well as showcasing emerging writing talent, from contemporary Chinese poets to Spanish writer Luna Miguel. Most of Damocle's creations are bilingual (including books in English) and many feature beautiful artwork created through collaborations with local and foreign artists.

CASA DEL PARMIGIANO
FOOD

Map p270 (☑041 520 65 25; www.aliani casadelparmigiano.it; Campo Cesare Battisti 214, San Polo; ⊘8am-1.30pm Mon-Wed, to 7.30pm Thu-Sat; ⬛Rialto-Mercato) Set suitably beside the appetite-piquing Rialto Market, cheery Casa del Parmigiano heaves with coveted cheeses like potent *parmigiano reggiano* aged three years, to rare, local Asiago Stravecchio di Malga. All are kept good

company by fragrant cured meats, *baccalà* (cod) and trays of marinated Sicilian olives. Drooling?

ALBERTO SARRIA
ARTS & CRAFTS

Map p270 (☑041 520 72 78; www.masksvenice. com; San Polo 777, San Polo; ⊘10am-7pm; ⬛San Stae) Go Gaga or channel Casanova at this atelier, dedicated to the art of masquerade for over 30 years. Sarria's *commedia dell'arte* masks are worn by theatre companies from Argentina to Osaka – ominous burnished black leather for dramatic leads, harlequin-chequered *cartapesta* (papier mâché) for comic foils, starting from around €20. Beyond the masks is a cast of one-of-a-kind marionettes.

VENEZIASTAMPA
ARTS & CRAFTS

Map p270 (☑041 71 54 55; www.veneziastampa. com; Campo Santa Maria Mater Domini 2173, Santa Croce; ⊘8.30am-7.30pm Mon-Fri, 9am-12.30pm Sat; ⬛San Stae) Mornings are best to catch the 1930s Heidelberg machine in action, but whenever you arrive, you'll find mementos hot off the proverbial press. Veneziastampa recalls more elegant times, when postcards were gorgeously lithographed and Casanovas invited dates upstairs to 'look at my etchings'. Pick your signature symbols – meteors, faucets, trapeze artists – for original bookplates and cards.

MURRA
ARTS & CRAFTS

Map p270 (☑041 523 40 30; Ruga degli Speziali 299, San Polo; ⊘10am-7.30pm; ⬛Rialto-Mercato) Hot copper and extremely careful handling

TALK, EAT, LIVE ITALIAN

You see a rental sign on a palace door and you start daydreaming: morning banter with the market *fruttivendoli* (greengrocers), lunchtime gossip with the neighbours at your local *bacaro* (hole-in-the-wall bar), perhaps an evening *ti amo* at a candlelit, canalside restaurant. There's no doubt that a grasp of Italian will enrich your experience of Venice.

If you're itching for a deeper Venetian connection, consider signing up for a language course with **Venice Italian School** (Map p270; ☑347 9635113, 340 7510863; www.veniceitalianschool.com; Campo San Stin 2504, San Polo; group course 1-/2-weeks €290/530, individual lessons per person €65; ☒San Tomà). Not only is the school run by Venetian brother and sister Diego and Lucia Cattaneo, it uses the broader classroom of Venice to draw out its students' burgeoning language skills.

Classes take place in the family house on Campo San Stin, where their biscuit-bearing father offers cheery Italian salutations. In the afternoon keener students convene in local bars for *aperitivo* where successful pronunciation brings platters of unusual *cicheti* (Venetian tapas) and glasses of limited-production wines; meanwhile others join Diego or Lucia in the backstreets chatting with craftspeople and artisans about their work.

All the courses are bespoke and can be organised for individuals, groups or families, and the school can also help arrange well-priced accommodation.

are the secrets to the embossed leather designs gracing journals, handbags and wallets in artisan Raffaella Murra's atelier. Choose from unique jewellery pieces, satchels detailed with Murano glass or leather roses, hand-sewn journals filled with artisanal Amalfi Coast paper, or a Venetian mask sans the kitsch factor.

DROGHERIA MASCARI   FOOD & DRINKS

Map p270 (☑041 522 97 62; www.imascari.com; Ruga degli Spezieri 381, San Polo; ☺8am-1pm & 4-7.30pm Mon, Tue & Thu-Sat, 8am-1pm Wed; ☒Rialto-Mercato) Ziggurats of cayenne, leaning towers of star anise and chorus lines of olive oils draw awestruck foodies to Mascari's windows. Indoors, chefs clutch truffle jars like holy relics, kids ogle candy in copper-lidded jars and dazed gourmands confront 50 different aromatic honeys. For small-production Italian *vino* – including Veneto cult producers like Giuseppe Quintarelli – don't miss the backroom *cantina*.

FRANCO FURLANETTO   ARTS & CRAFTS

Map p270 (☑041 520 95 44; www.ffurlanetto. com; Calle delle Nomboli 2768, San Polo; ☺10am-6pm Mon-Fri, to 5pm Sat; ☒San Tomà) Masks and violins inspire Franco's designs for *forcole* (gondola oarlocks) and *remi* (oars), hand-carved on-site from blocks of walnut, cherry and pear wood. There's a science to each creation, perfectly weighted and an-

gled to propel a vessel forward, but also a delicate art. For its sculptural finesse, Franco's work has been shown in New York's Metropolitan Museum of Art.

FARMACIA BURATI   COSMETICS

Map p270 (☑041 522 35 27; www.farmaciaburati. it; Campo San Polo 2012, San Polo; ☺9am-1pm & 3.30-7.30pm Mon-Fri, 9am-12.45pm Sat; ☒San Tomà) When you start feeling the effects of all those *spritz* sessions, pick up some healing herbs at this vintage pharmacy. Adorned with 19th-century woodwork and mosaics, it peddles an impressive selection of herbal teas, designed to target various ailments. A small range of cosmetics includes deeply moisturising lotions made using argan oil.

IL PAVONE DI
PAOLO PELOSIN   ARTS & CRAFTS

Map p270 (☑041 522 42 96; Campiello dei Meoni 1478, San Polo; ☺9.30am-7pm Tue, Thu, Sat & Sun, 10.45am-7pm Mon & Fri; ☒San Silvestro) Consider Paolo's hand-bound marbled-paper journals and photo albums a challenge: now it's up to you to create Venice memories worthy of such inspired workmanship. Recipe books are covered in violet and gold feather patterns, rippled blue sketchbooks inspire seascapes, and paper-wrapped pens seem to catch fire with flickers of orange and red.

EMILIO CECCATO   CLOTHING

Map p270 (☑041 522 27 00; www.emilio
ceccato.com; Sotoportego degli Oresi 16-17, San
Polo; ⊙10am-1.30pm & 2.30-7pm Mon-Sat, from
11am Sun; ⛴Rialto-Mercato) If you've been
eyeing up the natty striped T-shirts, devil-
ishly soft winter wool hats and crepe pants
sported by Venice's *gondolieri* then make a
beeline for official supplier Emilio Ceccato.
Here you'll find a huge selection of shirts,
pants and jackets all emblazoned with the
gondoliers super-cool logo. What's more,
proceeds from purchases are reinvested in
training programs and boatyards.

BOTTEGA ORAFA ABC   JEWELLERY

Map p270 (☑041 524 40 01; www.orafaabc.com;
Calle del Tentor 1839, Santa Croce; ⊙9.30am-
1pm & 3.30-7.30pm Tue-Sat; ⛴San Stae) Master of metals, Andrea d'Agostino takes his
influence from the Japanese technique
of *mokume gane* (meaning 'metal with
woodgrain'), masterful examples of which
are on display in the Asian gallery of Ca'
Pesaro. The result is rings, pendants and
bracelets with swirling multicoloured patterns that seem to capture the dappled lagoon waters for all time in silver and gold.

OTTICA VASCELLARI   FASHION & ACCESSORIES

Map p270 (☑041 522 93 88; www.otticavascellari.
it; Ruga Rialto 1030, San Polo; ⊙9am-12.30pm &
3-7.30pm Mon-Sat, closed Mon winter; ⛴San Silvestro) 🌿 Second-generation opticians and
first-class stylists, here the Vascellari family intuit eyewear needs with a glance at
your prescription and a long look to assess
your face shape and personal style. Angu-
lar features demand Vascellari's architectural eyewear with hand-finished two-tone
laminates, while delicate features are set off
with sleek specs of ecofriendly cotton-resin
– all for less than mass-market brands.

DECLARE   FASHION & ACCESSORIES

Map p270 (☑041 822 32 27; www.dclr.it; Calle
Seconda dei Saoneri 2671, San Polo; ⊙10.30am-
7.30pm; ⛴San Tomà) Declare's sleek black
fit-out provides a dramatic backdrop for
Emanuel Cestaro's and Omar Pavanello's
boldly hued, contemporary leathergoods.
Made by artisans using full-grain Tuscan
leather, these coveted, butter-soft creations
include origami-inspired wallets, slinky
clutch purses and totes, as well as effortlessly
stylish duffle and messenger bags. You'll find
a second branch in San Marco (p69).

GILBERTO PENZO   ARTS & CRAFTS

Map p270 (☑041 71 93 72; www.veniceboats.
com; Calle 2 dei Saoneri 2681, San Polo; ⊙9am-
1pm & 3-6pm Mon-Sat; ⛴San Tomà) Yes, you
actually can take a gondola home in your
pocket. Anyone fascinated by the models at
Museo Storico Navale (p130) will go wild
here, amid handmade wooden models of
Venetian boats, including some that are
seaworthy (or at least bathtub worthy). Signor Penzo also creates kits, so crafty types
and kids can have a crack at it themselves.

SABBIE E NEBBIE   GIFTS & SOUVENIRS

Map p270 (☑041 71 90 73; www.sabbienebbie.
com; Calle dei Nomboli 2768a, San Polo; ⊙10am-
12.30pm & 4-7.30pm Mon-Sat; ⛴San Tomà)
East–West trade-route trends begin here,
with chic cast-iron teapots, Japanese-
textile patchwork totes, and Orient-in-
spired ceramics by Rita Menardi. Trained
in design and graphics, owner Maria Teresa
Laghi has a sharp eye for beautiful, unique
and inspiring objects, making her shop especially popular with discerning locals.

CAMPIELLO CA' ZEN   ANTIQUES

Map p270 (☑329 4011625, 041 71 48 71; www.
campiellocazen.com; Campiello Zen 2581, San
Polo; ⊙9.30am-1pm & 3.30-8pm Tue-Sat, 3.30-
8pm Sun; ⛴San Tomà) Antique Murano glass
lamps are the last thing you'd want to cram
into your luggage – or so you thought before
you saw the 1940s Salviati silver chandelier
and the rare ultra-mod red Seguso lamp.
That golden Venini goblet seems safe to admire, but then here's a dangerous thought:
they ship.

I VETRI A LUME DI AMADI   GLASS

Map p270 (☑041 523 80 89; Calle Saoneri 2747,
San Polo; ⊙10am-1pm & 2.30-6pm Mon-Sat;
⛴San Tomà) Glass menageries don't get
more fascinating than the one created before your eyes by Signor Amadi. Fierce little glass crabs approach pink-tipped coral,
and glass peas spill from a speckled pea
pod. You might be tempted to swat at eerily
lifelike glass mosquitoes or (gently) prod
a snapping pelican. Venetian pets at their
low-maintenance best.

ANATEMA   FASHION & ACCESSORIES

Map p270 (☑041 524 22 21; www.anatema.it; Rio
Terà 2603, San Polo; ⊙10am-1.30pm & 3-7pm;
⛴San Tomà) Add a Venetian eye for colour to
a Japanese flair for sculptural fashion, and
here you have it: teal mohair tube scarves

that float around the collarbone like clouds, and pleated Thai and Italian silk shawls and bags in shimmering *cangiante* (dual-toned) shades. The Venetian-Japanese design duo behind Anatema brings out new collections each season, from sunhats to wool-felt brooches.

IL BAULE BLU   VINTAGE

Map p270 (⌨041 71 94 48; Campo San Tomà 2916a, San Polo; ⊙10.30am-12.30pm & 4-7.30pm Mon-Sat; ⬤San Tomà) A curiosity cabinet of elusive treasures where you can expect to stumble across anything from 1970s bubble sunglasses and vintage Murano *murrine* (glass beads) to vintage Italian coats and frocks in good condition. If travel has proved tough on your kid's favourite toy, first aid and kind words will be administered at the in-house teddy hospital.

GIUSEPPE TINTI   GLASS

Map p270 (⌨041 524 12 57; www.smtoriginal muranoglass.com; Campo San Cassian 2343, Santa Croce; ⊙9am-7.30pm; ⬤Rialto-Mercato) Watch Matteo turn molten glass into a colourful, cartoon-like fish with a blowtorch and very steady hands. The results are all around you in this tiny, packed corner bolthole: highly portable, affordable souvenirs, including elegant glass-bead necklaces infused with white and yellow gold, stackable glass-band rings, colourful bottle stoppers and playful glass magnets.

LABERINTHO   JEWELLERY

Map p270 (⌨041 710 0 17; www.laberintho.it; Calle del Scaleter 2236, San Polo; ⊙10am-12.30pm & 3-7pm Tue-Sat; ⬤San Stae) A token jewel in the window is a tantalising hint of the custom jewellery this versatile goldsmiths' atelier can create for you, with original designs that nod at Venice's seafaring Byzantine past: a nautilus-inspired ring inset with opal and turquoise mosaic, a square gold bracelet inlaid with ebony, a necklace of Murano glass seascapes that float on the collarbone like islands.

CÁRTE   ARTS & CRAFTS

Map p270 (⌨320 0248776; www.cartevenezia.it; Calle dei Cristi 1731, San Polo; ⊙10.30am-5.30pm; ⬤Rialto-Mercato) Venice's shimmering lagoon echoes in marbled-paper earrings and artist's portfolios, thanks to the steady hands and restless imagination of *carta marmorizzata* (marbled-paper) *maestra* Rosanna Corrò. After years restoring ancient Venetian books, Rosanna began creating her original, bookish beauties: tubular statement necklaces, op-art jewellery boxes, one-of-a-kind contemporary handbags, and even wedding albums.

MARE DI CARTA   BOOKS

Map p273 (⌨041 71 63 04; www.maredicarta. com; Fondamenta dei Tolentini 222, Santa Croce; ⊙9am-1pm & 3.30-7.30pm Mon-Wed, 9am-7.30pm Thu & Fri, 9am-12.30pm & 3-7.30pm Sat; ⬤Ferrovia) Sailors, pirates and armchair seafarers should navigate to this canalside storefront, which stocks every maritime map and sailor's-knot manual needed for lagoon exploration, boat upkeep and sealife spotting. If you're considering a sailing, kayaking or diving course or tour – who wouldn't after a few days on the lagoon? – stop here for information.

RIALTO BIOCENTER   FOOD & DRINKS

Map p270 (⌨041 529 35 15; Calle della Regina 2264, Santa Croce; ⊙8.30am-8pm Mon-Sat; ⬤San Stae) 🍃 For organic edibles, from baby food to biscuits plus sustainably produced wines, pop into Rialto Biocenter, an easy walk west of the Rialto Market.

Cannaregio

Neighbourhood Top Five

1 The Ghetto (p109) Exploring the historic island home/prison of Venice's Jewish community, which offered refuge from the Inquisition and sparked a Renaissance in thought.

2 Chiesa di Santa Maria dei Miracoli (p111) Discovering the marble-clad church that marked a turning point

in the city's ecclesiastical architecture.

3 Chiesa della Madonna dell'Orto (p111) Paying respects to the genius of Tintoretto at his parish church and burial place, a simple structure filled with the master's works.

4 Galleria Giorgio Franchetti alla Ca' d'Oro (p111)

Finding Grand Canal photo ops and misappropriated masterpieces in one of Venice's most glorious Gothic *palazzi*.

5 Canalside cicheti bars (p115) Experiencing the very Venetian delight of establishments like Vino Vero, where the snacking is as satisfying as the sipping.

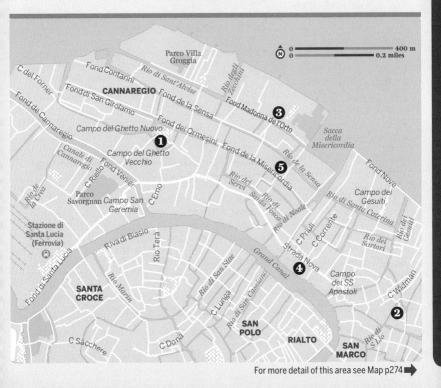

For more detail of this area see Map p274 ➡

Lonely Planet's Top Tip

Napoleon created the pedestrian boulevard that links the train station to the Rialto, and it's a lot like a highway, with rush-hour pedestrian traffic and fast-food and chain stores. At busy times you can avoid a few frustrating blocks by cutting through the Ghetto and following the sunny and scenic *fondamenta* (canal bank) running north of it.

✖ Best Places to Eat

➡ Pasticceria Dal Mas (p112)

➡ Osteria Boccadoro (p114)

➡ Trattoria da Bepi Già "54" (p113)

➡ Osteria da Rioba (p114)

For reviews, see p112. ➡

🍷 Best Places to Drink

➡ Vino Vero (p115)

➡ Timon (p115)

➡ Torrefazione Cannaregio (p115)

➡ Il Santo Bevitore (p115)

➡ Un Mondo di Vino (p115)

For reviews, see p115. ➡

🔒 Best Backstreet Buys

➡ Ca' Macana Atelier (p117)

➡ Nicolao Atelier (p116)

➡ Antichità al Ghetto (p118)

➡ L'Armadio di Coco Vintage Lab (p117)

For reviews, see p117. ➡

Explore: Cannaregio

Cannaregio doesn't have the sex appeal of San Marco, the youth of Dorsoduro or the working-class attitude of Castello. Rather, it's a well-balanced residential neighbourhood of unpretentious, patrician *palazzi* (mansions), picturesque *campi* (squares) and quiet canals. It also has some of the city's best local bars, restaurants and shops.

Settled in the 15th-century when Renaissance town planning was taking effect, Cannaregio is less of a maze than the medieval Rialto, its numerous canals cut in straight lines with broad, pedestrian-friendly *fondamente* (canal banks). The Strada Nova, created in 1871 by filling in canals, slices right through the neighbourhood.

From this pedestrian highway you can reach all of the area's sights: the churches of Madonna dell'Orto, Miracoli and Gesuiti, the Jewish Ghetto, with its historically important synagogues, and the impressive Gothic gallery of Ca' d'Oro. Come evening and you'll appreciate Cannaregio's understated charms even more as locals flock to sun-soaked bars and canalside restaurants along the Cannaregio, Ormesini and Sensa canals.

Local Life

➡**Canalside dining** Romance comes naturally to candlelit tables at Osteria da Rioba (p114) and Osteria L'Orto dei Mori (p114).

➡**Shopping secrets** Campo Santa Maria Nova hosts a monthly antiques market from spring to autumn.

➡**Serious about beer** Sightseers craving craft beers will find Venice's best brews at Il Santo Bevitore (p115).

➡**Neighbourhood nightlife** Cannaregio's timeless calm is broken at night by live music at Timon (p115), Al Parlamento (p116), Paradiso Perduto (p116) and Il Santo Bevitore (p115).

Getting There & Away

➡**Train** All services from the mainland stop at the Stazione di Santa Lucia (Ferrovia).

➡**Vaporetto** After the busy Ferrovia stop, there are two more Grand Canal stops in Cannaregio: San Marcuola (lines 1 and 2) and Ca' d'Oro (1). Lines 4.1, 4.2, 5.1 and 5.2 head from Ferrovia into the Canale di Cannaregio and on to Fondamente Nove. Line 3 heads directly from Ferrovia to all stops on Murano. From Fondamente Nove, lines 12 and 13 head to the northern islands.

➡**Traghetto** Gondolas cross the Grand Canal from Ca' d'Oro.

TOP SIGHT
THE GHETTO

This Cannaregio corner once housed a *getto* (foundry) – but its role as Venice's designated Jewish quarter from the 16th to 19th centuries gave the word a whole new meaning. From 1516 onwards, Jewish artisans and lenders tended to Venice's commercial enterprises by day, while at night and on Christian holidays they were restricted to the gated island of Ghetto Nuovo.

DON'T MISS

➡ Campo del Ghetto Nuovo
➡ Synagogue tour
➡ Museo Ebraico
➡ Memorial reliefs

PRACTICALITIES

➡ Map p274, C1
➡ 🚊 Guglie

Ghetto Life

Jewish people have lived in Venice from at least the 12th century, although it wasn't until 1516 that they were segregated in the Ghetto and subject to a strict sunset curfew. Unlike most European cities of the era, pragmatic Venice granted Jewish communities the right to practise certain professions key to the city's livelihood, including medicine, trade, banking, fashion and publishing.

When the Inquisition forced Jewish communities out of Spain in 1541, many fled to Venice. As new inhabitants crowded in, upper storeys were added to houses, creating mini-high-rises. As numbers grew, the Ghetto was extended into the neighbouring Ghetto Vecchio (Old Foundry) area, creating the confusing situation where the older Jewish area is called the New (Nuovo) Ghetto and the newer is the Old (Vecchio) Ghetto.

While the Ghetto was created as an act of segregation, over time it became a refuge in which Jewish culture and ideas thrived. It was the principal site of Hebrew publishing in Europe; Christians flocked to the Italian sermons of learned rabbi Leon da Modena, as well as rowdy Purim plays; and Ghetto literary salons attracted leading thinkers of all faiths.

When Napoleon conquered the Republic in 1797, the Jewish community experienced six months of freedom before the Austrian administration reimposed discriminatory restrictions. It wasn't until Venice joined with Italy in 1866 that full emancipation was gained. However, Mussolini's 1938 Racial Laws revived the earlier discrimination and in 1943 and 1944, 246 Jewish Venetians were deported to concentration camps; only eight survived. A **memorial** consisting of harrowing bas-reliefs and the names and ages of those killed lines two walls facing Campo del Ghetto Nuovo.

Museo Ebraico

At the Ghetto's heart, the **Museo Ebraico** (Jewish Museum; Map p274; 📞 041 71 53 59; www.museoebraico.it; adult/reduced €8/6, incl tour €12/10; 🕙 10am-7pm Sun-Fri Jun-Sep, to 5.30pm Sun-Fri Oct-May; 🚊 Guglie) explores the history of Venice's Jewish community and showcases its pivotal contributions to Venetian, Italian and world history. Opened in 1955, it has a small collection of finely worked silverware, precious textiles and other objects used in private prayer and to decorate synagogues, as well as early books published in the Ghetto during the Renaissance.

The museum visit can be combined with a highly recommended guided tour (departing hourly from 10.30am), which leads inside three of the Ghetto's historic synagogues: the Schola Tedesca, the Schola Canton and either the Schola Italiana (in summer) or the Schola Spagnola (in winter). The museum can also arrange tours to the Antico Cimitero Israelitico (p141) on the Lido.

WRITING ON THE WALL

On the wall at No 1131 Calle del Ghetto Vecchio, an official 1704 decree of the Republic forbids Jews who had converted to Christianity entry into the Ghetto, punishable by 'the rope [hanging], prison, galleys, flogging...and other greater punishments, depending on the judgment of their excellencies (the Executors Against Blasphemy)'. This was to prevent Jews from nominally converting in order to enjoy the freedom of Christians, while secretly continuing their Jewish observances.

Despite a 10-year censorship order issued by Rome in 1553, Jewish Venetian publishers contributed hundreds of titles popularising new Renaissance ideas on humanist philosophy, medicine and religion – including the first printed Qur'an.

TOP TIP

Although you can stroll around this peaceful precinct day and night, the best way to truly experience the Ghetto is to take one of the guided synagogue tours offered by the Museo Ebraico, departing hourly from 10.30am.

Synagogues

As you enter **Campo del Ghetto Nuovo** from the north, look up: atop private apartments is the wooden cupola of the 1575 **Schola Italiana** (Italian Synagogue; Map p274). The Italians were the poorest in the Ghetto, having fled from Spanish-controlled southern Italy, and their synagogue is starkly beautiful, with elegantly carved woodwork.

Recognisable from the square by its five long windows, the **Schola Tedesca** (German Synagogue; Map p274) has been the spiritual home of Venice's Ashkenazi community since 1528. By 16th-century Venetian law, only the German Jewish community could lend money, and the success of this enterprise shows in the handsome decor. The baroque pulpit and carved benches are topped by a gilded women's gallery, modelled after an opera balcony.

In the corner of the *campo*, behind the entrance to the Museo Ebraica, you'll spot the wonky wooden cupola of the **Schola Canton** (Corner Synagogue; Map p274), built c 1531 with gilded rococo interiors added in the 18th century. Though European synagogues typically avoid figurative imagery, this little synagogue makes an exception to the rule with eight charming landscapes inspired by Biblical parables.

In **Campo del Ghetto Vecchio**, Sephardic Jewish refugees raised two synagogues that are considered among the most elegant in northern Italy, having been rebuilt in the 17th-century, possibly under the direction of Baldassare Longhena. The **Schola Levantina** (Levantine Synagogue; Map p274), founded in 1541, has a magnificent woodworked pulpit (thought it's not usually open to the public), while the **Schola Spagnola** (Spanish Synagogue; Map p274), founded around 1580, shows just how Venetian the community had become, incorporating architectural flourishes such as high-arched windows and exuberant marble and carved-wood baroque interiors.

The Ghetto Today

In 2016 the Ghetto marked its 500th anniversary and used the occasion to embark on a fundraising campaign, generously supported by fashion designer Diane Von Furstenberg, to upgrade the museum and restore some of the most significant buildings.

Today few of Venice's 450-person Jewish community actually live in the Ghetto, but their children come to the *campo* to play, surrounded by the Ghetto's living legacy of bookshops, art galleries, religious institutions and kosher eateries. For information about local Jewish life, call into the **Jewish Community Info Point** (Map p274; ☎041 523 75 65; www.jvenice.org; ☺9.30am-5pm Mon-Fri).

⊙ SIGHTS

THE GHETTO
JEWISH SITE

See p109.

CHIESA DELLA
MADONNA DELL'ORTO
CHURCH

Map p274 (Campo de la Madonna de l'Orto 3520; adult/reduced €3/2; ⏱10am-5pm Mon-Sat; ⛴Orto) This elegantly spare 1365 brick Gothic church remains one of Venice's best-kept secrets. It was the parish church of Venetian Renaissance painter Tintoretto (1518–94), who filled the church with his paintings and is buried in the chapel to the right of the altar.

The church showcases two of Tintoretto's finest works: *Presentation of the Virgin in the Temple* and *Last Judgment,* where lost souls attempt to hold back a teal tidal wave while an angel rescues one last person from the ultimate *acqua alta* (high tide). It also had a Bellini masterpiece that was stolen in 1993 – note the empty space in the side chapel.

GALLERIA GIORGIO
FRANCHETTI ALLA CA' D'ORO
MUSEUM

Map p274 (☑041 520 03 45; www.cadoro. org; Calle di Ca' d'Oro 3932; adult/reduced €8.50/4.25; ⏱8.15am-2pm Mon, to 7.15pm Tue-Sun; ⛴Ca' d'Oro) One of the most beautiful buildings on the Grand Canal, 15th-century Ca' d'Oro's lacy arcaded Gothic facade is resplendent even without the original gold-leaf details that gave the palace its name (Golden House). Baron Franchetti (1865–1922) bequeathed this treasure-box palace to Venice, packed with his collection of masterpieces, many of which were originally plundered from Veneto churches during Napoleon's conquest of Italy. The baron's ashes are interred beneath an ancient purple porphyry column in the magnificent open-sided, mosaic-floored court downstairs.

Napoleon had excellent taste in souvenirs, including bronzes, tapestries, paintings and sculpture ripped (sometimes literally) from church altars. Most were warehoused at Milan's Brera Museum as Napoleonic war trophies until they were reclaimed by Venice for display here. Collection highlights include (when she's not touring the world)

CANNAREGIO SIGHTS

⊙ TOP SIGHT
CHIESA DI SANTA MARIA DEI MIRACOLI

When Nicolò di Pietro's *Madonna* icon started miraculously weeping in its outdoor shrine around 1480, crowd control became impossible. With public fundraising and marble scavenged from San Marco slag-heaps, this magnificent church was built (1481–89) to house the painting. Pietro and Tullio Lombardo's design dropped grandiose Gothic in favour of human-scale harmonies, introducing Renaissance church architecture to Venice.

The father-son team repurposed **polychrome marbles** plundered from Egypt to Syria for use on the sides of the Basilica di San Marco. Note the fine scrollwork capitols and Venetian fish-scale patterns framing veined-marble panels. If you look closely at the columns on either side of the sanctuary you'll spot angels and mermaids carved by Tullio Lombardo.

The lofty vaulted interior and domed apse seem effortless, but they're marvels of Renaissance engineering, achieved without the Gothic device of buttressing. In a prime example of Renaissance humanism, Pier Maria Pennacchi filled each of the 50 wooden coffered **ceiling panels** with a bright-eyed portrait of a saint dressed as a Venetian, just like a school yearbook.

DON'T MISS

➡ Pietro Lombardo's Renaissance design
➡ Tullio Lombardo's chancel staircase
➡ Pier Maria Pennacchi's 50 saints on the ceiling

PRACTICALITIES

➡ Map p274, G4
➡ Campo dei Miracoli 6074
➡ adult/reduced €3/1.50, free with Chorus Pass
➡ ⏱10.30am-4.30pm Mon-Sat
➡ ⛴Fondamente Nove

Titian's flushed, smouldering *Venus with a Mirror* (c 1550) and Mantegna's arrow-riddled *St Sebastian* (1490). There are also more depictions of the Madonna and Child than seems entirely reasonable.

Step outside onto Ca' d'Oro's double-decker *loggie* (balconies), where Grand Canal views framed by Gothic arcades make the city's most irresistible photo op.

A combined ticket (adult/reduced €10/5) is available including the Palazzo Grimani (p125). Admission is free on the first Sunday of each month.

I GESUITI   CHURCH

Map p274 (Santa Maria Assunta; ☑041 528 65 79; Salizada dei Specchieri 4882; €1; ☉10am-noon & 3.30-5.30pm; ⌷Fondamente Nove) Giddily over-the-top even by rococo standards, this glitzy 18th-century Jesuit church is difficult to take in all at once, with staggering white-and-green intarsia (inlaid marble) walls that look like a version of Venetian flocked wallpaper, marble curtains draped over the pulpit and a marble carpet spilling down the altar stairs. While the ceiling is a riot of gold-and-white stuccowork, gravity is provided by Titian's uncharacteristically gloomy *Martyrdom of St Lawrence,* on the left as you enter the church.

The sacristy is blanketed by 21 impressive works by Jacopo Palma di Giovane.

CHIESA DEI SCALZI   CHURCH

Map p274 (Chiesa di Santa Maria di Nazareth; ☑041 71 51 15; www.carmeloveneto.it; Fondamenta dei Scalzi 55-57; suggested donation €1; ☉7.30-11.50am & 4-7pm; ⌷Ferrovia) An unexpected outburst of baroque extravagance, this Longhena-designed church (built 1654–80) has a facade by Giuseppe Sardi rippling with columns and statues in niches. This is an unusual departure for Venice, where baroque ebullience was usually reserved for interiors of Renaissance-leaning buildings – and in fact it was a deliberate echo of a style often employed in Rome, intended to help make the Discalced (meaning 'barefoot', *scalzi* in Italian) Carmelites posted here from Rome feel more at home.

CHIESA DI SAN GEREMIA   CHURCH

Map p274 (☑041 71 61 81; Campo San Geremia 274; ☉9am-noon & 4.30-6.30pm; ⌷Ferrovia) This hefty, domed, 18th-century church contains the body of St Lucy (Santa Lucia), one of the early church's most famous mar-

tyrs, who was killed in Syracuse in AD 304. Her body was stolen from Constantinople in 1204 and moved to San Geremia after the Palladian church of Santa Lucia was demolished in the 19th century to make way for the train station. It's now displayed in a glass case in its own chapel, her face covered by a bronze mask.

LA SPEZIERIA
ALL'ERCOLE D'ORO   HISTORIC BUILDING

Map p274 (☑041 720 600; Campo Santa Fosca 2234; ☉9am-12.30pm & 3-7.30pm Mon-Fri, 9am-12.45pm Sat; ⌷Ca' d'Oro) **FREE** This perfectly preserved 17th-century *spezieria* (pharmacy) illustrates how Venetian medical advice was dispensed three centuries ago, with curatives in antique majolica jars lined up on hand-carved walnut shelves. The ornately panelled room is richly decorated with etchings of wise doctors hanging beneath a gilded wood-beam ceiling in the style of Sansovino. The room is now home to bespoke perfumery, the **Merchant of Venice**, where you can buy signature fragrances in hand-blown Murano glass bottles.

MUSEO WAGNER   MUSEUM

Map p274 (☑338 4164174; arwv@libero.it; Casinò di Venezia 2040; ☉by appointment; ⌷San Marcuola) **FREE** Richard Wagner survived the 20-year effort of composing his stormy Ring cycle only to expire in this gracious *palazzo,* now the casino (p117), in 1883. His suite – filled with musical scores and Wagner memorabilia – can be visited by pre-booked one-hour tours (available in Italian, English, German and French).

✗ EATING

★PASTICCERIA DAL MAS   BAKERY €

Map p274 (☑041 71 51 01; www.dalmaspasticceria.it; Rio Terà Lista di Spagna 150; pastries €1.30-6.50; ☉7am-9pm; ✗; ⌷Ferrovia) Our favourite Venetian bakery-cafe sparkles with mirrors, marble and metal trim, providing a fitting casket for the precious pastries displayed within. Despite the perpetual morning crush, the efficient team dispense top-notch coffee and *cornetti* (croissants) with admirable equanimity. Come mid-morning for mouth-watering, still-warm quiches. The hot chocolate is also exceptional – hardly surprising given its sister chocolate shop next door.

GELATERIA CA' D'ORO
GELATO €

Map p274 (📞041 522 89 82; Strada Nova 4273b; scoops €1.80; ⊙10am-10pm; 🚤Ca' d'Oro) Foot traffic stops here for spectacularly creamy gelato made in-house daily. For a summer pick-me-up, try the *granita di caffe con panna* (coffee shaved ice with whipped cream).

CANTINA AZIENDE AGRICOLE
VENETIAN €

Map p274 (📞333 3458811; Rio Terà Farsetti 1847a; meals €12, cicheti €1.50-1.80; ⊙9am-2.30pm & 4pm-midnight Mon-Sat; 🚤San Marcuola) For over 40 years Roberto and his sister Sabrina have run this *bacaro* (hole-in-the-wall bar), serving an impressive array of local wine to a loyal group of customers who treat the place much like a social club. Join them for a glass of Raboso and heaped platters of *lardo* (cured pork fat), cheese drizzled with honey, *polpette* (meatballs) and deep-fried pumpkin.

PANIFICIO VOLPE GIOVANNI
BAKERY €

Map p274 (📞041 71 51 78; www.facebook.com/PanificioVolpeGiovanni; Calle Ghetto Vecchio 1143; pastries €1.50-3; ⊙8.30am-noon Sun, 6.30am-7.30pm Mon-Fri; 🚤Guglie) Aside from unleavened pumpkin and radicchio bread, this kosher bakery sells unusual treats such as crumbly *impade* (biscuity logs flavoured with ground almonds) and *orecchiette di Amman* (little ears of Amman), ear-shaped pastries stuffed with chocolate, along with quite possibly the best *cornetti* (Italian-style croissants) in Venice.

OSTERIA DA ALBERTO
VENETIAN €

Map p274 (📞041 523 81 53; www.osteriadaalberto. it; Calle Larga Giacinto Gallina 5401; meals €27-37; ⊙noon-2.30pm & 6-11pm; 📶; 🚤Fondamente Nove) All the makings of a true Venetian *osteria* (casual tavern) – hidden location, casks of wine, chandeliers that look like medieval torture devices – plus fair prices on spaghetti *alla busara* (with shrimp sauce) or *alle seppie nere* (with tender squid in a squid-ink sauce), crispy fried Venetian seafood and seasonal *cicheti* (Venetian tapas). Service is friendly and efficient.

COCAETA
CRÊPES €

Map p274 (www.facebook.com/cocaeta; Fondamenta Savorgnan 548b; crêpes €3.50-8; ⊙vary; 📶; 🚤Crea) We're all for slow food, but this one-dude operation really does move at a glacial pace. Just as well that his crêpes are delicious and extremely cheap. No eggs,

---

CAMPO DEI MORI

A gent in an outsized turban called Sior Rioba has been hanging out at the corner of the **Campo dei Mori** (Square of the Moors) since the Middle Ages. The square's name is a misnomer as Rioba and his three buddies are believed to represent the Greek Mastelli family, 12th-century merchants from Morea. The Mastelli brothers became notorious for their eager participation in Doge Dandolo's sacking of Constantinople and, according to legend, Mary Magdalene herself turned them into stone.

---

milk or butter are used, so there's plenty of vegan options. In keeping with the whole slacker vibe, the hours are random; either take your chances or check the Facebook page.

RIZZO
BAKERY, DELI €

Map p274 (📞041 528 99 08; www.rizzovenezia. it; Strada Nova 3832a; ⊙7am-10pm; 🚤Ca' D'oro) One of six branches in Venice, this deli-style bakery serves up a tasty range of 'quality local street food' such as pizza slices, filled rolls, grilled *panini*, sandwiches and Venetian-style pastries.

AI PROMESSI SPOSI
VENETIAN €€

Map p274 (📞041 241 27 47; Calle d'Oca 4367; meals €29-37; ⊙6.30-11.30pm Mon & Wed, 11.30am-3pm & 6.30-11.30pm Tue & Thu-Sun; 🚤Ca' d'Oro) Bantering Venetians thronging the bar are the only permanent fixtures at this neighbourhood *osteria*, where ever-changing menus feature fresh Venetian seafood and Veneto meats at excellent prices. Seasonal standouts include *seppie in umido* (cuttlefish in rich tomato sauce) and housemade pasta, but pace yourself for cloudlike tiramisu and excellent semifreddo.

TRATTORIA DA BEPI GIÀ "54"
VENETIAN €€

Map p274 (📞041 528 50 31; www.dabepi.it; Campo SS Apostoli 4550; meals €24-37; ⊙noon-3pm & 7-10pm Fri-Wed; 🚤Ca' d'Oro) Much better than it looks, Da Bepi is a traditional trattoria in the very best sense. The interior is a warm, wood-panelled cocoon, and the service is efficient and friendly. Take their advice on the classic Venetian menu and order *spaghetti col nero di seppia* (with cuttlefish ink), grilled fish and a tiramisu that doesn't disappoint.

ALLE DUE GONDOLETTE
VENETIAN €€

Map p274 (☏041 71 75 23; www.alledue gondolette.com; Fondamente de le Capuzine 3016; meals €24-32; ⏱noon-2.30pm Mon-Thu, noon-2.30pm & 7-10.30pm Fri & Sat; ⛴Tre Archi) It's worth walking the extra mile to this humble traditional eatery for its pasta and *baccalà* (cod), either creamed with olive oil, lemon and parsley or *alla Vicentina* (braised with onions, anchovies and milk).

OSTERIA ALLA VEDOVA
VENETIAN €€

Map p274 (☏041 528 53 24; Calle del Pistor 3912; meals €28-30; ⏱11.30am-2.30pm & 6.30-10.30pm Mon-Wed, Fri & Sat, 6.30-10.30pm Sun; ⛴Ca' d'Oro) Culinary convictions run deep here at one of Venice's oldest *osterie* (1891), so you won't find *spritz* or coffee on the menu, or pay more than €2 to snack on a meatball. Enjoy superior seasonal *cicheti* with the local crowd at the bar, or call ahead for table service and strictly authentic Venetian dishes.

DALLA MARISA
VENETIAN €€

Map p274 (☏041 72 02 11; Fondamenta di San Giobbe 692b; set menu lunch €15, dinner €35-40; ⏱noon-2.15pm daily, 8-11pm Wed-Sat; ⛴Crea) At this Cannaregio institution, you'll be seated where there's room and get no menu – you'll have whatever Marisa's cooking. Serves are absurdly abundant and set meals include pasta, a main, sides, house wine and water. The food is simple; come for the local vibe, the reasonable prices and the chance to practise your Italian with whoever you're seated with.

ANICE STELLATO
VENETIAN €€

Map p274 (☏041 72 07 44; www.osterianice stellato.com; Fondamenta de la Sensa 3272; meals €40-48; ⏱11am-3.30pm & 6.30pm-midnight Wed-Sun; ⛴Sant'Alvise) Tin lamps, unadorned rustic tables and a small wooden bar set the scene for quality seafood and other Venetian specialties at this excellent canalside *bacaro*. You can munch on *cicheti* or go for the full à la carte menu and swoon over juicy scampi in *saor* (vinegar marinade) and grilled tuna. Reservations recommended.

★OSTERIA BOCCADORO
VENETIAN €€€

Map p274 (☏041 521 10 21; www.boccadoro venezia.it; Campiello Widmann 5405a; meals €40-

55; ⏱noon-3pm & 7-10pm Tue-Sun; ⛴Fondamente Nove) Birds sweetly singing in this *campo* are probably angling for your leftovers, but they don't stand a chance. Chef-owner Luciano's creative *crudi* (raw seafood) are two-bite delights and cloudlike gnocchi and homemade pasta is gone entirely too soon. Save room for luxurious desserts.

OSTERIA DA RIOBA
VENETIAN €€€

Map p274 (☏041 524 43 79; www.darioba.com; Fondamenta de la Misericordia 2553; meals €46-49; ⏱12.30-2.30pm & 7.30-11pm Tue-Sun; ⛴Orto) Taking the lead with fresh seafood and herbs pulled from the family's Sant'Erasmo farm, Da Rioba's inventive kitchen turns out exquisite plates as colourful and creative as the artwork on the walls. This is prime date-night territory. In winter, cosy up in the wood-beamed interior; in summer sit canalside. Reservations recommended.

VINI DA GIGIO
VENETIAN €€€

Map p274 (☏041 528 51 40; www.vinidagigio. com; Fondamenta San Felice 3268a; meals €47; ⏱noon-2pm & 7-10pm Wed-Sun; ⛴Ca' d'Oro) Both the food and the ambience couldn't be more Venetian in this pleasant canalside restaurant. Old beams and wood panelling provide a suitable backdrop for mixed seafood platters and tasty pasta dishes. Sadly the prices are quite Venetian too.

OSTERIA L'ORTO DEI MORI
ITALIAN €€€

Map p274 (☏041 524 36 77; www.osteriaortodei mori.com; Campo dei Mori 3386; meals €46-51; ⏱12.30-3.30pm & 7pm-midnight Wed-Mon; ⛴Orto) Not since Tintoretto lived next door has this neighbourhood seen so much action, thanks to this bustling *osteria*. Sicilian chef Lorenzo makes fresh pasta daily, including squid atop *tagliolini*. Fish-shaped lamps set a playful mood in an upmarket space.

ALGIUBAGIÒ
ITALIAN €€€

Map p274 (☏041 523 60 84; www.algiubagio.net; Fondamente Nove 5039; meals €50-60; ⏱9am-midnight Wed-Mon; ⏱; ⛴Fondamente Nove) Three monumental Murano chandeliers dangle from this swanky restaurant's exposed rafters but in summer you're going to want to nab one of the tables on the deck jutting over the water. The food is excellent, ranging from the traditional (including an excellent homemade *bigoli* pasta) to more modern fare (steak tartare with quail egg and truffle).

LOCAL KNOWLEDGE

FURTHER ADVENTURES IN WINE & CICHETI

Prosecco, Soave and Amarone aren't the only wines in town. Expand your happy-hour options with an immersion experience in Veneto wines led by an English-speaking sommelier from **Venetian Vine** (www.venetianvine.com; tastings €75 per person). Tasting sessions are held at Estro (p79) in Dorsoduro. Nan, who hosts the tastings, is also a dab hand at *voga* (the distinctive Venetian style of rowing) and is one of the tutors at Row Venice (p118). The brave (or the foolhardy) may be tempted to try her Cichetto Row: a gentle 2½-hour row between canalside bars (€240 for two people).

Landlubbers in search of a good backstreet *bacaro* (bar) crawl, should opt for fun and informed *cicheti* tours with Venetian home cook Monica Cesarato from Cook in Venice (p30). She'll ply you with more wine, cicheti and anecdotes than is seemly for one night and you'll no doubt end the evening toasting Venice with grappa-soaked grapes and chocolate 'salami'.

🍷 DRINKING & NIGHTLIFE

★VINO VERO — WINE BAR
Map p274 (📞041 275 00 44; www.facebook.com/vinoverovenezia; Fondamenta de la Misericordia 2497; ⏰11am-midnight Tue-Sun, from 6pm Mon; 🚤San Marcuola) Lining the exposed-brick walls of this superior wine bar are interesting small-production wines, including a great selection of natural and biodynamic labels. However it's the *cicheti* that really lifts this place beyond the ordinary, with arguably the most mouth-watering display of continually replenished, fresh *crostini* (open-face sandwiches) in the entire city. In the evenings the crowd spills out onto the canal.

★TIMON — WINE BAR
Map p274 (📞041 524 60 66; Fondamenta dei Ormesini 2754; ⏰6pm-1am; 🚤San Marcuola) Find a spot in the wood-lined interior or, in summer, on the boat moored out front along the canal and watch the motley parade of drinkers and dreamers arrive for seafood *crostini* and quality wines by the *ombra* (half-glass) or carafe. Musicians play sets canalside when the weather obliges.

★TORREFAZIONE CANNAREGIO — CAFE
Map p274 (📞041 71 63 71; www.torrefazionecannaregio.it; Rio Terà San Leonardo 1337; ⏰7am-7.15pm; 🚤Guglie) Venetians can't catch a train without a pit stop at this aromatic shopfront lined with brass-knobbed coffee bins. Since 1930, Venice's Marchi family has been importing speciality beans, roasted fresh daily in a washtub-size roaster behind the marble bar and ground to order. Service is as perky and efficient as you'd hope from such a well-caffeinated place.

★IL SANTO BEVITORE — PUB
Map p274 (📞335 8415771; www.ilsantobevitorepub.com; Calle Zancani 2393a; ⏰4pm-2am; 📶; 🚤Ca' d'Oro) San Marco has its glittering cathedral, but beer lovers prefer pilgrimages to this shrine of the 'Holy Drinker' for 20 brews on tap, including Trappist ales and seasonal stouts – alongside a big range of speciality gin, whisky and vodka. The faithful receive canalside seating, footy matches on TV, free wi-fi and the occasional live band.

★UN MONDO DI VINO — BAR
Map p274 (📞041 521 10 93; www.unmondodivinovenezia.com; Salizada San Canzian 5984a; ⏰11am-3pm & 5.30-11pm Tue-Sun; 🚤Rialto) Get here early for first crack at marinated artichokes and *sarde in saor* (sardines in tangy onion marinade), and to claim a few square inches of ledge for your plate and wineglass. There are dozens of wines offered by the glass, so take a chance on a freak blend or obscure varietal.

EL SBARLEFO — BAR
Map p274 (📞041 523 30 84; www.elsbarlefo.it; Salizada del Pistor 4556c; ⏰10am-11pm; 📶; 🚤Ca' d'Oro) All sorts sidle into this attractive little *cicheti* bar, from local hipsters to candidates for hip replacements, drawn by an excellent wine selection and a tasty array of snacks. The music meanders unpredictably from mellow jazz to early Elvis, but never at volumes to interrupt a decent chat.

CARNEVALE COSTUME HIRE

If you're wondering where Cinderella goes to find the perfect ball gown or Prince Charming his tights, look no further than **Nicolao Atelier** (Map p274; ☑041 520 70 51; www.nicolao.com; Fondamenta de la Misericordia 2590; ⊘9.30am-6pm Mon-Fri; ⛴San Marcuola). In his past life, Stefano Nicolao was an actor and an assistant costumier before finding his true calling as a scholar and curator of historical fashion, over 10,000 pieces of which are now stored in this Cannaregio studio.

If you're anxious about the correct cut or whether silk damask suits you better than crinoline, have no fear, his knowledge is prodigious. No wonder he's the best dressed star at the Regata Storica or that his shop is packed with customers buying and renting costumes for Carnevale. An exquisite handmade outfit will set you back €250 to €300 – and that's just to hire. Out of season they do brisk business catering to theatres, opera houses and films worldwide.

AL PARLAMENTO   BAR

Map p274 (☑041 244 02 14; www.facebook.com/alParlamento; Fondamenta Savorgnan 511; ⊘7.30am-1.30am; ☏; ⛴Crea) Entire university careers and international romances are owed to Al Parlamento's powerful espresso, 6pm-to-9pm happy-hour cocktails and excellent overstuffed *tramezzini* (triangular, stacked sandwiches). Draped ship ropes accentuate the canal views from the large windows at the front. Drop by in the evening and you might catch a live band or DJ set.

LA CANTINA   WINE BAR

Map p274 (☑041 522 82 58; Campo San Felice 3689; ⊘11am-11pm Mon-Sat; ⛴Ca' d'Oro) While you can sit down out the back for a serious seafood feast, we prefer to sample the wine and *cicheti* selection propped up at the bar or at one of the tables on the square fashioned from old wine barrels.

BAGATELA   BAR

Map p274 (☑328 7255782; www.bagatelavenezia.com; Fondamenta de le Capuzine 2925; ⊘6pm-1am Wed-Sun; ⛴Guglie) An unpretentious, popular, late-night hang-out crammed with Cannaregio locals, indie rockers and students, Bagatela offers bottled beers, cocktails, board games, sport on the TV and a rather disconcerting skull behind the bar. Pace your alcoholic intake with one of its legendary burgers.

DODO CAFFÈ   BAR

Map p274 (☑041 71 59 05; www.facebook.com/DodoCaffe; Fondamenta dei Ormesini 2845; ⊘8am-2pm & 5-8.15pm; ⛴San Marcuola) For sunsets as rosy as your *aperol spritz,* arrive early to snag canalside seating at this local favourite. The Dodo crew offer a warm welcome to strangers, along with generously stuffed *panini* and *tramezzini.*

BIRRE DA TUTTO IL MONDO O QUASI   BAR

Map p274 (☑041 71 58 34; Fondamenta dei Ormesini 2710; ⊘11am-4pm & 6pm-2am Mon-Sat; ⛴Orto) While the rest of Venice is awash in wine, 'Beers from Around the World or Almost' offers more than 100 brews, including reasonably priced bottles of speciality craft ales and local Birra Venezia. The cheery, beery scene often spills into the street – but keep it down, or the neighbours will get testy.

☆ ENTERTAINMENT

PARADISO PERDUTO   LIVE MUSIC

Map p274 (☑041 72 05 81; Fondamenta de la Misericordia 2540; ⊘11am-1am Thu-Mon; ⛴Orto) 'Paradise Lost' is a find for anyone craving a cold beer canalside on a hot summer's night. Although the restaurant is also popular, the Paradiso is particularly noted for its Monday night gigs; Chet Baker, Keith Richards and Vinicio Capossela have all played the small stage.

TEATRO MALIBRAN   THEATRE

Map p274 (☑041 965 19 75; www.teatrolafenice.it; Calle del Teatro 5873; ⛴Rialto) This pretty 17th-century theatre was built over the ruins of Marco Polo's *palazzo* (mansion). It now shares a classical music, opera and ballet program with La Fenice (p37), as well as hosting an intimate chamber-music season.

CASINÒ DI VENEZIA
CASINO

Map p274 (Ca' Vendramin Calergi; ☑041 529 71 11; www.casinovenezia.it; Calle Vendramin 2040; admission incl gaming token €10; ⊘11am-2.30am; ⚑San Marcuola) Founded in 1638, the world's oldest casino only moved into its current palatial home in the 1950s. The building certainly wasn't lucky for composer Richard Wagner, who died here in 1883; the Museo Wagner (p112) now occupies his suite. Slots open at 11am; to take on gaming tables, arrive after 3.30pm wearing your jacket and poker face. Arrive in style with a free water-taxi ride from Piazzale Roma. You must be at least 18 to enter the casino.

CIRCUITO CINEMA
GIORGIONE MOVIE D'ESSAI
CINEMA

Map p274 (☑041 522 62 98; www.comune. venezia.it/cinema; Rio Terà di Franceschi 4612; ⊘closed Tue; ⚑Fondamente Nove) Screenings of international film-festival winners, recently restored classics and family-friendly animations share top billing at this modern cinema in the heart of Venice. There are two screens (one tiny) and two or three evening screenings, plus matinees on Sunday.

🔒 SHOPPING

★CA' MACANA ATELIER
ARTS & CRAFTS

Map p274 (☑041 718 655; www.camacanaatelier. blogspot.it; Rio Terà San Leonardo 1374; ⊘9am-8pm; ⚑San Marcuola) Resist buying inferior mass-produced Carnevale masks until you've checked out the traditionally made papier-mâché and leather masks at this long-established shop, with a workshop right at its heart. The steampunk range is exactly as creepy as you'd hope.

★COIN
DEPARTMENT STORE

Map p274 (☑041 520 35 81; www.coinexcelsior. com; Ponte de l'Ogio 5787; ⊘10am-8pm; 🛜; ⚑Rialto) It's glitzy neighbour, Fondaco dei Tedeschi, gets all the attention these days but non-oligarchs will find Coin much more accessible. It's expensive but not stupidly so (especially during the legendary sales), and the range includes streetwear, famous brands and lesser known but top-quality local fashion.

GIANNI BASSO
STATIONERY

Map p274 (☑041 523 46 81; Calle del Fumo 5306; ⊘9am-1pm & 2-6pm Mon-Fri, 9am-noon Sat;

⚑Fondamente Nove) Gianni Basso doesn't advertise his letterpressing services: the clever calling cards crowding his studio window do the trick. Restaurant critic Gale Greene's title is framed by a knife and fork, and Hugh Grant's moniker appears next to a surprisingly tame lion. Bring cash to commission business cards, ex-libris, menus or invitations, and trust Signor Basso to deliver via post.

BALDUCCI BORSE
SHOES

Map p274 (☑041 524 62 33; www.balducciborse. com; Rio Terà San Leonardo 1593; ⊘9.30am-1pm & 2.30-7.30pm; ⚑San Marcuola) Venice isn't known for its leatherwork, but there's always an exception to the rule and Franco Balducci is it. Step through the door of his Cannaregio workshop and you can smell the quality of the hand-picked Tuscan hides that he fashions on the premises into glossy shoulder bags and women's boots.

L'ARMADIO DI COCO
VINTAGE LAB
VINTAGE

Map p274 (☑041 523 60 93; www.larmadiodicoco. it; Campo Santa Maria Nova 6029b; ⊘10.30am-7.30pm Mon-Sat; ⚑Rialto) For refined men's and women's vintage from the '30s to the '80s, look no further than 'Coco's closet'. Emerging designers also get rack space, making this a sure-fire place to hunt out unique and affordable fashion pieces.

VITTORIO COSTANTINI
GLASS

Map p274 (☑041 522 22 65; www.vittorio costantini.com; Calle del Fumo 5311; ⊘9.30am-

---

LOCAL KNOWLEDGE

SECRETS OF THE TRADE: CRAFT COURSES
....

As the ultimate merchant city, Venice has long been a creator and purveyor of luxury goods. To get an insight into this exclusive, creative world consider taking a course at one of Cannaregio's workshops, such as **Bottega del Tintoretto** (Map p274; ☑041 72 20 81; www. tintorettovenezia.it; Fondamenta dei Mori 3400; 5-day course incl lunch & materials €430; ⚑Orto) or **Fallani Venezia** (Map p274; ☑041 523 57 72; www.fallani venezia.com; Salizada Seriman 4875; 1/4/8hr courses €40/100/200; ⚑Fondamente Nove).

1pm & 2.15-5.30pm Mon-Fri; ⬛Fondamente Nove) 🏊 Kids and adults alike are thrilled at the magical, miniature insects, butterflies, shells and birds that Vittorio Costantini fashions out of glass using a lampwork technique. Some of these iridescent beetles have bodies made of 21 segments that need to be fused together with dazzling dexterity and speed.

ANTICHITÀ AL GHETTO   ANTIQUES

Map p274 (☎041 524 45 92; www.antichita alghetto.com; Calle del Ghetto Vecchio 1133/4; ⏰10am-noon & 2.30-7pm; ⬛Guglie) Instead of a souvenir T-shirt, how about taking home a memento of Venetian history: an ancient map of the canal, an etching of Venetian dandies daintily alighting from gondolas or an 18th-century cameo once worn by the most fashionable ladies in the Ghetto.

LEONARDO   JEWELLERY

Map p274 (Rio Terà San Leonardo 1703; ⏰9.30am-7.30pm; ⬛San Marcuola) This attractive shop stocks jewellery from some of the very best Murano glass artists, many of whom rarely sell outside their own showrooms. Chalcedony pendants in opal glass by Antonio Vaccari and contemporary statement necklaces by Igor Balbi are complemented by unique historical pieces, such as African murrine bead necklaces, so called as Venetian beads were widely traded throughout Africa.

FANNY   FASHION & ACCESSORIES

Map p274 (☎041 522 82 66; www.fannygloves.it; Rio Terà San Leonardo 1647; ⏰9.30am-7.30pm; ⬛San Marcuola) Fanny's rows of multicoloured gloves, each gripping its matching pair, is mildly disturbing (as is the brand name) but the quality of the soft leather is immediately apparent – and they're all made locally.

DOLCEAMARO   FOOD & DRINKS

Map p274 (☎041 523 87 08; Campo San Canzian 6051; ⏰10.30am-1.30pm & 4-8pm; ⬛Rialto) Call in for top-notch artisanal chocolate, regional wine, speciality Veneto grappa and other gourmet temptations, including aged balsamic vinegar and whole truffles.

DE SPAR TEATRO ITALIA   FOOD & DRINKS

Map p274 (www.despar.it; Rio Terà de la Maddalena 1976; ⏰8am-9pm; ⬛San Marcuola) In Venice, even the supermarkets are beautiful! Try not to be distracted by the painted ceilings and marbled walls while you hunt for milk and tea bags.

🏃 SPORTS & ACTIVITIES

ROW VENICE   BOATING

Map p274 (☎347 7250637; www.rowvenice.org; Fondamenta Gasparo Contarini; 90min lessons 1-2 people €85, 3/4 people €120/140; ⬛Orto) The next best thing to walking on water: rowing a traditional *batellina coda di gambero* (shrimp-tailed boat) standing up like gondoliers do. Tours must be pre-booked and commence at the wooden gate of the Sacca Misericordia boat marina.

SUP IN VENICE   WATER SPORTS

Map p274 (☎339 5659240; www.supinvenice. com; Fondamenta Contarini 3535; lesson from €60; ⏰Apr-Oct; ⬛Orto) Try your hand at stand-up paddleboarding in the Cannaregio canals; swimming is prohibited, so try to stay upright. More experienced boarders can join an island-to-island tour or paddle to a bar for a *spritz*.

BRUSSA IS BOAT   BOATING

Map p274 (☎041 71 57 87; www.brussaisboat. it; Fondamenta Labia 331; 7m boat per hour/day incl fuel €43/196; ⏰7.30am-5.30pm Mon-Fri, to 12.30pm Sat & Sun; ⬛Ferrovia) Aspiring sea captains can take on the lagoon (not the Grand Canal or canals in the historic centre) in a rented boat from Brussa. You don't need a licence, but you will be taken on a test run to see if you can manoeuvre and park; ask them to point out the refuelling stations on a map.

Castello

Neighbourhood Top Five

1 **Riva degli Schiavoni** (p129) Taking an early-morning or evening stroll along Castello's picturesque waterfront promenade.

2 **Zanipolo** (p123) Gawking at the sheer scale of this 14th-century church and admiring the master works of painting and sculpture contained within.

3 **Arsenale** (p121) Getting an insider's view during special events held within the Venetian Republic's vast honeycomb of a shipyard, once the world's best-kept industrial secret.

4 **Giardini Pubblici** (p124) Finding respite from brick and marble amid the leafy byways of Napoleon's formal gardens.

5 **Scuola Dalmata di San Giorgio degli Schiavoni** (p125) Basking in the golden glow of Carpaccio's paintings in the club rooms of the city's historic Dalmatian community.

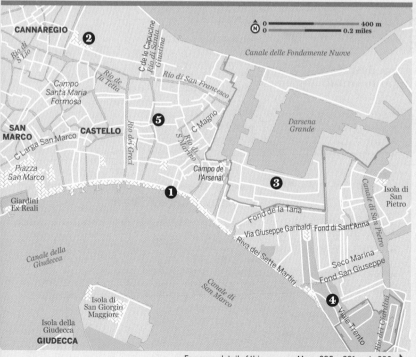

For more detail of this area see Map p280, p281 and p282

Lonely Planet's Top Tip

Venice is always best early in the morning or after the crowds thin in the evening. This is especially true of the Riva degli Schiavoni, which is packed from 11am to 7pm with day-trippers as cruises disgorge their madding crowds. But if you can get yourself out of bed, the seafront promenade is a magnificent and remarkably solitary spot for a morning constitutional. At the other end of the day, it is a spectacular sundowner spot.

✖ Best Places to Eat

➡ CoVino (p131)

➡ Met (p132)

➡ Il Ridotto (p132)

➡ Al Covo (p132)

➡ Trattoria Corte Sconta (p132)

For reviews, see p130.➡

☕ Best Places to Drink

➡ Bar Dandolo (p133)

➡ Al Portego (p133)

➡ Bacaro Risorto (p133)

➡ Strani (p133)

➡ Bar Terrazza Danieli (p133)

For reviews, see p133.➡

🔒 Best Places to Shop

➡ Atelier Alessandro Merlin (p134)

➡ Bragorà (p134)

➡ Ballarin (p135)

➡ Kalimala (p134)

➡ Banco Lotto 10 (p135)

For reviews, see p134.➡

CASTELLO

Explore: Castello

Stretching eastwards from San Marco, Castello is the city's most sprawling neighbourhood and exploring its entirety in one blast will test your walking shoes. Start with its most compelling sites – the masterfully grand Zanipolo church, Negroponte's rose-fringed Madonna in Chiesa di San Francesco della Vigna and Bellini's *Virgin Enthroned* in opulent Chiesa di San Zaccaria. All are within a stone's throw of San Marco and the Rialto.

Moving east, you'll reach the engine of the city's seafaring might: the extensive shipyards known as the Arsenale. While most of the complex is only open for special events, the boats displayed in the Padiglione delle Navi give a taste of the city's maritime history. East of the Arsenale lie working-class neighbourhoods around Via Garibaldi. You're most likely to hear the Venetian dialect here, and it's a great place for an *aperitivo* (pre-dinner drink).

Venice's glitzy waterfront promenade, the Riva degli Schiavoni, skirts the southern shore. It terminates in the Giardini Pubblici which springs to life during the Biennale. In Castello's easternmost reaches, visit Venice's first cathedral on the island of San Pietro del Castello before returning along the Riva dei Partigiani enjoying sweeping views of San Giorgio Maggiore.

Local Life

➡**Artist studios** Away from the main tourist areas, Castello's artisans are free to experiment. Don't miss Atelier Alessandro Merlin (p134) homoerotic ceramics and the wood workshop of Paolo Brandolisio (p134).

➡**Backstreet bars** Locals drop in all day for *cicheti* (bar snacks) at Bacaro Risorto (p133), Al Portego (p133) and Strani (p133).

➡**Outdoor living** *Nonne* (grandmothers) gather for afternoon gossip while their young charges kick balls across Campo Bandiera e Moro, Campo Zanipolo and Parco delle Rimembranze (p124).

Getting There & Away

➡**Vaporetto** Castello is encircled with *vaporetto* stops. Lines 4.1 and 4.2 service all stops as they loop around the eastern end of Venice; similarly 5.1 and 5.2 stop at all but Arsenale. Line 1 makes all the southern stops, linking them to the Grand Canal and the Lido. The busiest stop is San Zaccaria (also called San Marco San Zaccaria), with multiple jetties spread along the Riva degli Schiavoni.

ELEANOR SCRIVEN/GETTY IMAGES ©

TOP SIGHT
ARSENALE

For most of the year the public can only gaze and wonder at the grand portal and impassive walls surrounding this historic shipyard and still-functioning naval complex. However, the role the Arsenale has played in Venetian history cannot be underestimated. Founded in 1104, it quickly grew to become Europe's greatest naval installation and the largest productive complex in the world.

An Industrial Revolution

By its 15th- to 17th-century peak, the Arsenale employed up to 16,000 highly skilled workers, and was the very heart of Venice's mercantile and military power. A unique pre-industrial example of mass production, its centralised or-ganisation, standardised processes and stringent quality control all anticipate the modern factory. Not only was the Arsenale capable of turning out a new galley in a single day, its 45-hectare physical footprint occupied 15% of the city. Even today, it is completely surrounded by 3.2km of crenellated walls.

The Arsenale must have made an enormous impression, with its metalworking, timber cutting and boiling black pitch. Indeed, Dante used it as a model scene for hell in his *Divine Comedy*. Many streets in Castello are still named after its activities: Calle de la Pece (pitch), del Piombo (lead), de le Ancore (anchors) and de le Vele (sails).

Perhaps the most revolutionary aspect of the Arsenale was that it used canals as mov-ing assembly lines. The growing ship would move through the canals from one stage of construction to the next – a system that was not reproduced on such a scale until Henry Ford's 'revolutionary' car factory in the 20th century. As a result of this innovation, as many as 100 galleys could be in production at a single time. In addition, special consult-ants, such as Galileo, helped the Venetians rationalise production and build ships that could be equipped with increasingly powerful munitions. The treatise Galileo later wrote, drawing on his experience, is considered a seminal text of materials science.

DON'T MISS

➡ Porta Magna
➡ Padiglione delle Navi
➡ Special exhibitions

PRACTICALITIES

➡ Map p282, B2
➡ http://arsenale.comune.venezia.it
➡ 🚤 Arsenale

BUCINTORO

Seven centuries before *Pimp My Ride,* there was the *bucintoro.* The most lavish creation of the Arsenale, it was the doge's ceremonial galley. The most extravagant version was completed in 1727, and was entirely covered in gold leaf. It had seating for 90 people and required 168 oarsmen to manoeuvre. There's a scale model in the Museo Storico Navale (p130), plus a few original details salvaged after Napoleonic troops burned it in 1798.

At the core of the complex is the Arsenale Vecchio (Old Arsenal), which included storage for the *bucintoro.* Expansion in 1303–04 added La Tana to the Arsenale's southern flank. Used for rope-making, it was refashioned in 1579 by Antonio da Ponte (of Rialto Bridge fame). The Arsenale Nuovo (New Arsenal) was added in 1325, followed in 1473 by the Arsenale Nuovissimo (Very New Arsenal). In the 16th century, production of *galeazze* (large war vessels) required the creation of the deeper Canale delle Galeazze and the Gaggiandre (dry dock).

Porta Magna

Capped by a lion of St Mark that somehow eluded destruction by Napoleon's troops, the Arsenale's ornate landward **gate** (Map p282; Campo de l'Arsenal) is considered by many to be the earliest example of Renaissance architecture in Venice; it was probably built in 1460. A plaque on the wall celebrates the 1571 victory at Lepanto, and the fenced-in terrace was added in 1692. Below the statues is a row of carved lions; the biggest one, regally seated, was taken as booty by Francesco Morosini from the Greek port of Piraeus, which must have taken some doing. On the lion's left flank are some very faint Viking runes left behind by Norwegian mercenaries. They boast of their role in helping Byzantium quell a Greek rebellion – the mercenary equivalent of leaving behind a résumé.

Ships Pavilion

An annexe of the Museo Storico Navale, the **Padiglione delle Navi** (Map p282; ☎041 24 24; www.visit-muve.it; Fondamenta de la Madonna 2162c; adult/reduced €5/3.50; ◷2pm & 3.30pm Sat, 11am, 12.30pm, 2pm & 3.30pm Sun) is currently the only part of the Arsenale complex that's open to the public year-round. This vast 2000-sq-metre warehouse contains a fabulous collection of historic boats, including typical Venetian luggers, gondolas, racing boats, military vessels, a funerary barge and a royal motorboat. The most eye-catching is the *Scalé Reale,* an early 19th-century ceremonial vessel used to ferry King Vittorio Emanuele to Piazza San Marco in 1866 when Venice joined the nascent Kingdom of Italy. It was last used in 1959, when it brought the body of the Venetian pope Pius X to rest at St Mark's.

Exhibition Spaces

Biennale architecture and art exhibitions, as well as special events such as the **Arte Laguna Prize** (www.artelagunaprize.com; ◷Mar & Apr), are mounted in the **construction sheds** (Map p282; ▣Bacini) of the Arsenale. Shows offer a peek inside the former **Corderia** (where ships' cables were made), the **Artiglierie** (gun workshop) and the magnificent arcaded **Gaggiandre** (dry dock), which was fashioned from designs attributed to Jacopo Sansovino. Access to the public areas (as opposed to the military zone, which still operates within the complex) is from the north via the Celestia or Bacini *vaporetto* stops.

TOP SIGHT
ZANIPOLO

Commenced in 1333 but not finished until the 1430s, this vast Dominican church is similar in style and scope to the Franciscan Frari in San Polo, which was being raised at the same time. Both oversized structures feature red-brick facades with high-contrast detailing in white stone. After its completion, Zanipolo quickly became the go-to church for ducal funerals and burials.

Architecture
Named after two minor martyrs of early Christian Rome, Giovanni e Paolo – elided to San Zanipolo in Venetian – the church has a classic Italian Gothic style and a Latin cross plan. Its cavernous interior (90m by 38m) includes three naves and five aspes, which were designed to accommodate virtually the entire population of 14th-century Castello. Its 33m-high central nave is supported by 10 massive columns and reinforced by a clever series of cross-beams – necessary because of Venice's waterlogged soil. Typical of Italian Gothic and different from French Gothic, both the exterior and interior have a barnlike simplicity.

The Dominicans were booted out of their neighbouring friary during Napoleon's occupation and it was converted first into a military hospital and then into the civilian one that remains today. Zanipolo is now a parish church but is once again overseen by the Dominicans.

Artistic Masterpieces
In 1867 a fire destroyed paintings by Tintoretto, Palma di Giovanni, Titian and Bellini. Anti-Catholic arson was suspected, but nothing was proven. A second Bellini polyptych, on the second altar in the right aisle, survived intact. Depicting *SS Vincent Ferrer, Christopher and Sebastian,* the work has a vivid sensuousness that was to become a hallmark of Venetian painting.

Guido Reni's *San Giuseppe* is a rare expression of holy bonding, with Joseph exchanging adoring looks with baby Jesus. In the **Cappella del Rosario**, Paolo Veronese's *Assunta* ceiling depicts a rosy Madonna ascending a staggering staircase to be crowned by cherubim.

Rare 15th-century stained glass survives in the south transept. Created on Murano, it richly illuminates designs by Bartolomeo Vivarini and Girolamo Mocetto.

Tombs of the Dogi
Zanipolo was the site of all the doges' funerals from the middle of the 14th century onwards, and the walls are punctuated by 25 of their lavish tombs. From Pietro Lombardo's three-tier monument celebrating the *Ages of Man* for Pietro Mocenigo (1406–76) to the Gothic tomb of Michele Morosini (1308–82) and Andrea Tirali's bombastic *Tomba dei Valier* (1708), they provide an overview of the stylistic development of Venetian art.

The city's history is also on display. The tomb of Leonardo Loredan (1436–1521) shows him shielding Venice with his body against the invading League of Cambria. Sebastiano Venier (1496–1578), the admiral of the victorious fleet in the decisive naval battle of Lepanto in 1571 (and doge in his final year), is buried in the Cappella del Rosario.

TOP SIGHT
GIARDINI PUBBLICI

Venice's first public gardens were laid out between 1808 and 1812 on the orders of Napoleon, who decided the city needed a little breathing space – never mind that an entire residential district had to be demolished to make way for them. The park now stretches from Via Garibaldi, past the Garibaldi monument and through the Napoleonic gardens to Sant'Elena.

DON'T MISS
....

➜ Monument to the Partisan Woman
➜ Serra dei Giardini
➜ Venezuelan Pavilion

PRACTICALITIES
....

➜ Map p282, B4
➜ 🚤Giardini

Biennale Pavilions

A large portion of the gardens is given over to the Biennale exhibition arena, hosting international art (in odd years) and architecture (even years) events in 29 pavilions, each allocated to a different nation.

The pavilions tell a fascinating story of 20th-century architecture – not least because Venetian modernist master Carlo Scarpa contributed to the Biennale from 1948 to 1972, trying to make the best of Duilio Torres' Fascist 1932 Italian Pavilion, now the **Palazzo delle Esposizioni**. Scarpa is also responsible for the daring 1956 raw-concrete-and-glass **Venezuelan Pavilion** and the winsome, bug-shaped **Biglietteria** (Ticket Office).

The most recent addition is the 2015 **Australian Pavilion** by starchitects Denton Corker Marshall, the first new pavilion to be built in the garden for 20 years. A black granite box hidden intriguingly amid the foliage, it speaks of the imposition of European settlements on indigenous Australian lands.

Sadly, the entire exhibition area is usually closed to the public outside of the Biennale period.

Serra dei Giardini

This attractive iron-framed **greenhouse** (Map p282; 🗷041 296 03 60; www.serradeigiardini.org; Viale Garibaldi 1254; ☉10am-8pm; 🛜; 🚤Giardini) [FREE] was built in 1894 to house the palms used in Biennale events. It rapidly expanded into a social hub and a centre for propagation: many plants grown here adorned the municipal flowerbeds of the Lido and the ballrooms of aristocratic *palazzi* (mansions). Restored in 2010, it now has a cafe and hosts events, exhibitions and workshops.

Monument to the Partisan Woman

Located in the lapping water just along from the Riva dei Sette Martiri – where seven Venetian partisans were publicly executed by the Nazis in 1944 – lies the 1200kg bronze figure of a **woman** (Map p282; Riva dei Partigiani; 🚤Giardini Biennale). Sculpted by Augusto Murer, the figure lies on an arrangement of Istrian stone platforms designed by Carlo Scarpa to catch the eye as she appears and disappears beneath the rising and falling tide.

Parco delle Rimembranze

At the eastern limit of the gardens, on the island of Sant'Elena, is this **memorial park** (Map p282; Isola di Sant'Elena; 🚼; 🚤Sant'Elena) [FREE]. Planted with umbrella pines, each originally commemorating a fallen WWI soldier, it's a tranquil spot with postcard views of the Bacino di San Marco. Families gather here to sit on the benches, roller skate around the rink and play on the slides and swings. Apart from providing a shady respite in a crowded urban environment, it offers a real slice of Venetian life.

CASTELLO

◉ SIGHTS

ARSENALE   HISTORIC SITE
See p121.

ZANIPOLO   BASILICA
See p123.

GIARDINI PUBBLICI   GARDENS
See p124.

PALAZZO GRIMANI   MUSEUM
Map p280 (⌐041 520 03 45; www.palazzogrimani.
org; Ramo Grimani 4858; adult/reduced €5/2.50;
◷8.15am-7pm Tue-Sat, 2-7pm Sun; ⌷San Zaccaria)
The Grimani family built their Renaissance
palazzo (mansion) in 1568 to showcase their
extraordinary Graeco-Roman collection,
which was destined to become the basis of
the archaeological museum now housed in
the Museo Correr (p57). Unusually for Venice, the palace has a Roman-style courtyard,
which shed a flattering light on the archaeological curiosities. These days, the halls are
mainly empty, though their bedazzling frescoed interiors are reason enough to visit.

There is debate about who designed the
building. However, it's certain that Giovanni Grimani (1501–93) himself played a large
role in a design that consciously recalls the
glories of ancient Rome. Grimani also hired
a dream team of fresco painters specialis-
ing in fanciful grotesques and Pompeii-style
mythological scenes. Francesco Salviati applied the glowing, Raphael-style colours
he'd used in Rome's Palazzo Farnese, while
Roman painter Giovanni da Udine, considered among the brightest pupils of Raphael
and Giorgione, devoted three rooms to the
stories of Ovid.

The **Sala ai Fogliami** (Foliage Room) is
the most memorable room, though. Painted
by Mantovano, ceiling and walls are awash
with remarkably realistic plant and bird life.
They even include New World species that
had only recently been discovered by Europeans, including two that would come to be
staples of Venetian life: tobacco and corn.

A combined ticket (adult/reduced €10/5)
is available including access to Ca' d'Oro
(p111).

CHIESA DI SAN ZACCARIA   CHURCH
Map p280 (Campo San Zaccaria 4693; ◷10am-
noon & 4-6pm Mon-Sat, 4-6pm Sun; ⌷San Zaccaria) **FREE** When 15th-century Venetian girls

CASTELLO SIGHTS

◉ TOP SIGHT **SCUOLA DALMATA DI SAN GIORGIO DEGLI SCHIAVONI**

In the 15th century, Venice annexed Dalmatia – a coastal
region of present-day Croatia – and large numbers of
Dalmatian Croats, known locally as Schiavoni (Slavs),
emigrated to Venice. In a testament to Venetian plu-
ralism, they were granted their own *scuola* (religious
confraternity) in 1451. Around 1500, they began building
their headquarters, hiring Vittore Carpaccio (also of Dalmatian descent) to complete an extraordinary cycle of
paintings of Dalmatia's patron saints George, Tryphon
and Jerome.

Though Carpaccio never left Venice, his scenes
with Dalmatian backdrops are minutely detailed. But
their real brilliance is their engaging narrative power:
St George charges a lizard-like dragon across a Libyan
desert scattered with corpses; St Jerome leads his
tame-looking lion into a monastery, scattering friars like
a flock of lagoon birds; and St Augustine, watched by his
dog, is distracted from correspondence by a heavenly
voice informing him of Jerome's death.

Upstairs is a second chapel, with gilt detailing, a ceiling painted by Bastian de Muran and wall paintings from
the school of Palma il Giovane.

DON'T MISS

➤ Carpaccio's *St
George and the
Dragon*

➤ Carpaccio's *St
Jerome and the Lion*

➤ Carpaccio's *St Au-
gustine in his Study*

PRACTICALITIES

➤ Map p280, F5

➤ ⌐041 522 88 28

➤ Calle dei Furlani
3259a

➤ adult/reduced €5/3

➤ ◷1.30-5.30pm Mon,
9.30am-5.30pm Tue-
Sat, 9.30am-1.30pm Sun

➤ ⌷San Zaccaria

showed more interest in sailors than saints, they were sent to the convent adjoining San Zaccaria. The wealth showered on the church by their grateful parents is evident. Masterpieces by Bellini, Titian, Tintoretto and Van Dyck crowd the walls.

The star of the show is undoubtedly Giovanni Bellini's *Madonna Enthroned with Child and Saints* (1505), which graces an altar on the left as you enter, and glows like it's plugged into an outlet. Bellini was in his 70s when he painted it and had already been confronted by the first achievements of Giorgione (1477–1510), with his softer *sfumato* ('smokey') technique. Bellini's assimilation of the technique is clear in the sunlight that illuminates the saintly arrangement, infusing it with a sense of devout spirituality. The painting is such a treasure that Napoleon whisked it away to Paris for 20 years when he plundered the city in 1797.

To your right as you enter, the **Cappella di Sant'Atanasio** (admission €1.50) holds Tintoretto's *Birth of St John the Baptist,* while Tiepolo depicts the Holy Family fleeing to Egypt in a typically Venetian boat. Both hang above magnificently crafted choir stalls. Behind this chapel you'll find the Gothic **Cappella di San Tarasio** (also called the Cappella d'Oro, the golden chapel), with impressive Renaissance-style frescoes by Andrea del Castagno and Francesco da Faenza from the 1440s. Some original 12th-century mosaics can be seen by the altar, while a section of the original 9th-century mosaic floor is preserved under glass. Make sure you step down to the eerie flooded crypt, which houses the bodies of eight doges.

FONDAZIONE QUERINI STAMPALIA   MUSEUM
(℡041 2711411; www.querinistampalia.it; Campiello Querini Stampalia 5252; adult/reduced €4/2; ☺10am-6pm Tue-Sun; ⛴San Zaccaria) In 1869

LOVERS ALLEY

Under the arch of the covered passageway **Sotoportego dei Preti** (Map p280; ⛴Arsenale) is hidden a reddish, heart-shaped stone about the size of a hand. Local lore has it that couples that touch it together will remain in love forever. Not ready to commit just yet? This is also a nice private spot for a smooch.

Conte Giovanni Querini Stampalia made a gift of his ancestral 16th-century *palazzo* to the city on the forward-thinking condition that its 700-year-old library operate late-night openings. Downstairs, savvy drinkers take their *aperitivi* with a twist of high modernism in the Carlo Scarpa–designed garden, while the museum's temporary exhibitions add an element of the unexpected to the silk-draped salons upstairs.

Located in the upstairs apartments, the museum reflects the 18th-century tastes and interests of the count. Beneath the stuccoed ceilings you'll find rich furnishings and tapestries, Meissen and Sèvres porcelain, marble busts and some 400 paintings. Of these, many are dynastic portraits and conversation pieces, such as Alessandro and Pietro Longhi's genre scenes of masked balls, gambling dens and 18th-century bon vivants. It's a testimony to the richness of the collection that a lovely Tiepolo of St Francis clutching a crucifix is hidden in a small passageway off the bedroom.

Another standout is Giovanni Bellini's arresting *Presentation of Jesus at the Temple,* where the hapless child looks like a toddler mummy, standing up in tightly wrapped swaddling clothes. Other engaging pieces are the 39 winningly naïve *Scenes of Public Life in Venice* by Gabriele Bella (1730–99), which document the city and its customs during the period. Although somewhat crude in their realisation, the subject matter is fascinating.

CHIESA DI SAN FRANCESCO DELLA VIGNA   CHURCH
Map p280 (Campo San Francesco 2786; ☺8am-12.30pm & 3-7pm; ⛴Celestia) **FREE** Designed and built by Jacopo Sansovino, with a facade by Palladio, this enchanting Franciscan church is one of Venice's most underappreciated attractions. The Madonna positively glows in Bellini's *Madonna and Saints* (1507) in the **Cappella Santa**, just off the flower-carpeted cloister, while swimming angels and strutting birds steal the scene in the delightful *Virgin Enthroned* (c 1460–70) by Antonio da Negroponte, near the door to the right of the sanctuary. Bring €0.20 to illuminate them.

Palladio and the Madonna are tough acts to follow, but father-son sculptors Pietro and Tullio Lombardo make their own mark with their 15th-century marble reliefs that recount the lives of Christ and an assortment of saints. Housed in the **Cappella di**

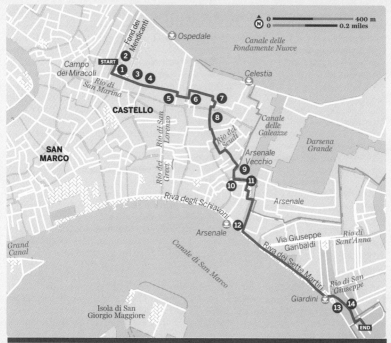

Neighbourhood Walk
Castello's Byways

START CAMPO ZANIPOLO (CAMPO SS GIOVANNI E PAOLO)
END GIARDINI PUBBLICI
LENGTH 2.5KM; TWO HOURS

Start in Campo Zanipolo, where you can't miss the **1 Bartolomeo Colleoni statue** (p130). Colleoni left the city a fortune on condition that a statue be built in his honour in Piazza San Marco. Venice bent the rules, erecting the statue in front of the **2 Scuola Grande di San Marco** (p128) instead. Next door is Gothic **3 Zanipolo** (p123).

A block east, pass the ornamented **4 Ospedaletto**, an orphanage chapel famous for its female musicians. Continue to stroll east down Barbaria de le Tole, past bric-a-brac haven **5 Ballarin** (p135) and across the canal in front of the **6 Liceo Scientifico**, with a fine Longhena facade.

Dog-leg left for Palladio's massive, classical **7 Chiesa di San Francesco della Vigna** , home to a fine Bellini and Antonio Negroponte's gorgeous *Virgin and Child Enthroned*.

Head under the colonnade lining the square to the south of the church and cross over Rio di San Francesco. To the left is the graffitied wall of **8 Laboratorio Occupato Morion** (p134). Continue past Campo de le Gatte and enter a tight nest of alleys, once housing workers of the **9 Arsenale** (p121). Turn right at Campo de le Gorne and follow the walls round to **10 Chiesa di San Martino** (p130). To the right of its doorway is a *bocca di leoni* (mouth of the lion), in which Venetians slipped denunciations of their neighbours.

Keep following the Arsenale's walls until you reach the **11 Porta Magna** (p122), considered the city's earliest example of Renaissance architecture. From here, turn southeast onto the **12 Riva degli Schiavoni** (p129) and gawk at the views across the Bacino. Stop to admire the **13 Monument to the Partisan Woman** (p124) before finishing your walk within the leafy confines of the **14 Giardini Pubblici** (p124).

VENICE'S SECRET WEAPON: ARSENALOTTI

In an early version of the assembly line, ships built in the Arsenale progressed through sequenced design phases, each staffed by *arsenalotti* (Arsenale workers) specialised in a particular aspect of construction, ranging from hull assembly and pitch application through to sail rigging. Women specialised in sails; children started apprenticeships at age 10, and did their part twisting hemp into rope.

But this wasn't a low-paid, low-status job. The *arsenalotti* were well remunerated, with cradle-to-grave fringe benefits. This helped keep them remarkably faithful to the Republic, and throughout Venetian history, *arsenalotti* repeatedly proved both their loyalty and their brawn during periods of war and rebellion. Using their proven shipbuilding techniques, they also constructed the vast *carena di nave* (ship's keel) ceilings you see in several Venetian churches.

Job requirements for *arsenalotti* included manual dexterity, strength and silence. Even in raucous Castello *bacari* (old-style bars), *arsenalotti* remained carefully vague about the specifics of their workday, in an 'I could tell you, but then I'd have to kill you' kind of way. Shipbuilding processes were top secret, and industrial espionage was considered an act of high treason, punishable by exile or death. For centuries the crenellated walls of the Arsenale hid the feverish activity inside from view. Even outside the walls, the *arsenalotti* tended to stick to their own kind. They intermarried, and even had their own market gardens to reduce contact with the rest of the city.

San Girolamo, just left of the altar, they are storytelling triumphs. Breezes seem to ripple through carved-marble trees, and lifelike lions seem ready to pounce right off the wall.

Outside, the free-standing *campanile* (bell tower) looks like the twin of the more famous one in Piazza San Marco. A portico of classical columns makes the surrounding *campo* (square) look like a proper ancient-Roman *agora* (marketplace). This makes a sociable setting for Venice's best annual block party, the **Festa di Francesco della Vigna**, when wine and rustic fare is served up in the church's stately shadow; it's usually held the third week in June.

CHIESA DI SAN GIORGIO DEI GRECI
CHURCH

Map p280 (☑041 523 95 69; www.ortodossia.it; Campo dei Greci 3412; ⊙9am-12.30pm & 2.30-4.30pm Mon & Wed-Sat, 9am-1pm Sun; ⛴San Zaccaria) FREE Greek Orthodox refugees who fled to Venice from Turkey with the rise of the Ottoman Empire built a church here in the 16th century, with the aid of a special dispensation to collect taxes on incoming Greek ships. The separate, slender bell tower was completed in 1603, though it began to lean right from the start. These days, it seems poised to dive into the canal.

Permission for a Greek confraternity was granted in the late 15th century in acknowledgment of the growing importance of the community in the city, which at its peak numbered around 4000. Greek scholars contributed greatly to Venice's dominance in the printing trade, and thereby to its eminence as a seat of Renaissance learning.

While the exterior is classically Venetian, the interior is Orthodox in style: the aisleless nave is surrounded by dark, wooden stalls and there's a *matroneo* (women's gallery). All eyes, however, are drawn to the golden iconostasis with its 46 icons, the majority of which are the work of 16th-century Cretan artist Michael Danaskinàs. More fascinating icons can be found in the neighbouring Museo delle Icone.

MUSEO DELLE ICONE
MUSEUM

Map p280 (Museum of Icons; ☑041 522 65 81; www.istitutoellenico.org; Campo dei Greci 3412; adult/reduced €4/2; ⊙9am-5pm; ⛴San Zaccaria) Glowing colours and all-seeing eyes fill this treasure box of some 80 Byzantine-style icons made in 14th- to 17th-century Italy. Keep your own eye out for the expressive *San Giovanni Climaco,* which shows the saintly author of a Greek spiritual guide distracted from his work by visions of souls diving into hell.

SCUOLA GRANDE DI SAN MARCO
NOTABLE BUILDING

Map p280 (www.scuolagrandesanmarco.it; Campo Zanipolo; ⊙9.30am-5.30pm; ⛴Ospedale) Instead of a simple Saturday father-son handyman project, sculptor Pietro Lombardo and his sons had something more ambitious in mind: a high-Renaissance polychrome marble facade for the most important confraternity in Venice. Mauro Codussi was brought in to put the finishing touches on this gem. Magnificent lions of St Mark prowl above the portals, while sculpted *trompe l'œil* perspectives beguile the eye. The *scuola* now serves as the main entrance to the Ospedale Civile, the city's public hospital.

RIVA DEGLI SCHIAVONI   WATERFRONT
Map p280 (San Zaccaria) Stretching east from San Marco, this broad waterfront avenue is one of the world's great promenades. Schiavoni (literally 'Slavs') refers to the people from Dalmatia (the coastal region of present-day Croatia, which once made up a substantial chunk of the Venetian republic) who settled here in medieval times.

CHIESA DI SAN LIO   CHURCH
Map p280 (Campo San Lio; ⊙9am-noon; Rialto) FREE Giandomenico Tiepolo sure knew how to light up a room. Duck into the atmospheric gloom of San Lio's baroque interior and, as your eyes adjust, look up at Tiepolo's magnificent ceiling fresco, *The Glory of the Cross and St Leo IX.* On your left by the main door is Titian's *Apostle James the Great,* but this church is better known for yet another Venetian artist: the great *vedutista* (landscapist) Canaletto, who was baptised and buried in this, his parish church.

Other highlights include a wonderful 15th-century Byzantine icon of the Madonna and Child.

CHIESA DI SANTA
MARIA FORMOSA   CHURCH
Map p280 (www.chorusvenezia.org; Campo Santa Maria Formosa 5267; adult/reduced €3/1.50, with Chorus Pass free; ⊙10.30am-7pm Mon-Sat; Rialto) Originally built as a thatch-roofed, wooden church in the 7th century, Santa Maria Formosa was refashioned by Mauro Codussi in 1492 with new baroque curves that make good on its name (literally 'Buxom St Mary'). The curious moniker is said to derive from a vision of the Madonna appearing in the form of a voluptuous woman to St Magnus, Bishop of Oderzo.

Continuing on the theme is Palma il Vecchio's polyptych of the forceful-looking St Barbara swathed in a billowing red cape atop an altar dedicated to the School of Shipbuilders, of whom she is patron saint. Also note the Byzantine icon of the Virgin of Lepanto near the main door.

BASILICA DI SAN
PIETRO DI CASTELLO   CHURCH
Map p282 (www.chorusvenezia.org; Campo San Pietro 2787; adult/reduced €3/1.50, with Chorus Pass free; ⊙10.30am-4.30pm Mon-Sat; San Pietro) As interesting as it is, St Peter's would be lucky to scrape into the top 10 of Venice's most impressive churches. Yet it served as the city's cathedral from 1451 until 1807, when Napoleon made the entirely reasonable decision that the Basilica di San Marco was a more worthy choice. St Peter's was founded in the 7th century; a rebuild nearly a thousand years later by one of Palladio's protégés resulted in the classical facade and large dome that stands today.

The most intriguing piece inside the church is **St Peter's Throne**, which according to legend was used by the Apostle in Antioch and once hid the Holy Grail. While the story has all the makings of a Dan Brown intrigue, there's very little truth to it: the intricately carved stone back is in fact made from a scavenged Muslim tombstone that postdates the saint's death by many centuries. Still, it seems a fitting tale for such a historic location, given that the island of San Pietro (originally known as Olivolo)

CASTELLO SIGHTS

THE VENETIAN BURBS: SANT'ELENA

At the easternmost reaches of central Venice, the island of Sant'Elena is rarely troubled by tourists. Most of it, with the exception of the 12th-century church and monastery of the eponymous saint, was built upon reclaimed swampland dredged up in the process of creating shipping lanes in the early 20th century.

The island took on its current aspect during the 1920s, when it was developed as the city's newest residential area. Deliberately eschewing the Modernist trends of its time, the middle-class apartments are echoes of the city's aristocratic palaces, although they lack the quirks and elegant decay that define the rest of Venice.

Today Sant'Elena is a quiet residential quarter and a favourite destination for joggers thanks to its shady byways and distinct lack of crowds.

was among the first to be inhabited in Venice, and the original church here was the seat of a Byzantine bishopric as early as 775.

The elegant **campanile** of white Istrian stone is older than the current church – it was designed by Codussi in the 15th century.

LA PIETÀ   CHURCH

Map p280 (🕿041 522 21 71; www.pietavenezia.org; Riva degli Schiavoni; €3, guided tours €10; ⊙9am-5pm Sat & Sun, tours noon Tue-Fri; 🛳San Zaccaria) Originally called Chiesa di Santa Maria della Visitazione but fondly nicknamed La Pietà, this harmonious church designed by Giorgio Massari is known for its association with the composer Vivaldi, who was concertmaster here in the early 18th century. Though the current church was built after Vivaldi's death, its acoustic-friendly oval shape honours his memory, and it is still used as a concert hall (p134).

BARTOLOMEO COLLEONI STATUE   MONUMENT

Map p280 (Campo Zanipolo; 🛳Ospedale) Bartolomeo Colleoni's galloping bronze equestrian statue is one of only two such public monuments in Venice – and an extraordinary example of early Renaissance sculpture. It commemorates one of Venice's most loyal mercenary commanders. From 1448, Colleoni commanded armies for the Republic, though in true mercenary form he switched sides a couple of times when he felt he'd been stiffed on pay or promotions.

On his death in 1474, Colleoni bequeathed 216,000 gold and silver ducats to Venice, on one condition: that the city erect a commemorative statue to him in Piazza San Marco. Since not even a doge had ever won such pride of place in Venice, the Senate found a workaround, placing the monument in front of the Scuola Grande di San Marco instead. Sculpted by Florentine master Andrea del Verrocchio (1435–88), it is embellished with Colleoni's emblematic *coglioni* (cullions or testicles) – a typically crude Renaissance pun. You can spot them on the base, looking like emphatic quotation marks.

CHIESA DI SAN GIOVANNI IN BRAGORA   CHURCH

Map p280 (🕿041 520 59 06; www.sgbattistainbragora.it; Campo Bandiera e Moro 3790; ⊙9.15-11.45am & 3.30-6pm Mon-Sat, 9.15-11.45am Sun; 🛳Arsenale) FREE This serene, 15th-century brick church harmonises Gothic and Renaissance styles with remarkable ease, set-

ting the tone for a young Antonio Vivaldi, who was baptised here. Look for Bartolomeo Vivarini's 1478 *Enthroned Madonna with St Andrew and John the Baptist,* which shows the Madonna bouncing a delighted baby Jesus on her knee.

MUSEO STORICO NAVALE   MUSEUM

Map p282 (Naval History Museum; www.visitmuve.it; Riva San Biagio 2148; 🛳Arsenale) At the time of research this museum, dedicated to Venice's seafaring history, was closed for renovations; in the meantime its collection of historic boats can be viewed in the Padiglione delle Navi (p122).

When the museum eventually reopens, its 42 rooms are likely to once again display scale models of Venetian-built vessels, sprawling galleries of fearsome weaponry, 17th-century dioramas of forts and ports, and a sumptuous model of the *bucintoro,* the doge's gilded ceremonial barge, destroyed by Napoleonic troops in 1798.

Although the minutiae of some of the exhibits will mostly be of interest to enthusiasts and specialists, the collection illustrates the incredible span of Venetian power across the Adriatic and Mediterranean over the centuries. In addition, it covers Italian naval history and memorabilia, from unification to the present day.

CHIESA DI SAN MARTINO   CHURCH

Map p282 (Campo San Martino 2298; ⊙9.45am-11.45am & 4.30-7pm Mon-Sat, 9.15-11.45am Sun; 🛳Arsenale) FREE Designed by Sansovino, the neighbourhood church of St Martin has a Greek-cross-shaped interior lined with eight chapels and topped by a *trompe l'œil* ceiling by Domenico Bruni.

✕ EATING

PASTICCERIA DA BONIFACIO   PASTRIES €

Map p280 (🕿041 522 75 07; Calle dei Albanesi 4237; pastries €1.10-2; ⊙7.30am-6.30pm Fri-Wed; 🛳San Zaccaria) Gondoliers and Venetian homemakers flock to this tiny bakery to devour the buttery, just-baked sweetness of almond croissants and take-home boxes of Venetian specialities such as *zaletti* (cornmeal biscuits with sultanas). As afternoon wanes, the bakery turns into a makeshift bar as locals pop in for the signature *spritz* (*prosecco* cocktail) and *mammalucchi* (deep-fried batter balls with candied fruit).

DIDOVICH
BAKERY, DELI €

Map p280 (☑041 523 00 17; Campo Santa Marina 5908; pastries €1.10, mains €8-10; ⊙7am-8pm Mon-Sat; ⛴Rialto) With outside seating on pretty Campo Santa Marina, cheerful Didovich offers the rare opportunity to sit down for a cooked breakfast. Otherwise, join the locals propping up the counter, sipping coffee and munching on croissants and *fritelle* (doughnuts). At lunchtime, sweets change to savouries with an option to take out portions of homemade pasta dishes or *polpette* (meatballs).

TRATTORIA ALLA
RAMPA DEL PIAVE
VENETIAN €

Map p282 (☑041 528 53 65; Fondamenta Sant'Anna 1135; meals €20; ⊙5am-4.30pm Mon-Sat; ⛴Giardini) Hidden behind a little working-class bar is a low-slung dining room serving up some of Venice's heartiest lunch specials. A largely male, Venetian crowd tucks in to massive portions of roasted meat and fish, accompanied by seasonal vegetables and plentiful hunks of bread. There's no menu but the unflappable waitresses will do their best to translate.

LE SPIGHE
VEGETARIAN €

Map p282 (☑041 523 81 73; Via Garibaldi 1341; meals €12-15; ⊙10.30am-2.30pm & 5.30-7.30pm Tue-Sat; ⚹; ⛴Giardini) All vegetarian, all organic and largely vegan, this tiny cafe-wholefood-shop offers a counter-full of salads and grains which are shovelled onto plates and sold by weight – haute cuisine this ain't. Either take it away to eat in the park or stake a place at the small communal table. The vegan chocolate muffins are surprisingly good.

CIP CIAP
PIZZA €

Map p280 (☑041 523 6621; Calle del Mondo Novo 5799a; pizza per 100g €1.50; ⊙9am-9pm Wed-Mon; ⛴Rialto) The cooks at this to-go pizza joint take their job seriously enough to dress in traditional chef's whites. Prices are based on weight; expect to pay about €3.50 for a decent slice.

★COVINO
VENETIAN €€

Map p280 (☑041 241 27 05; www.covinovenezia.com; Calle del Pestrin 3829; 3-course menu €39; ⊙12.30-3.30pm & 7pm-1am Thu-Mon; ☎; ⛴Arsenale) Tiny CoVino has only 14 seats but demonstrates bags of ambition in its inventive, seasonal menu inspired by the Venetian terroir. Speciality products are selected from Slow Food Presidio producers, and the charming waiters make enthusiastic recommendations from the interesting wine list. Only the set menu is available at dinner, but there's an à la carte selection at lunch.

AL GIARDINETTO DA SEVERINO
VENETIAN €€

Map p280 (☑041 528 53 32; www.algiardinetto.it; Salizada Zorzi 4928; meals €34-44; ⊙noon-3pm & 7-10pm Fri-Wed, closed Jan; ⛴San Zaccaria) Date nights don't come better than sitting among a sea of greenery in Al Giardinetto's vine-covered courtyard. For nearly 70 years the Bastianello-Parmesan family have run this restaurant in the former chapel of the 15th-century Palazzo Zorzi. In that time they've perfected traditional dishes such as crab pasta, bean soup and veal schnitzel.

TRATTORIA ALLA RIVETTA
VENETIAN €€

Map p280 (☑041 528 73 02; Salizada San Provolo 4625; meals €26-42; ⊙10am-10.30pm Tue-Sun; ⛴San Zaccaria) Tucked behind the Ponte San Provolo, this trattoria hums with the chatter of contented diners even in the dead of winter. It is staffed by a clutch of senior waiters in jovial red waistcoats, who'll cordially serve you platters of lagoon fare such as raw seafood antipasti, pasta with clams and *fritto misto* (mixed fried seafood).

OSTERIA RUGA DI JAFFA
OSTERIA €€

Map p280 (☑041 241 10 62; www.osteriarugadijaffa.it; Ruga Giuffa 4864; meals €29-41; ⊙7am-11pm; ⛴San Zaccaria) Hiding in plain sight on the busy Ruga Giuffa is this *osteria* (casual tavern) with artsy Murano wall lamps. You should be able to spot it by the *gondolieri* packing out the tables at lunchtime; they come to feast on the massive serves of pasta and delicious homemade bread. Be warned: there's no English menu.

OSTERIA ALLA STAFFA
VENETIAN €€

Map p280 (☑041 523 91 60; www.facebook.com/alla.staffa.it; Calle dell'Ospedale 6397a; meals €35-49; ⊙noon-3pm & 6.30-11pm; ⛴Ospedale) With fish fresh from the Rialto every morning and a preference for organic veg and cheese, chef Alberto's takes on Venetian classics have flavourful foundations. But this is traditional cooking taken to the next level, with artful presentation worthy of a modernist masterpiece.

LOCAL
VENETIAN €€€

Map p280 (☑041 241 11 28; www.ristorantelocal.com; Salizada dei Greci 3303; meals €75;

CASTELLO EATING

⊘noon-2pm & 7-10pm Thu-Mon, 7-10pm Wed; ✳; 🎗San Zaccaria) Although he's cooked in fine-dining establishments like Locanda Locatelli, Noma and the Cipriani, chef Matteo Tagliapietra grew up on the fisherman's island of Burano. As such his simple, seasonal cooking is rooted in the lagoon and his dishes, while creative, remain honest and flavourful. Highlights of the ever-changing menu include humble Gò risotto and the chocolate *barene* (sandbank) dessert.

TRATTORIA CORTE SCONTA VENETIAN €€€

Map p280 (☎041 522 70 24; www.cortescon tavenezia.it; Calle del Pestrin 3886; meals €44-53; ⊘12.30-2pm & 7-9.30pm Tue-Sat, closed Jan & Aug; ✳🖉; 🎗Arsenale) Well-informed visitors and celebrating locals seek out this vine-covered *corte sconta* (hidden courtyard) for its trademark seafood antipasti and imaginative house-made pasta. Inventive flavour pairings transform the classics: clams zing with ginger; prawn and courgette linguine is recast with an earthy dash of saffron; and the roast eel loops like the Brenta River in a drizzle of balsamic reduction.

IL RIDOTTO MODERN ITALIAN €€€

Map p280 (☎041 520 82 80; www.ilridotto.com; Campo SS Filippo e Giacomo 4509; meals €70-87; ⊘6.45-11pm Thu, noon-3pm & 6.45-11pm Fri-Tue; 🎗San Zaccaria) When the octopus starter looks so beautiful that it elicits gasps, there's no questioning how this small, elegant restaurant gained its Michelin star. Head chef Gianni Bonaccorsi is ably complemented by his Bangladeshi offsider Murshedul Haque, creating a menu that broadens the bounds of Italian cuisine. Tables spill out onto the square but the brick-lined interior is equally appealing.

AL COVO VENETIAN €€€

Map p280 (☎041 522 38 12; www.ristoranteal covo.com; Campiello de la Pescaria 3969; meals €42-67; ⊘12.45-3.30pm & 7.30pm-midnight Fri-Tue; ✳; 🎗Arsenale) Chef-owner Cesare Benelli has long been dedicated to the preservation of heritage products and lagoon recipes. Only the freshest seasonal fish gets the Covo treatment, accompanied by artichokes, aubergines, *cipollini* onions and mushrooms from the lagoon larders of Sant'Erasmus, Vignole, Treporti and Cavallino. Meat is also carefully sourced and much of it is Slow Food accredited.

MET MODERN ITALIAN €€€

Map p280 (☎041 524 00 34; www.metres taurantvenice.com; Riva degli Schiavoni 4149; 3-/5-/6-course meal €100/150/200; ⊘7-10.30pm Tue-Fri, 12.30-2.30pm & 7-10.30pm Sat & Sun; 🎗San Zaccaria) The Hotel Metropole's Michelin-starred restaurant offers an intriguing proposition: at each stage of their multicourse menu you can order a traditional Venetian dish or a theatrical modern interpretation using the same ingredients. The enthusiastic staff will ably assist you in your decision but, either way, you can't go wrong. Jellyfish-like Murano chandeliers add whimsy to an otherwise formal room.

ALLE TESTIERE VENETIAN €€€

Map p280 (☎041 522 72 20; www.osterialle testiere.it; Calle del Mondo Novo 5801; meals €49-57; ⊘12.30-3pm & 7-11pm Tue-Sat; 🎗Rialto) Make a reservation for one of the two evening sittings at this tiny restaurant and come prepared for one of Bruno Gavagnin's beautifully plated seafood feasts. Subtle spices such as ginger, cinnamon and orange zest recall Venice's trading past with the East.

WILDNER VENETIAN €€€

Map p280 (☎041 522 74 63; www.hotelwildner. com; Riva degli Schiavoni 4161; meals €44-55; ⊘noon-10pm Wed-Mon; 🎗San Zaccaria) Occupying a glass pavilion jutting out onto the Riva, Pensione Wildner's longstanding restaurant serves delicious takes on traditional Venetian dishes, such as octopus on lentils and veal liver on polenta. The waterfront position means that the prices are perhaps higher than they should be, but the lunch special (two courses and wine for €20) is a steal.

ALLE CORONE ITALIAN €€€

Map p280 (☎041 523 22 22; www.hotelaireali.com; Campo de la Fava 5527; meals €61-65; ⊘noon-2.30pm & 7-10.30pm; 🎗Rialto) The stupidly romantic view of gondolas floating past the windows helps to distract from the hotel-restaurant vibe of Ai Reali's dining room. The excellent food does its part too, particularly the mixed platter of *cicheti* (Venetian tapas). Venetian dishes are also showcased in the varied seafood selection on offer.

OSTERIA DI SANTA MARINA VENETIAN €€€

Map p280 (☎041 528 52 39; www.osteriadisan tamarina.com; Campo Santa Marina 5911; meals €60; ⊘7.30-10pm Mon, 12.30-2.30pm & 7.30-10pm Tue-Sat; ✳; 🎗Rialto) Don't be fooled by the casual piazza seating: this restaurant is saving up all the drama for your plate. Each course of the tasting menu brings two bites of reinvented local fare – prawn in a nest of shaved red pepper, artichoke and soft-shelled crab with squash *saor* marinade – while homemade pastas marry surprising flavours such as shrimp and chestnut ravioli.

🍷 DRINKING & NIGHTLIFE

⭐ BAR DANDOLO   COCKTAIL BAR
Map p280 (📞041 522 64 80; www.danielihotel venice.com; Riva degli Schiavoni 4196; ⊘9.30am-1.15am; 🛥San Zaccaria) Dress to the nines and swan straight past the 'hotel guests only' sign to the glamorous bar filling the grand hall of the 14th-century Palazzo Dondolo. Sparkles from Murano chandeliers reflect off the gilt edges and silk furnishings, while snappily dressed staff effortlessly descend with signature Vesper martinis and bottomless bowls of snacks.

BAR TERRAZZA DANIELI   BAR
Map p280 (📞041 522 64 80; www.danielihotel venice.com; Riva degli Schiavoni 4196; ⊘3-7pm May-Sep; 🛥San Zaccaria) Gondolas glide in to dock along the quay, while across the lagoon the white-marble edifice of Palladio's San Giorgio Maggiore turns from gold to pink in the waters of the canal: the late-afternoon scene from the Hotel Danieli's top-floor balcony bar definitely calls for a toast.

STRANI   BAR
Map p282 (📞041 099 14 34; www.straninvenice. it; Via Garibaldi 1582; ⊘7.30am-1am summer, noon-10pm winter; 🛥Giardini) There's always a party on at Strani thanks to its excellent selection of beers on tap, well-priced glasses of Veneto wines and platters of *sopressa* (soft salami). A plethora of *cicheti* keeps drinkers fuelled for late-night jam sessions.

EL RÈFOLO   BAR
Map p282 (Via Garibaldi 1580; ⊘noon-12.30am Tue-Sun; 🛥Giardini) Although the bars along Via Garibaldi may look interchangeable, the queue for El Rèfolo's pavement tables says otherwise. Part of the draw is the ever-friendly Massimiliano dispensing Italian microbrews and glasses of wine, as well as the plump sandwiches and summertime live music.

AL PORTEGO   BAR
Map p280 (📞041 522 90 38; Corte Spechiera 6014; ⊘11am-3pm & 5.30-10pm; 🛥Rialto) This walk-in closet somehow manages to distribute wine, craft beer and *cicheti* to the overflowing crowd of young Venetians in approximate order of arrival. Wine is cheap and plentiful, and the bar groans with classic nibbles. If that's not enough, make a dash for one of the five tables around the back where enormous plates of seafood are served.

BACARO RISORTO   BAR
Map p280 (Campo San Provolo 4700; ⊘8am-1am; 🛥San Zaccaria) Just a footbridge from San Marco, this shoebox of a corner bar overflowing with happy drinkers offers quality wines and abundant *cicheti,* including *crostini* (open-faced sandwiches) heaped with *sarde in saòr,* soft cheeses and melon tightly swaddled in prosciutto. Note that opening times are 'flexible'.

ROSA SALVA   CAFE
Map p280 (📞041 522 79 49; www.rosasalva.it; Campo Zanipolo 6779; ⊘8am-8pm; 🛥Ospedale) For over a century, Rosa Salva has been serving tea, pastries and ice creams to the passing trade on Campo Zanipolo. Inside the 1930s throwback interior, ladies take *tramezzini* (triangular, stacked sandwiches) and trays of *tè con limone* at marble-topped tables while, outside, sunseekers sip *spritz* and children slurp ice creams.

PARADISO   CAFE
Map p282 (📞041 241 39 72; Giardini Pubblici 1260; ⊘9am-7pm, later during Biennale; 🛥Giardini Biennale) This cheery yellow mini-*palazzo* is fuelled by a steady stream of coffee and cocktails that cost less than you'd expect given the designer chairs, waterfront terrace and lack of competition – this is the only cafe within reach of anyone in stilettos at the Biennale.

ENOTECA MASCARETA   WINE BAR
Map p280 (📞041 523 07 44; Calle Lunga Santa Maria Formosa 5183; ⊘7pm-2am Fri-Tue; 🛥Ospedale) Oenophiles love this traditional *enoteca* (wine bar) for its stellar wines by the glass, including big Amarones and organic 'cloudy' *prosecco,* one of them made by owner Mauro. If you're hungry, the excellent *taier misto* (platters of cured meats and cheeses) could pass for a light meal for two.

☆ ENTERTAINMENT

LABORATORIO
OCCUPATO MORION   LIVE MUSIC
Map p280 (www.facebook.com/laboratorioccu
patomorion; Salizada San Francesco 2951; ⚇Ce-
lestia) When not busy staging environmental protests or avant-garde performance art,
this counterculture social centre throws
one hell of a party, with performances by
bands from around the Veneto. Events are
announced on its Facebook page.

VENICE MUSIC GOURMET   MUSIC
(☏391 359 29 59; www.venicemusicgourmet.it; dinner, drinks & concert €110; ⊘7pm Thu & Fri; ⚇San
Zaccaria, Celestia) Hosted in historic palaces,
these gourmet musical evenings promise
stirring tunes from Vivaldi and Bach, as
well as Italian jazz legends, accompanied by
a multicourse dinner of lagoon delights. It's
exactly how Venetians past would have heard
the latest tracks amid a convivial group of
guests knocking back first-class glasses of
Franciacorta and forkfuls of *sarde in saor*
(grilled sardines in a sweet and sour sauce).

I VIRTUOSI ITALIANI   CLASSICAL MUSIC
Map p280 (☏041 522 11 20; www.chiesavivaldi.it; La
Pietà, Riva degli Schiavoni; adult/reduced €25/20;
⊘concerts 8.30pm; ⚇San Zaccaria) With fine
acoustics, soaring Tiepolo ceilings and a
long association with Vivaldi, La Pietà (p130)
makes an ideal venue for baroque music.
This ensemble delivers Vivaldi's *Four Seasons* in the venue it was first performed.

COLLEGIUM DUCALE   CLASSICAL MUSIC
Map p280 (☏041 98 42 52; www.collegiumducale.
com; Palazzo delle Prigioni 4209; tickets €28;
⚇San Zaccaria) Spend a perfectly enjoyable
evening in prison with this six-member
chamber orchestra, who perform Vivaldi's
Four Seasons in the grand hall rather than
the cells. On alternate nights opera singers
tackle everything from Mozart to Gerswhin.

🛍 SHOPPING

BRAGORÀ   FASHION & ACCESSORIES
Map p280 (☏041 319 08 64; www.bragora.it;
Salizada Sant'Antonin 3496; ⊘9.30am-7.30pm;
⚇Arsenale) Bragorà is a multipurpose space:
part shop, service centre and cultural hub.
Its upcycled products include beach bags
sewn out of boat sails, toy gondolas fash-
ioned from drink cans, belts made from

bike tyres and jewellery crafted from
springs. There's an excellent range of witty
tees on Venetian themes and you can even
print your own.

KALIMALA   SHOES
Map p280 (☏041 528 35 96; www.kalimala.it;
Salizada San Lio 5387; ⊘9.30am-7.30pm Mon-
Sat; ⚇Rialto) Sleek belts with brushed-steel
buckles, satchels, man-bags and knee-
high red boots: Kalimala makes beautiful
leather goods in practical, modern styles.
Shoes, sandals and gloves are crafted from
vegetable-cured cow hide and dyed in a
mix of earthy tones and vibrant lapis blues.
Given the natural tanning and top-flight
leather, the prices are remarkably reasonable, with handmade shoes starting at €135.

ATELIER ALESSANDRO MERLIN   HOMEWARES
Map p280 (☏041 522 58 95; Calle del Pestrin
3876; ⊘10am-noon & 3-7pm Mon-Thu & Sat,
3-7pm Fri & Sun; ⚇Arsenale) Enjoy your breakfast in the nude, on a horse or atop a jelly-
fish – Alessandro Merlin paints them all on
striking black and white cappuccino cups
and saucers. Homoerotic-art lovers will
recognise the influence of Tom of Finland
in his ultra-masculine, well-endowed, nude
dudes, but the *sgraffito* technique he uses
on some of his work dates back to Roman
times.

PAOLO BRANDOLISIO   ARTS & CRAFTS
Map p280 (☏041 522 41 55; Sotoportego Corte
Rota 4725; ⊘9am-1pm & 3-7pm Mon-Fri; ⚇San
Zaccaria) Beneath all the marble and gilt,
Venice is a city of wood long supported by
its carpenters, caulkers, oarmakers and
gilders. Master woodcarver Paolo Brandolisio continues the traditions, crafting the
sinuous *forcola* (rowlock) that supports the
gondolier's oar. Made of walnut or cherry
wood, each is crafted specifically for boat
and gondolier. Miniature replicas are on
sale in the workroom.

QSHOP   BOOKS, HOMEWARES
(☏041 523 44 11; www.querinistampalia.it;
Campiello Querini Stampalia 5252; ⊘10am-6pm
Tue-Sun; ⚇San Zaccaria) Aside from its sumptuous range of art and design books, the
shop of the Fondazione Querini Stampalia
(p126) offers a highly curated selection of
glass, jewellery, household items, silverware
and textiles. Pieces from design greats such
as Carlo Scarpa, Carlo Moretti and San Lorenzo sit beside the work of emerging talents.

BALLARIN   ANTIQUES

Map p280 (📞347 7792492; Calle del Cafetier 6482; ⏱10am-1pm & 4-6.30pm Mon-Sat; 🚤Ospedale) If you're looking for something distinctively Venetian, check out this Aladdin's cave. An old-fashioned dealer and artisan restorer, Valter Ballarin has a knack for tracking down period furnishings, hand-painted glassware, prints, books, toys and lamps. The best souvenir, though, is a handful of colourful, hand-blown glass flowers from dismembered Murano chandeliers.

OI VA VOI STUDIO   ARTS & CRAFTS

Map p282 (📞328 6072055; www.oivavoigallery. wordpress.com; Fondamenta di Sant'Anna 996a; ⏱10am-7pm Mon-Sat; 🚤Giardini) Artist-in-residence Roman Tcherpak has devised his own system of hand-printing digital images onto basically anything, including ceramics and leather. You can buy examples of his work here or enroll in an hour-long course (€70) where you'll create three or four pieces of your own. He also sells some deliciously creepy feather-covered masks come Carnevale time.

BANCO LOTTO 10   FASHION & ACCESSORIES

Map p280 (📞041 522 14 39; www.ilcerchiovenezia.it; Salizada Sant'Antonin 3478a; ⏱9.30am-7.30pm Mon-Sat, 10.30am-5pm Sun; 🚤Arsenale) Prison orange is out and plum silk velvet is in at this nonprofit boutique, whose hand-sewn fashions are the fruit of a retraining program at the women's prison on Giudecca. Designed and made by inmates, the smartly tailored jackets and handbags often incorporate opulent materials donated by Fortuny and Bevilacqua. Even La Fenice has dressed its divas in their ensembles.

AL CAMPANIL   JEWELLERY

Map p280 (📞041 523 57 34; Calle Lunga Santa Maria Formosa 5184; ⏱9.30am-12.30pm & 3.30-7.30pm Mon-Sat; 🚤Ospedale) Utilising traditional Murano techniques and materials, Sabina Melinato conjures up contemporary glass and costume jewellery. Her deco-inspired glass pendants are so highly polished they look like lacquerwork – just what you'd expect from a teacher at Murano's International School of Glass.

LIBRARIA AQUA ALTA   BOOKS

Map p280 (📞041 296 08 41; Calle Lunga Santa Maria Formosa 5176b; ⏱9am-8pm; 🚤Ospedale) Precarious stacks of books look at constant danger of collapse at this wonderfully rag-tag secondhand bookshop. Some books are displayed in a gondola – which must come in handy during floods – and you can even climb a stack for views over the back canal.

VIZIOVIRTÙ   CHOCOLATE

Map p280 (📞041 275 01 49; www.viziovirtu. com; Calle Forneri 5988; ⏱10am-7.30pm; 🚤Rialto) Work your way through Venice's most decadent vices at this Willy Wonka–esque shop, whose whisker-licking edibles include plague doctor masks. Ganache-filled chocolates come in a five-course meal of flavours, from barolo wine, pink pepper and balsamic vinegar to wild fennel and Earl Grey.

GIOVANNA ZANELLA   SHOES

Map p280 (📞041 523 55 00; www.giovannazanella.it; Calle Carminati 5641; ⏱1.30-8pm Mon-Sat; 🚤Rialto) Woven, sculpted and crested like lagoon birds, Zanella's shoes practically demand that red carpets unfurl before you. The Venetian designer custom-makes shoes, so the answer is always: yes, you can get those peep-toe numbers in yellow and grey, size 12, extra narrow – if, that is, you're willing to take out a second mortgage to pay for them.

I TRE MECANTI   FOOD

Map p280 (📞041 522 29 01; www.itremercanti.it; Campo de la Guerra 5364; ⏱11am-7.30pm; 🚤San Zaccaria) Stocked with wine, olive oil, jam and pasta, this excellent store has plenty of edible souvenirs that you can happily lug home with you but the reality is, most purchases don't make it out of the shop. That's because the legendary homemade macarons and jars of tiramisu demand immediate consumption.

🏃 SPORTS & ACTIVITIES

REALI WELLNESS SPA   SPA

Map p280 (📞041 241 59 16; www.hotelaireali. com; Campo de la Fava 5527; 4hr sessions €25; ⏱10am-9pm; 🚤Rialto) In this surprisingly spa-starved city, the Hotel ai Reali's spa offers a sanctuary of Asian-inspired wellness. Instead of being banished to the basement as is usually the case, the Reali's spa is on the top floor where light floods into the Turkish bath and soothes you in your 'emotional' shower. A range of Thai massages and beauty treatments is offered.

Giudecca, Lido & the Southern Islands

GIUDECCA | ISOLA DI SAN SERVOLO | ISOLA DI SAN LAZZARO DEGLI ARMENI | LIDO DI VENEZIA | PELLESTRINA

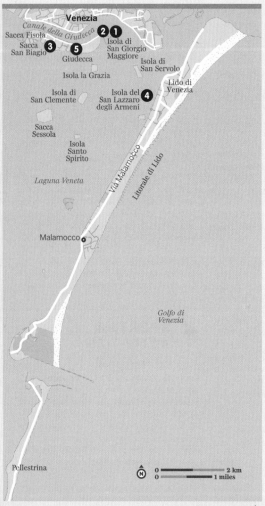

Neighbourhood Top Five

1 **Chiesa di San Giorgio Maggiore** (p138) Immersing yourself in the bright serenity of Palladio's eye-catching church and ascending its *campanile* (bell tower) for spectacular views of San Marco.

2 **Fondazione Giorgio Cini** (p139) Losing yourself in the garden maze, Longhena's elegant library and intriguing contemporary art exhibits.

3 **Giudecca** (p139) Soaking up the island's local-meets-luxe vibe – hopping between hotel spas, craft workshops, art galleries and bars frequented by residents and their four-legged friends.

4 **Monastero di San Lazzaro degli Armeni** (p141) Gaining insights from one of the resident Armenian monks as you tour around their island home.

5 **Chiesa del Santissimo Redentore** (p139) Giving thanks for Venice's ongoing survival in this impressive, art-filled church.

For more detail of this area see Map p283 and p284 ➡

Explore: Giudecca, Lido & the Southern Islands

Other cities have suburban sprawl; Venice has medieval monasteries floating in teal-blue waters. To the south, the seaward side of the lagoon is sheltered from the Adriatic by the Lido, for centuries the beach and bastion of the city. In the 19th century, it found a new lease of life as a bathing resort and a place of escape from the urban rigours of the Rialto. It's a quick 15-minute boat ride from San Marco, and many people decamp here for weeks in the summer. In winter, it's quiet and shuttered.

Smaller islands dot the foreground of memorable views back to San Marco: Isola delle Rose, San Lazzaro degli Armeni, San Servolo and San Giorgio Maggiore. In the past they served the Republic well as monasteries, quarantine stations, military hospitals and mental asylums.

Next to San Giorgio Maggiore lies Giudecca, Venice's unofficial seventh *sestiere* (district). It was once an aristocratic retreat and later the city's industrial centre; it now maintains an interesting balance between luxury and grit. You can easily visit both San Giorgio and Giudecca in half a day – weekends are best, when you can also tour the Fondazione Giorgio Cini.

Local Life

➡**Cicheti hot spots** Join artists and locals for generous *cicheti* (Venetian tapas) at La Palanca (p142), Da Cri Cri e Tendina (p144) and al Mercà (p143).

➡**Island pastimes** Join weekending locals on the Lido shooting rounds at Circolo Golf Venezia (p145) or, in summer, lazing on the beach.

➡**Giudecca's back alleys** Step away from the waterfront and discover public parks and tiny squares filled with youngsters kicking balls, oldies holding court on park benches and parents pushing prams.

Getting There & Away

➡**Vaporetto** Lines 2, 4.1 and 4.2 stop at all four Giudecca *vaporetto* stops. Line 2 also stops at neighbouring San Giorgio Maggiore. San Lazzaro and San Servolo are both served by line 20 from San Zaccaria. Lines 1, 2, 5.1, 5.2, 6, 8, 10 and 14 all call into Lido SME (Santa Maria Elisabetta), the island's main hub. Some seasonal services also stop at Lido San Nicolò and Lido Casino.

➡**Car ferry** Line 17 connects Tronchetto to Lido San Nicolò and Punta Sabbioni on the mainland.

➡**Bus** Bus 11 connects Lido to Pellestrina via a ferry.

Lonely Planet's Top Tip

Instead of braving the lines at San Marco's *campanile* (bell tower), seek out San Giorgio Maggiore's *campanile,* which offers comparable views for a fraction of the wait time.

✖ Best Places to Eat

➡ Trattoria Altanella (p142)
➡ La Palanca (p142)
➡ La Favorita (p143)
➡ Ristorante da Celeste (p143)
➡ Magiche Voglie (p143)

For reviews, see p142.➡

⊟ Best Places to Drink

➡ Skyline (p144)
➡ La Palanca (p142)
➡ Villa Laguna (p144)

For reviews, see p144.➡

🔒 Best Places to Shop

➡ Fortuny Tessuti Artistici (p144)
➡ Artigiani del Chiostro (p145)
➡ Cartavenezia (p145)
➡ Monastero di San Lazzaro degli Armeni (p141)

For reviews, see p144.➡

TOP SIGHT
CHIESA DI SAN GIORGIO MAGGIORE

Solar eclipses are only marginally more dazzling than the view of this abbey church (completed 1610), positioned for maximum impact on its own island facing San Marco. Palladio chose white Istrian stone to stand out against the blue lagoon waters, and set it at an angle to create visual drama while also ensuring that it catches the sun all afternoon.

Exterior

Palladio's facade gracefully solved the problem bedevilling Renaissance church design: how to graft a triangular pediment onto a Christian church, with its high, central nave and lower side aisles. Palladio's radical solution: use one pediment to crown the nave, and a lower, half-pediment to span both side aisles. The two interlock with rhythmic harmony, while prominent three-quarter columns, deeply incised capitals and sculptural niches create clever shadowplay. Above the facade rises a brick *campanile* (bell tower) with a conical copper spire and a cap of Istrian stone.

Interior

Likewise, the interior is a combination of brightness and serenity. Sunlight enters through high thermal windows and is diffused by acres of white stucco. Floors inlaid with white, red and black stone draw the eye toward the altar. With its rigorous application of classical motifs, it's reminiscent of a Roman theatre.

Two outstanding late works by Tintoretto flank the church's altar. On one side hangs his *Collection of Manna*; on the other side, *Last Supper* depicts Christ and his apostles in a scene that looks suspiciously like a 16th-century Venetian tavern, with a cat and dog angling for scraps.

DON'T MISS

➡ Tintoretto's *Collection of Manna* and *Last Supper*

➡ Views from the 60m-high bell tower

PRACTICALITIES

➡ Map p283, F1

➡ 🕿 041 522 78 27

➡ www.abbaziasan giorgio.it

➡ Isola di San Giorgio Maggiore

➡ bell tower adult/ reduced €6/4

➡ ⏰ 8.30am-6pm

➡ 🚤 San Giorgio Maggiore

⊙ SIGHTS

⊙ Giudecca

Giudecca's disputed history begins with its name. The name doesn't connote a historic Jewish enclave (as it does in parts of Southern Italy) but rather it probably derives from the Venetian *zudega,* meaning 'the judged' – referring to rebel aristocratic families banished here during the 9th century.

Michelangelo fled here from Florence in 1529, though by the time he arrived, the aristocratic Dandolo, Mocenigo and Vendramin families had transformed the island from a prison into a neighbourhood of garden villas. When the nobles headed inland in the 18th century to build villas along the Riviera Brenta, Giudecca's gardens gave way to factories, tenements and military barracks.

In recent years, these large abandoned spaces have attracted a new set of exiles – artists who can no longer afford the rent in central Venice.

CASA DEI TRE OCI   GALLERY
Map p283 (☎041 241 23 32; www.treoci.org; Fondamente de le Zitelle 43; adult/reduced €12/10; ⊙10am-6pm Wed-Mon; ⛴Zitelle) FREE Acquired by the Fondazione di Venezia in 2000, this fanciful neo-Gothic house was built in 1913 by artist and photographer Mario de Maria, who conceived its distinctive brick facade with its three arched windows (its namesake 'eyes'). It now houses his photographic archive and interesting exhibitions of contemporary art, especially photography.

CHIESA DEL
SANTISSIMO REDENTORE   CHURCH
Map p283 (Church of the Most Holy Redeemer; www.chorusvenezia.org; Campo del SS Redentore 194; adult/reduced €3/1.50, with Chorus Pass free; ⊙10.30am-4.30pm Mon-Sat; ⛴Redentore) Built to celebrate the city's deliverance from the Black Death, Palladio's *Il Redentore* was completed under Antonio da Ponte (of Rialto Bridge fame) in 1592. Inside there are works by Tintoretto, Veronese and Bassano, but the most striking is Paolo Piazza's 1619 *Venice's Offering for Liberation from the Plague of 1575–77,* near the door.

⊙ TOP SIGHT
FONDAZIONE GIORGIO CINI

In 1951, industrialist and art patron Vittorio Cini – a survivor of Dachau – acquired the monastery of San Giorgio and restored it in memory of his son, Giorgio Cini. The rehabilitated complex, now home to Cini's cultural foundation, is an architectural treasure incorporating a refectory and cloister by Palladio, and Baldassare Longhena's monumental staircase and 1671 library. Veronese's *Wedding Feast at Cana* once hung in Palladio's refectory, but was removed by Napoleon in 1797 and sent to the Louvre where it still resides (a copy hangs in its place).

Today the foundation continues the Benedictine tradition of scholarship; it became renowned for this during the Renaissance, when Florentine prince Cosimo de' Medici funded the creation of a library here. The Nuova Manica Lunga library now occupies the monk's former dormitory block.

Weekend tours take in all the highlights and allow you to stroll through the garden labyrinth and contemplate the tranquil Cypress Cloister, the oldest extant part of the complex, completed in 1526 by Andrea Buora. Check the website for exhibitions, events and performances in the open-air **Teatro Verde** (p144).

DON'T MISS
➡ Chiostro dei Cipressi
➡ Palladio's refectory
➡ Longhena's library

PRACTICALITIES
➡ Map p283, F1
➡ ☎347 3386426
➡ www.cini.it
➡ Isola di San Giorgio Maggiore
➡ adult/reduced €10/8
➡ ⊙tours 10am-5pm Sat & Sun
➡ ⛴San Giorgio Maggiore

LIDO STYLE

Between 1850 and WWI, the Lido became the world's most exclusive seaside resort and is still defined by the *stile liberty* (art nouveau) of the period. Walking itineraries around the most extravagant villas are available to download at www2.comune. venezia.it/lidoliberty.

Sensing an opportunity, canny business tycoon Nicolò Spada (founder of the Italian hotel group CIGA) started buying up Lido land, opening two vast, extravagant hotels, the **Hotel Excelsior** (✆041 526 02 01; www.hotelexcelsiorvenezia.com; Lungomare Marconi 41; r from €310; ☉Apr-Oct; ❇☎; ⚐Lido) and the **Grand Hotel des Bains** (Map p284; Lungomare Marconi 17; ⚐Lido SME), in 1908 and 1909 respectively. Giovanni Sardi's Excelsior, which sits directly on the beach, is a Veneto-Moorish fantasy palace with interiors decorated by Mariano Fortuny, while the more conservative Hotel des Bains, designed by Francesco Marsich, recalls the great luxury spas of Baden Baden. The latter was immortalised in Thomas Mann's best-selling novella *Death in Venice*, adapted for the screen by Luchino Visconti in 1971 and filmed in the hotel. Sadly it's now boarded up – an oversized symbol of the beach resort's fall from fashion.

Survival is never taken for granted in this tidal town, and to give thanks during the **Festa del Redentore**, Venetians have been making the pilgrimage across the canal on a shaky pontoon bridge from the Zattere since 1578.

GIUDECCA 795 GALLERY
Map p283 (✆340 8798327; www.giudecca795. com; Fondamenta San Biagio 795; ☉6-9pm Tue-Fri & Sun, 3.30-8pm Sat; ⚐Palanca) FREE Founded to promote local artists of all kinds, this quirky and welcoming gallery displays (and sells) a wide range of works by both established and young artists, most of whom have a strong connection with Venice itself.

LE ZITELLE CHURCH
Map p283 (Chiesa di Santa Maria della Presentazione; ✆041 260 19 74; Fondamenta de le Zitelle 33; ⚐Zitelle) Designed by Palladio in the late 16th century and built after his death, the Zitelle was a church and hospice for orphans and poor young women (*zitelle* is old local slang for 'old maids'). The doors are rarely open, but you can get a spa treatment in the adjoining convent and sleep in the orphanage. The luxury Palladio Hotel & Spa (p195) has creatively tweaked the original structure without altering Palladio's blueprint or the original cloister garden.

CHIESA DI SANT'EUFEMIA CHURCH
Map p283 (Fondamenta Sant'Eufemia 680; ☉8am-noon & 3-5pm Mon-Sat, 3-7pm Sun; ⚐Palanca) Four women saints were venerated in the original AD 890 church here, but Sts Dorothy, Tecla and Erasma weren't as popular as early Christian martyr Euphemia. She was thrown to hungry lions in Chalcedon (present-day Turkey), but after biting off her hand, the lions refused to eat her holy virgin flesh – a hungry bear was less forgiving. The simple Veneto-Byzantine structure you see today dates from 1371. Frescoes decorate the ceiling of the baroque interior.

◉ Isola di San Servolo

Step off *vaporetto* 20 from San Zaccaria amid the students of Venice International University and you'll be struck by the island's balmy beauty. But despite the exotic palms, San Servolo has long sent a chill down Venetian spines, serving as it did as the city's main insane asylum from the 18th century until 1978.

Home to Benedictine monks since the 9th century, the island's medicinal flora saw it granted an apothecary's license in 1719 so the monks could better supply the Republic's on-site military hospital. Not long afterwards, in October 1725, San Servolo's first 'insane' patient, Lorenzo Stefani, arrived, starting a trend among aristocratic families to have their afflicted relatives committed. At its peak, the asylum held hundreds of inmates, a large portion of them ex-ship's hands and Italian and Austrian servicemen, many of whom were simply suffering trauma or were afflicted by conditions caused by poverty and poor nutrition. A dedicated museum now documents their stories and some of the nightmarish 'treatments' practised on them.

MUSEO DEL MANICOMIO   MUSEUM
Map p284 (Insane Asylum Museum; ☑041 576 50 01; www.sanservolo.servizimetropolitani.ve.it; adult/reduced €6/4.50; ◷10.45am & 2pm Mon-Thu year-round, plus 3.30-6.30pm Fri, 11.30am-6.30pm Sat & Sun May-Sep; ⛴San Servolo) As well as a poignant photographic collection displaying portraits of patients, San Servolo's former asylum contains the full paraphernalia of psychiatric treatment of the day, including chains, handcuffs, cages for ice showers, early electrotherapy machines and a rare plethysmograph (the precursor of the lie detector). The visit also takes in a reconstructed anatomy theatre beside the church and the ancient pharmacy.

◉ Isola di San Lazzaro degli Armeni

Once the site of a Benedictine hospice for pilgrims and then a leper colony, this tiny island was given to Armenian monks fleeing Ottoman persecution in 1717. The entire island is still a working monastery, so access is by tour only.

**MONASTERO DI SAN
LAZZARO DEGLI ARMENI**   MONASTERY
Map p284 (☑041 526 01 04; adult/reduced €6/4.50; ◷tours 3.25pm; ⛴San Lazzaro) Tours of the historic Armenian island monastery start in its glittering church and are conducted by multilingual monks, who amply demonstrate the institution's reputation for scholarship. After passing through the 18th-century refectory, you'll head upstairs to the library. In 1789 the monks set up a polyglot printing press here and translated many scientific and literary works into Armenian. Those works are still housed in the 150,000-strong collection alongside curios from Ancient Egypt, Sumeria and India.

An Egyptian mummy and a 15th-century Indian throne are the rather quirky main features of the room dedicated to the memory of Lord Byron, who spent six months here in 1816 helping the monks to prepare an English-Armenian dictionary. True to his eccentric nature, he could often be seen swimming from the island to the Grand Canal.

Before you leave, stop in at the shop to purchase some Vartanush jam made from rose petals plucked in the monastery's exotic gardens.

Take the 3.10pm *vaporetto* number 20 from San Zaccaria to arrive in time for the tour; bookings aren't required.

◉ Lido di Venezia

The **Lido** (Map p284; ⛴Lido SME) is no longer the glamorous bolt-hole of Hollywood starlets and European aristocracy that it once was, but its groomed beaches, scattering of art nouveau buildings and summering Venetians sipping *prosecco* (sparkling white wine) beneath candy-striped awnings make it an interesting diversion on a hot day. However, the presence of cars and suburban sprawl can be jarring after the lost-in-time nature of central Venice, and in winter even fading glamour is in short supply.

ANTICO CIMITERO ISRAELITICO   CEMETERY
Map p284 (Ancient Jewish Cemetery; Riviera San Nicolò; tours €90; ⛴Lido San Nicolò) This overgrown garden was Venice's main Jewish cemetery from 1386 until the 18th century. Tombstones range in design from Venetian Gothic to distinctly Ottoman. Some bear the image of a lion, not of St Mark, but of Castile and León, brought to Venice on the armorials of Sephardic Jews expelled from Spain in 1492. The cemetery can only be visited on a guided tour, arranged through the Museo Ebraico (p109).

MALAMOCCO   VILLAGE
(Lido; ☐A or B) Pass over Ponte di Borgo to explore the canals and *calli* (lanes) of a less overwhelming lagoon town. A miniature version of Venice right down to the lions of St Mark on medieval facades, Malamocco was actually the lagoon capital from 742 to 811.

ⓘ LIDO ON BIKE

You can hire bikes from this **outlet** (☑041 526 80 19; www.lidoonbike.it; Gran Viale Santa Maria Elisabetta 21b; bicycle rental per 90min/day €5/9; ◷9am-7pm summer; ⛴Lido SME) near the Lido SME *vaporetto* stop. Bikes are offered at reasonable prices that include a helmet and a free map with recommended routes. Tandems and pedal cars are also available. ID is required for rental and the leader of the group must be 18 or over.

PINETA DEGLI ALBERONI   FOREST

Map p284 (▣A) Right at the southern tip of the island, the Alberoni pine forest slopes down to the Lido's wildest stretch of beach. These World Wildlife Fund–protected dunes and walking trails are the stuff of Shelley's poems and Byron's early-morning rides. The majority of the beach is open to the public.

⊙ Pellestrina

Stretching south of Lido and repeating its long, sinuous shape, Pellestrina reminds you what the lagoon might have been like if Venice had never been dreamed of. The 11km-island is home to three tight-knit fishing communities – San Pietro in Volta, Porto Secco and Pellestrina – strung out along the water's edge. There are no hotels, fancy shops or sun loungers here, and only a handful of restaurants and gelato shops – it's mainly just elderly women sitting on their porches and fishermen mending their nets.

Much of Pellestrina's seafront is lined by a remarkable feat of 18th-century engineering known as the *murazzi*. Although not immediately impressive to modern eyes, these massive sea walls represent Herculean handiwork from a pre-industrial age. Designed to keep high seas from crashing into the lagoon, they remain an effective breakwater even today. The island is also blissfully flat, making it ideal biking country. The scenic side faces the lagoon and is lined with fishermen's shacks built over beds of mussels.

Bus 11 travels from the Lido SME *vaporetto* stop to Pellestrina via a short hop on a ferry.

LOCAL KNOWLEDGE

EL PECADOR

No, you're not suffering from heatstroke – that really is a red, double-decker **bus** (Lungomare Gabriele d'Annunzio, Lido; sandwiches €2.50-5; h10am-2am Apr-Oct; Lido SME) parked up against the kerb. What's more it's dishing out the Lido's finest stuffed sandwiches and *spritz* (*prosecco* cocktails), so why not take a seat on the canopied top deck?

✗ EATING

✗ Giudecca

AL PONTIL DEA GIUDECCA   VENETIAN €

Map p283 (✆041 528 69 85; Fondamenta San Giacomo 197a; meals €16; ⊙noon-3pm Mon-Sat; ▣Redentore) Asking for a menu here is like asking for one at your grandma's house. Expect a generous plate of pasta, a meat or fish dish, a side dish, and a view of San Marco – if you get the one window seat. The bar is open for *cicheti* all day, but meals are only available at lunchtime.

★TRATTORIA ALTANELLA   VENETIAN €€

Map p283 (✆041 522 77 80; Calle de le Erbe 268; meals €38-47; ⊙12.30-2.30pm & 7.30-10.30pm Wed-Sun; ❄; ▣Redentore) Founded by a fisherman and his wife in 1920 and still run by the same family, this cosy restaurant serves fine Venetian fare such as potato gnocchi with cuttlefish and perfectly grilled fish. Inside, the vintage interior is hung with artworks, reflecting the restaurant's popularity with artists, poets and writers, while outside a flower-fringed balcony hangs over the canal.

★LA PALANCA   VENETIAN €€

Map p283 (✆041 528 77 19; Fondamenta Sant'Eufemia 448; meals €25-33; ⊙7am-8pm Mon-Sat; ▣Palanca) Locals of all ages pour into this humble bar for *cicheti*, coffee and *spritz*. However it's at lunchtime that it really comes into its own, serving surprisingly sophisticated fare like swordfish carpaccio with orange zest alongside more rustic dishes, such as a delicious thick seafood soup. In summer, competition for waterside tables is stiff.

TRATTORIA AI CACCIATORI   VENETIAN €€

Map p283 (✆328 736 33 46; www.aicacciatori.it; Fondamenta del Ponte Piccolo 320; meals €40-47; ⊙noon-3pm & 6.30-10pm Tue-Sun; ▣Palanca) If you hadn't guessed from the oversized gun hanging from the ceiling beams, the restaurant is named for the hunters who once bagged lagoon waterfowl. Dishes are hearty but sophisticated, including both game and local seafood.

HARRY'S DOLCI   VENETIAN €€€

Map p283 (✆041 522 48 44; www.cipriani.com; Fondamenta San Biagio 773; meals €80-120; ⊙11am-4pm Mon, to 11pm Wed-Sun summer;

LIDO BEACHES

A near-continuous stretch of sand is spread out alongside the seaward side of the Lido. The shallow gradient makes it ideal for toddlers but not great for adults and, despite its somewhat murky appearance, it has been granted Blue Flag status, certifying that the water quality is of a high standard for swimming.

There are only six 'free' beaches open to the public: the **spiaggia comunale** accessed through the **Blue Moon complex** (Piazzale Bucintoro 1; ⊙10am-6.30pm summer; ◉Lido SME), two north of here, one a little further south and two near the **Pineta degli Alberoni** (p142) at the southern end of the island.

The rest of the shoreline is occupied by *stabilimenti*: privately managed areas lined with wooden *capannas* (cabins), a relic of the Lido's 1850s bathing scene. Many of them are rented by the same families year in, year out or reserved for guests of seafront hotels. The *stabilimenti* also offer showers, sun loungers and umbrellas (€13 to €18) and small lockers. Rates drop a few euros after 2.30pm.

◉Palanca) The sun-washed Tiffany-blue canopy along the waterfront marks out this home away from home for the designer-sunglasses set. The service is low-key and the decor retro (think bistro chairs and subway tile), though the prices have more than kept up with inflation. In the early-evening, the pontoon seating is the perfect spot for an early evening peach bellini, with rosy views across the water to the Zattere.

✖ Lido di Venezia

MAGICHE VOGLIE   GELATO €
Map p284 (Gran Viale Santa Maria Elisabetta 47g; cones €2.50-4.50; ⊙10am-11.30pm summer; ◉Lido SME) The best ice cream in the Lido is made every morning on the premises at this family-owned gelateria. Mull over the soft peaks of new-world flavours such as acai berry and caja fruit, or plump for the classic purplish-black cherry or Sicilian pistachio.

**MERCATO SETTIMANALE
DEL LIDO**   MARKET €
Map p284 (Riviera di Corinto; ⊙7am-2pm Tue; ◉Lido SME) The Lido's open-air market is jam-packed with speciality food products. It is second only to the Rialto Market and has views across the lagoon to boot.

LA FAVORITA   VENETIAN, SEAFOOD €€
Map p284 (✆041 526 16 26; Via Francesco Duodo 33; meals €38-53; ⊙12.30-2.30pm & 7-10.30pm Fri-Sun, 7-10.30pm Tue-Thu; ◉Lido San Nicolò) La Favorita has been delivering long, lazy lunches, bottles of fine wine and impeccable service since 1955. The menu is full of traditional Venetian seafood dishes such

as *rombo* (turbot) simmered with cherry tomatoes and olives, crab *gnochetti* (mini-gnocchi) and classic fish risotto.

AL MERCÀ   VENETIAN €€
Map p284 (✆041 243 16 63; www.osteriaalmerca. it; Via Enrico Dandolo 17a; meals €28-40, set lunch 2-/3-courses €15/20; ⊙10.30am-3pm & 6.15-11pm Tue-Sun; ◉Lido SME) Located in the old Lido fish market, al Mercà is popular with students who come for the abundant *cicheti*, outdoor seating and well-priced wine by the glass. Snack at one of the counters or grab a seat in the *osteria* (casual tavern) for a traditional seafood meal. A good-value set menu is on offer for weekday lunch.

AL PONTE DI BORGO   VENETIAN €€
(✆041 77 00 90; Calle delle Mercerie 27, Malamocco; meals €31-40; ⊙12.30-2.30pm & 7-10pm Apr-Oct; ▣A, B) If you make it this far, you deserve to be rewarded with plates of sweet, briny crab served in its shell and garlicky bowls of *vongole* (clams). At weekends the shaded patio is crammed with locals and in the evening the bar serves typical *cicheti* with slugs of *prosecco*. Check lunch hours in low season, as it isn't always open.

✖ Pellestrina

RISTORANTE DA CELESTE   SEAFOOD €€€
(✆041 96 73 55; www.daceleste.it; Via Vianelli 625; meals €60-80; ⊙noon-2.30pm & 7-9.15pm Thu-Tue Mar-Oct; ▣11) Halfway along Pellestrina, this simple restaurant serves lagoon-fresh fish on its pontoon terrace. Go at sunset, when the rose-tinted sky kisses the glassy lagoon, and let Rossano guide

you through the best daily offerings from polenta with tiny shrimp to a whole host of cockles, clams, scallops, spider crab and – the house special – fish pie. Reservations essential.

🍷 DRINKING & NIGHTLIFE

⭐ SKYLINE   ROOFTOP BAR
Map p283 (📞041 272 33 11; www.skylinebarvenice.com; Fondamenta San Biagio 810, Giudecca; ⊗5pm-1am; 🚤Palanca) From white-sneaker cruise passengers to the €300-sunglasses set, the rooftop bar at the Hilton Molino Stucky wows everyone with its vast panorama over Venice and the lagoon. DJs spin tunes on Friday night year-round and on additional nights in summer, when the action moves to the deck and pool. There's occasional live music too.

VILLA LAGUNA   BAR
Map p284 (📞041 526 13 16; www.hotelvillalaguna.com; Via Sandro Gallo 6, Lido; ⊗7-10pm Tue-Sun; 🚤Lido) Sunset photo ops don't come any better than on the terrace of Villa Laguna. This restored, Habsburg holiday chalet is the only lagoon-facing hotel on the Lido and its west-facing terrace and lounge bar guarantees views of San Marco framed by a blushing pink sky.

DA CRI CRI E TENDINA   BAR
Map p284 (📞041 526 54 28; Via Sandro Gallo 159, Lido; ⊗11am-8pm; 🚌A) Leave the socialites at the Excelsior and head to this neighbourhood bar for Veneto wines, beers on tap and a counter full of tasty *cicheti*. It's best in summer when all the tables are set outside and local card sharks sip their *spritz* and goad each other loudly in Venetian. At lunchtime there's a huge selection of stuffed *panini*.

LION'S BAR   BAR
Map p284 (Al Leone d'Oro; Lungomare Marconi 31, Lido; ⊗during film festival 8am-3am; 🚌B) With its sexy baroque curves, stately porticoes and exuberant sunburst demilune above the door, the Lion's Bar is the Lido's most prestigious drinking den, although sadly it's only open during the film festival. Designed by Giovanni Sicher in the 1920s, it's a classic art nouveau extravagance with a sweeping staircase, mullioned windows and a large terrace.

☆ ENTERTAINMENT

TEATRO VERDE   THEATRE
Map p283 (www.cini.it; Isola di San Giorgio Maggiore; 🚤San Giorgio Maggiore) Set in the manicured grounds of the Fondazione Giorgio Cini (p139) is the outdoor Teatro Verde. It was built in the 1950s and is now used for summer performances of dance and music.

TEATRO JUNGHANS   THEATRE
Map p283 (📞041 241 19 74; www.accademiateatraleveneta.com; Campo Junghans 494, Giudecca; prices vary; ♿; 🚤Redentore) The experimental theatre of Venice's acting academy, nicknamed Teatro Formaggino (Little Cheese), seats 150 around its three-sided stage. But you're not expected to just sit there: Teatro Junghans offers workshops on costume design and *commedia dell'arte* (traditional masked theatre). If you'd rather leave that sort of thing to professionals, check the online calendar for performances.

PACHUKA   CLUB
Map p284 (📞041 770 147; www.pachuka.it; Via Umberto Klinger, Lido; ⊗hours vary; 🚤Lido San Nicolò) The most reliable of the Lido's summertime dance spots, this place right on the beach works year-round as a snack bar and pizzeria, but summer weekend nights it cranks up as a beachside dance club, too. Expect live music and DJ sets right on the beach.

🛍 SHOPPING

FORTUNY TESSUTI ARTISTICI   HOMEWARES
Map p283 (📞393 8257651; www.fortuny.com; Fondamenta San Biagio 805, Giudecca; ⊗10am-6pm Mon-Fri; 🚤Palanca) Marcel Proust waxed rhapsodic over Fortuny's silken cottons printed with art nouveau patterns. At the showroom attached to his still-functioning factory, visitors can browse 300 textile designs and purchase cushions, mirrors, notebooks, bowls and cloth rats. From April to September you can also tour the factory's garden and underground swimming pool. For more, head to Museo Fortuny (p58).

THE PALACE OF CINEMA

Eugenio Miozzi's rigid, Rationalist **Palazzo della Mostra del Cinema** (Map p284; www.labiennale.org; Lungomare Marconi 30; ⊡V) seems as ill-suited to the playboy Lido as a woolly bathing suit. But its severe Fascist lines were well in keeping with the ambitious modernism of the era, when business tycoon and Fascist minister Count Giuseppe di Volpi conceived of the film festival as a means of fostering the Lido's up-market tourism industry.

Inaugurated in August 1932 on the terrace of the Excelsior, the festival was the first of its kind (Cannes was a relative latecomer in 1946) and capitalised on the boom in the film-making industry. So great was its success, in fact, that Miozzi's *palazzo* (mansion) was commissioned within three years and remains the main festival venue – at least until the much-delayed new cinema is completed.

ARTIGIANI DEL CHIOSTRO   ARTS & CRAFTS
Map p283 (Campo San Cosma, Giudecca; ⊙hours vary; ⊡Palanca) The cloister of the former Convent of Sts Cosmas and Damian has been repurposed as a base for independent artisans to ply their craft. Each keeps their own hours and not all are open to the public, but loop around and you'll find traditional mask makers, antique restorers, artists, metal workers, glass-blowers and many, many cats.

CARTAVENEZIA   ARTS & CRAFTS
Map p283 (⊉041 524 12 83; www.cartavenezia.it; Campo di S Cosmo 621f, Giudecca; ⊙by appointment; ⊡Palanca) Paper is anything but two-dimensional here: paper maestro Fernando di Masone embosses and sculpts handmade cotton paper into seamless raw-edged lampshades, handbound sketchbooks, and paper versions of marble friezes that would seem equally at home in a Greek temple or a modern loft. White gloves are handy for easy, worry-free browsing; paper-sculpting courses are available by prior request.

🏃 SPORTS & ACTIVITIES

ACQUOLINA COOKING SCHOOL   COOKING
Map p284 (⊉041 526 72 26; www.acquolina.com; Via Lazzaro Mocenigo 10, Lido; half-/full-day courses €170/290; ⛟; ⊡Lido) These intimate cookery classes are held by Marika Contaldo in her flower-festooned Lido villa. Serious gourmets will want to consider the multiday culinary vacations, which include cookery lessons interspersed with market visits, lagoon cruises and trips to the Segusa glass factory. Otherwise, there are half- and

full-day taster courses, the latter including a morning trip to the Rialto Market.

PALLADIO SPA   SPA
Map p283 (⊉041 520 70 22; www.palladiohotelspa.com; Fondamenta de la Zitelle 33, Giudecca; ⊙Apr-Oct; ⊡Zitelle) When one too many grim airports has left you desperate for serenity, uplifting architecture and a serious scrub, head to this Palladio-designed former nunnery for a bath of milk, honey and rose petals (€90) with complimentary Jacuzzi and marble-steam-room access.

HELIAIR.IT   SCENIC FLIGHTS
Map p284 (⊉339 3342149; www.heliair.it; Aeroporto G Nicelli, Via Morandi 9; 10-30min tours per person €120-330) Lift off in Heliair's copters for an aerial view of the lagoon. Tours offer a unique perspective of the island jigsaw puzzle.

CIRCOLO GOLF VENEZIA   GOLF
Map p284 (⊉041 73 13 33; www.circologolfvenezia.it; Strada Vecchia 1, Alberoni, Lido; green fees weekdays/weekends €97/116; ⊙9am-6pm; ⊡A) The golf club sits on a 100-hectare site protected by the World Wildlife Fund. The original nine-hole course (there are now 18) was designed by Cruikshank of Glasgow in 1928 and incorporates the walls of the old Alberoni fort as key elements in a number of holes.

Photos of club regulars, such as the Duke of Windsor, still hang in the bar, although the club's most notorious guest was Adolf Hitler, who visited in 1934.

BAGNI ALBERONI   BEACH
Map p284 (⊉041 73 10 29; www.bagnialberoni.com; Strada Nuova dei Bagni 26, Lido; umbrella/sun-lounger/deck chair €8/8/5; ⊙8am-midnight Jun-Sep; ⛟; ⊡A) Sandy beach with changing cabins at the southern end of the Lido.

Venetian Artistry

Glass

Venetians have been working in crystal and glass since the 10th century, though fire hazards prompted the move of the city's furnaces to Murano in the 13th century. Trade secrets were so closely guarded that any glass-worker who left the city was considered guilty of treason. By the 15th century Murano glass-makers were setting standards that couldn't be equalled anywhere in the world. They monopolised the manufacture of mirrors for centuries, and in the 17th century their skill at producing jewel-bright crystal led to a ban on the production of false gems out of glass. Murano's history of innovation and high standard of artistry are well displayed at the island's **Museo del Vetro** (p151).

Today, on Murano centuries of tradition are upheld in Cesare Toffolo's winged goblets and Davide Penso's lampworked glass beads, while striking modern glass designs by Nason Moretti at ElleElle, Marina e Susanna Sent and Venini keep the tradition moving forward.

Paper

Embossing and marbling began in the 14th century as part of Venice's burgeoning publishing industry, but these bookbinding techniques and *ebru* (Turkish marbled paper) endpapers have taken on lives of their own. Artisan Rosanna Corrò of Cárte uses bookbinding techniques to create marbled, book-bound handbags and even furniture, while Cartavenezia turns hand-pulped paper into embossed friezes and free-form lamps. Gianni Basso uses 18th-century book symbols to make letter-pressed business cards with old-world flair, and you can watch a Heidelberg press in

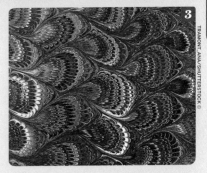

1. Glass-shop window display **2.** Lace-making **3.** Marbled paper

action at Veneziastampa, churning out menus and ex-libris (bookplates).

Textiles

Anything that stands still long enough in this city is liable to end up swagged, tasselled and upholstered. Venetian lace was a fashion must for centuries as Burano's **Lace Museum** (p152) attests, and Bevilacqua still weaves luxe tapestries (and donates scraps to nonprofit Banco Lotto 10 to turn into La Fenice costumes and handbags).

But the modern master of Venetian bohemian textiles is Fortuny, whose showroom on Giudecca features hand-stamped wall coverings created in strict accordance with top-secret techniques. But though the methods are secret, Fortuny's inspiration isn't: it covers the walls of his home studio, from Persian

armour to portraits of socialites who tossed aside their corsets for Fortuny's Delphi gowns – now available for modern boho goddesses at Venetia Studium.

TOP FIVE NON-TOURISTY SOUVENIRS

➡ Customised business cards at **Gianni Basso** (p117).

➡ Lilac smoking jacket with handprinted scarlet skulls from **Fiorella Gallery** (p68).

➡ Blown-glass soap-bubble necklaces from **Marina e Susanna Sent** (p83).

➡ Lux, hand-stamped velvet evening bags in gold and mulberry from **Venetia Studium** (p68).

➡ Bold, funky, cardboard-and-paper handbags from **Cárte** (p106).

Murano, Burano & the Northern Islands

ISOLA DI SAN MICHELE | MURANO | BURANO | MAZZORBO | TORCELLO | ISOLA DI SAN FRANCESCO DEL DESERTO | SANT'ERASMO | LE VIGNOLE | ISOLA DELLA CERTOSA

Neighbourhood Top Five

❶ Basilica di Santa Maria Assunta (p150) Engaging with visions of angels, saints and dastardly demons within the golden glow of ancient mosaics in the lagoon's oldest church.

❷ Murano (p151) Witnessing artistry in action at the island's glass-blowing showrooms and rewarding

the skill and originality with purchases of unique mementoes to take home.

❸ Burano (p152) Watching colourful houses shimmer with delight at their own reflections in the canals.

❹ Seafood feasts (p154) Enjoying the bounty of the lagoon at restaurants such as Venissa Osteria, where

there's the added bonus of vineyard views and extremely rare wine.

❺ Basilica dei SS Maria e Donato (p151) Checking out more golden mosaics, a spectacular ancient marbled floor and the added bonus of dragon bones.

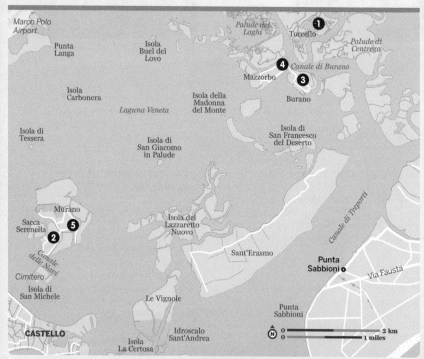

For more detail of this area see Map p285 and p286 ➡

Explore: Murano, Burano & the Northern Islands

A multitude of small islands dot the northern lagoon like shards of green glass splintering off the mainland. Refugees from the Roman city of Altinum escaped to safety on Torcello in the 5th century when the Mongol hordes descended. There they raised the first church of the lagoon, Santa Maria Assunta, decorating it with glittering mosaics telling cautionary tales in over a million hand-cut glass *tesserae*.

The northernmost islands remain sleepy places today, with only the pretty town of Burano attracting significant tourists. Few bother to cross the bridge to Mazzorbo, although those that do are amply rewarded with some of the region's best food and wine. Only the seriously intrepid visit the lost-in-time friary on San Francesco del Deserto, or the lagoon gardens on Sant'Erasmo and Vignole.

Much closer to Venice, the glass workshops of Murano continue to conjure writhing chandeliers and gem-bright jewellery from their red-hot furnaces – the modern heirs of Torcello's ancient mosaic makers.

Local Life

➡**Peaceful picnics** Pack a picnic to enjoy on Mazzorbo; in the meadow behind Basilica di Santa Maria Assunta (p150) on Torcello; or among the picturesque ruins of Forte Sant'Andrea on Le Vignole (p154).

➡**Beaches** Make a beeline for the tiny, remote beach on Sant'Erasmo or the vast beach at Lido di Jesolo (p155).

➡**Island sleepovers** Stay the night (p196) in one of the few inns on Torcello, Burano or Mazzorbo and experience the after-hours peace only locals usually enjoy.

Getting There & Away

➡**Vaporetto Murano** Services run every 10 minutes before 10pm and every 20 to 30 minutes thereafter. Murano has six stops, and lines 3, 4.1 and 4.2 loop around most of them. Lines 12 and 13 stop only at Faro before continuing on to the outlying islands. Aside from line 3 (train station direct), all other lines stop at Fondamente Nove.

➡**Vaporetto Mazzorbo, Burano & Torcello** Line 12 from Fondamente Nove and Murano-Faro serves Mazzorbo and Burano. Some boats also stop at Torcello; otherwise change to line 9 at Burano.

➡**Vaporetto Le Vignole & Sant'Erasmo** Line 13 heads here from Fondamente Nove via Murano-Faro.

➡**Alilaguna** Boats run from Marco Polo airport to Murano-Colonna.

Lonely Planet's Top Tip

➡ Hit the outer islands first (boats to Torcello take 50 minutes) before *vaporetti* get crowded, then work your way back to Murano, aiming to hit the shops as crowds start to thin out in the early evening. Murano is only 10 minutes from Venice, so it's fast and easy to reach if you need to return for more glass.

Best Lagoon Photo Ops

➡ Brightly painted houses reflected in Burano canals (p152)

➡ Far-flung lagoon views from the bell tower of Basilica di Santa Maria Assunta (p150)

➡ Cormorants holding their wings out to dry on Mazzorbo (p152)

For reviews, see p150.➡

Best Places to Eat

➡ Acquastanca (p154)
➡ Locanda Cipriani (p156)
➡ Venissa Osteria (p154)
➡ Ristorante da Omar (p155)

For reviews, see p154.➡

Best Places to Drink

➡ Osteria al Duomo (p154)
➡ Acquastanca (p154)
➡ Caffè-Bar Palmisano (p156)

For reviews, see p154.➡

 TOP SIGHT
BASILICA DI SANTA MARIA ASSUNTA

Life choices are presented in no uncertain terms in Santa Maria Assunta's vivid cautionary tale: look ahead to a golden afterlife amid saints and a beatific Madonna, or turn your back on her to face the wrath of a devil gloating over lost souls. In existence since the 7th century, this former cathedral is the lagoon's oldest Byzantine-Romanesque structure.

Madonna & Last Judgment Mosaics

The restrained brick exterior betrays no hint of the colourful scene that unfolds as you enter. The Madonna rises in the east like the sun above a field of Torcello poppies in the 12th-century apse mosaic, while the back wall vividly depicts the dire consequences of dodging biblical commandments. This extraordinary *Last Judgment* mosaic shows the Adriatic as a sea nymph ushering souls lost at sea towards St Peter, while a sneaky devil tips the scales of justice and the Antichrist's minions drag sinners into hell.

Chapel Mosaics & Other Key Works

The right-hand chapel is capped with another 12th-century mosaic showing Christ flanked by angels and Sts Augustine, Ambrose, Martin and Gregory amid symbolic plants: lilies (representing purity), wheat and grapes (representing the bread and wine of the Eucharist), and poppies (evoking Torcello's island setting).

The polychrome marble floor is another medieval masterpiece, with swirling designs and interlocking wheels symbolising eternal life. Saints line up atop the gilded iconostasis, their gravity foiled by a Byzantine screen teeming with peacocks, rabbits and other fanciful beasts.

DON'T MISS

➡ *Last Judgment* mosaic

➡ *Madonna* apse mosaic

➡ *Christ with Saints* mosaic in side chapel

➡ Iconostasis

➡ Views from the *campanile* (bell tower)

PRACTICALITIES

➡ Map p286, C4

➡ 📞 041 73 01 19

➡ Piazza Torcello, Torcello

➡ adult/reduced €5/4, incl museum €8/6, incl museum, audio guide & campanile €12/10

➡ ⏱ 10am-5pm

➡ 🚤 Torcello

SIGHTS

⊙ Isola di San Michele

This picturesque walled islet, positioned between Murano and the city, is Venice's main cemetery. *Vaporetti* 4.1 and 4.2 stop here, en route between Fondamente Nove and Murano.

CIMITERO DI
SAN MICHELE   CEMETERY

(◐7.30am-6pm Apr-Sep, to 4.30pm Oct-Mar; ⛴Cimitero) **FREE** Until Napoleon established a city cemetery on this little island, Venetians had been buried in parish plots across town – not an ideal solution in a watery city. Today, goths, incorrigible romantics and music lovers pause here to pay respects to Ezra Pound, Joseph Brodsky, Sergei Diaghilev and Igor Stravinsky. Pick up a map from the information point near the entrance and join them, but be aware, the map pinpointing the famous graves isn't accurate.

Architecture buffs stop by to see the Renaissance **Chiesa di San Michele in Isola** (open on weekday mornings), begun by Codussi in 1469, and the ongoing cemetery extension by David Chipperfield Architects, including the already completed **Courtyard of the Four Evangelists** – a concrete colonnade with basalt-clad walls engraved with Gospel quotes.

Note, this is a still functioning graveyard and Venetians are constantly dropping by to pay their respects to their loved ones buried here. Hence, photography and picnics aren't permitted.

⊙ Murano

Venetians have been working in glass since the 10th century, but due to the fire hazards of glass-blowing, the industry was moved to the island of Murano in the 13th century. Woe betide the glass-blower with wanderlust: trade secrets were so jealously guarded that any glass worker who left the city was guilty of treason and subject to assassination. Today, glass artisans continue to ply their trade at workshops all over the island, but particularly on Fondamenta dei Vetrai.

Murano is less than 10 minutes from Fondamente Nove by *vaporetto* and services are frequent.

BASILICA DEI SS
MARIA E DONATO   CHURCH

Map p285 (www.sandonatomurano.it; Campo San Donato,; ◐9am-6pm Mon-Sat, 12.30-6pm Sun; ⛴Museo) **FREE** Fire-breathing is the unifying theme of Murano's medieval church, with its astounding 12th-century gilded-glass apse mosaic of the Madonna made in Murano's *fornaci* (furnaces) and the bones of a dragon hanging behind the altar. According to tradition, this beast was slayed by St Donatus of Arezzo, whose mortal remains also rest here. The other masterpiece here is underfoot: a Byzantine-style 12th-century mosaic pavement of waving geometric patterns and peacocks rendered in porphyry, serpentine and other precious stones.

MUSEO DEL VETRO   MUSEUM

Map p285 (Glass Museum; ☎041 527 47 18; www.museovetro.visitmuve.it; Fondamenta Giustinian 8; adult/reduced €10/7.50, free with Museum Pass; ◐10am-5pm; ⛴Museo) Since 1861, Murano's glass-making prowess has been celebrated in Palazzo Giustinian (the seat of the Torcello bishopric from 1659 until its dissolution in 1818) and renovations finally do justice to the fabulous collection. On entry a video geeks out on the technical processes innovated on Murano, while upstairs eight rooms have beautifully curated displays of objects dating back to the 5th century BC.

From the glowing, back-lit cabinets of precious Syrian, Greek and Roman glassware in the **Origins** room, step into the **Salone Maggiore** (Grand Salon), where three enormous chandeliers appear to float beneath the frescoed ceiling in a room showcasing the Golden Age of glassmaking between the 14th and 17th century. Beyond, colour-themed rooms diverge into glassmaking fashions – etchings, mirrors, table pieces and imitation porcelain made from opaque glass – and the vast and profitable industry of Venetian beads, which were traded worldwide.

Back downstairs, rotating contemporary glass exhibits are on show in the **Spazio Coterie** just beyond the museum shop, which stocks a small selection of top-quality Murano glass gifts, jewellery and art books.

CHIESA DI SAN
PIETRO MARTIRE   CHURCH

Map p285 (www.sandonatomurano.it; Fondamenta dei Vetrai; ◐9am-5.30pm Mon-Fri, noon-5.30pm Sat & Sun; ⛴Museo) **FREE** Take a pause from glass shopping to check out *The Baptism of*

Christ, attributed to Tintoretto, in the 16th-century church of St Peter the Martyr.

◉ Burano & Mazzorbo

Once Venice's lofty Gothic architecture leaves you feeling overwhelmed, Burano brings you back to your senses with a reviving shock of colour. The 50-minute ferry ride on line 12 from the Fondamente Nove is packed with amateur photographers preparing to bound into Burano's backstreets, snapping away at pea-green stockings hung to dry between hot-pink and royal-blue houses.

Burano is famed for its handmade lace, which once graced the décolletage and ruffs of European aristocracy. Unfortunately the ornate styles and expensive tablewear fell out of vogue in lean post-WWII times and the industry has since suffered a decline. Some women still maintain the traditions, but few production houses remain; with a couple of notable exceptions, most of the lace for sale in local shops is of the imported, machine-made variety.

If you fancy a stroll, hop across the 60m bridge to Burano's even quieter sister island, Mazzorbo. Little more than a broad grassy knoll, Mazzorbo is a great place for a picnic or a long, lazy lunch. Line 12 also stops at Mazzorbo, and line 9 runs a shuttle between Burano and Torcello.

MUSEO DEL MERLETTO   MUSEUM
Map p286 (Lace Museum; ☑041 73 00 34; www.museomerletto.visitmuve.it; Piazza Galuppi 187; adult/reduced €5/3.50, with Museum Pass free; ☺10am-5pm; ⬢Burano) Burano's Lace Museum tells the story of a craft that cut across social boundaries, endured for centuries and evoked the epitome of civilisation reached during the Republic's heyday. From the triple-petalled corollas on the fringes of the Madonna's mantle in Torcello's 12th-century mosaics to Queen Margherita's spider-web-fine 20th-century mittens, lace-making was both the creative expression of female sensitivity and a lucrative craft.

Enter the exhibition downstairs with a video detailing the early origins of lace-making and its geographical spread from northern France to Bohemia, Malta and Turkey. Upstairs, four rooms cover the major developments from the 16th to the 20th century. Pattern books, journals, paintings, furniture and costumery place the evolving art in its historical context, starting with ecclesiastical garments and delicate *trinette* (accessories), and branching out into naughty, fringed underwear and sumptuously embroidered bodices shot through with silver thread.

In the final room, a group of local lacemakers often sit tatting and gossiping beneath pictures of the Lace School (where many of them learnt their craft), which was located here from 1872 to 1970. Don't be shy to ask questions about their work.

CHIESA DI SAN MARTINO   CHURCH
Map p286 (☑041 73 00 96; Piazza Galuppi; ☺8am-noon & 3-7pm; ⬢Burano) **FREE** This 16th-century church with a worryingly wonky *campanile* (bell tower) is worth a peek for Giambattista Tiepolo's 1725 *Crocifissione,* showing Mary gone grey with grief. The 19th-century Russian icon near the altar is the *Madonna di Kazan,* a masterpiece of enamelwork with bright, lifelike eyes.

CHIESA DI SANTA CATERINA   CHURCH
Map p286 (☑041 73 01 69; www.parrocchiadimazzorbo.weebly.com; Isola di Mazzorbo 32; ☺9am-7pm summer, to 5pm winter; ⬢Mazzorbo) Mazzorbo's late 13th-century Romanesque church of St Catherine is the only one of the island's 10 medieval churches to survive.

◉ Torcello

On the pastoral island of Torcello, sheep outnumber the 14 or so human residents. This bucolic backwater was once a Byzan-

---

REGATTA REVELRY

The biggest event in the northern lagoon calendar is the 32km **Vogalonga long row** (www.vogalonga.com) from Venice to Murano and Burano and back each May or June. It's a fabulously festive occasion when hundreds of enthusiasts take to the waters in their wooden *batèla* (flat-bottomed boat) and motorised boats are banned from the lagoon for the day.

Plan in advance and find a grassy picnic spot on Mazzorbo. If you'd like to have a go yourself get in touch with **Row Venice** (p118), who'll soon show you how to wield an oar like a gondolier.

tine metropolis of 20,000, but rivalry with its offshoot Venice and a succession of malaria epidemics systematically reduced its population. Of its original nine churches and two abbeys, all that remain are the Basilica di Santa Maria Assunta (p150) and the 11th-century Chiesa di Santa Fosca.

Not all line 12 *vaporetto* services stop at Torcello, but those that do provide a direct link to Burano, Mazzorbo, Murano and Fondamente Nove. The more frequent line 9 shuttles to and from Burano.

MUSEO DI TORCELLO MUSEUM
Map p286 (www.museoditorcello.provincia. venezia.it; Piazza Torcello; adult/reduced €3/1.50, incl basilica €8/6; ☺10.30am-5.30pm; ⏹Torcello) Occupying two buildings across the square from the Basilica di Santa Maria Assunta, this museum is dedicated to Torcello's bygone splendour. The main building, the 13th-century Palazzo del Consiglio, displays mainly religious art recovered from the island's many long-lost churches. The annexe focuses on ancient archaeological treasures, many of which were recovered from the abandoned Roman city of Altinum (Altino) on the mainland. The collection includes tiny Egyptian figurines, Etruscan bronzes, Greek pottery and some lovely Roman cameos.

CHIESA DI SANTA FOSCA CHURCH
Map p286 (Piazza Torcello; ☺10am-4.30pm; ⏹Torcello) Literally overshadowed by Torcello's famous basilica, to which it's connected by a colonnaded walkway, this interesting little round Byzantine-style church dates from the 11th century. It's relatively unadorned inside, with plain brick walls, a domed wooden roof and Corinthian columns in grey marble.

◉ Isola di San Francesco del Deserto

Given that the Venetian lagoon is situated on one of the most important bird migration routes in Europe, it seems only fitting that Francis of Assisi, the saint so famous for talking to birds, should have sought shelter here after his journey to Palestine in 1220. After the saint's death Jacopo Michiel, the owner of the island, donated it to the Franciscan order. In 1420 the friars were forced to desert the island (hence the name) due to rampant malaria, but

in 1856 Monsignor Portogruaro brought them back and here they have remained ever since.

Today, visits are only possible by prior arrangement with the **friary** (☏041 528 68 63; www.sanfrancescodeldeserto.it; donations appreciated; ☺9-11am & 3-5pm Tue-Sun) FREE, and are led by one of the brothers. As this is a place of prayer, visitors are kindly asked to speak in hushed tones as they are led around the two cloisters and into the serene chapel where St Francis himself is said to have prayed. Best of all are the peaceful, cypress-scented **gardens** with their dream-like views of Burano.

To get here you'll need to hire a private boat or water taxi (approximately €80 to €100 return for up to four people, including the 40- to 60-minute wait time) or book a seat aboard the 2.30pm shuttle from Burano operated by **Laguna Fla** (www.lagunaflaline.it; ☏347 9922959; return €10 min 4 people).

◉ Sant'Erasmo

Sant'Erasmo is known as the *orto di Venezia* (Venice's garden), and if you're visiting in early May, don't miss the **Festa del Carciofo Violetto**, when the island celebrates the first crop of its purple-hued artichokes. At 4.5km from tip to toe, Sant'Erasmo is as long as Venice, although it's just 1km at its widest point. Seven hundred and fifty farmers still plough its fields, supplying not only artichokes but also asparagus, squash, tomatoes and cardoons to the Rialto Market and Venice's restaurants.

Once a rural retreat for aristocrats, the island now provides a largely tourist-free refuge for Venetian families who moor their boats along its mudbanks and picnic on its narrow 'beaches'. Essential shots of coffee and pizza lunches are provided by the seasonal bar behind the beach, while bikes (€5 for two hours, €1 every hour thereafter) can be rented at the island's only accommodation, Il Lato Azzurro (p196).

Vaporetto 13 from Fondamente Nove and Murano docks at Capannone, Chiesa and Punto Vela. In summer, line 18 departs from Murano and the Lido and stops near the partly ruined **Torre Massimiliana** (Maximilian's Tower; Via dei Forti; ☺hours vary; ⏹Capannone), a 19th-century Austrian fort sometimes used for art exhibitions. There's a small beach nearby.

MURANO, BURANO & THE NORTHERN ISLANDS SIGHTS

⊙ Le Vignole

Welcome to the Venetian countryside! Together the two islands of Vignole Vecchie and Vignole Nuove produced the doge's wine, and their 50 inhabitants still live mainly from agriculture. Like that of nearby Sant'Erasmo, the landscape is covered in fields, groves and vineyards, and people are few and far between. *Vaporetto* 13 runs to Le Vignole from Fondamente Nove via Murano (Faro stop).

At the island's southeastern tip a promontory ends in the Isola di Sant'Andrea, the location of the best-preserved fort on the lagoon: 16th-century **Forte Sant'Andrea**.

⊙ Isola della Certosa

Once home to Carthusian monks (hence the island's name), La Certosa was the site of a grand monastery, its church graced with ducal tombs and rich artworks. All of that was lost, however, when the island was taken over by the military in the 19th century. Even its cloister was purchased by Prince Charles of Prussia and rebuilt in his summer castle in Berlin in 1850.

Today, thanks to EU funding and a public-private partnership, the island has been revived as a marina and lush public park under the **Vento di Venezia** (⌥041 520 85 88; www.ventodivenezia.it; ⛴Certosa) umbrella. The marina complex includes a hotel, an alfresco restaurant-bar and a sailing club, which runs regattas and a summertime Sail Camp for children.

At the time of writing, *vaporetto* line 4.1/4.2 stops on request in Certosa between 6am and 8pm, while 5.1/5.2 takes up the service after 8pm. This may change, however, so you're best to check before boarding.

✕ EATING & DRINKING

✕ Murano

OSTERIA LA PERLA – AI BISATEI ITALIAN €
Map p285 (⌥041 73 95 28; Campo San Bernardo 6; meals €16-22; ⊙11.30am-3pm Thu-Tue; ⛴Venier) Seek out this vintage *osteria* (casual tavern) where glass-blowers head for plates of *frittura mista* (mixed fried fish), seafood risotto and spaghetti *vongole* (with clams). If you're dining alone you're likely to be seated with a local – a good opportunity to practise your Italian, if you have any. Service is friendly and efficient, and the food, while simple, is very tasty.

★ACQUASTANCA MODERN ITALIAN €€
Map p285 (⌥041 319 51 25; www.acquastanca.it; Fondamenta Manin 48; meals €40-44; ⊙10am-11pm Mon & Fri, 9am-8pm Tue-Thu & Sat summer, 10am-10pm Mon & Fri, 10am-4pm Tue-Thu & Sat winter; ⛴Faro) A modern sensibility imbues both the decor and the menu at this wonderful little restaurant. A knowing array of old-fashioned Murano mirrors adorns a wall, while birds perch on artfully arranged twigs on another. Seafood features prominently on a menu that includes fresh flavour-filled takes on the classic Venetian bean soup, octopus with chickpeas and a panoply of pasta.

OSTERIA AL DUOMO ITALIAN €€
Map p285 (⌥041 527 43 03; www.osteriaalduomo.com; Fondamenta Maschio 20-21; meals €27-43; ⊙11am-10pm; 🐾; ⛴Museo) Opened in 1903 by the parish priest as a co-op grocery shop, this *osteria* is still collectively owned by 50 Muranese families. Don't be surprised, then, by the honest bowls of pasta and hands-down the best pizza in Venice – as you'd expect, considering the furnace they have to cook them in! In summer, sit out in the walled garden.

BUSA ALLA TORRE VENETIAN €€
Map p285 (⌥041 73 96 62; Campo Santo Stefano 3; meals €32-45, set menu €16; ⊙11.30am-3.30pm; ⛴Faro) Glassy-eyed shoppers are drawn to this classic eatery for its sunny disposition and set menu (not available Sunday). Arrive early for piazza seating with tempting views of glass showrooms, and settle in for seasonal lagoon treats like seafood soup and *sepie alla venexiana* (squid in black sauce).

✕ Burano & Mazzorbo

★VENISSA OSTERIA VENETIAN €€
Map p286 (⌥041 527 22 81; www.venissa.it; Fondamenta Santa Caterina 3, Mazzorbo; meals €40-47; ⊙noon-6pm Wed, Thu, Sun & Mon, noon-midnight Fri & Sat Apr-Oct; ⛴Mazzorbo) A more affordable companion piece to its Michelin-

WORTH A DETOUR

LIDO DI JESOLO

This 13km strand of golden sand on the mainland east of Venice is far and away Venetians' preferred beach – if they can be bothered with the travel time. Unlike its island namesake, this Lido looks to be booming, with upmarket apartments, shops selling designer eyewear, a water park, a large aquarium complex, and a stretch of colourful buildings housing kebab shops, pizzerias, bars and the odd top-notch restaurant, the best of which is **Ristorante da Omar** (☑042 19 36 85; www.ristorantedaomar.it; Via Dante Alighieri 21; meals €33-63; ☺noon-3.30pm & 7.30-10.30pm Thu-Tue).

Aside from the beach, the other attraction of Lido di Jesolo is its summertime nightclubs. Keep an eye out for flyers around Venice advertising club nights and beach concerts, often featuring international acts. Note that the main clubs are set back from the beach, about an hour's walk west from the bus station.

For more information on things to do and see in Jesolo, call into the **Casa del Turismo** (☑041 37 06 01; www.jesolo.it; Via XIII Martiri; ☺8.30am-6.30pm; ☑23a).

Getting to Lido di Jesolo takes about an hour by car. If you plan to come by public transport, ATVO has buses departing from Piazzale Roma roughly hourly from 6am until about 11pm (€8 return, 70 minutes). Another option is to catch a *vaporetto* (small passenger ferry) to Punta Sabbioni on the tip of the peninsula (lines 14, 15, 17 and 22) and then catch bus 23A (€3, 38 minutes).

If you're planning a club night, the problem is getting back. Taxis cost upwards of €80, so you might want to wait for the first buses. The 23A to Punta Sabbioni stops near the main clubs from around 5.20am.

starred sister, this upmarket *osteria* offers updates on Venetian classics such as marinated fish, duck pasta and *bigoli* (thick wholemeal pasta with anchovies). For an extra treat, splash out on a glass of Dorona, the prestigious golden-hued wine varietal only grown here. Make sure you save room for some of Venice's best desserts.

TRATTORIA DA PRIMO VENETIAN €€

Map p286 (☑041 73 55 50; www.trattoria-primoepaolo.it; Via Galuppi 285, Burano; meals €30-35; ☺noon-4pm Tue-Sun Feb-Dec; ☑Burano) Hiding in plain sight is unassuming looking da Primo. Don't be fooled, though. On entering you'll find a large canteen-style dining room panelled like the hull of a ship and filled with locals ordering plates of raw-fish antipasti and the speciality Gò fish risotto.

ALLA MADDALENA VENETIAN €€

Map p286 (☑041 73 01 51; www.trattoriamaddalena.com; Fondamenta di Santa Caterina 7b, Mazzorbo; meals €25-42; ☺noon-3pm & 7-9pm Fri-Wed; ☑Mazzorbo) Just a footbridge away from Burano's photo-snapping crowds are lazy seafood lunches on the island of Mazzorbo. Relax by the canal or in the garden out the back with fresh fish dishes and, during autumn hunting season, the signa-

ture pasta with wild-duck ragù. It pays to call ahead, as the hours are sporadic in the low-season.

VENISSA RISTORANTE MODERN ITALIAN €€€

Map p286 (☑041 527 22 81; www.venissa.it; Fondamenta Santa Caterina 3, Mazzorbo; 6-course menu €120; ☺12.30-4pm & 7-10pm Wed-Mon Apr-Oct; ☑Mazzorbo) The sleepy island of Mazzorbo is an unlikely setting for a Michelin-starred restaurant, and this one is unique in that it recruits a new chef each season with a brief to interpret afresh the produce from Venissa's extensive gardens and the bounty of the lagoon. The result is a consistently exciting multicourse experience, with views over the vines.

TRATTORIA AL GATTO NERO SEAFOOD €€€

Map p286 (☑041 73 01 20; www.gattonero.com; Fondamenta della Giudecca 88, Burano; meals €43-70; ☺noon-3pm & 7.30-10pm Tue-Sun; ☑Burano) Once you've tried the homemade *tagliolini* with spider crab, whole grilled fish and perfect house-baked biscuits, the ferry ride to Burano seems a minor inconvenience – a swim back here from Venice would be worth it for the mixed seafood grill alone. Call ahead and plead for canalside seating.

CAFFÈ-BAR PALMISANO CAFE

Map p286 (Via Galuppi 351, Burano; ⊙7am-9pm; 🚤Burano) Refuel with espresso and a toasted sandwich at this cafe on the sunny side of the street, and return later to celebrate photo-safari triumphs over *spritz* or wine with regular crowds of fishermen and university students.

✕ Torcello

★**LOCANDA CIPRIANI** VENETIAN €€€

Map p286 (📞041 73 01 50; www.locandacipriani. com; Piazza Torcello 29; meals €53-69; ⊙noon-3pm Wed-Mon Mar-Dec, plus 6-11pm Fri & Sat Apr-Sep; 🚤Torcello) Run by the Cipriani family since 1935, the Locanda is Harry's Bar gone rustic, with a wood-beamed dining room opening onto a pretty country garden. But standards are standards, so staff buzz about in dapper bow ties, theatrically silver serving every dish – even the pasta! The kitchen is just as precise, delivering pillowy gnocchi, perfectly cooked fish and decadent chocolate mousse.

✕ Isola della Certosa

IL CERTOSINO BAR

(📞041 520 00 35; www.ristoranteilcertosino. com; ⊙8.30am-9.30pm; 🚤Certosa) This restaurant-bar is worth it for the wonderful outdoor seating beneath giant white umbrellas and the Riviera vibe as it fills up with Superga-shod sailing enthusiasts, sipping on chilled Soave.

🛍 SHOPPING

Murano glass ranges from the sublime to the completely ridiculous, and you'll quickly see both as you walk down the main strip of showrooms on Fondamenta dei Vetrai. Sales staff will let you handle pieces if you ask first, but wield parcels and handbags with care – what you break, you buy. On sunny Burano, Via Galuppi is lined with lace shops. Look for 'fatto a Burano' (made in Burano) and 'Vero Artistico Murano' guarantees, since almost all of the less-expensive stock is imported.

🛍 Murano

VENINI GLASS

Map p285 (📞041 273 72 04; www.venini.it; Fondamenta dei Vetrai 47; ⊙9.30am-6pm Mon-Sat; 🚤Colonna) Even if you don't have the cash to buy a Venini, pop into this gallery to see Murano glass at its finest. Of the big houses, Venini remains the most relevant, having embraced modernist trends since the 1930s, and its enviable range is bolstered by collaborations with design greats such as Carlo Scarpa and Gae Aulenti.

★**ELLEELLE** GLASS

Map p285 (📞041 527 48 66; www.elleellemurano. com; Fondamenta Manin 52; ⊙10.30am-1pm & 2-6pm; 🚤Faro) Nason Moretti have been making modernist magic happen in glass since the 1950s, and the third-generation glass designers are in fine form in this showroom. Everything is signed, including an exquisite range of hand-blown drinking glasses, jugs, bowls, vases, tealight holders, decanters and lamps.

★**CESARE TOFFOLO** GLASS

Map p285 (📞041 73 64 60; www.toffolo.com; Fondamenta dei Vetrai 37; ⊙10am-6pm; 🚤Colonna) Mind-boggling miniatures are the trademarks of this Murano glass-blower, but you'll also find some dramatic departures: chiselled cobalt-blue vases, glossy black candlesticks that look like minarets, and drinking glasses so fine that they seem to be made out of air.

MARINA E SUSANNA SENT STUDIO GLASS

Map p285 (📞041 527 46 65; www.marinaesusan nasent.com; Fondamenta Serenella 20; ⊙10am-5pm Mon-Fri; 🚤Colonna) This striking space dedicated to the work of the pioneering Sent sisters is as sleek as their jewellery: white walls and huge picture windows flood the room with light, setting their signature bubble necklaces ablaze. The collection is displayed in colour groups and neatly stashed in drawers – don't be too shy to ask for assistance; there's a lot to see.

SALVADORE GLASS

Map p285 (📞041 73 67 72; Fondamenta dei Vetrai 128a; ⊙10.30am-6pm Mon-Sat; 🚤Colonna) This store specialises in light-hearted creations, including multicoloured drinking glasses and bead necklaces like strands of

VENISSA: A MAZZORBO RENAISSANCE

During the Renaissance, most of the wine served at Venice's high tables came from vineyards on the lagoon islands. The king of all was Dorona, a local varietal that was golden hued and imbued with the delicate flavours of peach and apricot.

Devastating floods all but wiped out the Dorona vines, and the wine of the doges was nearly lost for ever. That is, until Gianluca Bisol, a *prosecco* (sparkling white wine) producer from Valdobbiadene, heard of an ancient vineyard enclosed by medieval walls on Mazzorbo (p152). He rented the land from the city and set about rehabilitating the orchard and vegetable patches, restoring the brick-lined *peschiera* (cultivated fish pond), and reintroducing the rare Dorona grape from just 88 vines which had survived.

Once he'd reclaimed Venissa's garden and left it in the care of a team of Burano pensioners, he turned his attention to the farm buildings, which he converted into a contemporary six-room **guesthouse** (p196) and an **osteria**. Since then a Michelin-starred **restaurant** has been added in the garden.

The entire Mazzorbo operation is now managed by Gianluca's son Matteo, and his latest project has been the opening of **Casa Burano** (p196), an *albergo diffuso* (multi-venue hotel) with 13 rooms spread through five cottages on Burano.

tiny beach balls. Aspiring designers can create their own looks from individual glass beads.

FORNACE MIAN   GLASS
Map p285 (☑041 73 94 23; www.fornacemian.com; Fondamenta da Mula 143; ⊙9.30am-5.30pm; ⚱Venier) Shuffle past the typical Murano kitsch (parrots in trees etc) and you'll find one of the best ranges of classic stemware on the island. Samples are displayed in the showroom but everything's made to order and takes about 10 days to produce. Either call in early on in your trip, or arrange them to ship your purchases home.

DAVIDE PENSO   GLASS
Map p285 (☑041 527 56 59; www.davidepenso.com; Fondamenta Rivalonga 48; ⊙10am-6pm Mon-Sat; ⚱Museo) Davide Penso has taken the art of bead making to dizzying heights with exhibits at the Museo Correr, Boston's Fine Arts Museum and the San Marco Museum of Japan. Made using the lampworking process, each bead is worked into striking geometric forms and individually painted in matt modern colours.

🏠 **Burano**

EMILIA   ARTS & CRAFTS
Map p286 (☑041 73 52 99; www.emiliaburano.it; Via Galuppi 205; ⊙9.30am-7pm; ⚱Burano) Doyenne Emilia di Ammendola, a third-

generation lace-maker, has passed on her skills to her son and daughter who are continuing the family tradition in this flagship store, with branches in London and LA, and a partnership with Austin Martin. Prices befit the quality (ie out-of-this-world), but you can take away a tiny souvenir for €10. Upstairs there's a family museum.

🏃 **SPORTS & ACTIVITIES**

VENICE KAYAK   KAYAKING
(☑346 4771327; www.venicekayak.com; Vento di Venezia, Isola della Certosa; half-/full-day tours €90/120) Of all Venice's watery pursuits, kayaking is probably the best fun you can have without a license or the pirouetting skill of a gondolier. Well-planned tours take you into the warren of Venice's canals alongside police boats, fire boats and floating funeral hearses, or out to remote islands in the broad garden of the lagoon.

SCUOLA DEL VETRO ABATE ZANETTI   CULTURAL
Map p285 (☑041 273 77 11; www.abatezanetti.it; Calle Briati 8b, Murano; tours €20; ⊙4pm Tue & Thu; ⚱Faro) Murano's school of glass offers twice-weekly tours which include glassmaking demonstrations and a 40-minute film about the history of glass.

Magnificent Palladio

When it comes to coffee-table architecture, no one beats Andrea Palladio. As you flip past photos of his villas, your own problematic living space begins to dissolve, and you find yourself strolling through more harmonious country. Nature is governed by pleasing symmetries. Roman rigour is soothed by rustic charms. He managed to synthesise the classical past without doggedly copying it, creating buildings that were at once inviting, useful and incomparably elegant. From London to St Petersburg, his work – cleverly disseminated by his own 'Quattro Libri', a how-to guide for other architects – shaped the way Europe thought about architecture.

And yet when Palladio turned 30 in 1538, he was little more than a glorified stonecutter in Vicenza. His big break came when nobleman and amateur architect Giangiorgio Trissino recognised his potential and noticed his inclination towards mathematics. He introduced Palladio to the work of Roman architectural theorist Vitruvius, and sent him to Rome (1545–47) to sketch both crumbling antiquities and new works such as Michelangelo's dome for St Peter's.

Something mysterious happened on those trips, because when Palladio returned to Vicenza he was forging a new way of thinking about architecture – one that focused on the relationship between ratios to create spatial harmony. So a room in which the shorter wall was one-half (1:2), two-thirds (2:3) or three-quarters (3:4) the length of the longer would inevitably *feel* more satisfying because it was rationally harmonious. Like Pallas Athena, the goddess of wisdom, from whom he took his name,

1. La Rotonda (p169), Vicenza **2.** Teatro Olimpico (p169), Vicenza

Palladio's ideas seemed to spring fully formed from his head.

This search for perfection was never at odds with practicality. In his villas, he squeezed stables beneath elegant drawing rooms. Lacking funds to line San Giorgio Maggiore with marble, he came up with a superior solution: humble stucco walls that fill the church with an ethereal softness. Constraint provided the path to innovation.

A Palladian villa never masters its landscape like, say, Versailles. Palladio makes his mark tactfully, as if he has merely gathered the natural forces of the land and translated them into an ideal, and distinctly human, response. His Rotonda, for example, crowns a rise in the terrain, and looks out on it from four identical facades. Nothing like it had been built before. Yet when you see it *in situ*, it seems to be the inevitable outcome of the site itself.

PALLADIAN HIGHLIGHTS

➡ **Basilica Palladiana** (p169) Top-notch art gallery modelled on a Roman basilica.

➡ **La Rotonda** (p169) Palladio's most inspired design, copied the world over.

➡ **Villa di Masèr** (p172) Butter-yellow villa set against a green hillside; Palladio's prettiest composition.

➡ **Villa Foscari** (p161) River-facing facade with soaring Ionic columns that draw the eye and spirits upwards.

➡ **Palladio Museum** (Map p168; ☑0444 32 30 14; www.palladiomuseum.org; Contrà Porti 11, Vicenza; adult/reduced €8/6; ⊙10am-6pm Tue-Sun) Created by Howard Burns, the world authority on Palladio.

➡ **Teatro Olimpico** (p169) Palladio's visionary elliptical theatre.

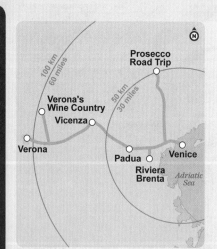

Day Trips from Venice

Riviera Brenta p161
See where 18th-century Venetian elites gambled away their summers in Palladian-style villas.

Padua (Padova) p163
A vibrant university town with a treasure trove of fresco cycles from its medieval golden age.

Vicenza p167
Palladio's adopted home is defined by the architect's classical restraint, while its countryside is dotted with his elegant villas.

Prosecco Country p171
Share a glass of *prosecco* with hard-working locals in one of the Veneto's most underrated areas.

Verona p174
Romeo and Juliet were fictional, but Verona's real history lives on in its Roman arena, Romanesque churches and Renaissance churches.

Verona's Wine Country p180
Valpolicella yields some of Italy's biggest, boldest reds, while Soave delivers crisp, refreshing whites.

Riviera Brenta

Explore

Every 13 June for 300 years, summer officially kicked off with a traffic jam along the Grand Canal, as a flotilla of fashionable Venetians headed to their villas along the banks of the Brenta. Every last ball gown and poker chair was loaded onto barges for dalliances that stretched until November. The annual party ended when Napoleon arrived in 1797, but 80 villas still strike elegant poses along the Brenta, and six of them are now open to the public at various times of the year.

The Best...

→**Sight** Villa Foscari
→**Place to Eat** Osteria da Conte (p162)
→**Place to Drink** I Molini del Dolo (p163)

Top Tip

All the villas along the Brenta show their best architectural face to the river, where boats arriving from Venice would dock. Even today the best way to experience the riviera is on a flat-bottomed riverboat.

Getting There & Away

→**Boat** Organised boat tours leave from both Venice and Padua.

→**Bus** ACTV's Venezia–Padova Extraurbane bus 53 leaves from Venice's Piazzale Roma about every half-hour, stopping at key Brenta villages en route to Padua.

→**Train** Venice–Padua services stop at Dolo (€3.40, 25 minutes, one to three per hour).

→**Car** Take SS11 from Mestre-Venezia towards Padua and take the A4 autostrada towards Dolo/Padua.

Need to Know

→**Area Code** ☑041
→**Location** 15km to 30km west of Venice

◉ SIGHTS

Many visitors opt to self-drive around the Riviera Brenta, but its network of cycling routes also makes it a great place to explore on two wheels.

VILLA FOSCARI   HISTORIC BUILDING

(☑041 520 39 66; www.lamalcontenta.com; Via dei Turisti 9, Malcontenta; €10; ☺9am-noon Tue & Sat Apr-Oct) The most romantic Brenta villa, the Palladio-designed, Unesco-listed Villa Foscari (built 1555–60) got its nickname La Malcontenta from a *grande-dame* of the Foscari clan who was reputedly exiled here for cheating on her husband – though these bright, highly sociable salons hardly constitute a punishment. The villa was abandoned for years, but Giovanni Zelotti's frescoes have now been restored to daydream-inducing splendour.

**VILLA WIDMANN
REZZONICO FOSCARI**   HISTORIC BUILDING

(☑041 547 00 12; Via Nazionale 420, Mira; €10; ☺9am-noon Tue & Sat May-Oct) To appreciate both gardening and Venetian-style social engineering, stop just west of Oriago at Villa Widmann Rezzonico Foscari. Originally owned by Persian-Venetian nobility, the 18th-century villa captures the Brenta's last days of rococo decadence, with Murano sea-monster chandeliers and a frescoed grand ballroom with upper viewing gallery. Head to the gallery to reach the upstairs ladies' gambling parlour where, according to local lore, villas were once gambled away in high-stakes games.

**VILLA BARCHESSA
VALMARANA**   HISTORIC BUILDING

(☑041 426 63 87; www.villavalmarana.net; Via Valmarana 11, Mira; adult/reduced €6/5; ☺10am-6pm Tue-Sun Mar-Oct, by appointment during winter) Debuting on the riviera in the 17th century, Villa Barchessa Valmarana was commissioned by Vicenza's aristocratic Valmarana family. You'll find

---

ⓘ BRENTA BY BIKE

The scenic Riviera Brenta plains make an easy, enjoyable bicycle ride, and you can speed past tour boats along 150km of cycling routes. **Rental Bike Venice** (p243) is a friendly bike-rental outlet with branches in many Veneto towns offering mountain and city bikes, plus pre-loaded GPS units (€10), guided tours (€80 per person), roadside assistance and advice in English on itineraries and local restaurants.

RIVER CRUISES

When Venetians set out from Piazza San Marco for the Brenta, many of them would step aboard the commodious barge *Il Burchiello*, which was drawn along the towpath by a team of horses. Goethe arrived on the lagoon in this fashion in 1786, and today a small fleet of modern *burchielli* ply the river between Venice and Padua (Padova).

There's no doubt that seeing the Brenta from the perspective of a boat (rather than through the snarl of Venetian and Padovan suburbs) is the best way to experience the river and its villas, most of which were designed to show their best face to the water. As you pass through the five locks and nine swing bridges, you'll appreciate the 15th-century hydraulic locks system, which diverted the main floodwaters of the river to Chioggia, putting a stop to the accumulation of silt in the lagoon.

Il Burchiello (☎049 876 02 33; www.ilburchiello.it; adult/reduced half-day cruise from €55/45, full day €99/55) is a modern luxury barge offering full-day cruises between Venice and Padua, stopping stopping at Malcontenta, Widmann (or Barchessa Valmarana) and Pisani villas. From Venice, cruises depart from Pontile della Pietà pier on Riva degli Schiavoni (Tuesday, Thursday and Saturday). From Padua, cruises depart from Pontile del Portello pier (Wednesday, Friday and Sunday).

them enjoying *la dolce vita* (the sweet life) in the villa's fanciful frescoes, painstakingly restored in 1964. These days, the elegant building is mainly used as a function centre, but is still fully accessible to the public.

VILLA PISANI NAZIONALE
HISTORIC BUILDING

(☎049 50 20 74; www.villapisani.beniculturali.it; Via Doge Pisani 7, Stra; adult/reduced €7.50/3.75, park only €4.50/2.25; ☉9am-8pm Tue-Sun Apr-Sep, to 6pm Oct, to 5pm Nov-Mar) To keep hard-partying Venetian nobles in line, Doge Alvise Pisani provided a Versailles-like reminder of who was in charge. The 1774, 114-room Villa Pisani Nazionale is surrounded by huge gardens, a labyrinthine hedge-maze, and pools to reflect the doge's glory. Here you'll find the bathroom with a tiny wooden throne used by Napoleon; the sagging bed where new king Vittorio Emanuele II slept; and, ironically, the reception hall where Mussolini and Hitler met in 1934 under Tiepolo's ceiling depicting the *Geniuses of Peace*.

Temporary exhibitions are held at the villa throughout the year, generally between March and October. Note that entry is free to EU citizens and on the first Sunday of the month.

VILLA FOSCARINI ROSSI
HISTORIC BUILDING

(☎049 980 10 91; www.museodellacalzatura.it; Via Doge Pisani 1/2, Stra; adult/reduced €7/5; ☉9am-1pm & 2-6pm Mon-Fri, 2.30-6pm Sat & Sun Apr-Oct, 9am-1pm Mon-Fri Nov-Mar) Well-

heeled Venetians wouldn't have dreamed of decamping to the Brenta without their favourite cobblers, sparking a local tradition of shoemaking. Today, 538 companies produce around 19 million pairs of shoes annually. Their lasting contribution is commemorated with a **Shoemakers' Museum** at this 18th-century villa, its collection including 18th-century slippers and kicks created for trendsetter Marlene Dietrich. Admission includes access to the villa's 17th-century *foresteria* (guesthouse), which wows with allegorical frescoes by Pietro Liberi and *trompe l'œil* effects by Domenico de Bruni.

✕ EATING & DRINKING

OSTERIA DA CONTE
VENETIAN €€

(☎049 47 95 71; www.osteriadaconte.it; Via Caltana 133, Mira; meals €25-35; ☉noon-2.30pm & 8-10.30pm Tue-Sat, noon-2.30pm Sun) An unlikely bastion of culinary sophistication lodged practically underneath an overpass, Da Conte has one of the most interesting wine lists in the region, plus creative takes on regional cuisine, from shrimps with black sesame and pumpkin purée to gnocchi in veal-cheek *ragù*. If it's on the menu, end your meal with the faultless *zabaglione* (egg and Marsala custard).

Da Conte lies 3.5km north of central Mira. The closest train station is Mira Mirano.

I MOLINI DEL DOLO WINE BAR
(www.molinidolo.com; Via Garibaldi 3, Dolo; meals €20-25; ⊙10am-2am Tue-Sun) Adorned with hulking wooden machinery, this atmospheric, canal-side wine bar occupies a restored 16th-century mill. Swill a coffee, or settle in with a regional *vino* and an interesting selection of cheeses and cured meats, from local *porchetta* to rustic *ventricina* salami from Italy's south. If the weather's warm, keep the waterwheel company on the alfresco patio.

Padua (Padova)

Explore

Though under an hour from Venice, Padua (Padova in Italian) seems a world away with its medieval marketplaces, Fascist-era facades and hip student population. As a medieval city-state and home to Italy's second-oldest university, Padua challenged both Venice and Verona for regional hegemony. A series of extraordinary fresco cycles recalls this golden age – including in Giotto's blockbuster Cappella degli Scrovegni, Menabuoi's heavenly gathering in the baptistry and Titian's *St Anthony* in the Scoletta del Santo. For the next few centuries, Padua and Verona challenged each other for dominance over the Veneto plains. But Venice finally settled the matter by occupying Padua permanently in 1405.

As a strategic military-industrial centre, Padua became a parade ground for Mussolini speeches, an Allied bombing target and a secret Italian Resistance hub (at its university).

The Best...

→ **Sight** Cappella degli Scrovegni
→ **Place to Eat** Belle Parti (p167)
→ **Place to Drink** Enoteca Il Tira Bouchon (p167)

Top Tip

Reservations are required to see Giotto's extraordinary Cappella degli Scrovegni (p163). Book a few weeks ahead for summer weekends and during school holidays.

Getting There & Away

→ **Car** the A4 (Turin–Milan–Venice–Trieste) passes to the north of town, while the A13 to Bologna starts south of town.

→ **Train** By far the easiest way to reach Padua from Venice (€4.15 to €14.90, 25 to 50 minutes, one to nine per hour). The station is about 500m north of Cappella degli Scrovegni and linked to the centre by Padua's monorail.

Need to Know

→ **Area Code** ⊘049
→ **Location** 37km west of Venice
→ **Tourist Office** (⊘0492 01 00 80; www.turismopadova.it; Vicolo Pedrocchi; ⊙9am-7pm Mon-Sat)

⊙ SIGHTS

★ **CAPPELLA DEGLI SCROVEGNI** CHAPEL
(Scrovegni Chapel; ⊘049 201 00 20; www.cappelladegliscrovegni.it; Piazza Eremitani 8; adult/reduced €13/8, night ticket €8/6; ⊙9am-7pm, night ticket 7-10pm) Padua's version of the Sistine Chapel, the Cappella degli Scrovegni houses one of Italy's great Renaissance masterpieces – a striking cycle of Giotto frescoes. Dante, da Vinci and Vasari all honour Giotto as the artist who ended the Dark Ages with these 1303–05 paintings, whose humanistic depiction of biblical figures was especially well suited to the chapel Enrico Scrovegni commissioned in memory of his father (who as a moneylender was denied a Christian burial).

ⓘ DISCOUNT PASS

A **PadovaCard** (€16/21 per 48/72 hours) gives one adult and one child under 14 free use of city public transport and access to almost all of Padua's major attractions, including the Cappella degli Scrovegni (plus €1 booking fee; reservations essential). PadovaCards are available at Padua tourist offices, Musei Civici agli Eremitani and the hotels listed in the PadovaCard section of the **tourist office** (⊘049 201 00 80; www.turismopadova.it; Vicolo Pedrocchi; ⊙9am-7pm Mon-Sat) website (www.turismopadova.it).

Padua

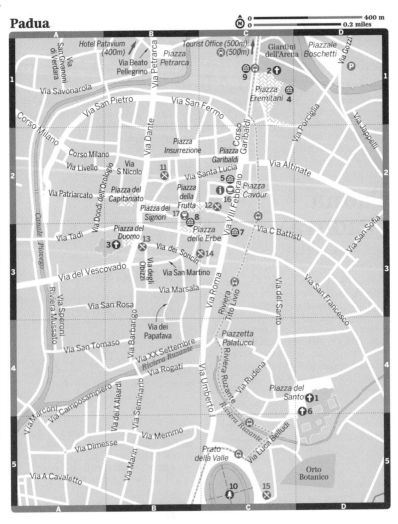

It's a simple brick building, with little indication from the outside of what lies within. It took Giotto two years to finish the frescoes which tell the story of Christ from Annunciation to Ascension. Scrovegni's chapel once adjoined the family mansion (demolished in 1824) – the city of Padua acquired the chapel in 1881.

Giotto's moving, modern approach helped change how people saw themselves: no longer as lowly vassals, but as vessels for the divine, however flawed. And where before medieval churchgoers had been accustomed to blank stares from saints perched on high thrones, Giotto introduced biblical figures as characters in recognisable settings. Onlookers gossip as middle-aged Anne tenderly kisses Joachim, and Jesus stares down Judas as the traitor puckers up for the fateful kiss. He also used unusual techniques such as building paint up into 3D forms. A 10-minute introductory video provides some helpful insights before you enter the church itself.

Book tickets at the Musei Civici agli Eremitani (p166), where you access the chapel, or at the tourist office. Chapel visits last 15 to 20 minutes (depending on the

Padua

◉ Sights

1 Basilica di Sant'Antonio D4
2 Cappella degli Scrovegni..................... C1
3 Duomo B3
4 Musei Civici agli Eremitani................. C1
5 Museo del Risorgimento e
   dell'Età Contemporanea C2
6 Oratorio di San Giorgio &
   Scoletta del Santo........................... D4
7 Palazzo del Bò C3
8 Palazzo della Ragione........................ B2
9 Palazzo Zuckermann.......................... C1
10 Prato della Valle................................. C5

⊗ Eating

11 Belle Parti... B2
12 Dalla Zita.. C2
13 Osteria Dal Capo B3
14 Osteria dei Fabbri.............................. C3
15 Zairo... C5

◉ Drinking & Nightlife

16 Caffè Pedrocchi.................................. C2
17 Enoteca Il Tira Bouchon.................... B2

time of year), plus another 10 minutes for the video. Arrive at least 15 to 30 minutes before your tour starts, or an hour before if you want to get round the Musei Civici agli Eremitani beforehand.

PALAZZO DELLA RAGIONE HISTORIC BUILDING
(☑049 820 50 06; Piazza delle Erbe; adult/reduced €6/4; ⊙9am-7pm Tue-Sun Feb–Oct, to 6pm Nov-Jan) Ancient Padua can be glimpsed in elegant twin squares (one the fruit market, the other the vegetable market) separated by the triple-decker Gothic Palazzo della Ragione, the city's tribunal dating from 1218. Inside Il Salone (the Great Hall), frescoes by Giotto acolytes Giusto de' Menabuoi and Nicolò Miretto depict the astrological theories of Padovan professor Pietro d'Abano, with images representing the months, seasons, saints, animals and noteworthy Paduans (not necessarily in that order).

The enormous 15th-century wooden horse at the western end of the hall was modelled on Donatello's majestic bronze *Gattamelata*, which still stands in Piazza del Santo. At the other end of the hall is a contemporary version of Foucault's *Pendulum*.

ORATORIO DI SAN GIORGIO & SCOLETTA DEL SANTO CHURCH
(☑049 822 56 52; Piazza del Santo; adult/reduced €5/4; ⊙9am-12.30pm & 2.30-7pm Apr-Sep, to 5pm Oct-Mar) Anywhere else, the fresco cycle of the Oratorio di San Giorgio and the paintings in the Scoletta del Santo would be considered highlights, but in Padua they must contend with Giotto's Scrovegni brilliance. This means you'll have Altichiero da Zevio and Jacopo Avanzi's jewel-like, 14th-century frescoes of St George, St Lucy and St Catherine all to yourself, while upstairs in the *scoletta* (confraternity house), Titian paintings are seldom viewed in such tranquillity.

BASILICA DI SANT'ANTONIO CHURCH
(Il Santo; ☑049 822 56 52; www.basilicadelsanto.org; Piazza del Santo; ⊙6.20am-6.45pm Mon-Sat, to 7.45pm Sun) **FREE** A pilgrimage site and the burial place of St Anthony of Padua (1193–1231), this huge church was begun in 1232, its polyglot style incorporating rising eastern domes atop a Gothic brick structure crammed with Renaissance treasures. Behind the high altar, nine radiating chapels punctuate a broad ambulatory homing in on the **Cappella delle Reliquie** (Relics Chapel), where the relics of St Anthony reside.

You'll also notice dozens of people clustering along the left transept waiting their turn to enter the **Cappella del Santo**, where Anthony's tomb is covered with requests and thanks for the saint's intercession in curing illness and recovering lost objects. The chapel itself is a light-filled Renaissance confection lined with nine panels vividly depicting the story of Anthony's life in extraordinary relief sculptures. The panels are attributed to the Padua-born Lombardo brothers and were completed around 1510.

Other notable works include the lifelike 1360s crucifix by Veronese master Altichiero da Zevio in the frescoed **Cappella di San Giacomo**; the wonderful 1528 sacristy fresco of St Anthony preaching to spellbound fish by a follower of Girolamo Tessari; and 1444–50 high altar reliefs by Florentine Renaissance master Donatello (ask guards for access).

Through the south door of the basilica you reach the attached monastery with its five wonderfully peaceful cloisters. The oldest (13th century) is the **Chiostro della Magnolia**, so called because of the magnificent tree in its centre. The complex also holds a large gift shop selling icons and St Anthony souvenirs to pilgrims.

DAY TRIPS FROM VENICE PADUA (PADOVA)

PRATO DELLA VALLE
PARK

(Prato della Valle) At the southern edge of the historical centre, this odd, elliptical garden was long used as a communal sportsground. Today it's a popular spot for locals wanting to soak up some summer rays and students swotting for exams. Framing the space is a slim canal lined by 78 statues of sundry great and good of Paduan history, plus 10 empty pedestals. Ten Venetian doges once occupied them, but Napoleon had them removed after he took Venice in 1797.

MUSEO DEL RISORGIMENTO E DELL'ETÀ CONTEMPORANEA
MUSEUM

(☑049 878 12 31; Galleria Pedrocchi 11; adult/reduced €4/2; ⊙9.30am-12.30pm & 3.30-6pm Tue-Sun) Since 1831, this neoclassical landmark has been a favourite of Stendhal and other pillars of Padua's cafe society for the heart-poundingly powerful coffee and *caffè correto* (coffee-based cocktails) served at its ground-floor cafe. The grand 1st floor – decorated in styles ranging from ancient Egyptian to imperial – houses the museum, recounting local and national history from the fall of Venice in 1797 until the republican constitution of 1848 in original documents, images and mementoes.

MUSEI CIVICI AGLI EREMITANI
MUSEUM

(☑049 820 45 51; Piazza Eremitani 8; adult/reduced €10/8; ⊙9am-7pm Tue-Sun) The ground floor of this monastery houses artefacts dating from Padua's Roman and pre-Roman past including some delicate glass, serviceable Roman surgical instruments and Etruscan bronze figures. Upstairs, a rambling but interesting collection boasts a few notable 14th- to 18th-century works by Bellini, Giorgione, Tintoretto and Veronese. Among the show-stoppers are a monster Brussels tapestry and an 18th-century painting by Georgio Fossati that shows the Prato della Valle when it was still a sportsground.

The museum is usually visited along with the Cappella degli Scrovegni (p163). Allow at least an hour to get round everything either before or after you see the chapel. The museum has a cloakroom and cafe.

PALAZZO ZUCKERMANN
GALLERY

(☑049 820 56 64; Corso di Garibaldi 33; adult/reduced €10/8; ⊙10am-7pm Tue-Sun) The ground and 1st floors of the early 20th-century Palazzo Zuckermann are home to the **Museo d'Arti Applicate e Decorative**, whose eclectic assortment of decorative and applied arts spans several centuries of flatware, furniture, fashion and jewellery. On the 2nd floor is the **Museo Bottacin**, a treasury of finely worked historic coins and medals, kept company by a modest collection of 19th-century paintings and sculpture.

DUOMO
CATHEDRAL

(☑049 65 69 14; Piazza del Duomo; baptistry €3; ⊙7.30am-noon & 4-7.30pm Mon-Sat, 7.30am-1pm & 4-7.30pm Sun & holidays, baptistry 10am-6pm) Built from a much-altered design of Michelangelo's, the rather industrial facade and whitewashed symmetry of Padua's cathedral is a far cry from its rival in Piazza San Marco. Pop in quickly for Giuliano Vangi's contemporary chancel crucifix and sculptures before visiting the adjoining 13th-century **baptistry**, a Romanesque gem frescoed with luminous biblical scenes by Giusto de' Menabuoi. Hundreds of saints congregate in the cupola, posed as though for a school graduation photo, exchanging glances and stealing looks at the Madonna.

PALAZZO DEL BÒ
HISTORIC BUILDING

(☑049 827 30 47; www.unipd.it/en/guidedtours; Via VIII Febbraio; adult/reduced €7/4; ⊙see website for tour times) This Renaissance *palazzo* (mansion) is the seat of Padua's history-making university. Founded by renegade scholars from Bologna seeking greater intellectual freedom, the university has employed some of Italy's greatest and most controversial thinkers, including Copernicus, Galileo, Casanova and the world's first female doctor of philosophy, Eleonora Lucrezia Cornaro Piscopia (her statue graces the stairs). Admission is on a 45-minute guided tour only, which includes a visit to the world's first **anatomy theatre**.

 ## EATING

DALLA ZITA
STREET FOOD €

(☑049 654 992; Via Gorizia 12; snacks €2-5, coffee €1; ⊙9am-8pm Mon-Fri) So small that around five people fill the place standing, this unmarked street-food bar is Padua's best spot when you need to eat on the hop. Choose from the large menu of sandwiches stuck to the wall in multicoloured sticky notes, or if your Italian and patience is up to it, customise your very own *panini*. Gets very busy at lunchtime.

ZAIRO ITALIAN €

(🖉049 66 38 03; www.zairo.net; Prato della Valle 51; pizzas €4-9.40, meals €25; ⊘noon-2.30pm & 7pm-1am Tue-Sun) The fresco above the kitchen door at this sweeping, chintzily over-the-top restaurant-pizzeria dates back to 1673, but most come for Zairo's long menu of cheap pizzas on a break from the Prato della Valle park on its doorstep.

OSTERIA DEI FABBRI OSTERIA €€

(🖉049 65 03 36; Via dei Fabbri 13; meals €30; ⊘noon-3pm & 7-11pm, closed Sun dinner) Rustic wooden tables, wine-filled tumblers and a single-sheet menu packed with hearty dishes keep things real at dei Fabbri. Slurp on superlative *zuppe* (soups) like sweet red-onion soup, or tuck into comforting meat dishes such as oven-roasted pork shank with Marsala, sultanas and polenta.

OSTERIA DAL CAPO OSTERIA €€

(🖉049 66 31 05; www.osteriadalcapo.it; Via degli Obizzi 2; meals €25-35; ⊘7-10.30pm Mon, 12.30-2.30pm & 7-10.30pm Tue-Sat) Rub elbows with locals – literally – at tiny tables precariously piled with traditional Venetian seafood and a few inspired novelties, such as *caviale di melanzane con bufala* (eggplant caviar with buffalo mozzarella atop crispy wafer bread). Reservations and a sociable nature advised.

★BELLE PARTI ITALIAN €€€

(🖉049 875 18 22; www.ristorantebelleparti.it; Via Belle Parti 11; meals €50; ⊘12.30-2.30pm & 7.30-10.30pm Mon-Sat) Prime seasonal produce, impeccable wines and near-faultless service meld into one unforgettable whole at this stellar fine-dining restaurant, resplendent with 18th-century antiques and 19th-century oil paintings. Seafood is the forte, with standout dishes including an arresting *gran piatto di crudità di mare* (raw seafood platter). Dress to impress and book ahead.

🍷 DRINKING & NIGHTLIFE

★CAFFÈ PEDROCCHI CAFE

(🖉049 878 12 31; www.caffepedrocchi.it; Via VIII Febbraio 15; ⊘8am-midnight Sun-Thu, to 1am Fri & Sat) This unmissable piece of olde worlde European cafe culture takes you back to the days when Stendhal held court here. The cafe is divided into three rooms, each one

TO MARKET

One of the most enjoyable activities in Padua (Padova) is browsing the markets in **Piazza delle Erbe** and **Piazza della Frutta**, which operate very much as they've done since the Middle Ages. Dividing them is the Gothic Palazzo della Ragione, whose arcades – known locally as **Sotto il Salone** (www.sotto ilsalone.it) – rumble with specialist butchers, cheesemakers, fishmongers, *salumerie* and fresh pasta producers. The markets are open all day, every day, except Sunday, although the best time to visit is before midday.

sporting huge maps of the world, high ceilings, simple tables and waiters scurrying central Europe–style. A white grand piano completes the scene.

ENOTECA IL TIRA BOUCHON WINE BAR

(🖉049 875 21 38; Sotto il Salone 23/24; ⊘10am-2.30pm & 5-9pm Mon-Sat) With a guiding French hand behind the bar, you can be sure of an excellent *prosecco,* Franciacorta or sauvignon at this traditional wine bar beneath Palazzo della Ragione's arcades. Locals crowd in for *spunci* (bread-based snacks), *panini* and a rotating selection of 12 wines by the glass. You'll find around 300 wines on the shelves, including drops from emerging winemakers.

Vicenza

Explore

When Palladio escaped an oppressive employer in his native Padua, few would have guessed the humble stonecutter would, within a few decades, transform not only his adoptive city but also the history of European architecture. By luck, a local count recognised his talents in the 1520s and sent him to study the ruins in Rome. When he returned to Vicenza, the autodidact began producing his extraordinary buildings, structures that marry sophistication and rustic simplicity, reverent classicism and bold innovation. His genius would turn Vicenza and its surrounding

Vicenza

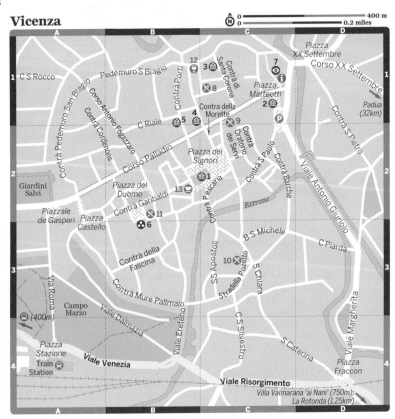

villas into one grand Unesco World Heritage Site. And yet, the Veneto's fourth-largest city is more than just elegant porticoes and balustrades – its dynamic exhibitions, bars and restaurants provide a satisfying dose of modern vibrancy.

The Best...
➡ **Sight** La Rotonda
➡ **Place to Eat** Al Pestello (p171)
➡ **Place to Drink** Bar Borsa (p171)

Top Tip
Palladio's Teatro Olimpico was built for live performances, and that is still the best way to absorb the complex harmonies of the space.

Getting There & Away
➡ **Train** Trains are the easiest way to reach Vicenza from Venice (€4.15 to €16, 45 to 80 minutes, up to five hourly). Trains also connect with Padua and Verona.

➡ **Car** Vicenza lies just off the A4 connecting Milan with Venice, while the SR11 connects Vicenza with Verona and Padua. Several large car parks ring the historic centre, including the underground Park Verdi just north of the train station (enter from Viale dell'Ippodromo).

Need to Know
➡ **Area Code** ☑ 0444
➡ **Location** 62km west of Venice
➡ **Tourist Office** (☑ 0444 32 08 54; www.vicenzae.org; Piazza Matteotti 12; ⊗ 9am-5.30pm)

Vicenza

⊚ **Sights**

⊗ **Eating**

⊖ **Drinking**

⊙ SIGHTS

★ PALAZZO LEONI MONTANARI   MUSEUM

(☏800 578875; www.gallerieditalia.com; Contrà di Santa Corona 25; adult/reduced €10/8, or with MuseumCard; ☺9.30am-7.30pm Tue-Sun, to 10.30pm Thu) An extraordinary collection of treasures await inside Palazzo Leoni Montanari, among them ancient pottery from Magna Graecia and grand salons filled with Canaletto's misty lagoon landscapes and Pietro Longhi's 18th-century satires. A recent addition is Agostino Fasolato's astounding *The Fall of the Rebel Angels,* carved from a single block of Carrara marble and featuring no less than 60 angels and demons in nail-biting battle. Topping it all off is a superb collection of 400 Russian icons.

★ LA ROTONDA   HISTORIC BUILDING

(☏049 879 13 80; www.villalarotonda.it; Via della Rotonda 45; villa/gardens €10/5; ☺villa 10am-noon & 3-6pm Wed & Sat mid-Mar–Oct, 10am-noon & 2.30-5pm Wed & Sat Nov–mid-Mar, gardens 10am-noon & 3-6pm Tue-Sun mid-Mar–Oct, 10am-noon & 2.30-5pm Tue-Sun Nov–mid-Mar) No matter how you look at it, this villa is a show-stopper: the namesake dome caps a square base, with identical colonnaded facades on all four sides. This is one of Palladio's most admired creations, inspir-

ing variations across Europe and the USA, including Thomas Jefferson's Monticello. Inside, the circular central hall is covered from the walls to the soaring cupola with *trompe l'œil* frescoes. Catch bus 8 (€1.30, €2 on board) from in front of Vicenza's train station, or simply walk (about 25 minutes).

★ TEATRO OLIMPICO   THEATRE

(☏0444 964 380; www.teatrolimpicovicenza.it; Piazza Matteotti 11; adult/reduced €11/8, or with MuseumCard; ☺9am-5pm Tue-Sun, to 6pm early Jul-early Sep) Behind a walled garden lies a Renaissance marvel: the Teatro Olimpico, which Palladio began in 1580 with inspiration from Roman amphitheatres. Vincenzo Scamozzi finished the elliptical theatre after Palladio's death, adding a stage set modelled on the ancient Greek city of Thebes, with streets built in steep perspective to give the illusion of a city sprawling towards a distant horizon.

Today, Italian performers vie to make an entrance on this extraordinary stage; check the website for opera, classical and jazz performances.

BASILICA PALLADIANA   GALLERY

(☏0444 22 21 22; www.museicivicivicenza.it; Piazza dei Signori; temporary exhibitions €10-13; ☺temporary exhibitions only) Now a venue for world-class temporary exhibitions, the Palladian Basilica is capped with an enormous copper dome reminiscent of the hull of an upturned ship. The building, modelled on a Roman basilica, once housed the law courts and Council of Four Hundred. Palladio was lucky to secure the commission in 1549 (it took his patron 50 years of lobbying the council), which involved radically restructuring the original, 15th-century *palazzo* and adding an ambitious double order of loggias, supported by Tuscan and Ionic columns topped by soaring statuary.

The building is also home to the elegant **Museo del Gioiello** (www.museodelgioiello.it; adult/reduced €6/4; ☺3-7pm Mon-Fri, 11am-7pm Sat & Sun) and its dazzling collection of historic and contemporary jewellery.

PALAZZO CHIERICATI   MUSEUM

(☏0444 22 28 11; www.museicivicivicenza.it; Piazza Matteotti 37/39; adult/reduced €7/5; ☺9am-5pm Tue-Sun, 10am-6pm Tue-Sun early Jul-early Sep) Vicenza's civic art museum occupies one of Palladio's finest buildings, designed in 1550. The ground floor, used for temporary exhibitions, is where you'll find the **Sala dal Firmamento** (Salon of the Skies) and its blush-inducing ceiling fresco of Diana and an up-skirted Helios by Domenico Brusasorci. Highlights in the upstairs galleries include Anthony Van Dyke's allegorical *The Four Ages* and Alessandro Maganza's remarkably contemporary *Portrait of Maddalena Campiglia*.

Another floor up is the private collection of the late marquis Giuseppe Roi, including drawings by Tiepolo and Picasso

VILLA VALMARANA
'AI NANI'   HISTORIC BUILDING
(0444 32 18 03; www.villavalmarana.com; Stradella dei Nani 8; adult/reduced €10/7; 10am-6pm) From La Rotonda, a charming footpath leads about 500m to the neoclassical elegance of Villa Valmarana 'ai Nani', nicknamed after the 17 statues of gnomes ('ai Nani') around the perimeter walls. Step inside for 1757 frescoes by Giambattista Tiepolo and his son Giandomenico. Giambattista painted the Palazzina wing with his signature mythological epics, while his offspring executed the rural, carnival and Chinese themes adorning the *foresteria* (guesthouse).

PALLADIO MUSEUM   MUSEUM
(Palazzo Barbarano; 0444 32 30 14; www.palladiomuseum.org; Contrà Porti 11; adult/reduced €8/6, or with MuseumCard; 10am-6pm Tue-Sun) To better understand architect Andrea Palladio and his legacy, explore the frescoed halls of this modern museum. Artefacts include historical copies of Palladio's celebrated *Quattro Libri dell'Architettura* (Four Books of Architec-

ture; 1570) and intriguing architectural models of his lauded *palazzi* and villas, as well as video footage of experts discussing various aspects of the maverick's craft and genius.

ROMAN CRIPTOPORTICO   RUINS
(347 9426020, 0444 326 880; athena_el@yahoo.it; Piazza del Duomo 6; 3-5pm Sat, 10am-12pm Sun) FREE Six metres below modern Vicenza lies one of the city's lesser-known historical treasures – a 1st-century Roman cryptoportico. Discovered during postwar reconstruction in 1954, it's the only private cryptoportico uncovered in northern Italy to date. If you are around at the weekend, it's a worth trip underground.

✖ EATING

★ SÒTOBOTEGA   VENETIAN €
(0444 54 44 14; www.gastronomiailceppo.com; Corso Palladio 196; meals €25, set tasting menus €26; 11.30am-3pm) Drop into cult-status deli **Gastronomia Il Ceppo** (prepared dishes per 100g from around €2.50; 8am-7.45pm Tue-Sat, 9am-2pm Sun) for picnic provisions, or head down into its cellar for sensational sit-down dishes like expertly crafted *bigoli* (a type of pasta) with the sauce of the day, or the star of the show, *bacalà alla vicentina*, Vicenza's signature codfish dish. Some 500 mostly Italian wines line the walls and transparent floor panels reveal an ancient Roman footpath and the foundations of an 11th-century dwelling. Book ahead or head in early.

'BIRDS' OF THE BANCA POPOLARE

Just off Corso Palladio, you'll find the headquarters of the Banca Popolare di Vicenza (People's Bank of Vicenza), housed rather ironically in Palladio's **Palazzo Thiene** (0444 339 216; www.palazzothiene.it; Contrà San Gaetano Thiene; 9am-5pm Wed-Fri by appointment only, closed Jul & Aug) FREE, which was fashioned for the aristocratic Thiene family in 1556. Purchased by the bank in 1872, the palace is now home to fine paintings, sculptures, and the world's largest collection of *oselle* (silver and gold coins minted by the doge each year and presented as a Christmas gift to all the noble families of the Great Council of Venice).

Originally, the gift was five mallards per family, but given the growing number of nobles and the declining number of mallards, in 1521 the Council decreed that the doge should mint a silver coin instead, hence the name, *oselle*, which is Venetian for bird.

Book in advance to see them along with the bank's frescoed salons, fine artworks and sculpture.

★ **OSTERIA IL CURSORE**　　OSTERIA €

(☎0444 32 35 04; www.osteriacursore.it; Stradella Pozzetto 10; meals €25; ⊙11am-3pm & 6pm-2am Mon & Wed-Sat, 11am-1pm & 6pm-2am Sun) A short walk from the city centre, behind a stained-glass door, this local institution serves up a thoroughly local scene where walls are hung with family photos and Tiffany & Co lamps illuminate the bar. Local diners keep one eye on the televised football match as they tuck into simple, tasty fare which includes local Vicenza dishes and pan-Italian favourites.

RIGHETTI SELF SERVICE　　VENETIAN €

(www.selfrighetti.it; Piazza del Duomo 3; meals €10-15; ⊙10am-3pm & 7-10pm Mon-Fri) This rare self-service restaurant offers an honest, daily changing menu of local pasta and meat for knock-down prices (*primi* €4, *secondi* €5), plus salads, desserts and cheap wine. Despite the abundance of seats, you'll be forced to join an Italian queue at feeding time when it's packed out. Outside prescribed mealtimes, staff can be very indifferent. No English spoken.

★ **AL PESTELLO**　　VENETIAN €€

(☎0444 32 37 21; Contrà San Stefano 3; meals €32; ⊙7.30-10pm Mon, Wed & Thu, noon-2pm & 7.30-10pm Fri-Sun; 🖘) Homely, brightly lit Al Pestello dishes out intriguing, lesser-known *cucina vicentina* such as *la panà* (bread soup), red-wine braised donkey and *bresaola* 'lollies' filled with grappa-flavoured Grana Padano and mascarpone. The kitchen is obsessed with local ingredients, right down to the Colli Berici truffles, while the collection of harder-to-find *digestivi* makes for an enlightening epilogue. Book ahead.

🍷 DRINKING & NIGHTLIFE

BAR BORSA　　BAR

(☎0444 54 45 83; www.barborsa.com; Basilica Palladiana, Piazza dei Signori 26; ⊙6pm-2am Mon, 10am-2am Tue-Sun; 🖘) Decked out in all manner of knick-knacks and flickering in candlelight, hip Borsa covers all bases, from coffee and juices to *aperitivo* and cocktails. Fresh, flavoursome food options span breakfast, brunch, lunch, snacks and dinner, with DJs spinning tunes on Fridays and Saturdays and jazz sessions almost any night of the week.

> **LOCAL KNOWLEDGE**
>
> ### VICENZA JAZZ
>
> Vicenza's biggest annual event is the **jazz festival** (☎0444-221 541; www. vicenzajazz.org; ⊙mid-May) that takes place at the Teatro Olimpico and at several other venues for a week in mid-May, attracting top names from the Italian scene.

The owners also run the cosy *enoteca* (wine bar) across the passageway; many choose a table in-between to make the most of both establishments.

PASTICCERIA SORARÙ　　CAFE

(☎0444 32 09 15; Piazzetta Palladio; ⊙7.30am-12.30pm & 3.30-7.30pm Mon, Tue, Thu & Fri, 7.30am-7.30pm Sat & Sun) Imbibe a bit of history at this tiny, marble-topped cafe-bar serving coffees, pastries, biscotti and snack-friendly *panini*. Olde-worlde jars of sweets line elaborately gilded shelves, while a row of more modern outdoor tables under arcading offer views of the Basilica Palladiana's elegant arches.

HELMUT　　BEER HALL

(www.helmutpub.com; Contrà Zanella 8; ⊙6.30pm-2am Tue-Sun) Industrial lighting, a sticky stone floor and battered tables set the scene at this earthy pub. Beer is the star attraction, with around 15 mostly European craft beers on tap, served to a hipster-ish 30- and 40-something crowd. Sud-soaking edibles include creative burgers (€7.50 to €13) made with beef from lauded local butcher Damini & Affini.

Prosecco Country

Explore

In the foothills of the Alps, the area between Conegliano and Valdobbiadene is the toast of the Veneto. The vine-draped hillsides hereabouts produce *prosecco*, a dry, crisp white wine made in *spumante* (bubbly), *frizzante* (sparkling) and still varieties. Visit local wineries for tastings to see what all the fizz is about.

The Best...

➡**Sight** Villa di Masèr

➡**Place to Eat** Locanda Baggio da Nino (p174)

➡**Place to Drink** Azienda Agricola Frozza

Top Tip

Running through a landscape of rolling vineyards, **La Strada di Prosecco** is a driving route that takes you from Conegliano to Valdobbiadene via some of the region's best wineries. A dedicated website (www.coneglianovaldobbiadene.it) provides an itinerary, background information on *prosecco,* and details about stops along the way.

Getting There & Away

➡**Car** Your own wheels are your best option for getting around the region at a reasonable pace and visiting wineries and farmstays. The A27 heads directly north from Mestre to Conegliano.

➡**Train** Head from Venice to the Mestre station, where there are two to three trains per hour to Conegliano (50 minutes, €4.40).

Need to Know

➡**Area Code** ☑0423

➡**Location** Conegliano is 53km north of Venice; Bassano del Grappa is 58km northwest of Venice

➡**Tourist Office** (☑0438 2 12 30; Via XX Settembre 132, Conegliano; ☺9am-1pm Tue & Wed, 9am-1pm & 2-6pm Thu-Sun)

◉ SIGHTS & ACTIVITIES

◉ Conegliano & Around

A sleepy, small town at the foothills of the Alps, Conegliano is the heart of the Veneto's *prosecco*-producing area and the surrounding hillsides are dotted with vineyards. Conegliano's *prosecco* was promoted to DOCG status in 2009, Italy's highest oenological distinction. The town is the starting point for a tasting detour along the Strada di Prosecco (Prosecco Rd) from Conegliano to the Valdobbiadene.

AZIENDA AGRICOLA BARICHEL WINE

(☑0423 97 57 43; www.barichel.it; Via Zanzago 9, Valdobbiadene) Like the prodigal son, ultra-marathon runner and vintner Ivan Geronazzo returned to his grandfather's vineyard in Valdobbiadene after years of working at larger, high capacity wineries. Here he tends his 7 hectares by hand, producing up to 60,000 bottles of natural, *frizzante*, extra dry and brut *prosecco* with a pale, straw-yellow colour and apple-and-pear fragrances. Prices range from €5 to €8 per bottle.

AZIENDA AGRICOLA FROZZA WINE

(☑0423 98 70 69; www.frozza.it; Via Martiri 31, Colbertaldo di Vidor) Galera vines have grown on this sunny Colbertaldo hillside for hundreds of years and six generations of the Frozza family have tended them since 1870. The result: *prosecco* with a remarkable fragrance and complexity. The 2011 brut is a particularly good vintage due to the dry summer. Expect fruity fragrances supported by a well-structured, mineral-rich body. Prices range from €5 to €8 per bottle.

WORTH A DETOUR

VILLA DI MASÈR

A World Heritage Site, the 16th-century **Villa di Masèr** (Villa Barbaro; ☑0423 92 30 04; www.villadimaser.it; Via Cornuda 7, Maser; adult/reduced €9/7; ☺10am-6pm Tue-Sat, from 11am Sun Apr-Oct, 11am-5pm Sat & Sun Nov-Mar; P) is a spectacular monument to the Venetian *bea vita* (good life). Designed by the inimitable Andrea Palladio, its sublimely elegant exterior is matched by Paolo Veronese's wildly imaginative *trompe l'œil* architecture inside. Vines crawl up the Stanza di Baccho; a watchdog keeps an eye on the painted door of the Stanza di Canuccio (Little Dog Room); and in a corner of the frescoed grand salon, the painter has apparently forgotten his spattered shoes and broom. You'll find it bedded down in a vineyard 7km northeast of Asolo.

○ Asolo

Known as the 'town of 100 vistas' for its panoramic hillside location, the medieval walled town of Asolo has long been a favourite of literary types. Robert Browning bought a house here, but the ultimate local celebrity is Caterina Corner, the 15th-century queen of Cyprus, who was given the town, its castle (now used as a theatre) and the surrounding county in exchange for her abdication. She promptly became queen of the literary set, holding salons that featured writer Pietro Bembo.

ROCCA   RUINS
(☎329 8508512; €2; ⊙10am-7pm Sat & Sun Apr-Jun, Sep & Oct, 10am-noon & 3-7pm Sat & Sun Jul & Aug, 10am-5pm Sat & Sun Nov-Mar) Perched on the summit of Monte Ricco and looking down on central Asolo are the hulking ruins of a fortress dating back to the 12th to early 13th centuries. The still-visible cistern well was constructed between the 13th and 14th centuries, while the heavily restored buttresses offer a breathtaking panorama that takes in soft green hills, snowcapped mountains and the industrious Po Valley.

MUSEO CIVICO DI ASOLO   MUSEUM
(☎0423 95 23 13; www.asolo.it; Via Regina Cornaro 74; adult/reduced €5/4; ⊙9.30am-12.30pm & 3-6pm Sat & Sun) In the Museo Civico you can explore Asolo's Roman past and wander through a small collection of paintings, including a pair of Tintoretto portraits. The museum also includes rooms devoted to Eleanora Duse (1858–1924) and British traveller and writer Freya Stark (1893–1993), who retreated to Asolo between Middle Eastern forays.

○ Bassano del Grappa

Bassano del Grappa sits with charming simplicity on the banks of the river Brenta as it winds its way free from Alpine foothills. The town is famous above all for its namesake spirit, grappa – a fiery distillation made from the discarded skins, pulp, seeds and stems from wine-making.

PRIMAVERA DEL PROSECCO

From mid-March to June, the Veneto's DOCG-denominated hills play host to the annual *prosecco* festival (www.primaveradelprosecco.it), which features a series of food and wine events showcasing the area's prized *prosecco superiore* and regional delicacies. Activities range from wine tasting and bike tours to guided walks and concerts. Check the website for details of what's on where. *Cin cin.*

POLI MUSEO DELLA GRAPPA   MUSEUM
(☎0424 52 44 26; www.poligrappa.com; Via Gamba 6; admission free, distillery guided tours €5; ⊙museum 9am-7.30pm, distillery guided tours 8.30am-1pm & 2-6pm Mon-Fri) Explore four centuries of Bassano's high-octane libation at this interactive museum, which includes tastings and the chance to tour the distillery of esteemed producer Poli (book tours online). Although grappa is made all over Italy, and indeed inferior versions are distilled well beyond the peninsula, the people of the Veneto have been doing it since at least the 16th century. In fact, an institute of grappa distillers was even created in Venice in 1601!

MUSEO CIVICO   MUSEUM
(☎0424 51 99 01; www.museibassano.it; Piazza Garibaldi 34; adult/reduced €5/3.50; ⊙10am-7pm) Bassano del Grappa's Museo Civico is beautifully housed around the cloisters of the Convento di San Francesco. Endowed in 1828 by the naturalist Giambattista Brocchi, the museum houses an extensive archaeological collection alongside 500 paintings, including masterpieces such as the 1545 *Flight into Egypt* by local son Jacopo Bassano.

PONTE DEGLI ALPINI   BRIDGE
Spanning the river is Palladio's photogenic 1569 covered bridge, the Ponte degli Alpini. Fragile as the wooden structure seems, it is cleverly engineered to withstand the rush of spring melt waters from Monte Grappa. It's always been critical in times of war: Napoleon bivouacked here for many months and during the Great War, the Alpine brigades adopted the bridge as their emblem.

✖ EATING & DRINKING

OSTERIA ALLA CANEVA
VENETIAN €

(☑335 542 35 60; Via G Matteotti 34, Bassano del Grappa; dishes €20-30; ☺9am-3pm Wed-Mon & 5.30pm-midnight Wed-Sun) Behind yellow-tinted glass lies this old-school favourite, with its hung pots, worn wooden tables and inter-generational regulars washing down rustic regional grub with a glass or three of *vino* from local wineries like Vigneto Due Santi di Zonta. Food options lean towards cured meats and pasta dishes like fettuccine with artichokes. For a light bite, don't miss the *baccala cicchetti* (salted cod tapas).

AL CASTELLO
CAFE €€

(☑0438 22 379; www.ristorantealcastello.it; Piazzale San Leonardo 7, Conegliano; meals €30-40; ☺8am-midnight Wed-Sun, to 2.15pm Mon) In the grounds of the Castello, the combination of well-executed pan-Italian food and the incredible views across the surrounding hills make this place a winner and well worth the hike uphill from the centre. Go for a full-blown meal involving duck *tagliata* (sliced grilled meat) with orange sauce or codfish Vicentina, or just for a coffee and cake stop to admire the Veneto panorama.

LOCANDA BAGGIO DA NINO
VENETO €€

(☑0423 529 648; www.locandabaggio.it; Via Bassane 1, Asolo; meals €30-40; ☺12.30-2.30pm Wed-Sun & 7.30-10pm Tue-Sun) Asolo's best restaurant is run by the Baggio family who welcome each guest personally and make sure only the finest ingredients go into the food they serve. The menu is a delightful read featuring suckling pig, guinea fowl, pizzas, octopus and lamb, and the family even make their own souvenirs and examples of local produce to take away.

VILLA CIPRIANI
MODERN ITALIAN €€€

(☑0423 52 34 11; www.villaciprianiasolo.com; Via Canova 298, Asolo; meals €60; ☺12.30-2.30pm & 8-10.30pm; ℗) The Ciprianis behind this Renaissance villa are the same as those in Venice, and they are just the latest in a long line of illustrious owners including the Guinnesses, the Galantis, and English poet Robert Browning. Now you, too, can enjoy the perfumed rose garden, not to mention the kitchen's seasonal, market-driven menus; the pasta dishes are particularly seductive.

NARDINI
BAR

(www.nardini.it; Ponte Vecchio 2, Bassano del Grappa; ☺8.30am-9.30pm) Flanking Bassano del Grappa's 16th-century Ponte degli Alpini, this historic distillery is a great place to grab a few bottles of Nardini's famous grappa, or to simply kick back with a glass of bitter-sweet *mezzo e mezzo*, a unique *aperitivo* made with Rabarbaro Nardini, Rosso Nardini, Cynar and soda water.

Follow the locals' lead and order a *crocchantino* (caramelised peanut bar), and make a restroom stop downstairs for a unique view of Palladio's famous wooden bridge.

Verona

Explore

Best known for its Shakespeare associations, Verona attracts a multinational gaggle of tourists to its pretty piazzas and knot of lanes, most in search of Romeo, Juliet and all that. But beyond the heart-shaped tack and Renaissance romance, Verona is a bustling centre, its heart dominated by a mammoth, remarkably well-preserved 1st-century amphitheatre, the venue for the city's annual summer opera festival. Add to that countless churches, a couple of architecturally fascinating bridges over the Adige, regional wine and food from the Veneto hinterland and some impressive art, and Verona shapes up as one of northern Italy's most attractive cities. Consider spending the night if you want to delve deeper – or explore Verona's remarkable wine country.

The Best...

➡ **Sight** Roman Arena

➡ **Place to Eat** Locanda 4 Cuochi (p179)

➡ **Place to Drink** Antica Bottega del Vino (p180)

Top Tip

The **VeronaCard** (€18/22 per 24/72 hours; www.tourism.verona.it), available at tourist sights, tobacconists and numerous hotels, offers access to most major monuments and churches, unlimited use of town buses, and discounted tickets to selected concerts and opera and theatre productions.

Getting There & Away

➡**Train** Verona Porta Nuova station is a major stop on the Italian rail network with direct services to numerous northern Italian towns and cities, including Venice (€8.85 to €27, 70 minutes to 2¼ hours, one to four hourly), Padua and Vicenza.

➡**Car** Verona is at the intersection of the A4 (Turin-Trieste) and A22 motorways.

➡**Bus** The intercity bus station is in front of the train station. Buses run to Padua, Vicenza and Venice.

Need to Know

➡**Area Code** 045
➡**Location** 120km west of Venice
➡**Tourist Office** (045 806 86 80; www.tourism.verona.it; Via degli Alpini 9; 10am-7pm Mon-Sat, to 3pm Sun)

 SIGHTS

★**ROMAN ARENA**   RUINS
(045 800 32 04; Piazza Brà; adult/reduced €10/7.50; 8.30am-7.30pm Tue-Sun, from 1.30pm Mon) Built of pink-tinged marble in the 1st century AD, Verona's Roman amphitheatre survived a 12th-century earthquake to become the city's legendary open-air opera house, with seating for 30,000 people. You can visit the arena year-round, though it's at its best during the summer opera festival. In winter months, concerts are held at the **Teatro Filarmonico** (045 800 28 80; www.arena.it; Via dei Mutilati 4; opera €23-60, concerts €25-50). From January to May and October to December, admission is €1 on the first Sunday of the month.

★**GIARDINO GIUSTI**   GARDENS
(045 803 40 29; Via Giardino Giusti 2; adult/reduced €8.50/5; 9am-8pm Apr-Sep, to 7pm Oct-Mar) Across the river from the historic centre, these sculpted gardens are considered a masterpiece of Renaissance landscaping, and named after the noble family that has tended them since opening them to the public in 1591. The vegetation is an Italianate mix of the manicured and natural, graced by soaring cypresses, one of which

the German poet Goethe immortalised in his travel writings.

According to local legend, lovers who manage to find each other in the gardens' petite labyrinth are destined to stay together. If you do, whisper sweet nothings while gazing out at the city from the *belvedere* (lookout), accessed from the back of the gardens. Forget the Casa di Giulietta, this is where the real romance is in Verona.

★**MUSEO DI CASTELVECCHIO**   MUSEUM
(045 806 26 11; https://museodicastelvecchio.comune.verona.it; Corso Castelvecchio 2; adult/reduced €6/4.50; 1.30-7.30pm Mon, 8.30am-7.30pm Tue-Sun) Bristling with fishtail battlements along the River Adige, Castelvecchio was built in the 1350s by Cangrande II. Severely damaged by Napoleon and WWII bombings, the fortress was reinvented by architect Carlo Scarpa, who constructed bridges over exposed foundations, filled gaping holes with glass panels, and balanced a statue of Cangrande I above the courtyard on a concrete gangplank. The complex is now home to a diverse collection of statuary, frescoes, jewellery, medieval artefacts and paintings.

★**GALLERIA D'ARTE MODERNA ACHILLE FORTI**   MUSEUM
(Palazzo della Ragione; 045 800 19 03; www.palazzodellaragioneverona.it; Cortile Mercato Vecchio; adult/reduced €4/2.50, incl Torre dei Lamberti €8/5; 10am-6pm Tue-Fri, 11am-7pm Sat & Sun) In the shadow of the Torre dei Lamberti, the Romanesque Palazzo della Ragione is home to Verona's jewel-box Gallery of Modern Art. Reached via the Gothic **Scala della Ragione** (Stairs of Reason), the collection of paintings and sculpture spans 1840 to 1940 and includes influential Italian artists such as Giorgio Morandi and Umberto Boccioni. Among the numerous highlights are Francesco Hayez' arresting portrait *Meditazione* (Meditation), Angelo Dall'Oca's haunting *Foglie cadenti* (Falling Leaves) and Ettore Berladini's darkly humorous *I vecchi* (Old Men).

The gallery's architectural pièce de résistance is the vaulted **Cappella dei Notai** (Chapel of Notaries), bursting with late 17th- and early 18th-century biblical scenes executed by Alessandro Marchesini, Giambattista Bellotti, Santo Prunati and Louis Dorigny.

Verona

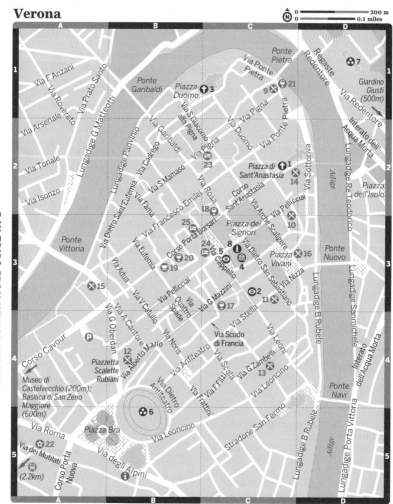

BASILICA DI SAN ZENO MAGGIORE

BASILICA

(www.basilicasanzeno.it; Piazza San Zeno; €2.50; ☑8.30am-6pm Mon-Sat, 12.30-6pm Sun Mar-Oct, 10am-1pm & 1.30-5pm Mon-Sat, 12.30-5pm Sun Nov-Feb) A masterpiece of Romanesque architecture, the striped brick and stone basilica was built in honour of the city's patron saint. Enter through the flower-filled cloister into the nave – a vast space lined with 12th- to 15th-century frescoes. Painstaking restoration has revived Mantegna's 1457–59 *Majesty of the Virgin* altarpiece, painted with such astonishing perspective that you actually believe there are garlands of fresh fruit hanging behind the Madonna's throne.

Under the rose window depicting the Wheel of Fortune you'll find meticulously detailed 12th-century bronze doors, which include a scene of an exorcism with a demon being yanked from a woman's mouth. Beneath the main altar lies a brooding crypt, with faces carved into medieval capitals and St Zeno's corpse glowing in a transparent sarcophagus.

Verona

TORRE DEI LAMBERTI TOWER
(☏045 927 30 27; Via della Costa 1; adult/reduced incl Galleria d'Arte Moderna Achille Forti €8/5, with VeronaCard €1; ◷10am-7pm) One of Verona's most popular attractions, this 84m-high watchtower provides panoramic views of Verona and nearby mountains. Begun in the 12th century and finished in 1463 – too late to notice invading Venetians – it sports an octagonal bell tower whose two bells retain their ancient names: Rengo once called meetings of the city council, while Marangona warned citizens of fire. A lift whisks you up two-thirds of the way but you have to walk the last few storeys.

PIAZZA DELLE ERBE SQUARE
(Piazza delle Erbe) Originally a Roman forum, Piazza delle Erbe is ringed with buzzing cafes and some of Verona's most sumptuous buildings, including the elegantly baroque **Palazzo Maffei**, which now houses several shops at its northern end. Just off the piazza, the monumental arch known as the **Arco della Costa** is hung with a whale's rib. Legend holds that the rib will fall on the first just person to walk beneath it. So far, it remains intact, despite visits by popes and kings.

BASILICA DI SANT'ANASTASIA BASILICA
(www.chieseverona.it; Piazza di Sant'Anastasia; €2.50; ◷9am-6pm Mon-Sat, 1-6pm Sun Mar-Oct, 10am-1pm & 1.30-5pm Mon-Sat, 1-5pm Sun Nov-Feb) Dating from the 13th to 15th centuries and featuring an elegantly decorated vaulted ceiling, the Gothic Basilica di Sant'Anastasia is Verona's largest church and a showcase for local art. The multitude of frescoes is overwhelming, but don't overlook Pisanello's story-book-quality fresco *St George and the Princess* above the entrance to the **Pellegrini Chapel**, or the 1495 holy water font featuring a hunchback carved by Paolo Veronese's father, Gabriele Caliari.

DUOMO CATHEDRAL
(☏045 59 28 13; Piazza Duomo; €2.50, combined Verona church ticket €6 or with VeronaCard; ◷10am-5.30pm Mon-Sat, 1.30-5.30pm Sun Mar-Oct, 10am-1pm & 1.30-5pm Mon-Fri, to 4pm Sat, 1.30-5pm Sun Nov-Feb) Verona's 12th-century cathedral is a striking Romanesque creation, with bug-eyed statues of Charlemagne's paladins Roland and Oliver, crafted by medieval master Nicolò, on the west porch. Nothing about this sober facade hints at the extravagant 16th- to 17th-century frescoed interior with angels aloft amid *trompe l'œil* architecture. At the left end of the nave is the **Cartolari-Nichesola Chapel**, designed by Renaissance master Jacopo Sansovino and featuring a vibrant Titian *Assumption*.

PONTE PIETRA

At the northern edge of the city centre, this bridge is a quiet but remarkable testament to the Italians' love of their artistic heritage. Two of the bridge's arches date from the Roman Republican era in the 1st century BC, while the other three were replaced in the 13th century. The ancient bridge remained largely intact until 1945, when retreating German troops blew it up. But locals fished the fragments out of the river, and painstakingly rebuilt the bridge stone by stone in the 1950s.

TEATRO ROMANO E MUSEO ARCHEOLOGICO
ARCHAEOLOGICAL SITE

(☑045 800 03 60; Regaste Redentore 2; adult/reduced €4.50/3, or with VeronaCard free; ◎8.30am-7.30pm Tue-Sun, 1.30-7.30pm Mon) Just north of the historic centre you'll find a **Roman theatre**. Built in the 1st century BC, it is cunningly carved into the hillside at a strategic spot overlooking a bend in the river. Take the lift at the back of the theatre to the former convent above, which houses an interesting collection of Greek and Roman pieces.

CASA DI GIULIETTA
NOTABLE BUILDING

(Juliet's House; ☑045 803 43 03; Via Cappello 23; adult/reduced €6/4.50, free with VeronaCard; ◎1.30-7.30pm Mon, 8.30am-7.30pm Tue-Sun) Juliet's house is a spectacle, but not for the reasons you might imagine – entering the courtyard off Via Cappello, you are greeted by a young multinational crowd, everyone milling around in the tiny space trying to take selfies with the well-rubbed bronze of Juliet. The walls are lined up to 2m high with love notes, many attached with chewing gum. Above you is the famous balcony, tourists taking their turn to have pics taken against the 'romantic background'.

🛏 SLEEPING

CASA SAN ZENO
GUESTHOUSE €

(☑045 807 01 09; Via Don Minzoni 50; s/d from €28/50; 🅿🛜) Buried deep within the Istituto Salesiano, a Catholic technical college, these student residence rooms are the best deal in Verona with clean bedrooms and bathrooms and strong wi-fi. There's a supermarket next door and several more a short walk away, plus regular buses head for Porta Nuova from nearby. The downsides are the strict 2pm to 8pm check-in and lack of breakfast.

To reach the Istituto Salesiano, take bus 13 from Porta Nuova to the Via San Marco stop.

★CORTE DELLE PIGNE
B&B €€

(☑333 7584141; www.cortedellepigne.it; Via Pigna 6a; s €60-110, d €90-150, tr €110-170, q €130-190; 🅿✳🛜) In the heart of the historic centre, this tiny three-room B&B is set around a quiet internal courtyard. It offers tasteful rooms and plenty of personal touches: sweets jars, luxury toiletries and even a Jacuzzi for one lucky couple.

HOTEL AURORA
HOTEL €€

(☑045 59 47 17; www.hotelaurora.biz; Piazzetta XIV Novembre 2; d €110-280, tr €130-300; ✳🛜) Overlooking Piazza delle Erbe, this friendly old Italian classic offers smart bedrooms, some with piazza views and all with classic wooden furniture and fresh, 21st-century bathrooms. The open-air terrace makes for a perfect spot to enjoy breakfast, or a lazy sundowner.

★HOTEL GABBIA D'ORO
HOTEL €€€

(☑045 59 02 93; www.hotelgabbiadoro.it; Corso Porta Borsari 4; d from €200; ✳🛜) One of the city's top addresses and also one of its most romantic, the Gabbia d'Oro features luxe rooms inside an 18th-century *palazzo* that manage to be both elegant and cosy. The rooftop terrace and central location are the icing on the proverbial cake.

🍴 EATING

HOSTARIA LA VECCHIA FONTANINA
TRATTORIA €

(☑045 59 11 59; www.ristorantevecchiafontanina.com; Piazzetta Chiavica 5; meals €20-25; ◎10.30-3.30pm & 6.30-midnight Mon-Sat) With tables on a pint-sized piazza, cosy indoor rooms and excellent food, this historic, knick-knack-filled eatery stands out from the crowd. The menu features typical Veronese dishes alongside a number of more unusual creations such as *bigoli con ortica e ricotta affumicata* (thick spaghetti with nettles and smoked ricotta) and several heavenly desserts. Queuing to get in is normal.

OSTERIA SOTTORIVA
OSTERIA €

(☑045 801 43 23; Via Sottoriva 9a; meals €15-20; ⏱11am-11pm) The last of the historic *osterie* (casual taverns) that once lined this riverside alley, Sottoriva still draws local crowds to rough-hewn tables under the arcade, with wine by the glass at fair prices, and traditional pork sausages and horse meatballs.

GELATERIA PONTE PIETRA
GELATO €

(Via Ponte Pietra 13; ⏱2.30-7.30pm Sep-Oct & Mar-May, to 10pm Jun-Aug, closed Nov-Feb) Impeccable gelato is made on the premises with alpine milk from Alto-Adige (Südtirol). Flavours like *bacio bianco* (white chocolate and hazelnut), candied orange with cinnamon, and *mille fiori* (cream with honey and bits of pollen gathered from local hillsides) are something a bit different.

PASTICCERIA MIOZZI
PASTRIES €

(☑045 927 50 18; Via A Diaz 7a; brioche €1.30; ⏱7am-8pm Mon-Sat, 7am-1pm & 3-7pm Sun) Not only home to Verona's plumpest brioche, sassy Miozzi peddles finger-licking pastries (including mini versions for those on a diet), biscotti and chocolates. The coffee is rich and aromatic, and there's a handful of tables for a leisurely pit stop.

★LOCANDA 4 CUOCHI
MODERN ITALIAN €€

(☑045 803 03 11; www.locanda4cuochi.it; Via Alberto Mario 12; meals €40, 3-course set menu €25; ⏱12.30-2.30pm & 7.30-10.30pm, closed lunch Mon-Wed; ☎) With its open kitchen, urbane vibe and hotshot chefs, you're right to expect great things from Locanda. Culinary acrobatics play second fiddle to prime produce cooked with skill and subtle twists. Whether it's perfectly crisp suckling pig lacquered with liquorice, or an epilogue of gianduja ganache with sesame crumble and banana, expect to to be gastronomically impressed.

OSTERIA DA UGO
VENETIAN €€

(www.osteriadaugo.com; Vicolo Dietro Sant'Andrea 1b; meals €25-30; ⏱noon-2.30pm & 7.30-10.30pm, closed Sun dinner) Lost in a backstreet away from the tourism, this *osteria* is a popular treat typically frequented at mealtimes by whole families. Surrounded by stained glass, elegantly laid tables and hundreds of wine bottles, enjoy a menu of Italian favourites as well as Vicenza-style codfish and tortellini with Lessinia truffles. Be prepared to queue to get a table during busy periods.

LA TAVERNA DI VIA STELLA
VENETO €€

(☑045 800 80 08; www.tavernadiviastella.com; Via Stella 5c; meals €30-35; ⏱12.15-2.30pm & 7.15-11pm, closed Wed & Mon evening) Brush past the haunches of prosciutto dangling over the deli bar and make your way into the dining room, decorated Tiepolo-style with rustic murals of chivalric knights and maidens. This is the place you'll want to sample traditional Veronese dishes such as *pastissada* (horse stew), tripe and DOP Lessinia cheeses from Monte Veronese.

★PESCHERIA I MASENINI
SEAFOOD €€€

(☑045 929 80 15; www.imasenini.com; Piazzetta Pescheria 9; meals €40-50; ⏱12.40-2pm & 7.40-10pm, closed Sun evening & Mon) Located on the piazza where Verona's Roman fish market once held sway, softly lit Masenini quietly serves up Verona's most imaginative,

DAY TRIPS FROM VENICE VERONA

VERONA'S OPERA FESTIVAL

On balmy summer nights, when 14,000 music lovers fill the Roman Arena during the opera festival and light their candles at sunset, expect goosebumps even before the performance starts. The **festival** (☑045 800 51 51; www.arena.it; Via Dietro Anfiteatro 6; ⏱late Jun–late Aug) was started in 1913 and is now the biggest open-air lyrical music event in the world. It draws international stars and the staging is legendary – highlights have included Franco Zeffirelli's lavish productions of *Carmen* and *Aida*.

Prices rise at weekends, ranging from €22 on unreserved stone steps and costing over €200 on the central gold seats. Performances usually start at 8.45pm or 9pm with locals booking their dinner table for after the show. Tucking into a preshow picnic on the unreserved stone steps is fine, so decant that wine into a plastic bottle (glass and knives aren't allowed), arrive early, rent a cushion and prepare for an utterly unforgettable evening.

BIKE TOURS

Simonetta Bike Tours (☎045 834 6104; www.simonettabiketours.it) operates a variety of pedal-powered jaunts around Verona, one involving cycling and rafting on the Adige. The company also arranges longer bike tours of the wine regions and even up to Lake Garda.

modern fish dishes. Inspired flavour combinations might see fresh sea bass carpaccio paired with zesty green apple and pink pepper, black-ink gnocchi schmoozing with lobster *ragù*, or sliced amberjack delightfully matched with crumbed almonds, honey, spinach and raspberries.

DRINKING & NIGHTLIFE

ANTICA BOTTEGA DEL VINO WINE BAR
(☎045 800 45 35; www.bottegavini.it; Vicolo Scudo di Francia 3; ⊙11am-1am) While *vino* is the primary consideration at this historic, baronial-style wine bar (the cellar holds around 18,000 bottles), the linen-lined tables promise a satisfying feed. Ask the sommelier to recommend a worthy vintage for your braised donkey, Vicenza-style codfish or Venetian liver – some of the best wines here are bottled specifically for the *bottega*.

ARCHIVIO COCKTAIL BAR
(☎345 816 9663; Via Rosa 3; ⊙8am-midnight Mon-Fri, from 9am Sat, from 11am Sun) Fragrant with aromatic cocktail ingredients, this side-street micro-bar is one of the best places for a night-launching drink. Imaginative mixology combines with craft beers to give a lot of choice to drinkers, and the friendly owner knows his tipples.

CAFE BORSARI COFFEE
(☎045 803 1313; Corso Porta Borsari 15d; ⊙7.30am-8.15pm) It might look like a ceramics shop from the outside, but open the door and you'll discover this magically minuscule coffee house that's been roasting its own coffee and supplying hot chocolate to four tables since 1969. Also sells quirky Christmas gifts year-round.

OSTERIA DEL BUGIARDO WINE BAR
(☎045 59 18 69; Corso Porta Borsari 17a; ⊙11am-midnight, to 1am Fri & Sat) Crowds converge at friendly Bugiardo for glasses of upstanding Valpolicella bottled specifically for the *osteria*. Feeling peckish? Order the yellow polenta with creamy gorgonzola and salami. On weekdays from November to January, pair a delicious Amarone with the very local *lesso e pearà* (boiled meat stew with a peppery beef, hen, bone-marrow and breadcrumb sauce).

TERRAZZA BAR AL PONTE BAR
(☎045 927 50 32; www.terrazzabaralponte.eu; Via Ponte di Pietra 26; ⊙9am-2am) Mingle with hip, young locals for *spritz* (*prosecco* cocktails) beneath the giant chandelier in this retro-cool bar. Come early enough and you might even nab a table on the tiny terrace overlooking the river and the Ponte Pietra.

Verona's Wine Country

Explore

A drive through Verona's hinterland is a lesson in fine wine. To the north and northwest are Valpolicella vineyards, which predate the arrival of the Romans, and east on the road to Vicenza lie the white-wine makers of Soave. You'll need a car to visit the vineyards, or you can sign up for a tour in Verona. Since vineyards are spread out, each region requires a full day for relaxed appreciation, including a long vinous lunch.

The Best...

➡**Sight** Villa della Torre
➡**Place to Eat** Osteria Numero Uno (p183)
➡**Place to Drink** Allegrini (p182)

Top Tip

If you don't want to rent a car, **Pagus** (☎327 796 53 80, 340 083 07 20; www.pagusvalpolicella.net; half/full day group tour €60-80) offers tours of Valpolicella and Soave, leaving regularly from Verona. Tours include visits to unusual, rural sites, impromptu rambles, lunches

BOERESCU/SHUTTERSTOCK ©

Soave vineyard.

in local restaurants and, of course, wine tastings. Tours can also be customised.

Getting There & Away

➤ **Car** A car is essential for getting to Valpolicella and even though Soave is accessible by public transport a car is needed for exploring the surrounding vineyards. Valpolicella, situated 20km northwest of Verona, can be reached via the SP1 and SP4; while Soave is a 40-minute drive east along the A4/E70 motorway.

Need to Know

➤ **Area Code** ✆045

➤ **Location** Soave and Valpolicella are 85km and 140km west of Venice, respectively

➤ **Tourist Offices Soave** (✆045 619 07 73; www.soaveturismo.it; Piazza Foro Boario l; ⏰10am-5pm Mon, 9am-6pm Tue-Fri, 9am-3pm Sat & Sun Apr-Oct, 9am-5pm Tue-Fri, to 2pm Sat & Sun Nov-Mar); **Valpolicella** (✆045 770 19 20; www.valpolicellaweb.it; Via Ingelheim 7, San Pietro in Cariano; ⏰9am-1pm Mon-Sat)

◉ SIGHTS & ACTIVITIES

◉ Soave

Southeast of Verona and an easy day trip, Soave serves its namesake DOC white wine in a storybook setting. The town is entirely encircled by medieval fortifications, including 24 bristling watchtowers guarding a medieval castle. Wine is the main reason to come here, with tastings available throughout the year.

CASTELLO DI SOAVE   HISTORIC BUILDING

(✆045 768 00 36; www.castellodisoave.it; adult/reduced €7/4; ⏰9am-noon & 3-6.30pm Tue-Sun Apr-Oct, 9am-noon & 2-4pm Nov-Mar) Built on a medieval base by Verona's fratricidal Scaligeri family, the Castello complex encompasses an early Renaissance villa, grassy courtyards, the remnants of a Romanesque church and the Mastio (the defensive tower apparently used as a dungeon): during restoration, a mound of human bones was unearthed here. The highlight for most, however, will be the panoramas of the surrounding countryside from the many rampart viewing points.

AZIENDA AGRICOLA COFFELE WINERY

(☑045 768 00 07; www.coffele.it; Via Roma 5; wine tasting €9-12; ☺9.30am-7.30pm Mon-Sat, 10am-1pm & 2-7pm Sun) Across from the old-town church, this family-run winery offers tastings of lemon-zesty DOC Soave Classico and an elegant, creamy DOC Coffele Ca' Visco Classico. The family also rents out rooms among vineyards a few kilometres from town. Book wine tastings in advance; at least a day ahead in winter and about a week ahead in summer.

★SUAVIA WINERY

(☑045 767 50 89; www.suavia.it; Via Centro 14, Fittà; ☺9am-1pm & 2.30-6.30pm Mon-Fri, 9am-1pm Sat & by appointment; ℗) Soave is not known as a complex white, but this trail-blazing winery, located 8km outside Soave via the SP39, has been changing the viticul-tural landscape in recent years. Don't miss DOC Monte Carbonare Soave Classico, with its mineral, ocean-breeze finish.

◉ Valpolicella

The 'valley of many cellars', from which Valpolicella gets its name, has been in the business of wine production since the ancient Greeks introduced their *passito* technique (the use of partially dried grapes) to create the blockbuster flavours we still enjoy in the region's Amarone and Recioto wines.

Situated in the foothills of Monte Lessini, the valleys benefit from a happy microclimate created by the enormous body of Lake Garda to the west and cool-ing breezes from the Alps to the north. No wonder Veronese nobility got busy build-ing weekend retreats here. Many of them, like the extraordinary Villa della Torre, still house noble wineries, while others have been transformed into idyllic places to stay and eat.

VILLA DELLA TORRE HISTORIC BUILDING

(☑045 683 20 70; www.villadellatorre.it; Via della Torre 25, Fumane; villa guided tours €10, with wine tasting & snack €30-40; ☺villa tours 11am & 4pm Mon-Sat by appointment; ℗) The jewel in the Allegrini crown, this historic villa dates to the mid-16th century and was built by intellectual and humanist Giulio della Torre. Numerous starchitects contributed to its construction: the classi-cally inspired peristyle and fish pond are

attributed to Giulio Romana (of Palazzo Te fame), the chapel to Michele Sanmicheli, and the monstrous, gaping-mouthed fire-places to Bartolomeo Ridolfi and Giovanni Battista Scultori.

ALLEGRINI WINERY

(☑045 683 20 11; www.allegrini.it; Via Giare 9/11, Fumane; wine tasting & cellar tour €20, tour of villa €10, tour of villa with wine tasting & snack €30-40; ☺cellar tour & wine tasting 10.30am & 3.30pm Mon-Fri by appointment, villa tours 11am & 4pm Mon-Sat by appointment; ℗) The Allegrini family have been tending vines in Fumane, Sant'Ambrogio and San Pietro since the 16th century, and have been one of the leading wineries of the Valpolicella region. Pride of place goes to the *cru* wines produced from Corvinia and Rondinella grapes grown on the La Grola hillside (La Poja, La Grola and Palazzo della Torre). Wine tastings in the historic 16th-century **Villa della Torre** are a fabulous experience.

VILLA MOSCONI BERTANI WINERY

(☑045 602 07 44; www.mosconibertani.it; Via Novare, Arbizzano; tours €10, tastings from €20; ☺wine tastings & tours 2pm & 4pm Sun-Fri, 10am Tue-Sun) This grand winery housed in a small chateau offers both wine tastings and tours of the building. There is a choice of four tasting sessions, most of them in-volving superior Valpolicello wines such as Lepia Soave Doc, Amarone Classico Docg and Torre Pieve Chardonnay. Afterwards, take a turn around the sumptuously ro-mantic chateau gardens.

ZÝMĒ WINERY

(☑045 770 11 08; www.zyme.it; Via Cà del Pipa 1, San Pietro in Cariano; wine tastings €15; ☺shop 9am-5pm Mon-Sat, tastings by appointment 9am-noon & 2-6pm Mon-Sat) An award-winning winery with striking contemporary archi-tecture by Moreno Zurlo, an ancient quarry turned cellar, and a reputation for bold, big-blend wines. The most famous of these is Zýmē's signature Harlequin, a thrilling, opulent IGP wine made using 15 local grape varieties (11 red, four white). Book wine tastings in advance; around three weeks for Saturday tastings, and around 10 days for weekday tastings.

PIEVE DI SAN GIORGIO CHURCH

(☑347 248 67 87; www.sangiorgiodivalpolicella.it; Piazza della Pieve, San Giorgio di Valpolicella; ☺7am-6pm) FREE In the tiny hilltop vil-

DAY TRIPS FROM VENICE VERONA'S WINE COUNTRY

OVERNIGHTING IN VALPOLICELLA

If you'd like to extend your wine tour consider overnighting at the vineyard-cum-relais **Massimago** (☑045 888 01 43; Via Giare 21, Mezzane di Sotto; wine tastings from €10, 2-person apt €120-150, 4-person apt €220-250; ⊙9am-6pm Mon-Fri, by appointment Sat & Sun; ℗). Dynamic hostess Camilla Chauvenet took over the winery when she was just 20 years old and has since been turning out lighter, more modern versions of the classics, including an unusual rosé and sparkling variety. The on-site four-room relais is as elegant and refined as the wines. Call ahead for wine tastings, which are preferred in the afternoon.

lage of San Giorgio, around 6km northwest of San Pietro in Cariano, you'll find this fresco-filled, cloistered 8th-century Romanesque church. Not old enough for you? In the little garden to its left you can also see a few fragments of an ancient Roman temple.

✖ EATING & DRINKING

★**LOCANDA LO SCUDO**   MODERN ITALIAN €€
(☑045 768 07 66; www.loscudo.vr.it; Via Cavergnino 9, Soave; meals €35; ⊙noon-2.30pm & 7.30-10.30pm Tue-Sat, noon-2.30pm Sun; 🛜) Just outside the medieval walls of Soave, Lo Scudo is half country inn and half high-powered gastronomy. Cult classics include a risotto of scallops and porcini mushrooms, though – if it's on the menu – only a fool would resist the extraordinary dish of tortelloni stuffed with local pumpkin, Grana Padano, cinnamon, mustard and Amaretto, and topped with crispy fried sage.

Above the restaurant, the owners rent out four bright, lovely rooms (single/double €85/95) that continue the theme of countrified sophistication.

★**OSTERIA NUMERO UNO**   OSTERIA €€
(☑045 770 13 75; www.osterianumero1.com; Via Flaminio Pellegrini 2, Fumane; meals €15-30; ⊙noon-2.30pm & 7-10.30pm Thu-Mon, noon-2.30pm Tue) The archetypal *osteria* with a wooden bar packed with overall-clad vintners and delicious aromas wafting

out of the kitchen. Glasses of Valpolicella (around 120 types) range from just €2 to €5 for a good Amarone. Pair them with salty speck and belly-filling duck with wild garlic and gnocchi.

★**ENOTECA DELLA VALPOLICELLA**   VENETIAN €€
(☑045 683 91 46; www.enotecadellavalpolicella. it; Via Osan 47, Fumane; meals €25; ⊙noon-2.30pm Sun, noon-2.30pm & 7.30-10pm Tue-Sat) Gastronomes flock to the town of Fumane, just a few kilometres north of San Pietro in Cariano, where an ancient farmhouse has found renewed vigour as a rustically elegant restaurant. Put your trust in gracious owners Ada and Carlotta, who will eagerly guide you through the day's menu, a showcase for fresh, local produce.

Among the more unusual dishes is a risotto made using local Recioto wine and shredded chocolate. The 700-bottle wine list is an oenophile's dream.

TRATTORIA CAPRINI   TRATTORIA €€
(☑045 750 05 11; www.trattoriacaprini.it; Via Zanotti 9, Torbe; meals €30; ⊙noon-2.30pm & 7-10pm Thu-Tue) A little north of Negrar in the hamlet of Torbe, family-run Caprini serves heart-warming fare you wish your mamma could make. Many menu items are homemade, including the delicious *lasagnetta* with hand-rolled pasta, and a *ragù* of beef, tomato, porcini and *finferlo* mushrooms. Downstairs, beside the fire of the old *pistoria* (bakery), you can sample some 200 Valpolicella labels.

Sleeping

Venice was once known for charmingly decrepit hotels where English poets quietly expired, but new design-literate boutique hotels are spiffing up historic palaces. In peak seasons quality hotels fill up fast. In summer, many people decamp to the Lido where prices are more reasonable and swimming is an option at the end of hot days in the Rialto.

More Options than Ever

Venice offers plenty of luxe hotels along the Grand Canal and Riva degli Schiavone, and there's also a growing inventory of boutique sleeps. At the same time, the internet has made it much easier for locals to rent out their homes (or extra rooms) and short-term rentals are increasingly popular.

For budget travellers, Venice offers a range of hostels (called *foresterie*). Some bunks even have canal or garden views. During summer, university housing also opens to tourists.

Location, Location, Location

Although Venice is a small city, getting around it amid tourist crowds and on slow *vaporetti* (small passenger ferries) can take time, so plan where you stay carefully. Easy access to the Grand Canal or a convenient *vaporetto* stop is key, although San Marco has all the best sights, and *sestiere* (districts) such as Dorsoduro, Cannaregio and Castello have all the best restaurants and bars. For those on a budget, Giudecca, Murano and the Lido are all within 15 to 30 minutes of the Rialto and are cheaper, quieter and more authentically Venetian.

Season Matters

In low season – November, early December, and January to March (except around New Year's, Carnevale and Easter) – you can expect discounts of 20% or more off peak rates. Even in high season, midweek rates tend to be lower than weekend ones. By contrast, expect to pay a hefty premium during Carnevale, New Year's and Easter.

Rates cited here should be considered a guide, since hotels often make constant adjustments according to season, day of week and holidays of varying importance.

Amenities

In general, rooms tend to be small in Venice – and sometimes dark or awkwardly shaped as per the quirks of ancient *palazzi* (mansions). Unless otherwise stated, guestrooms come with private bathroom, often with a shower rather than a bathtub. Business centres are rarely well equipped, even in swanky hotels. Only a few large hotels have a pool – mostly on the Lido or private islands. While increasingly available, wi-fi doesn't always penetrate thick stone walls and may only be available in common areas.

Buyer Beware

Not all hotels in Venice are grand: some are cramped, frayed and draughty, with lackadaisical service. Budget and midrange places around the train station tend to be especially dreary – sometimes despite glowing internet 'reviews'. Note also that many hotels boast of 'Venetian-style' rooms. Sometimes this implies real antiques and Murano chandeliers, but it can mean a kitsch version of baroque in rooms whose former charms have been remodelled out of existence.

Lonely Planet's Top Choices

Cima Rosa (p192) A stylish contemporary bolt-hole with Grand Canal views.

Al Ponte Antico (p193) A silk-swathed *palazzo* (mansion) with views of the Rialto Bridge.

Oltre Il Giardino (p191) Stylish secret-garden hideaway in the heart of Venice.

Hotel Palazzo Barbarigo (p192) Dark, plush elegance right on the Grand Canal.

Corte di Gabriela (p188) Cool, contemporary interiors framed by 19th-century elegance.

Best by Budget

€

Allo Squero (p192) Cannaregio home comforts.

Le Terese (p188) A home from home with two architect-styled rooms.

Albergo San Samuele (p187) Rock-bottom prices right by Palazzo Grassi.

Generator (p195) Contemporary hostel with canal views.

€€

Locanda Ca' Le Vele (p192) Boutique B&B with a heavy dose of Venetian glam.

Venice Halldis Apartments (p192) Light, bright, well-priced, Scandi-style modern apartments.

Oltre Il Giardino (p191) A romantic garden retreat once home to Alma Mahler's widow.

Residenza de L'Osmarin (p193) A true B&B with quilted bedspreads and a slap-up breakfast.

Casa Burano (p196) Pastel-coloured cottages full of locally crafted furnishings.

€€€

Gritti Palace (p188) Grand Canal rooms in a doge's palace.

Al Ponte Antico (p193) Old-world glamour accompanied by gracious service.

Hotel Palazzo Barbarigo (p192) Seductive rooms with fainting couches.

Best Boutique Hotels

Corte di Gabriela (p188) Design greats bring palace living into the 21st century.

Hotel Palazzo Barbarigo (p192) A decadent concoction of smokey mirrors and curvaceous deco accents.

Cima Rosa (p192) Grand Canal living with an eye to contemporary styling.

Hotel Moresco (p190) Restrained Venetian style and a spoiling walled garden.

Best for Romance

Al Ponte Antico (p193) A Grand Canal hideaway worthy of Casanova.

Oltre Il Giardino (p191) Effortless elegance with a whimsical, artistic soul.

Locanda Cipriani (p196) Rustic style and a garden full of roses.

Ca' Maria Adele (p190) High baroque interiors and an intimate, hushed atmosphere.

Best for Heritage

Gritti Palace (p188) A prestigious, landmark hotel full of opulent details.

Palazzo Abadessa (p193) A frescoed palace ready for romance since 1540.

Hotel Palazzo Barbarigo (p192) Boudoir glamour in a 16th-century palace.

NEED TO KNOW

Prices

The following price ranges refer to a double room with bathroom. Unless otherwise stated, breakfast is included in the price.

€	less than €110
€€	110–200
€€€	over €200

Reservations

➡ Book ahead at weekends and during high season.

➡ The best, and best-value, hotels are always in high demand; book well ahead.

➡ Check individual hotel websites for online deals.

➡ Confirm arrival at least 72 hours in advance in high season.

Getting to Your Hotel

➡ Pack light to better negotiate twisting alleys and footbridges.

➡ Try to arrive during daylight to avoid getting lost in night-time Venice.

➡ Get directions from your hotel, plus a detailed map.

➡ Water taxis can be worth the price for night arrivals or if you're heavily laden.

Breakfast

Except in higher-end places, breakfast tends to be utilitarian. *Affittacamere* (rooms for rent) generally don't offer breakfast because of strict dining codes. However, you're never far from a great local cafe.

SLEEPING

Where to Stay

NEIGHBOURHOOD	FOR	AGAINST
San Marco	Historic and design hotels in central location, optimal for sightseeing and shopping.	Rooms often small with little natural light; streets crowded and noisy in the morning; fewer good restaurant options.
Dorsoduro	Lively art and student scenes, with design hotels near museums and seaside getaways along Zattere.	Lively student scene can mean noise echoing from Campo Santa Margherita until 2am, especially on weekends.
San Polo & Santa Croce	Top value on spacious B&Bs and opulent boutique hotels with prime local dining, the Rialto Market, drinking and shopping; convenient to train and bus.	Easy to get lost in maze of streets, and it may be a long walk to major sights and a *vaporetto* (small passenger ferry) stop.
Cannaregio	Venice's best deals on B&Bs with character and hotels convenient to the train and bus stop, with canal-bank happy hours and restaurants frequented by locals.	Long walk or *vaporetto* ride to San Marco sightseeing; pedestrian traffic between train station and Rialto.
Castello	Calmer and fewer tourists as you move away from San Marco; good budget options close to San Marco and the park.	The eastern fringes near Sant'Elena are far away from key sights and devoid of services.
Giudecca, Lido & the Southern Islands	Good value for money; beaches within walking distance in summer; fewer tourists.	Far from the action, especially at night; must rely on expensive *vaporetti* and less frequent services at night.
Murano, Burano & the Northern Islands	Murano is a crowd-free, good-value alternative base within 10 minutes of Cannaregio. Outer islands are remote, but great for gourmet weekend retreats.	Limited eating and drinking options; outer islands are far from Venice; very quiet in low season.

🛏 San Marco

ALBERGO SAN SAMUELE   HOTEL €

Map p266 (☑041 520 51 65; www.hotelsansamu
ele.com; Salizada San Samuele 3358; r from
€99, s/d without bathroom €72/81; @🛜; 🛥San
Samuele) These neat and friendly digs offer
10 recently renovated rooms at reasonable
prices, three of which share bathrooms.
There's no air-con and breakfast isn't
served, but there's free tea and coffee and
you're steps away from cafe-fringed Campo
San Stefano.

LOCANDA ART DÉCO   HOTEL €

Map p266 (☑041 277 05 58; www.locandaartdeco.
com; Calle de le Botteghe 2966; s/d from €78/101;
❄🛜; 🛥Sant'Angelo) Rakishly handsome,
cream-coloured guestrooms with terrazzo
marble floors, antique tables and comfy
beds in wrought-iron bed frames. Wood-
beamed lofts are romantic hideaways, if you
don't mind low ceilings and stairs.

★REZIDENZA CORTE ANTICA   B&B €€

Map p266 (☑335 1863555; www.residenzacorte
antica.com; Calle Frutarol 2876; r from €119; ❄🛜;
🛥Accademia) A tasteful renovation showcases the ancient wooden beams and stone
staircases of this historic Venetian house,
hidden down a small lane at the far end of
the San Marco quarter. Each of the three
romantic guestrooms is simply decorated
with white walls and linen, and antique-
style beds – including one four-poster.

★B&B AL TEATRO   B&B €€

Map p266 (☑333 9182494; www.bedandbreak
fastalteatro.com; Fondamenta de la Fenice 2554;
r from €165; 🛜; 🛥Giglio) With La Fenice for
your neighbour and a chorus of singing
gondolieri passing beneath your windows,
you'll need to book early to nab one of the
three rooms in Eleonora's 15th-century
family home. Inside, old-world elegance
meets a minimalist style with white linen
and Murano chandeliers. Eleonora hosts
breakfast every morning tossing out recommendations over freshly brewed coffee.

HOTEL FLORA   HOTEL €€

Map p266 (☑041 520 58 44; www.hotelflora.it;
Calle dei Bergamaschi 2283a; s/d from €134/151;
❄🛜❄; 🛥Giglio) Down a lane from glitzy
Calle Larga XXII Marzo, this ivy-covered
retreat quietly outclasses brash designer
neighbours with its delightful tearoom and

breakfasts around the garden fountain. Guestrooms feature antique mirrors, fluffy duvets
atop hand-carved beds and tiled en-suite
bathrooms with apothecary-style amenities.
Damask-clad superior rooms overlook the
garden. Strollers and kids' teatime are complimentary; babysitting available.

HOTEL AL CODEGA   HOTEL €€

Map p266 (☑041 241 32 88; www.hotelalcodega.
com; Corte del Forno Vecchio 4435; s/d from
€104/137; ❄🛜; 🛥Rialto) Unicorns are easier
to find in Venice than a quiet, bright, affordable hotel, five minutes' walk to Piazza San
Marco – yet here you have it. This flower-
trimmed yellow inn takes pride of place in
a hidden-away square, reached through a
sotopòrtego (passageway) off a quiet lane.
Rooms are romantic, if not overly large,
with swagged curtains and marble-clad
bathrooms.

CA' DEL NOBILE   HOTEL €€

Map p266 (☑041 528 34 73; www.cadelnobile.
com; Rio Terà de le Colonne 987; r from €149;
❄🛜❄; 🛥Rialto) Move over, Casanova – Ca'
del Nobile makes romantic getaways easy.
The exposed-brick Casanova room has a
canopied bed; cosy standards have wood-
beamed ceilings and sleigh beds; deluxe
rooms have room for daybeds and cribs.

GIÒ & GIÒ   B&B €€

Map p266 (☑347 3665016; www.giogioven
ice.com; Calle de le Ostreghe 2439; s/d from
€140/150; ❄🛜; 🛥Giglio) Restrained baroque
sounds like an oxymoron, but here you
have it: burl-wood bedsteads, pearl-grey
silk draperies, polished parquet floors and
spotlit art. Packaged breakfasts are available in the shared kitchen. Ideally located
near Piazza San Marco, along a side canal;
angle for rooms overlooking the gondola
stop, and wake to choruses of '*Volare, oh-
oh-oooooh!*'

HOTEL AI DO MORI   HOTEL €€

Map p266 (☑041 520 48 17; www.hotelaido
mori.com; Calle Larga San Marco 658; s/d from
€90/130, without bathroom from €60/110;
❄🛜; 🛥San Zaccaria) Artist's garrets just
off Piazza San Marco, each as snug as an
Arsenale ship's cabin. Book ahead to score
upper-floor rooms with sloped wood-
beamed ceilings, parquet floors, wall tapestries and close-up views of basilica domes
and the clock tower's Do Mori (bell ring-
ers) in action. Ask for No 11, with a private

terrace – but pack light, because there's no lift.

LOCANDA CASA PETRARCA   B&B €€

Map p266 (☑041 520 04 30; www.casapetrarca. com; Calle Schiavine 4386; r with/without bathroom from €120/100; ❄️🛜; 🚊San Marco) A budget option with heart and character, this family-run place offers seven unfussy, sparkling rooms in a historic brick apartment building, with breakfast serenades from passing gondolas. Five rooms have air-con and en-suite bathrooms; rooms facing the side canal are brighter and slightly bigger. Fair warning: the route to nearby Piazza San Marco is lined with tempting boutiques.

★GRITTI PALACE   HOTEL €€€

Map p266 (☑041 79 46 11; www.thegrittipalace. com; Campo di Santa Maria del Giglio 2467; r from €874; ❄️🛜; 🚊Giglio) Guests at the Gritti Palace on the Grand Canal don't have to leave their balconies to go sightseeing: this landmark 1525 doge's palace sports Landmark Grand Canal rooms with Rubelli silk damask lining, antique fainting couches, stucco ceilings, hand-painted vanities and bathrooms sheathed in rare marble.

★CORTE DI GABRIELA   HOTEL €€€

Map p266 (☑041 523 50 77; www.cortedigabriela. com; Calle dei Avvocati 3836; r from €270; ❄️🛜; 🚊Sant'Angelo) Yes, Corte di Gabriela is a 19th-century *palazzo,* but there's nothing old or traditional about its 11 rooms, which inventively play with the palace's historic features, combining frescoed ceilings and terrazzo floors with contemporary design pieces, high-spec finishes and a modern colour palette. The views are undeniably romantic, and the atmosphere sophisticated.

LOCANDA ORSEOLO   B&B €€€

Map p266 (☑041 520 48 27; www.locandaorseolo. com; Corte Zorzi 1083; r from €200; ❄️🛜; 🚊San Marco) Hide out behind Piazza San Marco: no one will know but the *gondolieri,* who regularly row past the lobby. Consistently warm greetings and cosy wood-trimmed rooms – some with vintage-kitsch Carnevale murals – make this the ideal launch pad.

NOVECENTO   BOUTIQUE HOTEL €€€

Map p266 (☑041 241 37 65; www.novecento. biz; Calle del Dose 2683/84; r from €200; ❄️🛜; 🚊Giglio) Sporting a boho-chic look, the Novecento is a real charmer. Its nine individually designed rooms ooze style with Turkish kilim pillows, Fortuny draperies and 19th-century carved bedsteads. You can mingle with creative fellow travellers around the honesty bar, while outside, its garden is a lovely spot to linger over breakfast.

PALAZZO PARUTA   HOTEL €€€

Map p266 (☑041 241 08 35; www.palazzoparuta.com; Campo San Anzolo 3824; r from €233; ❄️🛜; 🚊Sant'Angelo) Kissing frogs won't get you princely palace getaways like this: lantern-lit courtyard staircases beckon to silken boudoir bedrooms with mirrored bedsteads and Carrara marble en-suite bathrooms. Museum-worthy suites feature velvet-draped beds, stuccoed ceilings and parquet or terrazzo floors; ask for canal views. Breakfasts seduce gourmets with freshly squeezed juices, local cheeses, cured meats, fresh pastries, pancakes and eggs.

BLOOM   B&B €€€

Map p266 (☑340 1498872; www.bloom-venice. com; Campiello Santo Stefano 3470; r from €208; ❄️🛜; 🚊Sant'Angelo) Occupying the top floor of a historic home overlooking Santo Stefano, Bloom has glam-rock rooms in shocking scarlet, fuchsia and gold damask, with leather bedsteads and breakfast on a sunny terrace. Downstairs, sister property Settimo Cielo (Seventh Heaven) is artfully romantic. A third sibling, Locanda Fiorita, is a cheaper option, with some single rooms and shared bathrooms.

🛏 Dorsoduro

★LE TERESE   B&B €

Map p276 (☑041 523 17 28; www.leterese.com; Campiello Tron 1902; d €80-100; 🛜; 🚊San Basilio) Join architectural duo Antonella and Mauro in their 18th-century granary on the Rio Terese for a dose of local living. There are just two rooms overlooking the canal and both are furnished in understated style with comfortable beds, Persian rugs and modernist furniture. The large, marble tiled bathroom is shared, which just adds to the home-from-home feeling.

SILK ROAD   HOSTEL €

Map p276 (☑388 1196816; www.silkroadhostel. com; Calle Corteloto 1420e; dm €50-60, d €100-120; 🛜; 🚊San Basilio) Breathe easy along the Giudecca Canal in this clean, hassle-free hostel, complete with communal kitchen and, best of all, no curfew. Both of the airy, four-bed dorms (one mixed gender, one female-only) come with water views, and there's one private room to boot. The hostel is down the block from a supermarket, canalside cafes and gelaterie, plus handy *vaporetto* stops.

B&B LEONARDO
B&B €

Map p276 (☑347 6805871; www.bebleonardo. com; Calle delle Botteghe 3153; d €60-180, tr €80-250; ✹ 🛜; ⬤Ca' Rezzonico) Take a break from baroque in this serene, simple retreat overlooking Ca' Rezzonico's formal garden. Two snug, shipshape guestrooms await upstairs (no lift), with TVs stashed in deco dressers and compact private bathrooms. Rates rarely hit maximum and a basic breakfast is included.

★PENSIONE ACCADEMIA VILLA MARAVEGE
INN €€

Map p276 (☑041 521 01 88; www.pensioneaccademia.it; Fondamenta Bollani 1058; d €190-260; ✹🛜🛗; ⬤Accademia) Step through the ivy-covered gate of this 17th-century garden villa just off the Grand Canal, and you'll forget you're a block from the Accademia. Although some of the 27 guestrooms are rather small, all are effortlessly elegant, with parquet floors, antique desks and shiny bathrooms – one even comes with four-poster bed, wood-beamed ceilings and glimpses of the canal.

Ask to stay in Thelma, a superior double with its own patch of greenery, named after a regular who loved reading in the garden. Buffet breakfasts are served on the lawn in summer, sunsets are toasted with a complimentary drink at the bar, and garden swings for two promise romance under the stars. Wheelchair-accessible rooms and

wheelchair use upon request. Laundry service available for an additional fee.

HOTEL GALLERIA
INN €€

Map p276 (☑041 523 24 89; www.hotelgalleria. it; Campo della Carità 878a; s €120-150, d €200-290; 🛜🛗; ⬤Accademia) Smack on the Grand Canal alongside the Ponte dell'Accademia is this classic hotel in a converted 18th-century mansion decked out with floral silk wallpaper and imposing period furnishings. Book ahead, especially for rooms 7 and 9, small doubles overlooking the Grand Canal. Room 10 sleeps six and comes with an original ceiling fresco.

LOCANDA SAN BARNABA
B&B €€

Map p276 (☑041 241 12 33; www.locanda-sanbarnaba.com; Calle del Traghetto 2785-6; s €90-115, d €140-185; ✹🛜; ⬤Ca' Rezzonico) The stage is set for intrigue at this 16th-century *palazzo*, with its frescoed grand salon, hidden courtyard garden and cupboards concealing a secret staircase. Ask for the romantic wood-beamed Poeta Fanatico room; Campiello, with skylight views of a neighbouring bell tower; or the superior Il Cavaliere e la Dama, for 18th-century frescoed ceilings and balconies dangling over the canal.

PALAZZO GUARDI
B&B €€

Map p276 (☑041 296 07 25; www.palazzoguardi venice.com; Calle del Pistor 995; d €150-230; ✹@🛜🛗; ⬤Accademia) Relive the Renaissance at 15th-century Palazzo Guardi, right around the corner from Accademia – you're never more than a minute away from a Titian masterpiece or glass of Amarone. Dashing baroque-style guestrooms with modern bathrooms accommodate two to five guests,

---

RENTALS & BOOKING SERVICES

For longer stays and groups of three or more, renting an apartment is an economical option that gives you the freedom to cook your own meals. To rent a studio for yourself, expect to pay €800 to €1200 per month.

Luxrest Venice (Map p280; ☑041 296 05 61; www.luxrest-venice.com; Ponte del Pistor 5990, Castello) Carefully curated, hand-picked selection of apartments.

Lonely Planet (www.lonelyplanet.com/italy/venice/hotels) Expert author reviews, user feedback, booking engine.

Venice Prestige (www.veniceprestige.com) The crème de la crème of Venetian apartments to rent in aristocratic *palazzi* (mansions) in the best locations in town.

Views on Venice (☑041 241 11 49; www.viewsonvenice.com) A comprehensive selection of apartments picked for their personality, character and view, of course.

but only the suites and breakfast room have canal vistas worthy of a Guardi painting.

LA CHICCA
B&B €€

Map p276 (☑041 522 55 35; www.lachicca-venezia.com; Calle Franchi 644; d €170; ❄🐕; ⛴Accademia) Neatly wedged among Dorsoduro's trifecta of museums – Accademia, Peggy Guggenheim and Punta della Dogana – yet all you'll hear at night in this elegant B&B is the lapping of the canal at the end of the *calle*. Hosts Sabrina and Massimo are helpful, their Venetian damask-clad, terrazzo-floored guestrooms spacious and blessedly uncluttered after a museum binge.

LA CALCINA
HOTEL €€

Map p276 (☑041 520 64 66; www.lacalcina.com; Zattere 780; s €100-130, d €185-250; ❄@🐕; ⛴Zattere) Upgrade from ordinary seaside resorts to La Calcina, with breezy roof-garden breakfasts, a canalside restaurant, and panoramas of Palladio's Redentore church across Giudecca Canal. Antique armoires and brocade bedspreads come as standard in parquet-floored guestrooms. Bathrooms are clean though tired and uninspiring. Book ahead for waterfront rooms – especially No 2, where John Ruskin wrote his classic *The Stones of Venice* (1876).

CA' DELLA CORTE
B&B €€

Map p276 (☑041 71 58 77; www.cadellacorte.com; Campo Surian 3560; d €110-185; ❄🐕🚌; ⛴Piazzale Roma) Live like a Venetian in this 16th-century family home with a Liberty frescoed salon, piano room, self-service bar, top-floor terrace, and breakfast delivered to your room. Stay in wood-beamed garrets, chandelier-lit superior rooms or feng shui eco-rooms. Sporty types should ask helpful staff to organise sailing, tennis and horse-riding on the Lido; babysitting and shiatsu massage are also available.

★HOTEL MORESCO
BOUTIQUE HOTEL €€€

Map p276 (☑041 244 02 02; www.hotelmoresco venice.com; Fondamente del Passamonte 3499; d €280-390; ❄; ⛴Piazzale Roma) A complimentary glass of *prosecco* (sparkling white wine) at check-in and a daily *aperitivo* (pre-dinner drinks) hour in the walled garden will give you an idea of the welcoming and friendly service you'll encounter at this lovely hotel. Rooms are similarly well cared for with fine fabrics, elaborate wallpapers, plush sofas and sleek modern bathrooms.

Staff can help with all manner of things, and do.

CA' MARIA ADELE
BOUTIQUE HOTEL €€€

Map p276 (☑041 520 30 78; www.camariaadele.it; Rio Terà dei Catecumeni 111; d €380-640; ⛴Salute) If your vision of Venice includes a Grand Canal palace full of crushed velvet, gold wallpaper, mad Murano chandeliers and marbled bathrooms then this decadent boutique hotel is for you. It's quietly situated overlooking a canal and offers an impressive level of personal service. Unsurprisingly it's full of lovebirds who can be found canoodling on the 2nd-floor terrace.

CA' PISANI
DESIGN HOTEL €€€

Map p276 (☑041 240 14 11; www.capisanihotel.it; Rio Terà Antonio Foscarini 979a; d €230-370; ❄@🐕; ⛴Accademia) Sprawl out in style right behind the Accademia, and luxuriate in sleigh beds, Jacuzzi tubs and walk-in closets. Mood lighting and sound-proofed walls make downstairs deco-accented rooms right for romance; families will appreciate top-floor rooms with sleeping lofts. Venetian winters require in-house Turkish steam baths, while summers mean roof-terrace sunning and patio breakfasts. A hushed, elegant, antiques-laced retreat.

🛏 San Polo & Santa Croce

AL GALLION
B&B €

Map p270 (☑380 4520466, 041 524 47 43; www.algallion.com; Calle Gallion 1126, Santa Croce; d €75-110; 🐕; ⛴Riva de Biasio) A couple of bridges away at train station hotels, weary tourists wait at front desks – but at this 16th-century family home, you'll be chatting and sipping espresso in the living room. The whitewashed guestroom (which can be divided in two and turned into a quad) is handsomely furnished with walnut desks, cheerful yellow bedspreads, terrazzo floors and host Daniela's family art collection. Breakfasts are homemade spreads; tasty, affordable restaurants abound nearby.

L'IMBARCADERO
HOSTEL €

Map p270 (☑328 5880102; http://imbarcadero.hostelvenice.net; Calle Zen 1268, Santa Croce; dm €59; ⊙reception 8.30am-10pm; 🐕; ⛴Riva de Biasio) A five-minute walk from the train station, this friendly hostel in Santa Croce offers worn but comfortable mixed and female-only dorms with single beds and the occasional Grand Canal view. Prices include a buffet breakfast, use of a communal kitchen and wi-fi.

★ OLTRE IL GIARDINO   BOUTIQUE HOTEL €€

Map p270 (☑041 275 00 15; www.oltreilgiardino-venezia.com; Fondamenta Contarini 2542, San Polo; d €180, ste €230-280; ❄ 🐾; 🚤San Tomà) Live the dream in this garden villa, the 1920s home of Alma Mahler, the composer's widow. Hidden behind a lush walled garden, its six high-ceilinged guestrooms marry historic charm with modern comfort: marquetry composer's desks, candelabras and 19th-century poker chairs sit alongside flat-screen TVs and designer bathrooms, while outside, pomegranate trees flower.

LA VILLEGGIATURA   B&B €€

Map p270 (☑041 524 46 73; www.lavilleggiatura.it; Calle dei Boteri 1569, San Polo; d €175-210; 🐾; 🚤Rialto-Mercato) Barbara and Francesca's ebullient personalities are on display in this charming B&B where six large, light-filled rooms are decorated with verve around different opera themes. The choicest rooms are on the *piano nobile* (main floor) and enjoy pretty views, king-sized beds and generous bathrooms with bath-tubs. Breakfast is taken at a communal table where guests are pampered by their genial hostesses.

AL PONTE MOCENIGO   HOTEL €€

Map p270 (☑041 524 47 97; www.alpontemocenigo.com; Fondamenta Rimpetto Mocenigo 2063, Santa Croce; d €160-185; ❄ 🐾; 🚤San Stae) A doge of a deal near the Grand Canal, just steps from the San Stae *vaporetto* stop, with prime dining and a handful of museums nearby. Reached via a petite bridge, this little oasis offers elegant guestrooms, some with Murano chandeliers illuminating high wood-beamed ceilings, four-poster beds, gilt-edged armoires and salon seating. Ask for a room overlooking Rio San Stae or the courtyard.

CA' ANGELI   BOUTIQUE HOTEL €€

Map p270 (☑041 523 24 80; www.caangeli.it; Calle del Traghetto de la Madoneta 1434, San Polo; d €165-240; ❄ 🐾; 🚤San Silvestro) Murano glass chandeliers, a Louis XIV love-seat and namesake 16th-century angels set a refined tone at this restored, canalside *palazzo*. Guestrooms are a picture with beamed ceilings, antique carpets and big bathrooms, while the dining room looks out onto the

Grand Canal. Breakfast includes organic products where possible.

DOMINA HOME CA' ZUSTO   BOUTIQUE HOTEL €€

Map p270 (☑041 524 29 91; www.dominavacanze.it; Campo Rielo 1358, Santa Croce; d €195-250; ❄ 🐾🛜; 🚤Riva di Biasio) Gothic goes pop at this palace, whose stately Veneto-Byzantine exterior disguises a colourful wild streak. Designer Gianmarco Cavagnino serves up 22 mod-striped, harem-styled suites named after Turkish princesses. Pedestal tables flank baroque beds fit for pashas, and Jacuzzis soothe frazzled darlings in the deluxe rooms. Wi-fi is only available on the 1st floor.

HOTEL AL DUCA   HOTEL €€

Map p270 (☑041 812 30 69; www.alducadivenezia.com; Fontego dei Turchi 1739, Santa Croce; d/apt €175/225; ❄ @ 🐾🛜; 🚤San Stae) Bedrooms swagged with red damask and black Murano chandeliers are Venetian bordellochic, honouring the courtesans that once ruled nearby Rialto backstreets, but the all-bronze guestrooms are serene Serenissima retreats. Get an insider's view of Venice at the family-friendly kitchenette apartments, conveniently close to Campo San Giacomo dell'Orio happy hours. Reception is open 24 hours; babysitting, laundry and wheelchair-accessible rooms are available.

PENSIONE GUERRATO   PENSION €€

Map p270 (☑041 528 59 27; www.hotelguerrato.com; Calle Drio la Scimia 240a, San Polo; d/tr/q €145/165/185, apt €160-280; ❄ 🐾; 🚤Rialto-Mercato) In a 1227 tower that was once a hostel for knights headed to the Third Crusade, the smart guestrooms here haven't lost their sense of history – some have frescoes or glimpses of the Grand Canal. Sparkling modern bathrooms, a prime Rialto Market location and helpful owners add to the package. No lift.

The owners also have three good-value apartments with kitchens, sleeping four to six people.

★CIMA ROSA
B&B €€€

Map p270 (☑373 7495041; www.cimarosaven ezia.com; Calle Tron 1958, Santa Croce; d €245-385; ⊛♨; ⛴San Stae) Although many B&Bs promise a 'living in Venice' experience, Cima Rosa, in the northern reaches of Santa Croce, delivers it in spades. There are just three suites and two doubles in this 15th-century *palazzo*, all with beamed ceilings, romantic pastel wall washes and stunning Grand Canal views. Breakfast in the stylish downstairs lounge. Let owner Brittany plan you an insider's itinerary.

★HOTEL PALAZZO BARBARIGO
DESIGN HOTEL €€€

Map p270 (☑041 74 01 72; www.palazzobarbarigo. com; Grand Canal 2765, San Polo; d €240-440; ⊛☎; ⛴San Tomà) Brooding, chic and seductive, Barbarigo delivers 18 plush guestrooms combining modern elegance and intrigue – think dark, contemporary furniture, sumptuous velvets, feathered lamps and the odd fainting couch. Whether you opt for a suite overlooking the Grand Canal (get triple-windowed Room 10) or a standard room overlooking Rio di San Polo, you can indulge in the sleek bathrooms, positively royal breakfasts and smart, attentive service.

🛏 Cannaregio

★ALLO SQUERO
B&B €

Map p274 (☑041 523 69 73; www.allosquero. it; Corte dello Squero 4692; r from €100; ☎♨; ⛴Fondamente Nove) Dock for the night at this historic gondola *squero* (shipyard), converted into a garden retreat. Gondolas float right by the windows of two of the rooms. All have their own bathrooms, although one is accessed from the corridor. Hosts Andrea and Hiroko offer Venice-insider tips over cappuccino and pastry breakfasts in the fragrant, wisteria-filled garden. Cots and cribs available.

WE CROCIFERI
HOSTEL, APARTMENT €

Map p274 (☑041 528 61 03; www.we-gastameco. com; Campo dei Gesuiti 4878; s/tw/apt from €20/72/109; ⊛☎; ⛴Fondamente Nove) In contrast to the bombastic Gesuiti church next door, this convent-turned-barracks-turned-hostel provides minimalist, white rooms overlooking a cloister. Used as university digs throughout the year, there's a friendly vibe to the place with an on-site cafe (breakfast isn't included), bar, laundry and communal kitchen.

CA' DOGARESSA
BOUTIQUE HOTEL €

Map p274 (☑041 275 9441; www.cadogaressa. com; Fondamenta di Cannaregio 1018; r annexe/ hotel from €85/105; ⊛@☎; ⛴Guglie) Venetian charm abounds at this family-run canalside inn. Rooms have princess beds, gilt mirrors, chandeliers and modern bathrooms. The views from the roof terrace and breakfasts by the canal in summer are memorable perks. An annexe around the corner can be rented as a three-bedroom apartment or as individual rooms; breakfast isn't offered and the bathrooms are shared.

★VENICE HALLDIS APARTMENTS
APARTMENT €€

Map p274 (☑024 795 22 00; www.venicehalldisa partments.com; Calle Priuli dei Cavalletti 96t; apt from €189; ⊛☎; ⛴Ferrovia) Modern apartment blocks are a rarity in central Venice, but this converted factory offers spacious, chic, well-equipped units which are surprisingly quiet, despite being just across a canal from the train station. Treats include laundry facilities, spacious wardrobes and showers with adjustable mood lighting which double as Turkish baths. The only downsides are the hard beds and no reception.

★LOCANDA CA' LE VELE
B&B €€

Map p274 (☑041 241 39 60; www.locandalevele. com; Calle de le Vele 3969; r/ste from €130/183; ⊛☎; ⛴Ca' d'Oro) The lane may be quiet and the house might look demure but inside it's Venetian glam all the way. The six guestrooms are a surprisingly stylish riot of terrazzo floors, damask furnishings, Murano glass sconces and ornate gilded beds with busy covers. Pay a little extra for a canal view.

3749 PONTE CHIODO
B&B €€

Map p274 (☑041 241 39 35; www.pontechiodo. it; Calle de la Racchetta 3749; r from €130; ⊛☎; ⛴Ca' d'Oro) This charming little B&B offers six sweet rooms with period furnishings, views over the canal and a private front garden. It takes its name from the bridge at the back door – the only remaining one without parapets. All bridges in Venice were once like this before too many drunks took the plunge and the government decreed new safety measures.

CASA BASEGGIO
B&B €€

Map p274 (☑348 3432069; www.casabaseggio.it; Fondamenta dell'Abazia 3556; r from €110; 🛜🖶; ⬢Orto) *Venexianárse* (become Venetian) at this family home converted to a B&B in a quiet Cannaregio corner, handy to happy-hour hot spots. The house is situated in a wing of the Misericordia abbey and from the 1st-floor bedroom there are views through the cypresses into the abbey garden. As well as two bedrooms upstairs, there's a self-contained flat on the ground floor.

GIARDINO DEI MELOGRANI
HOTEL €€

Map p274 (☑041 822 61 31; www.pardesrimonim. net; Campo del Ghetto Nuovo 2874; s €80-150, d €100-200; ❄🛜; ⬢Guglie) Run by Venice's Jewish community, to which all proceeds go, the 'Garden of Pomegranates' is a sparkling kosher residence located right at the heart of the Ghetto. However you don't have to be Jewish to enjoy the 20 bright modern rooms, with artwork themed around local plants. Some have canal views while others face the square.

CA' POZZO
HOTEL €€

Map p274 (☑041 524 05 04; www.capozzoinn. com; Calle de Ca' Pozzo 1279; s/d from €105/165; ❄@; ⬢Guglie) Recover from Venice's sensory onslaught at this low-slung minimalist-chic hotel hidden down a dead-end lane near the Ghetto. Sleek, contemporary guestrooms feature platform beds, abstract artwork and cube-shaped bathroom fixtures.

★AL PONTE ANTICO
BOUTIQUE HOTEL €€€

Map p274 (☑041 241 19 44; www.alponteantico. com; Calle dell'Aseo 5768; r from €320; ❄🛜; ⬢Rialto) Like a courtesan's boudoir, this 16th-century *palazzo* is swathed in damask wall coverings, heavy silk curtains and thick, plush carpets. A smiling host greets you at the padded, golden reception desk and whisks you up large, unabashedly lavish rooms with enough gilt to satisfy Louis XIV. In the evening, romance blossoms on the terrace, framed by views of Rialto Bridge.

★PALAZZO ABADESSA
BOUTIQUE HOTEL €€€

Map p274 (☑041 241 37 84; www.abadessa.com; Calle Priuli 4011; r from €245; ❄🛜; ⬢Ca' d'Oro) Evenings seem enchanted in this opulent 1540 *palazzo*, with staff fluffing pillows, plying guests with *prosecco*, arranging water taxis to the opera and plotting irresistible marriage proposals. Classic guestrooms feature kingly beds, silk-damask-clad walls, Murano glass lamps and wood-beamed ceilings. Frescoed superior rooms have 18th-century vanities and canal vistas. Breakfast is served in the tree-shaded, lily-perfumed garden.

🛏 Castello

B&B SAN MARCO
B&B €

Map p280 (☑041 522 75 89; www.realvenice.it; Fondamenta San Giorgio dei Schiavoni 3385l; r with/without bathroom €135/105; ❄; ⬢San Zaccaria) Alice and Marco welcome you warmly to their home overlooking Carpaccio's frescoed Scuola Dalmata. The 3rd-floor apartment (no lift), with its parquet floors and large windows, is furnished with family antiques and offers photogenic views over the terracotta rooftops and canals. The hosts live upstairs, so they're always on hand with great recommendations.

ALLOGGI BARBARIA
B&B €

Map p280 (☑041 522 27 50; www.alloggibarbaria. it; Calle de le Capucine 6573; r from €80; ❄🛜; ⬢Ospedale) Located near the Fondamente Nove, this *pensione* isn't easy to find – but that's part of its charm, and so are the intrepid fellow travellers you'll meet over breakfast on a shared balcony. All six rooms are simple but tidy, bright and airy.

RESIDENZA DE L'OSMARIN
B&B €€

Map p280 (☑347 4501440; www.residenzadelosmarin.com; Calle Rota 4960; r from €170; ❄🛜; ⬢San Zaccaria) This B&B is good value, especially considering it is barely 300m from Piazza San Marco. Rooms – one with a roof terrace and another with a courtyard-facing terrace – are quaintly decorated with quilted bedspreads, painted wardrobes and period furnishings. The hosts make guests feel warmly welcome with slap-up breakfasts of homemade cakes, brioche and platters of ham and cheese.

HOTEL LE ISOLE
HOTEL €€

Map p280 (☑041 522 89 11; www.hotel-leisole.it; Campo San Provolo 4661; r from €185; ❄@🛜; ⬢San Zaccaria) Barely a stone's throw from San Marco, this small, friendly hotel offers good value. Arranged around a vine-clad central courtyard, rooms are understated and elegant with wooden floors, Venetia

Studium lamps, Fortuny-style fabrics, cable TV and gleaming marble bathrooms. Breakfast is similarly generous: a buffet loaded with cold cuts, fruit and cakes, with eggs to order from the kitchen.

CA' DEI DOGI
BOUTIQUE HOTEL €€

Map p280 (☑041 241 37 51; www.cadeidogi.it; Corte Santa Scolastica 4242; s/d from €95/165; ❄☎; ⬛San Zaccaria) Even the nearby Bridge of Sighs can't dampen the high spirits of the sunny Ca' dei Dogi, with guestroom windows sneaking peeks into the convent cloisters next door. Streamlined, modern rooms look like ship cabins, with tilted wood-beamed ceilings, dressers that look like steamer trunks, and compact mosaic-covered bathrooms – ask for the one with the terrace and Jacuzzi.

HOTEL SANT'ANTONIN
HOTEL €€

Map p280 (☑041 523 16 21; www.hotelsantantonin.com; Fondamenta dei Furlani 3299; r from €185; ❄☎♿; ⬛San Zaccaria) Enjoy patrician pleasures at this 16th-century *palazzo* perched on a canal near the Greek church. Grand proportions make for light, spacious rooms with cool terrazzo floors, geranium-draped balconies, frescoed ceilings and impressive furnishings. Trip down the stone staircase and out into one of the largest private gardens in Venice, complete with a pretty stone pergola and gurgling fountain.

HOTEL SANT'ELENA
HOTEL €€

Map p282 (☑041 271 78 11; www.hotelsantelena.com; Calle Buccari 10; s/d from €185/190; ❄@☎♿; ⬛Sant'Elena) Once a convent, then a navy-owned holiday resort for admirals and now a Best Western, this hotel's quiet location, spacious halls, grassy cloister and ample, window-lined rooms are unusual for Venice. Inside, a minimalist, modern style complements the 1930s Brutalist makeover while providing a high level of comfort and facilities. Families are particularly well catered for.

PALAZZO SCHIAVONI
APARTMENT €€

Map p280 (☑041 241 12 75; www.palazzoschiavoni.com; Fondamenta dei Furlani 3288; apt from €140; ❄☎♿; ⬛San Zaccaria) The refurbishment of this 15th-century *palazzo* into an apartment hotel retained many of its period features while paying close attention to guest comforts. Apartments are kitted out with kitchens and generous living spaces.

AI CAVALIERI DI VENEZIA
HOTEL €€€

Map p280 (☑041 241 10 64; www.hotelaicavalieri.com; Calle Borgolocco 6108; r from €315; ❄☎; ⬛Rialto) Venetian glam is dialled up to the max in this luxurious *palazzo* hotel, yet it somehow avoids slipping into tackiness. Rooms are dripping in gilt, silk damask wall coverings and sparkling Murano chandeliers – and with canals on two sides, you've got an excellent chance of a watery view.

HOTEL DANIELI
HOTEL €€€

Map p280 (☑041 522 64 80; www.danielihotelvenice.com; Riva degli Schiavoni 4196; s/d from €435/445; ❄☎; ⬛San Zaccaria) As eccentric and luxurious as Venice itself, the Danieli has attracted bohemians, minor royalty and their millionaire lovers for over a century. The hotel sprawls through three landmark buildings: the frescoed, antique-filled, 14th-century *casa vecchia* (old house), built for Doge Enrico Dandolo; the 18th-century, gilt-to-the-hilt *casa nuova* (new house); and the Danielino, a Fascist edifice with a modern-luxe interior redesign.

AQUA PALACE
LUXURY HOTEL €€€

Map p280 (Palazzo Scalfarotto; ☑041 296 04 42; www.aquapalace.it; Calle de la Malvasia 5492; r from €250; ❄☎; ⬛Rialto) With its exotic, spice-route vibe and burnished colour palate of gold, bronze and grey, the Aqua Palace is a heady mix of modern amenities and Eastern romance. Expect aristocratic proportions in the suites: acres of weighty fabric and bathrooms marbled within an inch of their lives. Complete with its own private gondola pier, this is the hotel for lovebirds.

IQS
DESIGN HOTEL €€€

Map p280 (☑041 241 00 62; www.thecharminghouse.com; Campiello Querini Stampalia 4425; ste from €310; ❄@☎; ⬛San Zaccaria) These achingly cool suites designed by Mauro Mazzolini are arranged around an ancient Gothic courtyard and hung with modern art. All four of them look out on the vivid waters of the Rio di Santa Maria Formosa, made even more luminous by the deliciously dark colour palate of the high-design interiors.

🛏 Giudecca, Lido & the Southern Islands

LE GARZETTE
B&B €

Map p284 (☑041 712 16 53; www.legarzette.it; Lungomare Alberoni 32, Lido; r €100-120; ☉summer; P ✱ ⊕; ⊡A) Nestled amid gardens overflowing with radicchio, fennel, pumpkins and courgettes is the rust-red *agriturismo* (farmstay accommodation) of Renza and Salvatore. Book for lunch at the traditional restaurant downstairs (lunch/dinner €50/70; also open to non-guests), then retire to your comfortable room for a nap on your 19th-century bed as herb-scented sea breezes waft through the window. Bicycles are provided for free.

GENERATOR   HOSTEL €

Map p283 (🕿041 877 82 88; www.generatorhostels.com; Fondamenta de la Croce 86, Giudecca; dm/r from €35/155; ✱@🛜; ⚓Zitelle) Generator rocks a sharp, contemporary interior including a fabulous kooky-kitsch bar-restaurant with crazy wallpaper, Murano chandeliers and a pool table. Try to score a bunk by the window – you might even wake up to a San Marco view. Sheets, blanket and a pillow are provided; breakfast is an additional €4.50.

OSTELLO JAN PALACH   HOSTEL €

Map p283 (🕿041 522 13 21; www.ostellojanpalach. it; Fondamenta di San Giacomo 186, Giudecca; r €80, dm/s/tw without bathroom €27/65/70; ☼Jul & Aug; 🛜; ⚓Redentore) Once school's out, this university halls of residence does duty as a hostel offering shared and private twin rooms and a large communal kitchen. Rooms are simply and clinically furnished with a bed, study desk and the odd poster or two. The views of the Zattere and Salute, though, are superb.

CAMPLUS LIVING REDENTORE   HOSTEL €

Map p283 (🕿041 522 53 96; www.camplusliving. it; Calle de le Cape 194, Giudecca; r €50; 🛜; ⚓Redentore) The rigorous monastic lives of the Redentore's Capuchin monks were surely eased by the view from their cells over the olive-tree- and palm-shaded garden. A revamp now gives access to 50 simple, ensuite rooms with kitchen and laundry facilities to boot.

★AL REDENTORE
DI VENEZIA   APARTMENT €€

Map p283 (🕿041 522 94 02; www.alredentore divenezia.com; Fondamenta del Ponte Longo 234a, Giudecca; apt from €167; ✱🛜⊕; ⚓Redentore) These fully serviced apartments blend modern facilities with antique-style furnishings, and then throw in travertine bathrooms, top-quality pillows, high-end

bath products and divine views across the water to San Marco.

VILLA INES   B&B €€

Map p284 (🕿041 526 72 26; www.villa-ines. com; Via Lazzaro Mocenigo 10, Lido; r from €130; P ✱🛜⊕; ⚓Lido SME) Gardens surround this quintessential Liberty-style villa. It belongs to the Seguso family, one of Murano's most famous glass-blowing dynasties, so the fittings are predictably top-notch: Seguso chandeliers, enormous damask-clad beds, flat-screen TVs and Jacuzzi bathtubs. Hostess Marika is a chef and runs the Acquolina Cooking School (p145) on-site.

BELMOND HOTEL CIPRIANI   HOTEL €€€

Map p283 (🕿041 24 08 01; www.belmond.com; Fondamenta de le Zitelle 10, Giudecca; r from €1280; ☼Apr-Oct; ✱🛜🏊; ⚓Zitelle) The heart-stoppingly expensive Cipriani offers 95 luxurious rooms and suites – all with private balconies overlooking flower-filled gardens – along with Venice's best swimming pool and a Michelin-starred restaurant.

JW MARRIOTT VENICE   HOTEL €€€

(🕿041 852 13 00; www.jwvenice.com; Isola delle Rose; d €360-485; ☼spa 9.30am-8pm; ✱🛜🏊⊕) Set on a 16-hectare private island, 20 minutes from Piazza San Marco, the Marriott's Venetian hotel is a bucolic haven in the lagoon. While Matteo Thun's contemporary, minimalist interiors and rooms are elegant in the extreme, it's the rooftop spa and pools (indoor and outdoor), with their four-poster loungers and unimpeded views across the lagoon, that really steal the show.

The spa, gym and pools (there's a third larger outdoor pool in the gardens) are open to non-hotel guests, who can access the island via the free shuttle from San Marco Giardinetti. The spa offers a variety of packages from basic use of the facilities to a range of massages (€125 to €170), hammam treatments (€90), and half- and full-day programs (from €220).

PALLADIO HOTEL & SPA   HOTEL €€€

Map p283 (🕿041 520 70 22; www.palladiohotel spa.com; Fondamenta de le Zitelle 33, Giudecca; r from €240; ☼Apr-Oct; ✱🛜; ⚓Zitelle) Splash out on a stay in a serene, Palladio-designed former convent with San Marco views, a private boat service and a superb spa. These premises once housed nuns and orphans but now offer heavenly comfort in 37 rosy, serenely demure guestrooms, many with garden terraces or canal views. Head downstairs for local organic breakfast buffets and spa treatments (p145).

ALBERGO QUATTRO FONTANE HOTEL €€€

Map p284 (☑041 526 02 27; www.quattrofontane.com; Via Quattro Fontane 16, Lido; s/d from €175/205; ☉Apr-Oct; P🅿✳@🛜🚼; 🛜V) Strange but true: this alpine chalet is just a stone's throw from Lido beaches. Parts of the main building date to the 16th century, when it was a casino frequented by royalty. Rooms are large and unabashedly retro in the 1970s annexe; the original building offers more traditional quarters with wrought-iron beds. Service can be variable.

🛏 Murano, Burano & the Northern Islands

VENICE CERTOSA HOTEL HOTEL €

(☑041 277 86 32; www.ventodivenezia.it; Isola della Certosa; s/d from €70/90; ✳@🛜; 🚤Certosa) Nautical talk abounds at the outdoor breakfast tables at La Certosa's activity-focused hotel before guests head off on jogging trails, sailing courses or kayak tours. Rooms are practical, unfussy and a little institutional feeling. Throughout the day the sailing fraternity and marina workers drop in at the bar and restaurant, but at night there's not a lot of action.

IL LATO AZZURRO B&B €

(☑041 523 06 42; www.latoazzurro.it; Via Forti 13, Sant'Erasmo; dm/s/d €27/55/80; @🛜🚼; 🚤Capannone) 🌿 Sleep among the artichokes on Venice's garden isle of Sant'Erasmo in a red-roofed country villa, 25 minutes by boat from central Venice. Spacious guestrooms with wrought-iron beds open onto a wraparound verandah. Meals are largely homegrown, bicycles are available, and the lagoon laps at the end of the lane – bite-prone guests should bring mosquito repellent.

★VILLA LINA B&B €€

Map p285 (☑041 527 53 58; www.villalinavenezia.com; Calle Dietro gli Orti 12, Murano; s/d from €110/170; ☉Mar-Dec; ✳🛜🚼; 🚤Colonna) Finding 16th-century Villa Lina in the grounds of the Nason Moretti glassworks is like chancing upon a wonderful secret. The home of Carlo Nason and his wife Evi has a mod 1950s vibe and is scattered with Carlo's glass designs. Bedrooms are large,

comfortable and contemporary, and the flower-filled garden backs directly on to the Serenella canal.

★MURANO PALACE HOTEL €€

Map p285 (☑041 73 96 55; www.muranopalace.com; Fondamenta dei Vetrai 77, Murano; d €110-180; ✳🛜; 🚤Colonna) Come here for designer fabulousness at an outlet price. Jewel-toned colour schemes and (naturally) Murano glass chandeliers illuminate high-ceilinged, wooden-floored rooms, and there are free drinks and snacks in the minibar. Expect canal views and unparalleled art-glass shopping in the vicinity, but eerie calm once the shops close around 6pm.

★CASA BURANO COTTAGE €€

(☑041 527 22 81; www.casaburano.it; Burano; r from €180; ✳🛜) Wake up in one of Burano's famous candy-coloured houses, courtesy of the stylish folks at Venissa who have converted five classic homes into an *albergo diffuso* – basically a spread-out hotel. There's no reception or breakfast service; you'll be met at the ferry and led to your canalside cottage. Rooms are spacious and chic, showcasing the work of local craftspeople.

VENISSA INN €€

Map p286 (☑041 527 22 81; www.venissa.it; Fondamenta di Santa Caterina 3, Mazzorbo; r from €180; ☉Mar-Nov; ✳✳🛜; 🚤Mazzorbo) Gourmet getaways are made in the shade of the vineyards at Venissa, which offers some of the lagoon's best dining as well as six Scandinavian-chic rooms under the farmhouse rafters. Breakfast is included, and given the kitchen (p155) has a Michelin star, you can be assured that it will be worth getting out of bed for.

LOCANDA CIPRIANI INN €€€

Map p286 (☑041 73 01 50; www.locandacipriani.com; Piazza Torcello 29, Torcello; s/d/ste €140/220/300; ☉Wed-Mon Mar-Dec; ✳; 🚤Torcello) Not much has changed since this rustic wine shop was transformed into a country inn in 1934 by Harry's Bar founder Giuseppe Cipriani. The six spacious rooms are more like suites, with stocked libraries and easy chairs in lieu of TVs for a true literary retreat. You're bound to find inspiration for your next novel in Hemingway's favourite room, Santa Fosca, with its original creaky oak floors and balcony overlooking the garden.

Understand Venice & the Veneto

Venice Today

It seems that everyone wants a piece of Venice, from selfie-stick-wielding tourists and foreign entrepreneurs to self-interested politicians and the rising Adriatic Sea. As La Serenissima sails further into the 21st century, new (and revisited) challenges are stirring up some rather choppy seas. How does a city reconcile its magnetism with its fragility, its individuality with an increasingly homogenised, globalised world?

Best on Film

Casino Royale (2006) James Bond hits the Grand Canal.

Pane e Tulipani (Bread and Tulips; 2000) An AWOL housewife starts life anew in Venice.

Casanova (1976) Fellini's take on Venice's famous seducer with Donald Sutherland.

Don't Look Now (1973) A couple's demons follow them to Venice in Nicolas Roeg's taut thriller.

Death in Venice (1971) Luchino Visconti takes on Thomas Mann's story of an infatuation and a deadly outbreak of disease.

Best in Print

Stabat Mater (Tiziano Scarpa; 2009) Winner of Italy's top literary prize; based on Antonio Vivaldi's orphan-girl orchestra.

Shakespeare in Venice (Alberto Toso Fei and Shaul Bassi; 2007) Local legends intertwined with Shakespearean dramas.

Watermark (Joseph Brodsky; 1992) The Nobel Laureate's 17-year fascination with Venice spills onto every page.

Venice, an Interior (Javier Marías; 1988) A tale of how history and imagination have shaped Venice.

#Venexodus

Tempers are fraying in La Serenissima as the rising tide of tourism – 25 million per annum – threatens to overwhelm the city. Of the 54,976 residents who remain in the historic centre (down from 102,000 in 1976), life in the world's most beautiful city is woeful, featuring low-wage employment, lack of affordable housing, neglected civic infrastructure, political disenfranchisement and a declining quality of life.

Top of the list of grievances is the lack of affordable housing, which is forcing young Venetians out of their island home and over to mainland Mestre from where 40,000 of them currently commute. The liberalisation of the rental sector in 2013 and the growth of home-rental websites mean fewer and fewer apartments are available to rent. After all, when tourists will pay €1000 a week to rent an apartment, renting to locals for a quarter of the price is hardly an enticing prospect.

Soaring real-estate prices have also precipitated the closure of essential businesses, from bakeries to hardware stores. Most of these are replaced by fast-food outlets and souvenir shops selling cheap, foreign-made trinkets. More worryingly, schools and libraries are underfunded; fish stalls at the Pescaria are disappearing due to lack of customers; valuable public properties (such as islands, parks and palaces) are sold off to cover city debts; and even the maternity ward at the Ospedale Civile is threatened with closure.

These challenges are propelling an increasing number of grassroots organisations – including Venessia (venessia.com), Generazione90 (facebook.com/generazione90), Venezia Cambia (veneziacambia.org) and We Are Here Venice (wearherevenice.org) – to raise public awareness and lobby politicians to take action. Their chief demands: immediate measures to tackle the housing crisis; a complete ban of cruise ships from the lagoon; regulation on the speed and number of boats; and the creation of a sustainable, long-term tourism strategy.

A Showdown at Unesco

Venice now faces the threat of being placed on Unesco's Endangered Heritage Sites list, after a damning report on the degradation of the city was issued by Icomos (International Council on Monuments and Sites) in 2015.

In order to avoid the highly embarrassing listing and uncomfortably close monitoring of the city by Unesco, Venice needs to come up with a plan for the protection of the city, its inhabitants and the lagoon environment. In February 2017, Mayor Brugnaro announced the €457 million 'Pact of Venice' aimed at revitalising the city, although concrete action has been minimal to date. But young Venetians and campaigners won't be ignored this time. Many travelled to Krakow in July 2017 to witness the Unesco vote and remind the world that Venice is not a cultural theme park but a living, breathing city.

The Changing Shape of Venice

As the population of Venice dwindles, the Metropolitan City of Venice has grown to encompass 2.6 million people. This newly designated area, approved in 2014, includes the urban agglomerations of Padua, Treviso and Venice and replaces the old province, which previously incorporated Venice, Mestre and the communities bordering the lagoon. The change aims to improve coordination in regional governance and upgrade the area's economic base.

On the face of it, this seems sensible given that many of the issues Venice faces are exacerbated by a lack of coordination between the original 21 municipalities. But Venetians are wary of the change, afraid that the highly specific issues facing the lagoon city will be lost in broader, regional concerns and a further political drive to pursue growth over sustainability. Already, the demographic disparity between Venice and Mestre (30:70) puts the concerns of the historic centre in second place.

In response to this, Venice plans to hold a fifth referendum on the separation of the cities of Venice and Mestre. It argues that the issue is self-governance of the unique city rather than 'separation'. Many people in Mestre are also in favour of the split arguing that they, too, need autonomy to shift the perception that Mestre is a suburban dormitory without specific needs and identity. Ideally, both sides would like to see two independent, but interdependent, cities with a networked economy rooted in sustainability that recognises Venice's special status. It's a hopeful vision and one that residents are committed to realising.

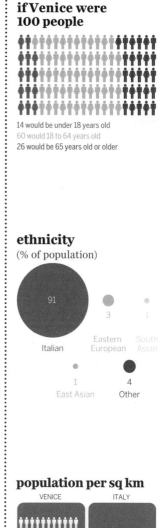

if Venice were 100 people

14 would be under 18 years old
60 would 18 to 64 years old
26 would be 65 years old or older

ethnicity
(% of population)

91 Italian
3 Eastern European
1 South Asian
1 East Asian
4 Other

population per sq km

VENICE   ITALY

† ≈ 200 people

History

For centuries Venice dominated trade on the Mediterranean through wily diplomacy, assisted by its mighty navy. When its maritime empire passed its high-water mark, Venice refused to concede defeat on the world stage. Instead the city itself became a stage, attracting global audiences with its vivid painting, baroque music, opera, independent thinkers and parties without parallel. In its audacious 1000-year history, Venice has not only remained above sea level, but repeatedly risen to the occasion.

From Swamp to Empire

A malarial swamp seems like a strange place to found an empire, unless you consider the circumstances. The Veneti, who had dominated this northern part of the Adriatic coast since at least 800 BC, had been Roman citizens since 49 BC and were not in the habit of war. But between the 5th and 6th centuries AD, when Visigoths, Huns and Lombards started to sack Veneto towns such as Altinum and Aquileia, many Veneti fled to the murky wetlands of the lagoon. They settled first on the island of Torcello before spreading out to the surrounding islands and finally the Rivoalto (meaning 'high bank', shortened to Rialto).

In *The Wings of the Dove* (1902), a dapper con man and sickly heiress meet in Venice, with predictable consequences – but Henry James' gorgeous storytelling makes for riveting reading.

By AD 466, these nascent island communities had elected tribunes and formed a loose federation. When Emperor Justinian claimed Italy's northeast coast for the Byzantine (Eastern Roman) Empire in 540, Venetia (roughly today's Veneto region) sent elected representatives to the regional Byzantine headquarters in Ravenna. This council reported to the capital, Constantinople (today's İstanbul), but as Byzantine power waned in the early 8th century, Venice seized the opportunity for independence.

In 726 the people of Venice elected Orso Ipato as their *dux* (Latin for leader), or doge (duke) in the Venetian dialect, the first of 118 elected Venetian doges that would lead the city for more than 1000 years. Like some of his successors, Orso tried to turn his appointment into a hereditary monarchy. He was assassinated for overstepping his bounds. At first, no one held the doge's hot seat for long: Orso's successor, Teodato, managed to transfer the ducal seat to Malamocco in 742 before

TIMELINE	c 1500 BC	AD 452	7th–9th Centuries
	Celtic Veneti tribes, possibly from Anatolia (in present day Turkey), arrive in northeast Italy to inhabit the region now known as the Veneto.	The Huns, led by Attila, sack the Roman cities of Aquileia and Altinum on the mainland, and their inhabitants take refuge in the islands of the lagoon.	Glass-making furnaces on Torcello get fired up, creating the cathedral's Byzantine glass-mosaic masterpieces.

being deposed. Gradually the office of the doge was understood as an elected office, kept in check by two councillors and the Arengo (a popular assembly).

When the Franks invaded the lagoon in 809, they were surprised by resistance led by Agnello Partecipazio from Rivoalto, a shallow area of the lagoon inaccessible to most seafaring vessels. Partecipazio's success led to his election as doge and the establishment of a fortress on the eventual site of the Palazzo Ducale. Thus the cluster of islets around Rivoalto became the focus of community development. Land was drained, earth was lifted above the tides with wooden pylons driven into the soft silt, and soon Venetians rose above their swampy circumstances.

War & Spoils

Once terra firma was established, Venice set about shoring up its business interests. When consummate diplomat Pietro Orseolo was elected doge in 991, he positioned Venice as a neutral party between the western Holy Roman Empire and the Byzantine Empire controlled by Constantinople, and won the medieval equivalent of most-favoured-nation status from both competing empires.

Even at the outset of the Crusades, Venice maintained its strategic neutrality, continuing to trade with Muslim leaders from Syria to Spain while its port served as the launching pad for crusaders bent on wresting the Holy Land from Muslim control. With rivals Genoa and Pisa vying for lucrative contracts to equip crusaders, Venice established the world's first assembly lines in the Arsenale, capable of turning out a warship a day. Officially, La Serenissima ('The Most Serene'; the Venetian Republic) remained above the fray, joining crusading naval operations only sporadically – and almost always in return for trade concessions.

With Venice starting to have a hold on the Byzantine economy, emperor Manuele Comnenus played on Venetian-Genoese rivalries, staging an 1171 assault on Constantinople's Genoese colony and blaming it on Constantinople's Venetian residents, who were promptly clapped into irons. Venice sent a fleet to the rescue, but the crew contracted plague from stowaway rats, and the ships limped home without having fired a shot.

Meanwhile, Venice was under threat by land from Holy Roman Emperor Frederick Barbarossa's plans to force Italy and the pope to recognise his authority. But after several strikes, Barbarossa found northern Italy a tough territory to control. When his army was struck by plague in 1167, Barbarossa was forced to withdraw to Pavia – only to discover

726	828	957	1094
Orso Ipato becomes the first Venetian doge. The Byzantines consider Ipato's election an act of rebellion, and are not devastated by Ipato's assassination in 737.	According to legend, the corpse of St Mark the Evangelist is smuggled from Alexandria (Egypt) to Venice in a shipment of pork. St Mark is adopted as the patron saint of Venice.	Holy Roman Emperor Otto the Great recognises key trading rights for Venice, cutting the Byzantine Empire out of Venice's increasingly lucrative deals.	Basilica di San Marco is completed. The doge's Chiesa d'Oro (Church of Gold) stands for the glory of Venice, St Mark and a brain trust of Mediterranean artisans.

THE STOLEN SAINT

By the 9th century, Venice had all the makings of an independent trading centre – ports, a defensible position against Charlemagne and the Franks, leadership to settle inevitable trade disputes – but no glorious shrine to mark the city's place on the world map. So Venice did what any ambitious, God-fearing medieval city would do: it procured a patron saint. Under Byzantine rule, St Theodore (San Teodoro) had fulfilled the role. But according to local legend, the evangelist St Mark (San Marco) had visited the lagoon islands and been told by an angel that his body would rest there – and some Venetian merchants decided to realise this prophecy.

In AD 828, Venetian smugglers stole St Mark's body from its resting place in Alexandria (Egypt), apparently hiding the holy corpse in a load of pork to deter inspection by Muslim customs officials. Venice summoned the best artisans from Byzantium and beyond to enshrine these relics in an official ducal church that would impress visitors with the power and glory of Venice. The usual medieval construction setbacks of riots and fires thrice destroyed exterior mosaics and weakened the underlying structure, and St Mark's bones were misplaced twice in the mayhem. With Basilica di San Marco under construction, the winged lion of St Mark was officially adopted as the emblem of the Venetian empire, symbolically setting Venice apart from Constantinople and Rome.

---

that 15 Italian city-states, including Venice, had formed the Lombard League against him. Barbarossa met with spectacular defeat, and even worse, excommunication. Venice quickly recognised that it could only handle one holy war at a time, and through diplomatic manoeuvres, convinced Pope Alexander III and the repentant emperor to make peace in Venice in 1177.

The Dodgy Doge

For fast-talking, even the shrewdest Venetian merchant couldn't top Doge Enrico Dandolo. The doddering nonagenarian might have seemed like an easy mark to Franks seeking Venice's support in the Fourth Crusade, but Doge Dandolo drove a hard bargain: Venice would provide a fleet to carry 30,000 crusaders, but not for less than 84,000 silver marks – approximately double the yearly income of the king of England at the time.

Only one-third of the proposed Frankish forces turned up in Venice the following year, and their leaders couldn't pay. But Venice had the ships ready, and figured it had kept its side of the bargain. To cover the balance due, Doge Dandolo suggested that the crusaders might help Venice out with a few tasks on the way to Palestine. This included invading Dalmatia and a detour to Constantinople in 1203 that would

1172	1203–04	1271	1297
Venice establishes a Maggior Consiglio (Great Council), instituting a form of communal civic leadership that limits the powers of the doge.	Doge Dandolo promises to transport Frankish crusaders to the Holy Land but heads to Constantinople; his forces massacre and pillage, then return to Venice with booty.	Traders Nicolò and Matteo Polo depart for Xanadu with Nicolò's 20-year-old son, Marco. They return in 1295 and Marco's account of Kublai Khan's court causes a sensation.	Membership of the Maggior Consiglio is restricted to only those whose families are already members, creating a hereditary ruling elite.

last a year, while Venetian and Frankish forces thoroughly pillaged the place.

Finally Doge Dandolo claimed that Constantinople had been suitably claimed for Christendom – never mind that it already was under Christian rule. At age 96, the doge declared himself 'Lord of a Quarter and a Half-Quarter of the Roman Empire' of Byzantium. This title conveniently granted Venice three-eighths of the spoils, including the monumental gilt-bronze horses in Basilica di San Marco. Venetian ships opted to head home loaded with booty instead of onward to Christian duty, leaving the Franks to straggle onwards to the Crusades.

Venice Versus Genoa

The puppet emperor Doge Dandolo put on the throne in Constantinople didn't last long: the Genoese conspired with the Byzantines to overthrow the pro-Venetian regime. Having taken Constantinople for all it was worth, Venice set its sights on distant shores. Through the overland trip of native son Marco Polo to China in 1271–91, Venetian trade routes extended all the way to China. Rival Genoa's routes to the New World were proving slower to yield returns, and the impatient empire cast an envious eye on Venice's spice and silk-trade routes.

In 1372 Genoa and Venice finally came to blows over an incident in Cyprus, initiating eight years of maritime warfare that took a toll on Venice. To make matters worse, plague decimated Venice in the 1370s. Genoa's allies Padua and Hungary took the opportunity to seize Venetian territories on the mainland, and in 1379 a Genoese fleet appeared off the Lido. Venetian commander Carlo Zeno's war fleet had been sent out to patrol the Mediterranean, leaving the city outflanked and outnumbered.

But the Genoese made a strategic mistake: instead of invading, Genoa attempted to starve out the city. With stores of grain saved for just such an occasion, Venice worked day and night to build new ships and defences around the islands. Mustering all of Venice's might, Venetian commander Vittore Pisani mounted a counter-attack on the Genoese fleet – but his forces were inadequate. All hope seemed lost, until ships flying the lion of St Mark banner appeared on the horizon: Carlo Zeno had returned. Venice ousted the Genoese, exerting control over the Adriatic and a backyard that stretched from Dalmatia (Croatia) to Bergamo (northern Italy).

Rats & Redemption

As a maritime empire, ships came and went through Venice's ports daily, carrying salt, silks, spices and an unintentional import: rats infested

---

Those found guilty of crimes against the doge were bludgeoned or decapitated. Severed heads were placed atop columns outside the Palazzo Ducale and sundry parts displayed in sestieri *(districts) for exactly three nights and four days, until they started to smell.*

HISTORY FROM SWAMP TO EMPIRE

Byzantine Splendour

Basilica di San Marco (San Marco)

Basilica di Santa Maria Assunta (Torcello)

Basilica dei SS Maria e Donato (Murano)

1309	1310	1348–49	1386
For opening defying Rome's orders, Venice is excommunicated from the Church for the first time. Through its wealth and negotiation skills, Venice convinces Rome to relent.	With rebellion afoot, a temporary security force called the Consiglio dei Dieci (Council of Ten) is convened; it lasts almost five centuries, effectively running Venice for two.	A horrific bout of the Black Death hits Venice, killing some 60% of the population. Venetian doctors observe that the worst-hit areas are by Dorsoduro's docks, where rats arrive.	A Jewish cemetery is established on the Lido in 1386, with land granted by the state. The cemetery remains in use until Mussolini's racial laws are imposed in 1938.

with fleas carrying bubonic plague. In 1348 the city was still recovering from an earthquake that had destroyed houses and drained the Grand Canal, when the plague struck. Soon as many as 600 people were dying every day, and undertakers' barges raised the rueful cry: *'Corpi morti! Corpi morti!'* (Bring out your dead!). Within a year, more than 50,000 Venetians died.

No one was sure how the disease had spread, but Venice took the unprecedented step of appointing three public health officials to manage the crisis. Observing that outbreaks seemed to coincide with incoming shipments, Venice decided in 1403 to intercept all incoming ships arriving from infected areas on Isola di Lazzaretto Vecchio. Before any ship was allowed to enter the city, it was required to undergo inspection, and its passengers had to wait for a *quarantena* (40-day period) while Venetian doctors monitored them for signs of plague. This was the world's first organised quarantine station, setting a precedent that has saved untold lives from plague and other infectious diseases since.

While the plague struck Italy's mainland as many as 50 more times before 1500, the outbreaks often seemed to miraculously bypass Venice. The city's faithful chalked up their salvation to divine intervention, and built the spectacular churches of Il Redentore and Basilica di Santa Maria della Salute as monumental thanks.

Traders & Traitors

Like its signature Basilica di San Marco, the Venetian empire was dazzlingly cosmopolitan. Venice turned arrivals from every nation and creed into trading partners with a common credo: as long as everyone was making money, cultural boundaries need not apply. Dalmatians, Armenians, Turks, Greeks and Germans became neighbours along the Grand Canal, and Jewish and Muslim refugees and other groups widely persecuted in Europe settled into established communities in Venice.

Commerce provided a common bond. At the height of Venice's maritime prowess, 300 shipbuilding companies in the Arsenale had 16,000 employees. By the mid-15th century, Venice's maritime ventures had left the city swathed in golden mosaics, rustling silks and incense. In case of trade disputes or feuds among neighbours, La Serenissima instigated a complex political system of checks, balances and elections, with the doge as the executive presiding over council matters.

Yet inside the red-velvet cloak of its ruling elite, Venice was hiding an iron hand. Venice's shadowy secret service, the Consiglio dei Dieci (Council of Ten), thwarted conspiracies by deploying Venetian James Bonds throughout the city and major European capitals. Venice had no qualms about spying on its own citizens, and trials, torture and execu-

Individual Venetians involved in the sacking of the Christian cities of Zadar and Constantinople during the Fourth Crusade were excommunicated from the Church in 1202. However, on five subsequent occasions between 1284 and 1606, the Pope placed the entire city under an interdict (restricting sacraments) for openly defying orders.

1403	1470	1492	1494
The world's first quarantine stations are established with proceeds from Venice's salt monopoly, saving lives by limiting contact with the bubonic plague.	Cyprus is the latest of Venice's conquests, which stretch from Bergamo, along the Adriatic to the Aegean. They also have trading outposts in Jaffa, Beirut and Alexandria.	Genoese Cristoforo Colombo's voyage kicks off the age of discovery and Venice's long slide into obsolescence, as the Portuguese and Spanish bypass its customs controls.	Aldo Manuzio founds Aldine Press, introducing mass-market paperbacks, including Dante's *Divine Comedy*. By 1500, one in six books published in Europe is printed in Venice.

tions were carried out in secret. Still, compared with its neighbours at the time, Venice remained a haven of tolerance.

Friendly Foes

Never mind that Venice sacked Constantinople, or that Constantinople sided with Genoa against Venice: warfare wasn't enough to deter the two maritime powers from doing brisk business. When Constantinople fell to Ottoman rule in 1453, business carried on as usual. The rival powers understood one another very well; the Venetian language was widely spoken across the eastern Mediterranean.

After Suleiman the Magnificent captured Cyprus in 1571, Venice sensed its maritime power slipping, and allied with the papal states, Spain and even arch-rival Genoa to keep the Ottoman sultan at bay. The same year a huge allied fleet (much of it provided by Venice) routed the Turks off Lepanto (Greece) and Sebastiano Venier and his Venetian fleet sailed home with 100 Turkish women as war trophies.

Legend has it that when Turkish troops took over the island of Paros, the prisoners of war included Cecilia Venier-Baffo, who was apparently the illegitimate daughter of Venice's noble Venier family, a niece of the doge, and possibly the cousin of Sebastiano (of Lepanto fame). Cecilia became the favourite wife of Sultan Salim II in Constantinople, and when he died in 1574 she took control as Sultana Nurbani (Princess of Light). Regent of Sultan Murad III, she was a faithful pen pal of Queen Elizabeth I of Britain and Catherine de Medici of France. According to historian Alberto Toso Fei, the Sultana's policies were so favourable to Venetian interests that the Venetian senate set aside special funds to fulfil her wishes for Venetian specialities, from lapdogs to golden cushions. Genoa wasn't pleased by her favouritism, and in 1582 she was poisoned by what appeared to have been Genoese assassins.

The Age of Decadence

While Italy's city-states continued to plot against one another, they were increasingly eclipsed by marriages cementing alliances among France, England and the Habsburg Empire. As it lost ground to these European nation-states and the seas to pirates and Ottomans, Venice took a different tack, and began conquering Europe by charm.

Sensations & Scandals

Venice's star attractions were its parties, music, women and art. Nunneries in Venice held soirées to rival those in its *ridotti* (casinos), and Carnevale lasted up to three months. Claudio Monteverdi was hired as choir director of San Marco in 1613, introducing multipart harmonies

In 1444 the second incarnation of the Rialto Bridge collapsed under the weight of spectators watching a wedding flotilla. It took 148 years before the current stone replacement by Antonio da Ponte was completed.

HISTORY THE AGE OF DECADENCE

Landmarks of Multicultural Venice

The Ghetto (Cannaregio)

Museo delle Icone (Castello)

Scuola Dalmata di San Giorgio degli Schiavoni (Castello)

Monastero di San Lazzaro degli Armeni (Southern Islands)

1498	1501	1508	1516
Portuguese explorer Vasco da Gama sails around the Cape of Good Hope, and the boom in trans-Atlantic trade shuts out many Venetian merchants.	The Magistrato alle Acque is created in order to maintain and regulate the delicate hydrological balance of the lagoon, on which Venice's security and fortune is built.	The Holy Roman Empire, papal states, Spain and France form the League of Cambrai against Venice – but with Venice cutting side deals, ensuing war doesn't change the map much.	A proclamation declares that Jewish residents of Venice are to live in a designated zone called the Ghetto, with the gates closed and guarded after dark.

and historical operas with crowd-pleasing tragicomic scenes. Monteverdi's style of opera caught on: by the end of the 17th century, Venice's season included as many as 30 operas.

New orchestras required musicians, but Venice came up with a ready workforce: orphan girls. Circumstances had conspired to produce an unprecedented number of Venetian orphans: on the one hand was the plague, and on the other were scandalous masquerade parties and flourishing prostitution. Funds poured in from anonymous donors to support *ospedaletti* (orphanages), and the great baroque composers Antonio Vivaldi and Domenico Cimarosa were hired to lead orphan orchestras. The Venetian state took on the care and musical training of the city's orphan girls, who earned their keep by performing at public functions and *ospedaletti* fund-raising galas. Visiting diplomats treated to orphan concerts were well advised to tip the orphan performers: you never knew whose illegitimate daughter you might be insulting otherwise.

Pulling Rank: The Pope & the Doge

Rome repeatedly censured Venice for depicting holy subjects in an earthy, Venetian light, and for playing toe-tapping tunes in churches – but such censorship was largely ignored. According to late 16th-century gossip, Cardinal Camillo Borghese had a beef with the Venetian ambas-

Venetian party planners outdid themselves with the 1574 reception for King Henry III of France. The king's barge was greeted with glass-blowers performing on rafts, bevvies of Venetian beauties dressed in white, a 1200-dish meal and decorations provided by an all-star committee of Palladio, Veronese and Tintoretto.

VENICE'S HONEST COURTESANS

High praise, high pay and even high honours: Venice's *cortigiane oneste* were no ordinary strumpets. An 'honest courtesan' earned the title not by offering a fair price, but by providing added value with style, education and wit that reflected well on her patrons. They were not always beautiful or young, but *cortigiane oneste* were well educated, dazzling their admirers with poetry, music, philosophical insights and apt social critiques. In the 16th century, some Venetian families of limited means spared no expense on their daughters' educations: beyond an advantageous marriage or career, educated women who become *cortigiane oneste* could command prices 60 times those of the average *cortigiana di lume* ('courtesan of the lamp' – streetwalker).

Far from hiding their trade, a catalogue of 210 of Venice's *piu honorate cortigiane* (most honoured courtesans) was published in 1565, listing contact information and going rates, payable directly to the courtesan's servant, her mother or, occasionally, her husband. A *cortigiana onesta* might circulate in Venetian society as the known mistress of one or more admirers, who compensated her for her company rather than services rendered, and with an allowance rather than pay per hour. Syphilis was an occupational hazard, and special hospices were founded for infirm courtesans.

1571	1575–76	1630	1669
Venice and the Holy League of Catholic states defeat Ottoman forces at the naval Battle of Lepanto, thanks in part to a technical advantage: cannons and guns versus archers.	Plague claims many lives, including Titian's. Quarantine aids Venice's recovery; a new painting cycle by Tintoretto is dedicated to San Rocco, patron saint of the plague-stricken.	The plague kills a third of Venice's population within 16 months. With few leaders surviving, Venice allows wealthy Venetians to buy their way into the Golden Book of nobles.	The Venetian colony of Crete is lost to the Ottoman Turks, yet the two powers continue to trade with one another – despite repeated objections from Rome.

sador to Rome, Leonardo Donà, ever since the two exchanged heated words in the Roman halls of power. The cardinal hissed that, were he pope, he'd excommunicate the entire Venetian populace. 'And I would thumb my nose at the excommunication', retorted Donà.

As fate would have it, by 1606 cardinal and ambassador were promoted to Pope Paul V and doge, respectively. Rome had never appreciated Venice's insistence on reserving a degree of control over Church matters, and when Venice claimed that zoning laws required its approval of Church expansion plans within the city, Pope Paul V issued a papal bull excommunicating Venice. As promised, Doge Donà defied the bull, ordering all churches to remain open on Venetian territory. Any church that obeyed the bull would have its doors permanently closed, property seized and clergy exiled from Venice.

Venetian-born monk and philosopher Paolo Sarpi convincingly argued Venice's case, claiming Venice's right to self-determination came directly from God, not through Rome. Before the excommunication could cause further loss of Church property in Venice, or other Catholic territories became convinced by Sarpi's argument, Pope Paul V rescinded his bull.

But the power struggle didn't stop there. Venice conducted an official 1767 audit of 11 million golden ducats in revenues rendered to Rome in the previous decade, and decided to cut its losses: 127 Veneto monasteries and convents were closed, cutting the local clerical population in half and redirecting millions of ducats to Venice's coffers.

Red Lights, White Widows & Grey Areas

While Roman clerics furiously scribbled their disapproval, Venetian trends stealthily took over drawing rooms across the continent. Venetian women's lavish finery, staggering platform shoes up to 50cm high and masculine quiff hairdos scandalised visiting European nobility, until Venice felt obliged to enact sumptuary laws preventing women from wearing manly hairstyles and blinding displays of jewels on dipping décolletages. Venetian noblewomen complained to the doge and the pope, and the restrictions were soon dropped.

With trade revenues and the value of the Venetian ducat slipping in the 16th century, Venice's fleshpots brought in far too much valuable foreign currency to be outlawed. Instead, Venice opted for regulation and taxation. Rather than baring all in the rough-and-ready streets around the Rialto, prostitutes could only display their wares from the waist up in windows, or sit bare-legged on window sills. Venice decreed that to distinguish themselves from noblewomen who increasingly dressed like them, ladies of the night should ride in gondolas with red

Many Venetians dropped the mask of propriety altogether, openly cohabiting with lovers year-round and acknowledging illegitimate heirs in their wills. By the 18th century, less than 40% of Venetian nobles bothered with the formality of marriage.

Venice's former leper colony of San Lazzaro degli Armeni became a monastery, founded by Armenian refugees in 1717, and frescoed Palazzo Zenobio remains an Armenian cultural centre and popular venue for concerts and Carnevale.

1678	1703	1718	1797
Venetian scholar Elena Lucrezia Cornaro Piscopia is the first woman to receive a university degree in Europe, gaining her doctorate in philosophy at the University of Padua.	Antonio Vivaldi becomes the musical director at La Pietà, composing many concertos for the resident orchestra comprised of orphan girls.	Venice and Austria sign the Treaty of Passarowitz with the Ottoman Empire, splitting prime coastal territory and leaving Venice with nominal control and some Ionian islands.	Napoleon conquers the Venetian Republic. The segregation of Jewish Venetians comes to an end, briefly, until restrictions are reimposed by the Austrians.

lights. By the end of the 16th century, the town was flush with some 12,000 registered prostitutes, creating a literal red-light district.

Beyond red lights ringing the Rialto, 16th to 18th-century visitors encountered broad grey areas in Venetian social mores. As free-spirited, financially independent Venetian women took lovers, there became a certain fluidity surrounding the definition of a *cortigiana* (courtesan). With their husbands at sea for months or years, Venice's 'white widows' took young, handsome *cicisbei* (manservants) to tend their needs. Not coincidentally, Venetian ladies occasionally fell into religious fervours entailing a trimester-long seclusion.

One of Italy's most beloved graphic novels, *Corto Maltese in Fables of Venice* (originally published in 1967) follows Hugo Pratt's cosmopolitan sea captain as he cracks the mysteries of the *calli* (lanes).

From Occupation to Revolution

When Napoleon arrived in 1797, Venice had been reduced by plague and circumstances from its 16th-century peak population of around 190,000 to fewer than 140,000 people. Venetian warships managed to deter one French ship by the Lido, but when Napoleon made it clear he intended to destroy the city if it resisted, the Maggior Consiglio (Great Council) decreed the end of the Republic. The doge reportedly doffed the signature cap of his office with a sigh, saying, 'I won't be needing this anymore'. Rioting citizens were incensed by such cowardice, but French forces soon ended the insurrection, and began systematically plundering the city.

Though Napoleon only controlled Venice sporadically for a total of about 11 years, on and off, the impact of his reign is still visible. Napoleon grabbed any Venetian art masterpiece that wasn't nailed down, lifted restrictions on the Jewish Ghetto and filled in canals in order to create wider streets to facilitate the movement of troops and commerce. Napoleon lost control of Venice to the Austrians in 1814, and two years later one-quarter of Venice's population was destitute.

But Austria had grand plans for the city, and expected impoverished Venetians to foot the bill. They were obliged to house Austrian soldiers, who spent off-duty hours indulging in their new happy-hour invention, the *spritz* (a prosecco-and-bitters cocktail). Finding their way back home afterwards was a challenge in Venetian *calli* (lanes), so the Austrians implemented a street-numbering system. To improve shipping access for reinforcements and supplies, they dredged and deepened entrances to the lagoon, and began a train bridge in 1841 – all with Venetian labour and special Venetian taxes. To make way for the new train station in 1846, *scuole* (religious confraternities), a palace and the church containing the body of St Lucy were demolished.

When a young lawyer named Daniele Manin suggested reforms to Venice's puppet administration in 1848, he was tossed into prison –

1807	1814	1836	1840
Napoleon suppresses religious orders to quell dissent. Some churches are eventually reconsecrated – but many aren't, serving instead as archives or tourist attractions.	Austria takes Venice as a war trophy and imposes order with thousands of troops, a house-numbering system and heavy taxes that push Venice to the brink of starvation.	Fire guts Venice's legendary public opera house, but a new version soon rises from the ashes. When La Fenice (The Phoenix) burns again in 1996, an exact replica is rebuilt.	At La Serenissima's height, Venice's fabled Golden Book of nobles includes more than 1200 families – but by 1840, all but 200 are destitute and subsisting on charity.

PRINCE OF PLEASURE

Never was a hedonist born at a better time and in a more appropriate place. Eighteenth-century Venice was well into its new career as the pleasure capital of Europe when Giacomo Casanova (1725–98) arrived on the scene. He was abandoned as a young boy, and became a gambler and rake while studying law in Padua. He graduated by age 17 to take up a position with the Church in Venice, but adventuring soon became Casanova's primary career. His charm won him warm welcomes into the homes of wealthy patrons – and the beds of their wives, lovers and daughters.

Venice was a licentious place, but some political limits still applied. Casanova's dalliances with Freemasonry and banned books were considered nothing less than a threat to the state. After an evening foursome with the French ambassador and a couple of nuns, Casanova was arrested on the nebulous charge of 'outrages against religion' and dragged to the Palazzo Ducale's dreaded attic prison. Sentenced to five years in a flea-infested cell, Casanova complained bitterly, and promptly escaped through the roof of his cell, entered the palace, and breezed past the guards in the morning.

Casanova fled Venice to make his fortune in Paris and serve briefly as a French spy. But his extracurricular habits caused him no end of trouble: he went broke in Germany, survived a duel in Poland, fathered and abandoned several children, and contracted venereal diseases in England. Late in life, he returned to Venice as a celebrity, and served the government as a spy – but he was exiled for publishing a satire of the nobility. He wound up as a librarian in an isolated castle in Bohemia, where boredom drove him to finally write his memoirs. In the end, he concludes, 'I can say I have lived'.

sparking a popular uprising against the Austrians that would last 17 months. Austria responded by bombarding and blockading the city. In July, Austria began a 24-day artillery bombardment, raining some 23,000 shells down on the city and its increasingly famished and cholera-stricken populace, until Manin finally managed to negotiate a surrender to Austria with a guarantee of no reprisals. Yet the indignity of Austria's suppression continued to fester, and when presented with the option in 1866, the people of Venice and the Veneto voted to join the new independent kingdom of Italy under King Vittorio Emanuele II.

Life During Wartime

Glamorous Venice gradually took on a workaday aspect in the 19th century, with factories springing up on Giudecca, along the fringes of Cannaregio and around Mestre and Padua, and textile industries setting up shop around Vicenza and Treviso. As an increasingly strategic industrial area, Venice began to seem like a port worth reclaiming. But when Austro-Hungarian forces advanced on Venice, they were confronted

1846	1848	1866	1895
The first train crosses to the mainland. The feat is bittersweet: churches are demolished for the station, trains bring occupying Austrian troops and Venetians foot the bill.	Daniele Manin leads an anti-Austrian rebellion and declares Venice a republic for 17 months. Austrians retake the city in 1849, and Venice remains under Austrian control for 17 years.	Venice and the Veneto join the new Kingdom of Italy. The unification of Italy is complete when Rome is made the capital in 1870.	The first Biennale reasserts the city's role as global taste maker. Other nations are eventually invited, though a provocative Picasso is removed from the Spanish Pavilion in 1910.

by Italy's naval marines. Two days after Italy declared war on Austria in 1915, air raids on the city began, and would continue intermittently throughout WWI until 1918. Venice was lucky: the bombardments caused little damage.

When Mussolini rose to power after WWI, he was determined to turn the Veneto into a modern industrial powerhouse and a model Fascist society – despite Venice's famously laissez-faire outlook. Mussolini constructed a roadway from the mainland to Venice, literally bringing the city into line with the rest of Italy. While Italy's largest Fascist rallies were held in Padua, with up to 300,000 participants, Italian Resistance leaders met in Padua's parks to plot uprisings throughout northern Italy. When Mussolini's grip on the region began to weaken during WWII, partisans joined Allied troops to wrest the Veneto from Fascist control.

Venice emerged relatively unscathed from Allied bombing campaigns that targeted mainland industrial sites, and was liberated by New Zealand troops in 1945 – but the mass deportation of Venice's Jewish population in 1943 had all but annihilated that historic community. When the Veneto began to rebound after the war, many Venetians left for the mainland, Milan and other postwar economic centres. The legendary lagoon city seemed mired in the mud, unable to reconcile its recent history with its past grandeur, and unsure of its future.

Keeping Venice Afloat

No one comes to Venice and fails to be struck by the uniqueness of the city. However, fewer people consider the utterly unique character of the lagoon in which it stands, despite the fact that it is the only lagoon in the world to have retained its equilibrium for over 1000 years.

Master of the Waters

By its very nature a lagoon is an unstable system, tending either towards erosion or, if the silt-bearing rivers prevail, towards swamps and then fields. In order to prevent either of these two fates, the Republic of Venice brought to bear all its resources and technological know-how and enforced them autocratically under the aegis of the Magistrato alle Acque (Master of the Waters), which was established in 1501. This specially empowered office had absolute responsibility for ensuring the hydraulic health of the lagoon.

Between the 14th and 16th centuries when the Brenta, Sila and Piave rivers threatened to overwhelm the lagoon with silt, the magistrates ordered they be rerouted. Later, in the 18th century, they engineered the construction of Pellestrina's impressive *murazzi* (sea wall). To ensure

1907	1918	1932	1933
Under the Italian government, the Magistrato alle Acque becomes part of the Ministry of Public Works and operational functions are devolved to the Consorzio Venezia Nuova.	Austro-Hungarian planes drop almost 300 bombs on Venice in WWI, but their aim is off, resulting in mercifully little loss of life or damage.	The world's first film festival is initially considered a dubious ploy for attention, but Greta Garbo, Clark Gable and 23,000 movie-goers prove the formula a success.	Mussolini opens the Ponte della Libertà (Freedom Bridge) from Mestre to Venice. The 3.85km-long, two-lane highway remains the only access to Venice by car.

the ebb and flow of the tides dealt effectively with the city's sewage, the three mouths to the sea were kept open just enough; and ships were required to unload cannons and cargo at Pola and the Lido to reduce weight in order to navigate the *ghebbi* (capillary canals) that ensured the city's security against both enemies and the force of the tidal influx. Anyone who sunk *briccole* (navigation poles) without permission was sent directly to prison, and in 1505 the Senate enacted a fine of 100 ducats (a colossal amount) for any unauthorised person who tampered with the lagoon in any way. Through this careful management the lagoon not only survived but thrived.

When the Republic fell in 1797 the unified management of the lagoon collapsed. Instead, Napoleonic, Austrian and Italian governments introduced new systems that validated the concept of private property. A third of the lagoon was reclaimed for agricultural use and aquaculture, and in 1917 the industrial zone of Marghera was constructed. To allow cargo ships to access Marghera, a deep water channel, the Vittorio Emanuele, was dug in 1925, with two additional channels – the Malamocco Canal and the Canale dei Petroli – dredged in the mid-1960s.

As the area into which high tides could expand and the area of absorbent capillary canals was reduced the level of the *acque alte* (high waters) increased. Then in 1966, a catastrophic flood hit. For hours the waters reached more than 2m above sea level and the world feared that Venice would drown. Fifty organisations worldwide rallied to preserve the city, raising €50 million to cover 1500 restoration projects. Unesco took fright at the threatened loss and in 1987 awarded Venice and its lagoon World Heritage status.

Modern Lagoon Politics

More importantly for the city, in 1973, Italy passed the first 'special' law for Venice wherein the Italian state recognised the vital task of maintaining the lagoon in order to safeguard the city from environmental disaster. Debates were held, studies commissioned and it was agreed that any further reduction in the area of the lagoon should be forbidden. A plan to build a third industrial zone was abandoned and ideas were discussed as to how best to regulate the increased force of the tides.

It was decided to commission a system of barriers – MoSE (Modulo Sperimentale Elettromeccanico) – at the three mouths of the lagoon, which could be raised to prevent flooding during high tides. Initial costs were estimated at €1.5 billion with a completion date set for 1995. Since then decades of controversy have ensued, ending in the exposure of a huge corruption scandal in 2014 that saw the arrest of the city mayor, undermined the scientific soundness of the idea and resulted in the

The Water Magistrate was the second-most important person of the Republic, and his word was law on anything to do with the lagoon. On his investiture, the doge presented him to the people with these words: 'Weigh him, pay him, and, if he makes a mistake, hang him'.

1943	1948	1955	1966
Under the Nazi occupation 256 Jewish Venetians are rounded up and deported to concentration camps. A memorial in Campo del Ghetto Nuovo commemorates those who perished.	Peggy Guggenheim arrives with major modernists, renewing interest in Italian art, reclaiming Futurism from the Fascists and championing Venetian abstract expressionism.	Venice opens Italy's first museum of Jewish history, the Museo Ebraico, in the historic Ghetto. The museum opens The Ghetto's synagogues and the Lido cemetery to visitors.	Record floods cause widespread damage and unleash debate on measures to protect Venice. Its admirers around the world rally to save the city, and rescue its treasures from lagoon muck.

dissolution of the 500-year-old Magistrato alle Acque, also implicated in the scandal. Some academics and hydrologists argue that relying on the mechanical fix of MoSE is an inadequate solution for a dynamic system like a lagoon, which needs constant regulation and effective, unitary environmental planning, as the Republic once provided. MoSE is now not expected to be fully completed until 2022 and the price tag has risen to over €5 billion.

But just as public opinion questions the efficacy of MoSE as a solution, Venice faces another rising tide – the boom in tourism. In 1999, cruise-ship passengers accounted for only 100,000 visitors a year to Venice. By 2012 the Port Authority published figures of 2.26 million arrivals. In protest, Venetians took to the Giudecca Canal in rowboats, symbolically blocking the entry of ships they argue endanger the very foundations of their city. The Port Authority countered that the city relies on the cruise industry to support 5000 jobs and the lagoon has never been a natural environment, but has always been adapted to serve the principal source of Venetian power – its port. In 2014, the protestors won a brief ban on outsized ships (over 96,000 gross tons) entering the lagoon, plus a limit on smaller ships to five per day. However, by January 2015 that ban had been overturned. In 2016 there were further protests, with locals blockading the canal with gondolas and other small craft. Their cause was taken up by Unesco, which has threatened to place Venice on their list of endangered heritage sites unless the big ships are banned.

Venice sorely misses the dedicated, centralised governance of the Republic – the lagoon now covers four provinces and is dependent on the policies and post-crisis finances of nine different city and town councils. Venice also has to negotiate over the direct stake of the national government in its museums, airport, railway station and port. As a result the city and its lagoon continue to degrade, with the city estimated to be sinking at a rate of 2mm a year. The floor of the lagoon on which Venice stands may gradually be washed out to sea, transforming the lagoon into a bay, with the city in danger of subsidence or actual collapse into the water as the foundations are undermined.

As a cosmopolitan port city, Venice has always been a crowded place. Today, the city accommodates a daily average of around 144,000 residents and visitors combined, which falls short of the 190,000 residents the city housed at its 16th-century peak.

1973	1996	2003	2014
Italy's first 'special' law for Venice is enacted. It promises to protect urban settlements while maintaining the physical continuity of the lagoon.	La Fenice burns down for the second time; two electricians are found guilty of arson. A €90-million replica of the 19th-century opera house is completed in 2003.	Prime Minister Silvio Berlusconi launches construction of Modulo Sperimentale Elettromeccanico (MoSE) to prevent flooding from rising water levels.	MoSE is mired in scandal. Venice mayor Giorgio Orsoni is arrested, the city council suspended and the venerable office of Magistrato alle Acque is dissolved.

Architecture

So what exactly is Venetian architecture? Everyone has a pet period in Venice's chequered architectural history, and hardly anyone agrees which is Venice's defining moment. Ruskin waxed rhapsodic about Venetian Gothic and detested Palladio; Palladians rebuffed baroque; fans of regal rococo were scandalised by the Lido's louche Liberty (Italian art nouveau); and pretty much everyone recoiled at the inclinations of industry to strip Venice of ornamentation. Now that the latest architectural trend is creative repurposing, it's all making a comeback.

Engineering Marvels

Over the centuries, Venetian architecture has evolved into such a dazzling composite of materials, styles and influences that you might overlook its singular defining feature: it floats. Thousands of wooden pylons sunk into lagoon mud support stone foundations, built up with elegant brickwork and rustic ceiling beams, low *sotoportegi* (passageways) and lofty loggias, grand water gates and hidden *cortile* (courtyards). Instead of disguising or wallpapering over these essential Venetian structural elements, modern architects have begun highlighting them. With this approach, the Fondazione Giorgio Cini converted a naval academy into a cultural centre, Tadao Ando turned Punta della Dogana customs houses into a contemporary-art showplace, and Renzo Piano transformed historic Magazzini del Sale (salt warehouses) into a rotating gallery space for Fondazione Vedova. With original load-bearing supports and brickwork exposed to public admiration, Venice's new-old architecture seems more fresh and vital than ever.

Veneto-Byzantine

If Venice seems to have unfair aesthetic advantages, it did have an early start: cosmopolitan flair has made Venetian architecture a standout since the 7th century. While Venice proper was still a motley, muddy outpost of refugee settlements, the nearby island of Torcello was a booming Byzantine trade hub of 20,000 to 30,000 people.

At its spiritual centre was the Basilica di Santa Maria Assunta, which from afar looks like a Byzantine-style basilica on loan from Ravenna. But look closely: those 7th-to-9th-century apses have Romanesque arches, and the iconostasis separating the central nave from the presbytery is straight out of an Eastern Orthodox church. Back in Torcello's heyday, traders from France, Greece or Turkey could have stepped off their boats and into this church, and all felt at home. But to signal to visitors that they had arrived in a powerful trading centre, Santa Maria Assunta glitters with 12th-to-13th-century golden mosaics.

Excavations have revealed Torcello glassworks dating from the 7th century, and those furnaces would have been kept glowing through the night to produce the thousands of tiny glass *tesserae* (tiles) needed to create the mesmerising *Madonna* hovering over the altar – not to mention the rather alarmingly detailed *Last Judgment* mosaic, with hellfire licking at the dancing feet of the damned.

More than 1000 years of architectural history is covered on the short trip down the Grand Canal, lined with 200 palaces that range from Venetian Gothic with Moorish flourishes (the Ca' d'Oro) to postmodern neoclassical (Palazzo Grassi).

VENICE'S MOST CONTROVERSIAL BRIDGES

Ponte di Calatrava Officially known as Ponte della Costituzione (Constitution Bridge), Spanish architect Santiago Calatrava's contemporary bridge between Piazzale Roma and Ferrovia was commissioned for €4 million in 1999, and for a decade was variously denounced as unnecessary, inappropriate, wheelchair-inaccessible and torture for anyone with luggage. Though the bridge cost more than triple the original estimate, it also received private backing, hence its local nickname 'Benetton Bridge'.

Ponte di Rialto The original 1255 wooden structure burned during a 1310 revolt, and its replacement collapsed under spectators watching a 1444 wedding parade. The state couldn't gather funds for a 1551 stone bridge project pitched for by Palladio, Sansovino and Michelangelo, and the task fell to Antonio da Ponte in 1588. Cost overruns were enormous: as the stonework settled, the bridge cracked, and legend has it that only a deal with the Devil allowed da Ponte to finish by 1592.

Ponte dei Pugni (Bridge of the Fists) Turf battles were regularly fought on this Dorsoduro bridge between residents of Venice's north end, the Nicolotti, and its south end, the Castellani. Deadly brawls evolved into full-contact boxing matches, with starting footholds marked in the corners of the bridge. Bouts ended with fighters bloodied, bruised and bobbing in the canal. King Henry III of France apparently enjoyed the spectacle, but escalation into deadly knife fights in 1705 ended the practice.

Ponte delle Tette 'Tits Bridge' got its name in the late 15th century, when neighbourhood prostitutes were encouraged to display their wares in the windows of buildings above the bridge instead of taking their marketing campaigns to the streets. According to contemporary logic, this display was intended to curb a dramatic increase in sodomy.

Ponte dei Sospiri Built by Antonio Contino in 1600 and given its 'Bridge of Sighs' nickname by Lord Byron, the bridge connects the upper storeys of the Palazzo Ducale and Priggione Nove (New Prisons). According to Byron's conceit, doomed prisoners would sigh at their last glimpse of lovely Venice through the bridge's windows – but as you'll notice on Palazzo Ducale tours, the lagoon is scarcely visible through the stonework-screened windows.

Breakout Byzantine Style

When Venice made its definitive break with the Byzantine empire in the 9th century, it needed a landmark to set the city apart, and a platform to launch its golden age of maritime commerce. Basilica di San Marco captures Venice's grand designs in five vast gold mosaic domes, refracting stray sunbeams like an indoor fireworks display. Even today, the sight elicits audible gasps from crowds of international admirers. The basilica began with a triple nave in the 9th century but, after a fire two wings were added to form a Greek cross, in an idea borrowed from the Church of the Holy Apostles in Constantinople. The finest artisans from around the Mediterranean were brought in to raise the basilica's dazzle factor to jaw-dropping, creating the 11th-to-13th-century marble relief masterpieces over the Romanesque entry arches and the intricate Islamic geometry of the 12th to 13th-century inlaid semiprecious stone floors.

Since the basilica was the official chapel of the doge, every time Venice conquered new territory by commerce or force, the basilica displayed the doge's share of the loot – hence the walls of polychrome marble pilfered from Egypt and 2nd-century Roman bronze horses looted from Constantinople's hippodrome in 1204. The basilica's ornament shifted over the centuries from Gothic to Renaissance, but the message to visiting dignitaries remained the same: the glory above may be God's, but the power below rested with the doge.

Romanesque

Romanesque was all the rage across Western Europe in the 9th century, from the Lombard plains to Tuscany, southern France to northeast Spain, and later, Germany and England. While the materials ranged from basic brick to elaborate marble, Romanesque rounded archways, barrel-vaulted ceilings, triple naves and calming cloisters came to define early-medieval church architecture. This austere, classical style was a deliberate reference to the Roman Empire and early martyrs who sacrificed all for the Church. But in case the architecture failed to send the message, sculptural reliefs were added, heralding heroism on entry portals – and putting the fear of the devil into unbelievers, with angels and demons carved into stone capitals in creepy crypts.

As Venice became a maritime empire in the 13th century, many of the city's smaller Byzantine and early Romanesque buildings were swept away to make room for International Gothic grandeur. The finest examples of Romanesque in the Veneto – and possibly in northern Italy – are Verona's vast 12th to 14th-century Basilica di San Zeno Maggiore and Padua's frescoed jewel of a Romanesque Baptistry. Within Venice, Romanesque simplicity awaits at Chiesa di San Giacomo dell'Orio.

Venetian Gothic

Soaring spires and flying buttresses rose above Paris in the 12th century, making the rest of Europe suddenly seem small and squat by comparison. Soon every European capital was trying to top Paris with Gothic marvels of their own, featuring deceptively delicate ribbed cross-vaulting that distributed the weight of stone walls and allowed openings for vast stained-glass windows.

Europe's medieval superpowers used this grand international style to showcase their splendour and status. Venice one-upped its neighbours not with height but by inventing its own version of Gothic. Venice had been trading across the Mediterranean with partners from Lebanon to North Africa for centuries, and the constant exchange of building materials, engineering innovations and aesthetic ideals led to a creative cross-pollination in Western and Middle Eastern architecture. Instead of framing windows with the ordinary ogive (pointed) arch common to France and Germany, Venice added an elegantly tapered, Moorish flourish to its arches, with a trilobate (three-lobed) shape that became a signature of Venetian Gothic at Ca' d'Oro.

Brick Gothic

While Tuscany, like France and Germany, used marble for Gothic cathedrals, Venice showcased a more austere, cerebral style with clever brickwork and a Latin cross plan at I Frari, completed in 1443 after a century's work, and Zanipolo, consecrated in 1430. The more fanciful brick Madonna dell'Orto was built on 10th-century foundations, but its facade was lightened up with lacy white porphyry ornament in 1460–64. This white stone framing red brick may have Middle Eastern origins: the style is pronounced in Yemen, where Venice's Marco Polo established trade relations in the 13th century.

Secular Gothic

Gothic architecture was so complicated and expensive that it was usually reserved for churches in wealthy parishes – but Venice decided that if it was good enough for God, then it was good enough for the doge. A rare and extravagant secular Gothic construction, the Palazzo Ducale was built in grand Venetian Gothic style beginning in 1340, with

Wagering which of Venice's brick *campanile* (bell towers) will next fall victim to shifting *barene* (mud banks) is a morbid Venetian pastime – but don't bet on the leaning tower of San Giorgio dei Greci, which has slouched ever since 1592. San Marco's *campanile* stood ramrod-straight until its 1902 collapse.

refinements and extensions continuing through the 15th century. The palace was just finished when a fire swept through the building in 1577, leaving Venice with a tricky choice: rebuild in the original *gotico fiorito* (flamboyant Gothic) style, or go with the trendy new Renaissance style proposed by Palladio and his peers. The choice was Gothic, but instead of brick, the facade was a puzzlework of white Istrian stone and pink Veronese marble with a delicate, lofty white loggia facing the Grand Canal. In 1853, critic and unabashed Gothic architecture partisan John Ruskin called the Palazzo Ducale the 'central building of the world'.

While the doge's palace is a show-stopper, many Venetian nobles weren't living too shabbily themselves by the 14th century. Even stripped of its original gilding, the Ca' d'Oro is a Grand Canal highlight. The typical Venetian noble family's *palazzo* (palace) had a water gate that gave access from boats to a courtyard or ground floor, with the grand reception hall usually on the *piano nobile* ('noble' or 1st floor). The *piano nobile* was built to impress, with light streaming through double-height loggia windows and balustraded balconies. The 2nd floor might also feature an elegant arcade topped with Venetian Gothic marble arches and trefoils, with crenellation crowning the roofline like a whimsical tiara.

> **Most Divine Religious Buildings**
> ....
> Basilica di San Marco (San Marco)
> ....
> Chiesa di San Giorgio Maggiore (Southern Islands)
> ....
> Chiesa di Santa Maria dei Miracoli (Cannaregio)
> ....
> Schola Spagnola (Cannaregio)

Renaissance

For centuries Gothic cathedrals soared to the skies, pointing the eye and aspirations heavenward – but as the Renaissance ushered in an era of reason and humanism, architecture became more grounded and rational. Venice wasn't immediately sold on this radical new Tuscan world view, but the revival of classical ideals was soon popularised by the University of Padua and Venetian publishing houses.

With the study of classical philosophy came a fresh appreciation for strict classical order, harmonious geometry and human-scale proportions. A prime early example in Venice is the 1489 Chiesa di Santa Maria dei Miracoli, a small church and great achievement by sculptor-architect Pietro Lombardo (1435–1515) with his sons Tullio and Antonio. The exterior is clad in veined multicolour marbles apparently 'borrowed' from Basilica di San Marco's slag-heap, kept in check by a steady rhythm of Corinthian pilasters. The stark marble interiors set off a joyous profusion of finely worked sculpture, and the coffered ceiling is filled in with portraits of saints in contemporary Venetian garb. This is ecclesiastical architecture come down to earth, intimate and approachable.

Sansovino's Humanist Architecture

Born in Florence and well versed in classical architecture in Rome, Jacopo Sansovino (1486–1570) was a champion of the Renaissance as Venice's *proto* (official city architect). His best works reveal not just a shift in aesthetics but a sea change in thinking. While the Gothic ideal was a staggeringly tall spire topped by a cross, his Biblioteca Nazionale Marciana was a role-model Renaissance landmark: a low, flat-roofed monument to learning, embellished with statues of great men. Great men are also the theme of Sansovino's Scala dei Giganti in the Palazzo Ducale, a staircase reserved for Venetian dignitaries and an unmistakable metaphorical reminder that in order to ascend to the heights of power, one must stand on the shoulders of giants.

Instead of striving for the skies, Renaissance architecture reached for the horizon. Sansovino changed the skyline of Venice with his work on 15 buildings, including the serenely splendid Chiesa di San Francesco della Vigna, completed with a colonnaded facade by Palladio and

Venetians avoid walking between the San Marco pillars, where criminals were once executed. According to legend, anyone wandering between these pillars will meet an untimely demise – doomed Marin Falier was beheaded eight months after supposedly passing between them to accept the post of doge.

sculptural flourishes by Pietro and Tullio Lombardo. Thankfully, however, one of Sansovino's most ambitious projects never came to fruition: his plan to turn Piazza San Marco into a Roman forum.

Renaissance Palaces

As the Renaissance swept into Venice, the changes became noticeable along the Grand Canal: pointed Gothic arcades relaxed into rounded archways, repeated geometric forms and serene order replaced Gothic trefoils, and palaces became anchored by bevelled blocks of rough-hewn, rusticated marble. One Renaissance trendsetter was Bergamo-born Mauro Codussi (c 1440–1504), whose pleasing classical vocabulary applied equally to churches, the 15th-century Torre dell'Orologio (Clock Tower) and several Grand Canal palaces, including Ca' Vendramin Calergi, better known today as Casinò di Venezia.

Michele Sanmicheli (1484–1559) was from Verona but, like Sansovino, he worked in Rome, fleeing its sacking in 1527. The Venetian Republic kept him busy engineering defence works for the city, including Le Vignole's Forte Sant'Andrea, also known as the Castello da Mar (Sea Castle). Even Sanmicheli's private commissions have an imposing imperial Roman grandeur; the Grand Canal's Palazzo Grimani (built 1557–59) incorporates a triumphal arch on the ground floor, and feels more suited to its current use as the city's appeal court than a 16th-century pleasure palace. Sanmicheli is also occasionally credited with the other Renaissance Palazzo Grimani in Castello, along with Sansovino – but Venetian Renaissance man Giovanni Grimani seems to have mostly designed his own home as a suitably classical showcase for his collection of ancient Roman statuary, now in the Museo Correr.

Palladio

As the baroque began to graft flourishes and curlicues onto basic Renaissance shapes, Padua-born Andrea Palladio (1508–80) carefully stripped them away, and in doing so laid the basis for modern architecture. His facades are an open-book study of classical architecture, with rigorously elemental geometry – a triangular pediment supported by round columns atop a rectangle of stairs – that lends an irresistible logic to the stunning exteriors of San Giorgio Maggiore and Il Redentore.

Critic John Ruskin detested Renaissance architecture in general and Palladio in particular, and ranted about San Giorgio Maggiore in his three-volume book *The Stones of Venice* (1851–53): 'It is impossible to conceive a design more gross, more barbarous, more childish in conception, more servile in plagiarism, more insipid in result, more contemptible under every point of rational regard.' But don't take his word for it: Palladio's blinding white Istrian-stone facades may seem stoic from afar, but up close they become relatable, with billowing ceilings and an easy grace that anticipated baroque and high modernism.

Baroque & Neoclassical

In other parts of Europe, baroque architecture seemed lightweight: an assemblage of frills and thrills, with no underlying Renaissance reason or gravitas. But baroque's buoyant spirits made perfect sense along the Grand Canal, where white-stone party palaces with tiers of ornament looked like floating wedding cakes. Baldassare Longhena (1598–1682) stepped into the role as the city's official architect at a moment when the city was breathing a sigh of relief at surviving the Black Death, and he provided the architectural antidote to Venice's dark days with the white bubble-dome of Basilica di Santa Maria della Salute.

Top Palladio Designs

....

Chiesa di San Giorgio Maggiore (Southern Islands)

....

Chiesa del Santissimo Redentore (Giudecca)

....

Facade of Chiesa di San Francesco della Vigna (Castello)

....

Le Zitelle (Giudecca)

Architectural historians chalk up Longhena's unusual octagon base and dome to the influence of Roman shrines and cabbala diagrams, and the church's geometric stone floors are said to have mystical healing powers. Santa Maria della Salute's exterior decoration evokes pagan triumphal arches, with statues posing triumphantly on the facade and reclining over the main entrance. The building has inspired landscape artists from Turner to Monet, leading baroque-baiting Ruskin to concede that 'an architect trained in the worst schools, and utterly devoid of all meaning or purpose in his work may yet have such natural gift of massing and grouping as will render all his structures effective when seen from a distance'.

Although Ruskin deemed Longhena's fanciful facade of hulking sculptures at the Ospedaletto 'monstrous', baroque fans will think otherwise. Another Longhena-designed marvel is Ca' Rezzonico, a wonder of sunny salons graced with spectacular Tiepolo ceilings. Soaring grandeur and mystical geometry in the interior of the Ghetto's Schola Spagnola have led many to attribute it to Longhena, too.

Venice's first bridge to the mainland was built by the Austrians at Venetian taxpayers' expense in 1841–46, enabling troop and supplies transport by railway. Propped up by 222 arches, the bridge spans 2.7km. Explosives were originally planted under the piers, to be detonated in case of emergency.

Neoclassicism & Napoleon

Venice didn't lose track of Renaissance harmonies completely under all that ornament, and in the 18th century muscular neoclassicism came into vogue. Inspired by Palladio, Giorgio Massari (c 1686–1766) created the Chiesa dei Gesuati as high theatre, setting the stage for Tiepolo's *trompe l'œil* ceilings. He built the gracious Palazzo Grassi with salons arranged around a balustraded central light well, and brought to completion Longhena's Ca' Rezzonico on the Grand Canal.

Napoleon roared into Venice like a bully in 1797, itching to rearrange its face. The emperor's first order of architectural business was demolishing Sansovino's Chiesa di Geminiano to construct a monument in his own glory: the Ala Napoleonica (now Museo Correr) by Giovanni Antonio Selva (1753–1819). Napoleon had an entire district with four churches bulldozed to make way for the Giardini Pubblici and Via Garibaldi in Castello. Though Napoleon ruled Venice for only 11 years, French boulevards appeared where there were once churches across the city. Among others, Sant'Angelo, San Basilio, Santa Croce, Santa Maria Nova, Santa Marina, San Mattio, San Paterniano, San Severo, San Stin, Santa Ternita and San Vito disappeared under the ambitious Gallic ruler.

The 20th Century

After Giudecca's baroque buildings were torn down for factories and the Ferrovia (train station) erected, the city took decades to recover from the shock. Venice reverted to 19th-century *venezianitá,* the tendency to tack on exaggerated Venetian elements from a range of periods – a Gothic trefoil arch here, a baroque cupola there. Rather than harmonising these disparate architectural elements, interiors were swagged in silk damask and moodlit with Murano chandeliers. The resulting hodgepodge seemed to signal the end of Venice's architectural glory days.

From Liberty Flounce to Fascist Sobriety

After nearly a century dominated by French and Austrian influence, Venice let loose on the Lido with the bohemian decadence of *stile liberty* (Liberty style, or Italian art nouveau). Ironwork vegetation wound around balconies of seaside villas and wild fantasy took root at grand hotels, including Giovanni Sardi's 1898–1908 Byzantine-Moorish Excelsior and Guido Sullam's garish Ausonia & Hungaria. Eclectic references to Japanese art, organic patterns from nature and past Venetian styles give Lido buildings cosmopolitan flair with *stile liberty* tiles, stained glass, ironwork and murals.

By the 1930s, the Liberty party was well and truly over. The Fascists arrived to lay down the law on the Lido, applying a strict, functional neoclassicism even to entertainment venues such as the 1937–38 Palazzo della Mostra del Cinema and the former Casinò. Fascist architecture makes occasional awkward appearances in central Venice too, notably the Hotel Bauer and the extension to the Hotel Danieli, which represent an architectural oxymoron: the strict Fascist luxury-deco hotel.

Scarpa's High Modernism

The Biennale introduced new international architecture to Venice, but high modernism remained mostly an imported style until it was championed by Venice's own Carlo Scarpa (1906–78). Instead of creating seamless modern surfaces, Scarpa frequently exposed underlying structural elements and added unexpectedly poetic twists. At Negozio Olivetti, mosaic and water channels mimic *acqua alta* (high tide) across the floor, a floating staircase makes ascent seem effortless, and internal balconies jut out mid-air like diving boards into the infinite. Scarpa's concrete-slab Venezuelan Pavilion was ahead of its time by a full half-century, and inevitably steals the show at Biennales. High modernist architecture aficionados make pilgrimages outside Venice to see Scarpa's Brioni Tomb near Asolo, and Castelvecchio in Verona. Scarpa's smaller works can be spotted all over Venice: the cricket-shaped former ticket booth at the Biennale, the entry and gardens of Palazzo Querini Stampalia, spare restorations to the doorway of the Accademia, the elegant *boiserie* (panelling) inside the Aula Mario Baratto at Ca' Foscari, as well as the playful main gate at the Università Iuav di Venezia – Tolentini.

Next to bridges, Venice's most common architectural features are its *poggi* (well-heads). Before Venice's aqueduct was constructed, more than 6000 wells collected and filtered rainwater for public use. Even today, overflow happy-hour crowds at neighbourhood *bacari* (bars) schmooze and toast around 600 surviving ancient watering holes.

Contemporary Venice

Modernism was not without its critics, especially among Venice's preservationists. But when a disastrous flood hit Venice in 1966, architecture aficionados around the globe put aside their differences, and aided Venetians in bailing out *palazzi* and reinforcing foundations across the city. With the support of Unesco and funding from 24 affiliated organisations worldwide, Venice has completed over 1500 restoration projects in 40 years.

Today the city is open to a broader range of styles, though controversy is never far behind. Divisive projects that never left the drawing board include a 1953 design for student housing on the Grand Canal by Frank Lloyd Wright, Le Corbusier's 1964 plans for a hospital in Cannaregio, Louis Kahn's 1968 Palazzo dei Congressi project for the Giardini Pubblici, and the 2011 Palais Lumière, a three-finned skyscraper proposed by fashion designer Pierre Cardin and his architect nephew Rodrigo Basilicati. Planned for the industrial, mainland area of Porto Marghera, the 60-storey project ignited widespread opposition in Venice, with many Venetians arguing that its enormous scale and sci-fi design was highly inappropriate in the historic lagoon. Old also triumphed over new in the 2003 reconstruction of La Fenice, which opted for a €90 million replica of the 19th-century opera house instead of an edgier, modernised version proposed by the late architect Gae Aulenti.

1. Mosaic, Basilica di San Marco (p50) 2. Palazzo Ducale (p53) 3. Basilica di San Marco 4. Basilica di Santa Maria della Salute (p76)

Architectural Marvels

➜ **Basilica di San Marco** (p50) Only if angels and pirates founded an architecture firm could there ever be another building like Venice's cathedral. Saints tip-toe across gold mosaics inside bubble domes, gilded horses pilfered from Constantinople gallop off the loggia, and priceless marbles lining the walls and floors are on exceedingly long-term loan from Syria and Egypt. Awed glee ensues.

➜ **Basilica di Santa Maria della Salute** (p76) The sublime white dome defies gravity, but thousands of wooden poles underfoot are doing the heavy lifting. Posts sunk deep into lagoon mud create an ingenious foundation for Baldassare Longhena's white Istrian stone masterpiece, influenced by mystical cabbala designs and rumoured to have curative powers.

➜ **Palazzo Ducale** (p53) Town halls don't get grander than this pink palace. Other medieval cities reserved Gothic graces for cathedrals, but Venice went all out to impress visiting dignitaries and potential business partners with pink Veronese marble and gilt staircases – you'd never guess there were spies and prisoners hidden upstairs.

➜ **Biennale Pavilions** (p124) International relations never looked better than in Venice's Giardini Pubblici, where Biennale pavilions are purpose-built to reflect national architectural identities from Hungary (futuristic folklore hut) to Korea (creative industrial complex). Venetian modernist Carlo Scarpa steals the show with his Venezuelan Pavilion.

➜ **Chiesa di Santa Maria dei Miracoli** (p111) Small with outsized swagger, this corner church is a masterpiece of Renaissance repurposing. Pietro Lombardo and sons worked wonders from San Marco's marble slag-heap, creating a gleaming, aquarium-like space where carved mermaids and miracle-working Madonnas seem right at home.

Old is the New New

Despite the constraints of history, strict building codes, and the practical challenges of construction with materials transported by boat, lifted by crane and hauled by handcart, a surprising number of projects have turned Venice into a portfolio of contemporary architecture.

MIT-trained Italian architect Cino Zucchi kicked off the creative revival of Giudecca in 1995 with his conversion of 19th-century brick factories and waterfront warehouses into art spaces and studio lofts. A decade later, a triangular WWII bunker and bombs warehouse found new purpose as Teatro Junghans, a hot spot for experimental theatre.

London-based firm David Chipperfield Architects has breathed new life into the cemetery island of San Michele with its sleek contemporary extensions. Among them is the House of the Dead, a bold, basalt-clad burial complex consisting of four open courtyards. The most striking of these is the Courtyard of the Four Evangelists. Featuring a black concrete colonnade, the courtyard's walls and pavement are inlaid with text from the gospels. The next stage of the project will see a new island flanking the existing one. Separated by a canal, this supporting island is set to include gardens at water level and a series of elegant, sculpted mausoleums.

Meanwhile, rebirth of the artistic kind underscores Fondazione Giorgio Cini's redevelopment of the monastary on Isola di San Giorgio Maggiore, one that has transformed the island into a global cultural centre. Among its numerous features is a garden maze dedicated to Argentine writer Jorge Luis Borges behind the Palladian cloisters, as well as a dormitory turned humanities library to complement Baldassare Longhena's original 17th-century science library. Across the Canale di San Marco, the continuing evolution of Venice's historic Arsenale shipyards has seen its medieval assembly-line sheds turned into fetching Biennale art galleries.

French billionaire art collector François Pinault hired Japanese minimalist architect Tadao Ando to repurpose two historic buildings into settings for his contemporary-art collection. Instead of undermining their originality, Ando's careful repurposing showcases the muscular strength of Giorgio Masari's 1749 neoclassical Palazzo Grassi in San Marco and Venice's late 17th-century Punta della Dogana customs houses in Dorsoduro. Around the corner from Punta della Dogana, Pritzker Prize–winning architect Renzo Piano reinvented the Magazzini del Sale as a showcase for the Fondazione Vedova, an art foundation dedicated to abstract Venetian painter Emilio Vedova. Similar to Ando's approach, Renzo's conversion embraces the building's original essence, with historic roof trusses and brick walls integral elements of the modern makeover. Within this clear, uncluttered historical template, Piano added his respectful modern touches. The most unique of these is a conveyor system of 10 robotic arms, designed to rotate the gallery's art works like a team of cyborg curators. Renzo's transformation is only fitting: Venice's salt monopoly was once its dearest treasure, but now its ideas are its greatest asset.

Culture and commerce co-exist in Dutch architect Rem Koolhaas' recent redevelopment of the Fondaco dei Tedeschi, steps away from the Rialto Bridge in San Marco. Once a base for German merchants, the revamped 16th-century *palazzo* now houses a department store, contemporary frescoes, a publicly accessible rooftop, as well as dedicated public and cultural spaces. The highly publicised incorporation of non-commercial spaces into the project aimed to appease its opponents, who argued that the historical building's retail conversion undermines Venice's heritage.

Best Modern Design

Biennale pavilions
(Castello)

Punta della
Dogana
(Dorsoduro)

Negozio Olivetti
(San Marco)

Fondazione Giorgio Cini (Southern
Islands)

Palazzo Grassi
(San Marco)

The Arts

By the 13th century, Venice had already accomplished the impossible: building a glorious maritime empire on a shallow lagoon. But its dominance didn't last. Plague repeatedly decimated the city in the 14th century, new trade routes to the New World bypassed Venice and its tax collectors, and the Ottoman Empire dominated the Adriatic by the mid-15th century. Yet when Venice could no longer prevail by wealth or force, it triumphed on even loftier levels, with art, music, theatre and poetry.

Visual Arts

The sheer number of masterpieces packed into Venice might make you wonder if there's something in the water here, but the reason may be simpler: historically, Venice tended not to starve its artists. Multiyear commissions from wealthy private patrons, the city and the Church offered creatives a sense of security. Artists were granted extraordinary opportunities to produce new artwork without interference, with the city frequently declining to enforce the Inquisition's censorship edicts. Instead of dying young, destitute and out of favour, painters such as Titian and Giovanni Bellini survived into their 80s to produce late, great works. The side-by-side innovations of emerging and mature artists created schools of painting so distinct they still set Venice apart from the rest of Italy – and the world.

Early Venetian Painting

Once you've seen the mosaics at Basilica di San Marco and Santa Maria Assunta in Torcello, you'll recognise key aspects of early Venetian painting: larger-than-life religious figures with wide eyes and serene expressions floating on gold backgrounds and hovering inches above Gothic thrones. Byzantine influence is clearly present in *Madonna and Child with Two Votaries,* painted c 1325 by Paolo Veneziano (c 1300–62) and on display at the Gallerie dell'Accademia: like stage hands parting theatre curtains, two angels pull back the edges of a starry red cloak to reveal a hulking Madonna, golden baby Jesus, and two tiny patrons.

By the early 15th century, Venetian painters were breaking with Byzantine convention. *Madonna with Child* (c 1455) by Jacopo Bellini (c 1396–1470) in the Accademia is an image any modern parent might relate to: bright-eyed baby Jesus reaches one sandalled foot over the edge of the balcony, while a seemingly sleep-deprived Mary patiently pulls him away from the ledge. Padua's Andrea Mantegna (1431–1506) took Renaissance perspective to extremes, showing bystanders in his biblical scenes reacting to unfolding miracles and martyrdoms with shock, awe, anger, and even inappropriate laughter.

Tuscan painter Gentile da Fabriano was in Venice as he was beginning his transition to Renaissance realism, and apparently influenced the young Murano-born painter Antonio Vivarini (c 1415–80), whose *Passion* polyptych in Ca' d'Oro shows tremendous pathos. Antonio's brother, Bartolomeo Vivarini (c 1432–99), created a delightful

Turbaned figures appear across Venice on the corners of Campo dei Mori, on diamond-encrusted jewels at Sigfrido Cipolato, and propping up I Frari funerary monuments. Misleadingly referred to as Mori (Moors), some represent Venetians from Greek Morea, others Turkish pirates, and others enslaved Africans who rowed merchant ships.

The winged-lion symbol of Mark the Evangelist, Basilica di San Marco (p50)

altarwpiece in I Frari showing a baby Jesus wriggling out of the arms of the Madonna, squarely seated on her marble Renaissance throne.

Venice's Red-Hot Renaissance

Jacopo Bellini's sons used a new medium that would revolutionise Venetian painting: oil paints. The 1500 *Miracle of the Cross at the Bridge of San Lorenzo* by Gentile Bellini (1429–1507) at the Accademia shows the religious figure not high on a throne or adrift in the heavens, but floating in the Grand Canal, with crowds of bystanders stopped in their tracks in astonishment. Giovanni Bellini (c 1430–1516) takes an entirely different approach to his Accademia *Annunciation,* using luminous reds and oranges to focus attention on the solitary figure of the kneeling Madonna awed by an angel arriving in a swish of rumpled drapery.

From Venice's guild of painters emerged some of art history's greatest names, starting with Giovanni Bellini's apt pupils: Giorgione (1477–1510) and Titian (c 1488–1576). The two worked together on the frescoes that once covered the Fondaco dei Tedeschi (only a few fragments remain in the Palazzo Grimani), with teenage Titian following Giorgione's lead. Giorgione was a Renaissance man who wrote poetry and music, is credited with inventing the easel, and preferred to paint from inspiration without sketching out his subject first, as in his enigmatic, Leonardo da Vinci–style 1508 *La tempesta* (The Storm) at the Gallerie dell'Accademia.

When Giorgione died at 33, probably of the plague, Titian finished some of his works – but young Titian soon set himself apart with brushstrokes that brought his subjects to life, while taking on a life of their own. At Basilica di Santa Maria della Salute, you'll notice Titian started out a measured, methodical painter in his 1510 *Saint Mark on the Throne.* After seeing Michelangelo's expressive *Last Judgment,* Titian let it rip: in his final 1576 *Pietà* he smeared paint onto canvas with his bare hands.

Winged lions carved onto Venetian facades symbolise St Mark, Venice's patron, but some served sinister functions. In the 1500s, the Consiglio dei Dieci (Council of Ten) established *bocca dei leoni* (lion's mouths) – stone lions' heads with slots for inserting anonymous denunciations of neighbours for crimes ranging from cursing to conspiracy.

But even for a man of many masterpieces, Titian's 1518 altarpiece *Assunta* (Ascension) at I Frari is nothing short of enigmatic, mysteriously lighting up the cavernous space with solar-like energy. Vittore Carpaccio (1460–1526) rivalled Titian's reds with his own sanguine hues – hence the dish of bloody beef cheekily named in his honour by Harry's Bar – but it was Titian's *Assunta* that cemented Venice's reputation for glowing, glorious hues.

Not Minding Their Manners: Venice's Mannerists

Although art history tends to insist on a division of labour between Venice and Florence – Venice had the colour, Florence the ideas – the Venetian School had plenty of ideas that repeatedly got it into trouble. Titian was a hard act to follow, but there's no denying the impact of Venice's Jacopo Robusti, aka Tintoretto (1518–94), and Paolo Cagliari from Verona, known as Veronese (1528–88).

A crash course in Tintoretto begins at Chiesa della Madonna dell'Orto, his parish church and the serene brick backdrop for his action-packed 1546 *Last Judgment*. True-blue Venetian that he is, Tintoretto shows the final purge as a teal tidal wave, which lost souls are vainly trying to hold back, like human MoSE barriers. A dive-bombing angel swoops in to save one last person – a riveting image Tintoretto reprised on the upper floor of the Scuola Grande di San Rocco. The artist spent some 15 years creating works for San Rocco, and his biblical scenes read like a modern graphic novel. Tintoretto sometimes used special effects to get his point across, enhancing his colours with a widely available local material: finely crushed glass.

Veronese's colours have a luminosity entirely their own, earning him Palazzo Ducale commissions and room to run riot inside Chiesa di San Sebastiano – but his choice of subjects got him into trouble. When Veronese was commissioned to paint the *Last Supper* (in the Gallerie dell'Accademia) his masterpiece ended up looking suspiciously like a Venetian shindig, with apostles in Venetian dress mingling freely with Turkish merchants, Jewish guests, serving wenches, begging lapdogs and (most shocking of all) Protestant Germans. When the Inquisition demanded he change the painting, Veronese refused to remove the offending Germans and altered scarcely a stroke of paint, simply changing the title to *Feast in the House of Levi*. In an early victory for freedom of expression, Venice stood by the decision.

The next generation of Mannerists included Palma il Giovane (1544–1628), who finished Titian's *Pietá* after the master's death and fused Titian's early naturalism with Tintoretto's drama. Another Titian acolyte who adopted Tintoretto's dramatic lighting was Jacopo da Ponte from Bassano del Grappa, called Bassano (1517–92). Bassano's work is so high contrast and high drama, at first glance you might wonder how black-velvet paintings wound up in the Gallerie dell'Accademia, Chiesa di San Giorgio Maggiore and Bassano del Grappa's Museo Civico.

A Blast of Baroque

By the 18th century, Venice had endured plague and seen its ambitions for world domination dashed – but the city repeatedly made light of its dire situation in tragicomic art. Pietro Longhi (1701–85) dispensed with lofty subject matter and painted wickedly witty Venetian social satires, while Giambattista Tiepolo (1696–1770) turned religious themes into a premise for dizzying ceilings with rococo sunbursts. Ca' Rezzonico became a show place for both their talents, with an entire salon of Longhi's drawing-room scenarios and Tiepolo's *trompe l'œil* ceiling masterpieces.

Instead of popes on thrones, portraitist Rosalba Carriera (1675–1757) captured her socialite sitters on snuffboxes, and painted in a medium she pioneered: pastels. Her portraits at Ca' Rezzonico walk a fine line between Tiepolo's flattery and Longhi's satire, revealing her sitters' every twinkle and wrinkle.

As the 18th-century party wound down, the Mannerists' brooding theatricality merged with Tiepolo's pastel beauty in works by Tiepolo's son, Giandomenico Tiepolo (1727–1804). His 1747–49 *Stations of the Cross* in Chiesa di San Polo takes a dim view of humanity in light colours, illuminating the jeering faces of Jesus' tormentors. Giandomenico used a lighter touch working alongside his father on the frescoes at Villa Valmarana 'ai Nani' outside Vicenza, covering the walls with Chinese motifs, rural scenes and Carnevale characters.

The Vedutisti

Many Venetian artists turned their attention from the heavens to the local landscape in the 18th century, notably Antonio Canal, aka Canaletto (1697–1768). He became the leading figure of the *vedutisti* (landscape artists) with minutely detailed *vedute* (views) of Venice that leave admiring viewers with vicarious hand cramps. You might be struck how closely Canalettos resemble photographs – and, in fact, Canaletto created his works with the aid of a forerunner to the photographic camera, the *camera oscura* (camera obscura). Light entered this instrument and reflected the image onto a sheet of glass, which Canaletto then traced. After he had the outlines down, he filled in exact details, from lagoon algae to hats on passers-by.

Vedute sold well to Venice visitors; they were like rich man's postcards. Canaletto was backed by the English collector John Smith, who introduced the artist to such a vast English clientele that only a few of his paintings can be seen in the Veneto today, in Venice's Gallerie

Top Art Workshops

Various hands-on workshops during the Biennale (Castello)

....

Printing and engraving at Bottega del Tintoretto (Cannaregio)

....

Screenprinting at Fallani Venezia (Cannaregio)

....

Painting Venice lessons (citywide)

TOP FIVE ARTISTS IN RESIDENCE

Albrecht Dürer (1471–1528) Dürer left his native Nuremberg for Venice in 1494, hoping to see Venetian experiments in perspective and colour that were the talk of Europe. Giovanni Bellini took him under his wing, and once Dürer returned to Germany in 1495, he began his evolution from Gothic painter into Renaissance artist. When Dürer returned to Venice in 1505, he was feted as a visionary.

JMW Turner (1775–1851) Turner was drawn to Venice three times (in 1819, 1833 and 1840), fascinated by the former merchant empire that, like his native England, had once commanded the sea. His hazy portraits of the city are studies in light at different times of day; as he explained to art critic John Ruskin, 'atmosphere is my style'. Ruskin applauded the effort, but in London many critics loathed Turner's work.

James Whistler (1834–1903) The American painter arrived in Venice in 1879, bankrupt and exhausted after a failed libel case brought against John Ruskin. He rediscovered his verve and brush in prolific paintings of the lagoon city, returning to London in 1880 with a formidable portfolio that re-established his reputation.

John Singer Sargent (1856–1925) A lifelong admirer of Venice, the American visited at a young age and became a part-time resident from 1880 to 1913. His intimate knowledge of the city shows in his paintings, which capture new angles on familiar panoramas and illuminate neglected monuments.

Claude Monet (1840–1926) The French artist turned up in Venice in 1908, and immediately found Impressionist inspiration in architecture that seemed to dissolve into lagoon mists and shimmering waters. Despite claiming that the city was too beautiful to paint, he set brush to 37 canvases during his short sojourn.

dell'Accademia and Ca' Rezzonico, and further afield in Vicenza's Palazzo Leoni Montanari. Canaletto's nephew Bernardo Bellotto (1721–80) also adopted the *camera oscura* in his painting process, though his expressionistic landscapes use strong *chiaroscuro* (shadow and light contrasts). His paintings hang in the Accademia alongside *San Marco Basin with San Giorgio and Giudecca* by Francesco Guardi (1712–93), whose Impressionistic approach shows Venice's glories reflected in the lagoon. Among the last great *vedutisti* was Venetian Impressionist Emma Ciardi (1879–1933), who captured Venetian mysteries unfolding amid shimmering early-morning mists in luminous landscapes at Ca' Rezzonico and Ca' Pesaro.

Lucky Stiffs: Venetian Funerary Sculpture

Bookending Venice's accomplishments in painting are its sculpted marvels. The city kept its sculptors busy, with 200 churches needing altars and the fire-prone Palazzo Ducale requiring near-constant rebuilding for 300 years, not to mention the almost endless chiselling of tombs for nobles with political careers cut short by age, plague and intrigue. The tomb of Doge Marco Corner in Zanipolo by Pisa's Nino Pisano (c 1300–68) is a sprawling wall monument with a massive, snoozing doge that somewhat exaggerated his career: Corner was doge for less than three years.

Venice's Pietro Lombardo (1435–1515) and his sons Tullio (1460–1532) and Antonio (1458–1516) sculpted heroic, classical monuments to short-lived doges: Nicolo Marcello, doge for a year (1473–74), Pietro Mocenigo (1474–76) and Andrea Vendramin (1476–78). This last gilded marble monument was probably completed under Tullio, who literally cut corners: he sculpted the figures in half relief, and chopped away part of Pisano's Corner tomb to make room for Vendramin. Tullio's strong suit was the ideal beauty of his faces, as you can see in his bust of a young male saint at Chiesa di Santo Stefano.

The most prominent sculptor to emerge from the Veneto is Antonio Canova (1757–1822), whose pyramid tomb intended for Titian at I Frari would become his own funerary masterpiece. Mourners hang their heads and clutch one another, scarcely aware that their diaphanous garments are slipping off; even the great winged lion of St Mark is curled up in grief. Don't let his glistening Orpheus and Eurydice in Museo Correr fool you: Canova's seamless perfection in glistening marble was achieved through rough drafts modelled in gypsum, displayed at the Museo Canova near the hilltop town of Asolo.

Venetian Modernism

The arrival of Napoleon in 1797 was a disaster for Venice and its art. During his Kingdom of Italy (1806–14), Napoleon and his forces knocked down churches and systematically plundered Venice and the region of artistic treasures. Some works have been restored to Venice, including the bronze horses of Basilica di San Marco that arguably belong in İstanbul, given that Venice pilfered them from Constantinople. Yet even under 19th-century occupation, Venice remained a highlight of the Grand Tour, and painters who flocked to the city created memorable Venice cityscapes.

After joining the newly unified Italy in 1866, Venice's signature artistic contribution to the new nation was Francesco Hayez (1791–1882). The Venetian painter paid his dues with society portraits but is best remembered for Romanticism and frank sexuality, beginning with *Rinaldo and Armida* (1814), in the Gallerie dell'Accademia. Sexuality and Italian patriotism underline Hayez' brooding *Meditation* (1851) in

Top Five for Modernism

Peggy Guggenheim Collection (Dorsoduro)

Ca' Pesaro (Santa Croce)

Fondazione Prada (Santa Croce)

Fondazione Giorgio Cini (Isola di San Giorgio Maggiore)

Museo Fortuny (San Marco)

Verona's Galleria d'Arte Moderna, a work driven by the artist's frustration at the failed pro-unification battles of 1848.

Never shy about self-promotion, Venice held its first Biennale in 1895 to reassert its role as global taste maker and provide an essential corrective to the brutality of the Industrial Revolution. A garden pavilion showcased a self-promoting, studiously inoffensive take on Italian art – principally lovely ladies, pretty flowers, and lovely ladies wearing pretty flowers. Other nations were granted pavilions in 1907, but the Biennale retained strict control, and had a Picasso removed from the Spanish Pavilion in 1910 so as not to shock the public with modernity.

A backlash to Venetian conservatism arose from the ranks of Venetian painters experimenting in modern styles. Shows of young artists backed by the Duchess Felicita Bevilacqua La Masa found a permanent home in 1902, when the Duchess gifted Ca' Pesaro to the city as a modern-art museum. A leader of the Ca' Pesaro crowd was Gino Rossi (1884–1947), whose brilliant blues and potent symbolism bring to mind Gauguin, Matisse and the Fauvists, and whose later work shifted toward Cubism. Often called the Venetian van Gogh, Rossi spent many years in psychiatric institutions, where he died. Sculptor Arturo Martini (1889–1947) contributed works to Ca' Pesaro ranging from the rough-edged terracotta *Prostitute* (c 1913) to his radically streamlined 1919 gesso bust.

Top Five for Contemporary Art

Venice Biennale (Castello)

Peggy Guggenheim Collection (Dorsoduro)

Ca' Pesaro (Santa Croce)

Punta della Dogana (Dorsoduro)

Palazzo Grassi (San Marco)

From Futurism to Fluidity

In 1910, Filippo Tommaso Marinetti (1876–1944) threw packets of his manifesto from the Torre dell'Orologio (Clock Tower) promoting a new vision for the arts: futurism. In the days of the doge, Marinetti would have been accused of heresy for his declaration that Venice (a 'magnificent sore of the past') should be wiped out and replaced with a new industrial city. The futurists embraced industry and technology with their machine-inspired, streamlined look – a style that Mussolini co-opted in the 1930s for his vision of a monolithic, modern Italy. Futurism was conflated with Mussolini's brutal imposition of artificial order until championed in Venice by a heroine of the avant-garde and refugee from the Nazis: American expat art collector Peggy Guggenheim, who recognised in futurism the fluidity and flux of modern life.

Artistic dissidents also opposed Mussolini's square-jawed, iron-willed aesthetics. Emilio Vedova (1919–2006) joined the Corrente movement of artists, which openly opposed Fascist trends in a magazine shut down by the Fascists in 1940. After WWII, Vedova veered towards abstraction, and his larger works are now in regular robot-assisted rotation at the Magazzini del Sale. Giovanni Pontini (1915–70) was a worker who painted as a hobby until 1947, when he discovered Kokoschka, van Gogh and Rouault, who inspired his empathetic paintings of fishermen.

Venetian Giuseppe Santomaso (1907–90) painted his way out of constrictive Fascism with lyrical, unbounded abstract landscapes. Rigidity and liquidity became the twin fascinations of another avant-garde Italian artist – Unesco-acclaimed, Bologna-born and Venice-trained video artist Fabrizio Plessi (b 1940). His 1970s *Arte povera* (Poor Art) experiments in humble materials, while his multimedia installations feature Venice's essential medium: water.

The fluidity that characterises Venice and its art continues into the 21st century, with new art galleries in San Marco and Giudecca showing a range of landscapes, abstraction, video and installation art.

Music

Over the centuries, Venetian musicians developed a reputation for playing music as though their lives depended on it, which at times wasn't far from the truth. In its trade-empire heyday, La Serenissima had official musicians, including the distinguished directorship of Flemish Adrian Willaert (1490–1562) for 35 years at Capella Ducale. But when the city fell on hard times in the 17th to 18th centuries, it discovered its musical calling.

With shrinking trade revenues, the state took the quixotic step of underwriting musical education for orphan girls, and the investment yielded unfathomable returns. Among the *maestri* hired to conduct orphan orchestras was Antonio Vivaldi (1678–1741), whose 30-year tenure yielded hundreds of concertos and popularised Venetian baroque music across Europe. Visitors spread word of extraordinary performances by orphan girls, and the city became a magnet for novelty-seeking moneyed socialites. Modern visitors to Venice can still experience music and opera performed in the same venues as in Vivaldi's day – *palazzi* (palaces), churches and *ospedaletti* (orphanages) such as La Pietà, where Vivaldi worked – sometimes with 18th-century instruments.

Opera

Today's televised talent searches can't compare to Venice's knack for discovering talents like Claudio Monteverdi (1567–1643), who was named the musical director of the Basilica di San Marco and went on to launch modern opera. Today, opera reverberates inside La Fenice and across town in churches, concert halls and *palazzi* – but until 1637 you would have needed an invitation to hear it. Opera and most chamber music were the preserve of the nobility, performed in private salons.

Then Venice threw open the doors of the first public opera houses. Between 1637 and 1700, some 358 operas were staged in 16 theatres to meet the musical demands of a population of 140,000. Monteverdi wrote two standout operas, *Il ritorno di Ulisse al suo paese* (The Return of Ulysses) and *L'Incoronazione di Poppea* (The Coronation of Poppaea), with an astonishing range of plot and subplot, strong characterisation and powerful music. Critical response couldn't have been better: he was buried with honours in I Frari.

A singer at the Basilica di San Marco under Monteverdi, Pier Francesco Cavalli (1602–76) became the outstanding 17th-century Italian opera composer, with 42 operas. With his frequent collaborator Carlo Goldoni and Baldassare Galuppi (1706–84), he added musical hooks to *opera buffa* (comic opera) favourites like *Il filosofo di campagna* (The Country Philosopher).

Classical Music

Get ready to baroque-and-roll: Venetian classical musicians are leading a revival of 'early music' from medieval through to Renaissance and baroque periods, with historically accurate arrangements played *con brio* (with verve) on period instruments. Venetian baroque was the rebel music of its day, openly defying edicts from Rome deciding which instruments could accompany sermons and what kinds of rhythms and melodies were suitable for moral uplift. Venetians kept right on playing stringed instruments in churches, singing along to bawdy *opera buffa* and writing compositions that were both soulful and sensual.

Modern misconceptions about baroque being a polite soundtrack to wedding ceremonies are smashed by baroque 'early music' ensembles. Among Vivaldi's repertoire of some 500 concertos is his ever-popular *The Four Seasons,* instantly recognisable from hotel lobbies and ringtones – but you haven't heard summer lightning strikes or icy winter rainfall until you've heard it played *con brio* by Interpreti Veneziani.

Venetian venues make all the difference. The pleasure palace of Palazzetto Bru Zane is now restored to its original function: concerts

It's not all Vivaldi in Venice. The Venice Jazz Club features tribute nights year-round, and during July's Venice Jazz Festival, you may luck into a performance by Venetian saxophonist and composer Giannantonio De Vincenzo or Venetian trumpeter-musicologist Massimo Donà.

to flirt and swoon over, with winking approval from Sebastiano Ricci's frolicking, frescoed angels. Seek out programs featuring Venetian baroque composer Tomaso Albinoni (1671–1750), especially the exquisite *Sinfonie e concerti a 5*. For a more avant-garde take on classical music, look for works by Bruno Maderna (1920–73) or Luigi Nono (1924–90).

Literature

In a surprising 15th-century plot twist, shipping magnate Venice became a publishing empire. Johannes Gutenberg cranked out his first Bible with a movable-type press in 1455, and Venice became an early adopter of this cutting-edge technology, turning out the earliest printed Quran. Venetian printing presses were in operation by the 1470s, with lawyers settling copyright claims soon thereafter. Venetian publishers printed not just religious texts but histories, poetry, textbooks, plays, musical scores and manifestos.

Early Renaissance author Pietro Bembo (1470–1547) was a librarian, historian, diplomat and poet who defined the concept of platonic love and solidified Italian grammar in his *Rime*. Bembo collaborated with Aldo Manuzio on an invention that revolutionised reading and democratised learning: the Aldine Press, which introduced italics and paperbacks, including Dante's *La divina commedia*. By 1500, nearly one in six books published in Europe was printed in Venice.

Poetry

Shakespeare has competition for technical prowess from Veneto's Petrarch (aka Francesco Petrarca; 1304–74), who added wow to Italian woo with his eponymous sonnets. Writing in Italian and Latin, Petrarch applied a strict structure of rhythm (14 lines, with two quatrains to describe a desire and a sestet to attain it) and rhyme (no more than five rhymes per sonnet) to romance the idealised Laura. He might have tried chocolates instead: Laura never returned the sentiment.

Posthumously, Petrarch became idolised by Rilke, Byron, Mozart and Venice's *cortigiane oneste* (well-educated 'honest courtesans'). Tullia d'Aragona (1510–56) wrote Petrarchan sonnets that conquered men: noblemen divulged state secrets, kings risked their thrones to beg her hand in marriage, and much ink flowed in panegyric praise of her hooked nose.

Written with wit and recited with passion, poetry might get you a free date with a high-end courtesan, killed, or elected in Venice. Leonardo Giustinian (1388–1446) was a member of the Consiglio dei Dieci (Council of Ten) who spent time off from spying on his neighbours writing poetry in elegant Venetian-inflected Italian, including *Canzonette* (Songs) and *Strambotti* (Ditties). Giorgio Baffo (1694–1768) was a friend of Casanova's whose risqué odes to the posterior might have affected his political career elsewhere – but in Venice, he became a state senator. To experience his bawdy poetry, head to Taverna da Baffo, where his ribald rhymes may be chanted by night's end.

One of Italy's greatest poets, Ugo Foscolo (1778–1827) studied in Padua and arrived in Venice as a teenager amid political upheavals. Young Foscolo threw in his literary lot with Napoleon in a 1797 ode to the general, hoping he would revive the Venetian Republic, and even joined the French army. But Napoleon considered Foscolo a dangerous mind, and Foscolo ended his days in exile in London.

In trying to describe the Inferno to contemporary readers c 1307, Dante compared it to Venice's Arsenale, with its stinking vats of tar, sparks flying from hammers and infernal clamour of 16,000 labourers working nonstop on its legendary ship-assembly lines.

Memoirs

Life on the lagoon has always been stranger than fiction, and Venetian memoirists were early bestsellers. Venice-born Marco Polo (1254–1324) captured his adventures across central Asia and China in memoirs entitled *Il Milione* (c 1299), as told to Rustichello da Pisa. The book achieved bestseller status even before the invention of the printing press, each volume copied by hand. Some details were apparently embellished along the way, but his tales of Kublai Khan's court remain riveting. In a more recent traveller's account, *Venezia, la Città Ritrovata* (Venice Rediscovered; 1998), Paolo Barbaro (1922–2014) captures his reverse culture shock upon returning to the lagoon city.

Memoirs with sex and scandal sold well in Venice. 'Honest courtesan' Veronica Franco (1546–91) kissed and told in her bestselling memoir, but for sheer *braggadocio* (boasting) it's hard to top the memoirs of Casanova (1725–98). Francesco Gritti (1740–1811) parodied the decadent Venetian aristocracy in vicious, delicious *Poesie in dialetto Veneziano* (Poetry in the Venetian Dialect) and satirised the Venetian fashion for memoirs with his exaggerated *My Story: The Memoirs of Signor Tommasino Written by Him, a Narcotic Work by Dr Pifpuf.* Modern scandal, corruption and a cast of eccentric Venetians drive *The City of Falling Angels* by John Berendt (b 1939), an engrossing account of life in Venice following the devastating fire that gutted La Fenice in 1996.

Modern Fiction

Venetian authors have remained at the forefront of modern Italian fiction. The enduring quality of Camillo Boito's 1883 short story *Senso* (Sense), a twisted tale of love and betrayal in Austrian-occupied Venice, made it a prime subject for director Luchino Visconti in 1954. Mysterious Venice proved the ideal setting for Venice's resident expat American mystery novelist Donna Leon (b 1942), whose inspector Guido Brunetti uncovers the shadowy subcultures of Venice, from island fishing communities *(A Sea of Troubles)* to environmental protesters *(Through a Glass Darkly)*. But the pride of Venice's literary scene is Tiziano Scarpa (b 1963), who earned the 2009 Strega Prize, Italy's top literary honour, for *Stabat Mater,* the story of an orphaned Venetian girl learning to play violin under Antonio Vivaldi.

Film

Back in the 1980s, a Venice film archive found that the city had appeared in one form or another in 380,000 films – feature films, shorts, documentaries, and other works archived and screened at the city's Casa del Cinema. But Venice's photogenic looks have proved a mixed blessing. This city is too distinctive to fade into the background, so the city tends to upstage even the most photogenic co-stars (which only partly excuses 2010's *The Tourist*).

Since Casanova's escapades and a couple of Shakespearean dramas unfolded in Venice, the lagoon city was a natural choice of location for movie versions of these tales. In the Casanova category, two excellent accounts are Alexandre Volkoff's 1927 *Casanova* and Federico Fellini's 1976 *Casanova,* starring Donald Sutherland. Oliver Parker directed a 1995 version of *Othello,* but the definitive version remains Orson Welles' 1952 *Othello,* shot partly in Venice, but mostly on location in Morocco. Later adaptations of silver-screen classics haven't lived up to the original, including Michael Radford's 1994 *The Merchant of Venice* starring Al Pacino as Shylock, and Swedish director Lasse Hallström's 2005 *Casanova,* with a nonsensical plot but a charmingly rakish Heath Ledger in the title role.

After WWII, Hollywood came to Venice in search of romance, and the city delivered as the backdrop for Katharine Hepburn's midlife Italian love affair in David Lean's 1955 *Summertime.* Of all his films, Lean claimed this was his favourite, above *Lawrence of Arabia* and *Doctor Zhivago.*

Eighteenth-century Venetian *grande dame* Isabella Teotochi Albrizzi was practically wedded to her literary salon: when her husband received a post abroad, she got her marriage annulled to remain in Venice, and continue her discussions of poetry with the patronage of a new husband, her *cicisbeo* (manservant-lover) in devoted attendance.

Locals confirm that yes, Signora Hepburn did fall into that canal, and no, she wasn't happy about it. Gorgeous Venice set pieces compensated for some dubious singing in Woody Allen's musical romantic comedy *Everyone Says I Love You* (1996). But the most winsome Venetian romance is Silvio Soldini's *Pane e tulipani* (Bread and Tulips; 2000), a tale of an Italian housewife who restarts her life as a woman of mystery in Venice, trying to dodge the detective-novel-reading plumber hot on her trail.

More often than not, romance seems to go horribly wrong in films set in Venice. It turns to obsession in *Morte a Venezia* (Death in Venice), Luchino Visconti's 1971 adaptation of the Thomas Mann novel, and again in *The Comfort of Strangers* (1990), featuring Natasha Richardson and Rupert Everett inexplicably following Christopher Walken into shadowy Venetian alleyways. A better adaptation of a lesser novel, *The Wings of the Dove* (1997) was based on the Henry James novel and mostly shot in the UK, though you can scarcely notice behind Helena Bonham Carter's hair.

Venice has done its best to shock movie-goers over the years, as with Nicolas Roeg's riveting *Don't Look Now* (1973) starring Donald Sutherland, Julie Christie, and Venice at its most ominous and depraved. *Dangerous Beauty* (1998) is raunchier but sillier, a missed opportunity to show 16th-century Venice through the eyes of a courtesan.

Always ready for action, Venice made appearances in *Indiana Jones and the Last Crusade* (1989) and *Casino Royale* (2006), whose Grand Canal finale was shot in Venice with some help from CGI – don't worry, no Gothic architecture was harmed in the making of that blockbuster. To see the latest big film to make a splash in Venice, don't miss the Venice International Film Festival.

Venice's first movie role dates from the earliest days of cinema, as the subject of the 1897 short film *A Panoramic View of Venice*. However, as Venice was complicated and expensive for location shooting, classics set in Venice, such as the Astaire-Rogers vehicle *Top Hat*, were shot in Hollywood backlots.

VENICE'S BESTSELLING WOMEN WRITERS

At a time when women were scarcely in print elsewhere in Europe, Venetian women became prolific and bestselling authors in subjects ranging from mathematics to politics. Works from over 100 Venetian women authors from the 15th to 18th centuries remain in circulation today. Among the luminaries of their era:

Writer Sara Copia Sullam (1592–1641) A leading Jewish intellectual of Venice's Accademia degli Incogniti literary salon, Sullam was admired for her poetry and spirited correspondence with a monk from Modena. A critic accused her of denying the immortality of the soul, a heresy punishable by death under the Inquisition. Sullam responded with a treatise on immortality written in two days; her manifesto became a bestseller. Sullam's writings remain in publication as key works of early modern Italian literature.

Philosopher Isotta Nogarola (c 1418–66) The Verona-born teen prodigy corresponded with Renaissance philosophers and was widely published in Rome and Venice. An anonymous critic published attacks against her in 1439, claiming 'an eloquent woman is never chaste' and accusing her of incest. But she continued her correspondence with leading humanists and, with Venetian diplomat Ludovico Foscarini, published an influential early feminist tract: a 1453 dialogue asserting that since Eve and Adam were jointly responsible for expulsion from Paradise, women and men must be equals.

Musician and poet Gaspara Stampa (1523–54) A true Renaissance intellectual, Stampa was a renowned lute player, literary-salon organiser, and author of published Petrarchan sonnets openly dedicated to her many lovers. Historians debate her livelihood before she became a successful author; some claim she was a courtesan.

Dr Elena Lucrezia Cornaro Piscopia (1646–84) Another prodigy, Piscopia became the first female university doctoral graduate in Europe in 1678 at the University of Padua, where a statue of her now stands. Her prolific contributions to the intellectual life of Venice are commemorated with a plaque outside Venice's city hall.

Theatre

Venice is an elaborate stage and, whenever you arrive, you're just in time for a show. Sit on any *campo* (square), and the *commedia dell'arte* (featuring masked archetypes) and *opera buffa* (comic opera) commence, with stock characters improvising variations on familiar themes: graduating university students lurching towards another round of toasts, kids crying over gelato fallen into canals, neighbours hanging out laundry gossiping indiscreetly across the *calle* (lane). Once you've visited Venice, you'll have a whole new appreciation for its theatrical innovations.

Commedia dell'Arte

During Carnevale, *commedia dell'arte* conventions take over, and all of Venice acts out with masks, extravagant costumes and exaggerated gestures. It may seem fantastical today, but for centuries, this was Italy's dominant form of theatre. Scholars attribute some of Molière's running gags and Shakespeare's romantic plots to the influence of *commedia dell'arte* – although Shakespeare would have been shocked to note that in Italy, women's parts were typically played by women. But after a couple of centuries of *commedia dell'arte*, 18th-century Venice began to tire of bawdy slapstick. Sophisticated improvisations had been reduced to farce, robbing the theatre of its subversive zing.

Comedy & Opera Buffa

As the public tired of *commedia dell'arte,* Carlo Goldoni (1707–93), a former doctor's apprentice, occasional lawyer and whipsmart librettist, entered the scene offering some serious tragic opera. But of his 160 plays and 80 or so *libretti,* he remains best loved for *opera buffa,* unmasked social satires that remain ripe and delicious: battles of the sexes, self-important socialites getting their comeuppance, and the impossibility of pleasing one's boss.

Goldoni was light-hearted but by no means a lightweight; his comic genius and deft wordplay would permanently change Italian theatre. His *Pamela* (1750) was the first play to dispense with masks altogether, and his characters didn't fall into good or evil archetypes: everyone was flawed, often hilariously so. Some of his most winsome roles were reserved for women and *castrati* (male soprano countertenors), from his early 1735 adaptation of Apostolo Zeno's *Griselda* (based on Boccaccio's *Decameron,* with a score by Vivaldi) to his celebrated 1763 *Le donne vendicate* (Revenge of the Women). Princess Cecilia Mahony Giustiniani commissioned this latter work, in which two women show a preening chauvinist the error of his ways with light swordplay and lethal wordplay.

But one Venetian dramatist was not amused. Carlo Gozzi (1720–1806) believed that Goldoni's comedies of middle-class manners were prosaic, and staged a searing 1761 parody of Goldoni – driving Goldoni to France in disgust, never to return to Venice. Gozzi went on to minor success with his fairy-tale scenarios, one of which would inspire the Puccini opera *Turandot.* But Gozzi's fantasias had little staying power, and eventually he turned to...comedy.

Meanwhile, Goldoni fell on hard times in France, after a pension granted to him by King Louis XVI was revoked by the Revolution. He died impoverished, though at his French colleagues' insistence, the French state granted his pension to his widow. But Goldoni got the last laugh: while Gozzi's works are rarely staged, Goldoni regularly gets top billing along with Shakespeare at the city's main theatre, Teatro Goldoni.

The Biennale Teatro (www.labiennale.org/en/theatre) is a showcase for experimental theatre, drawing on Venice's 400-year tradition of risk-taking performance. Avant-garde troupes and experimental theatres such as Teatro Junghans and Laboratorio Occupato Morion also bring new plays, performance art and choreography to Venetian stages.

The Fragile Lagoon

White ibis perch on rock outcroppings, piles of lagoon crab are hauled into the Pescaria (Fish Market), and waters change like mood rings from teal blue to oxidised silver: life on the lagoon is extraordinary, and extraordinarily fragile. When gazing across these waters to the distant Adriatic horizon, the lagoon appears to be an extension of the sea. But with its delicate balance of salty and fresh water, *barene* (mudbanks) and grassy marshes, the lagoon supports a unique aquaculture.

What is the Lagoon?

The lagoon is a 550-sq-km shallow dish, where ocean tides meet freshwater streams from alpine rivers. It's protected by a slender 50km arc of islands, which halt the Adriatic's advances. Between Punta Sabbioni and Chioggia, three *bocche di porto* (port entrances) allow the sea entry into the lagoon. When sirocco winds push ocean waves toward the Venetian gulf, *acque alte* (high tides) ensue. These seasonal tides help clear the lagoon of extra silt and maintain the balance of its waters.

Since 1930 an estimated 20% of bird life has disappeared, 80% of lagoon flora has gone and lagoon water transparency has dropped 60%.

The Venetian lagoon is the second-largest wetland in Europe and the largest in the Mediterranean Basin, and its highly productive ecosystem supports some 200,000 birds and unique lagoon species. Like all lagoons, it is a continually evolving environment although through careful interventions, it is one of the only survivors of a system of estuarine lagoons that in Roman times extended from Ravenna to Trieste. In fact, the word *laguna* (lagoon) is Venetian.

Environmental & Manmade Challenges

Until the 20th century, human intervention engineered the lagoon's survival against environmental forces. However, maintaining its delicate balance has become fraught with difficulty in the post-industrial era. In the 1920s, Marghera, at the southern end of the lagoon, was developed into an industrial zone centred on chemical plants and oil refineries. With few regulations, these factories released dioxins and heavy metals into the water, radically disturbing the delicate ecosystem. Although strict environmental laws put an end to the practice in the 1980s, the lagoon is still plagued by non-biodegradable pollutants from this era which contribute to phytoplankton and macroalgal blooms.

In addition, to facilitate the passage of modern tankers to Marghera, deep channels were dredged in the 1960s, the most damaging being the 12m-deep, 100m-wide Canale dei Petroli. The passage of boats through these channels has resulted in strong transverse currents across the lagoon. The currents flatten the *ghebbi* (capillary canals) and erode the sandbanks that have historically acted to dissipate the force of the tidal influx. In a 2006 report highlighting their destruction, Lidia Fersuoch, president of NGO Italia Nostra Venezia (www.italianostravenezia.org),

---

THE TIDE IS HIGH

The alarm from 16 sirens throughout the city is a warning that *acqua alta* (high tide) is expected to reach the city within two to four hours. Venetians aren't often surprised: most monitor Venice's Centro Maree 48-hour tidal forecast at www.comune.venezia. it for high-tide warnings between November and April. When alarms sound, it's not an emergency situation but a temporary tide that principally affects low-lying areas. Within five hours, the tide usually ebbs.

One even tone (up to 110cm above normal): barely warrants a pause in happy-hour conversation.

Two rising tones (up to 120cm): you might need *stivali di gomma* (rubber boots).

Three rising tones (around 130cm): check Centro Maree to see where *passarelle* (gangplank walkways) are in use.

Four rising tones (140cm and up): shops close early, everyone slides flood barriers across their doorsteps.

---

argued that the lagoon's sandbanks were 'in need of protection as much as the churches and palaces of the city'.

Well drilling by coastal industries in the 1960s and the lowering of the mainland water table has also caused the *caranto* (the layer of clay that forms the base of the lagoon) to subside, while the reduction in the lagoon's salt marshes from 255 sq km in the 17th century to 47 sq km by 2003 has allowed unobstructed wind to whip up large waves that further destabilise the lagoon bed. The effect of all this: a downward-eroding, sediment-exporting system that is slowly turning the lagoon into a marine bay and posing a critical danger to the city.

To add to this already complex picture, global climate change is now also being felt in the lagoon, with rising temperatures threatening increased levels of CO_2 in the water causing acidification and anaerobic episodes – a factor that will be made worse if the lagoon is further isolated from the sea through the use of MoSE. Furthermore, Unesco has projected end-of-century sea-level rises could be anywhere between 26cm and 100cm, although Venice itself could only survive a rise of 60cm.

Mobile Flood Barriers (MoSE)

The hot topic of the last three decades in Venice has been the mobile-flood-barrier project known as MoSE (Modulo Sperimentale Elettromeccanico; Experimental Electromechanical Module). These 78 inflatable barriers 30m high and 20m wide are intended to seal the three *bocche di porto* whenever the sea approaches dangerous levels. However, since its proposal in 1988 both the science and the management of the project have been dogged by controversy, culminating, in 2014, in the exposure of a corruption scandal in which the city mayor, the main contractor (Consorzio Venezia Nuova) and the government body responsible for the lagoon (Magistrato alle Acque) were implicated.

Despite an original completion date of 1995, MoSE remains a work in progress and a tentative completion date is now slated for June 2018. In the meantime, costs have ballooned from €1.5 billion to €5.5 billion. In addition the 2014 corruption scandal further undermined the project's credibility and even its supporters now concede that it offers only a temporary solution, since it does nothing to address the issue of erosion, and if sea levels rise frequently enough above the 110cm barrier trigger, the gates may be closed so often as to compromise the entire lagoon.

Furthermore, tests of the barriers conducted in 2013 were not without problems. While the barriers were raised effectively, they could not be lowered due to a build up of debris, which had to be cleared by divers. And, a 2017 report by the Ministry of Infrastructure pointed out issues with the degradation of critical hinge components that are more susceptible to corrosion than originally thought, and may not be replaceable due to their location on the seabed. Locals despair of the vast expense and everyone wonders where the €50 to €80 million per year required to maintain and manage the system will come from, if and when it ever becomes operational.

No Grandi Navi (No Big Ships)

High waters aren't the only concern. Venice's foundations are taking a pounding as never before, with new stresses from wakes of speeding motorboats and mega cruise ships as well as pollution. When pollution and silt fill in shallow areas, algae takes over, threatening building foundations and choking out other marine life. The increase in the salt content of the lagoon also corrodes stone foundations and endangers unique lagoon aquaculture.

The spike in cruise ships entering the Bacino di San Marco (around 600 each year) has created new environmental threats. So severe is the concern, that Unesco has repeatedly threatened to place Venice on their list of Endangered Heritage Sites. Critics like Venice's No Grandi Navi (No Big Ships) committee also oppose cruise-ship entry for introducing pollution to the lagoon. In response, the Port Authority maintains that the cruise industry is a vital provider of local jobs and revenue, generating 3% to 4% of Venice's GDP. While Fincantieri, an Italian public company with a major construction yard in Marghera, is one of the biggest shipbuilding companies in the world.

In order to find a solution to the current situation, the Italian government is currently considering three proposals. Two of them, the Contorta Project and Trezze Project, involve dredging further environmentally damaging deep canals to reroute cruise ships away from Piazza San Marco; the third, Venis Cruise Project, which passed an environmental study in early 2017, recommends building a new dock terminal at the Lido. The lagoon, meanwhile, was placed on Europa Nostra's 'Most Endangered' list (www.7mostendangered.eu/2016-list) in 2016, with a passionate plea from president Plácido Domingo to remind the world that Venice cannot survive without its lagoon.

ARPAV (www.arpa.veneto.it), the Veneto's regional agency for environmental protection has demonstrated that cruise ships are a major contributor to air pollution in Venice. Every ship pollutes as much as 14,000 cars. As of October 2016, the only limitations on cruise ships was the use of fuel containing 1.5% sulphur (1500 times higher than the limits allowed on land).

Survival Guide

Transport

ARRIVING IN VENICE

Most people arrive in Venice by train, plane and, more controversially, cruise ship. There is a long-distance bus service to the city and it is also possible to drive to Venice, though you have to park at the western end of the city and then walk or take a *vaporetto* (small passenger ferry).

Flights, tours and rail tickets can be booked online at lonelyplanet.com/bookings.

Marco Polo Airport

Venice's main international airport, **Marco Polo Airport** (☑flight information 041 260 92 60; www.veniceairport. it; Via Galileo Gallilei 30/1, Tessera), is 12km east of Mestre.

Inside the terminal you'll find ticket offices for water taxis and Alilaguna water bus transfers, an ATM, currency exchange offices, a **left luggage office** (per item per 24hr €6; ⊘5am-9pm) and a Vènezia Unica **tourist office** (☑041 24 24; www. veneziaunica.it; Arrivals Hall; ⊘8.30am-7pm) where you can pick-up pre-ordered travel cards and a map.

Alilaguna Airport Shuttle

Alilaguna (☑041 240 17 01; www.alilaguna.it; airport transfer one-way €15) operates four water shuttles that link the airport with various parts of Venice at a cost of €8 to Murano and €15 to all other landing stages. Passengers are permitted one suitcase and one piece of hand luggage. All further bags are charged at €3 per piece. Expect it to take 45 to 90 minutes to reach most destinations; it takes approximately 1¼ hours to reach Piazza San Marco. Lines include the following:

Linea Blu (Blue Line) Stops at the Lido, San Marco, Stazione Marittima and points in-between.

Linea Rossa (Red Line) Stops at Murano and the Lido.

Linea Arancia (Orange Line) Stops at Stazione Santa Lucia, Rialto and San Marco via the Grand Canal.

Linea Gialla (Yellow Line) Stops at Murano and Fondamente Nove.

Bus

Azienda del Consorzio Trasporti Veneziano (ACTV; ☑041 272 21 11; www.actv. it) Runs bus 5 between Marco Polo Airport and Piazzale Roma (€8, 30 minutes, four per hour) with a limited number of stops en route. Alternatively, a bus+*vaporetto* ticket covering the bus journey and a one-way

CLIMATE CHANGE & TRAVEL

Every form of transport that relies on carbon-based fuel generates CO_2, the main cause of human-induced climate change. Modern travel is dependent on aeroplanes, which might use less fuel per kilometre per person than most cars but travel much greater distances. The altitude at which aircraft emit gases (including CO_2) and particles also contributes to their climate change impact. Many websites offer 'carbon calculators' that allow people to estimate the carbon emissions generated by their journey and, for those who wish to do so, to offset the impact of the greenhouse gases emitted with contributions to portfolios of climate-friendly initiatives throughout the world. Lonely Planet offsets the carbon footprint of all staff and author travel.

vaporetto trip within a total of 90 minutes costs €14.

Azienda Trasporti Veneto Orientale (ATVO; ☏0421 59 46 71; www.atvo.it; Piazzale Roma 497g, Santa Croce; ☺6.40am-7.45pm) Runs a direct bus service between the airport and **Piazzale Roma** (Map p273) (€8, 25 minutes, every 30 minutes from 8am to midnight). At Piazzale Roma you can pick up the ACTV *vaporetti* to reach locations around Venice.

Water Taxi

The dock for water transfers to the historic centre is a 10-minute walk from the arrivals hall via a raised, indoor walkway accessed on the 1st floor of the terminal building. Luggage trolleys (requiring a €1 deposit) can be taken to the dock.

Private water taxis can be booked at the **Consorzio Motoscafi Venezia** (☏041 240 6712; www.motoscafivenezia.it; ☺9am-6pm) or **Veneziataxi** (☏information 328 238 9661; www.veneziataxi.it) desks in the arrivals hall, or directly at the dock. Private taxis cost from €110 for up to four passengers and all their luggage. Extra passengers (up to a limit of 12 or 16) carry a small surcharge.

If you don't have a large group, there is also the option of a shared **Venice Shuttle**. This is a shared water taxi and costs from €25 per person with a €6 surcharge for night-time arrivals. Seats should be booked online at www.venicelink.com. Boats seat a maximum of eight people and accommodate up to 10 bags. Those opting for a shared taxi should be aware that the service can wait for some time to fill up and has set drop-off points in Venice; only private transfers will take you directly to your hotel.

Land Taxi

A taxi from the aiport to Piazzale Roma costs €50; the taxi rank is located by the bus station. From there you can either hop on a vaporetto or pick up a water taxi at the nearby Fondamente Cossetti.

Treviso Airport

Ryanair and some other budget airlines use **Treviso Airport** (☏0422 31 51 11; www.trevisoairport.it; Via Noalese 63), about 5km southwest of Treviso and a 26km, one-hour drive from Venice.

Bus

Barzi Bus Service (☏0422 68 60 83; www.barziservice.com) The most direct service to Tronchetto in Venice (€12, 40 minutes, one to two per hour from 8am to 10.30pm) from where you can jump on the monorail to Piazzale Roma. Buy tickets on the bus or at the desk in the arrivals hall.

Azienda Trasporti Veneto Orientale (ATVO;☏0421 59 44; www.atvo.it) Offers a service to Mestre and Piazzale Roma in Venice (€12, one hour, one to two per hour from 5.30am to 11.30pm), but it takes a more circuitous route than Barzi Bus Service.

Train & Taxi

Line 6 of **ACTT** (☏0422 58 83 11; www.mobilitadimarca.it) connects Treviso Airport with Treviso train station (€1.30, 20 minutes, two to three an hour from 6am to 10.30pm), from where there are frequent services to Santa Lucia train station in Venice (€3.35, 30 to 40 minutes, half hourly).

Taxi

Taxis from Treviso Airport to Venice cost €90.

Venezia Santa Lucia Train Station

Trains run frequently to Venice's **Santa Lucia train station** (www.veneziasantalucia.it; Fondamenta Santa Lucia, Cannaregio), which appears as 'Ferrovia' on signs within Venice. The station has a helpful **tourist office** (☏041 24 24; www.veneziaunica.it; ☺7am-9pm; ⊠Ferrovia) opposite platform 3 where you can obtain a map and buy *vaporetto* tickets, and a **left luggage depot** (☏041 78 55 31; ☺6am-11pm) opposite platform 1.

Local trains linking Venice to the Veneto are frequent, reliable and remarkably inexpensive, including Padua (€4.15, 25 to 50 minutes, three to four per hour) and Verona (€8.85, 1¾ hours, three to four per hour). Expensive, high-speed Le Frecce trains also serve these Veneto destinations, but are a better option for longer journeys to Milan (€60, 2½ hours) and Rome (€86 to €117, 3¾ hours).

Train tickets can be purchased at self-serve ticketing machines in the station, online at www.trenitalia.it and www.raileurope.com, or through travel agents. When buying train tickets, be sure to specify Venezia Santa Lucia (VSL), for the station in central Venice, as opposed to Venezia Mestre.

Validate your ticket in the orange machines on station platforms before boarding your train. Failure to do so can result in a hefty on-the-spot fine when the inspector checks tickets on the train.

Vaporetto & Water Taxi

Vaporetti (p242) connect Santa Lucia train station with all parts of Venice. There is also a handy water-taxi rank just out front if you are heavily laden.

Venezia Mestre Train Station

Venezia Mestre (Piazzale Pietro Favretti) station is located on the mainland in Mestre directly across the channel from Venice. Trains, which take 10 to 12 minutes, and an ATVO shuttle bus connect the two stations.

Other services from the station include high-speed Le Frecce and Italo trains connecting Venice with Rome, Milan and Florence, as well as Eurocity trains to Munich.

Inside the station you'll find a tourist information office, currency exchange and a **left-luggage depot** (per piece 1st 5hr €6, next 6hr €0.90, thereafter per hour €0.40; ⏱8am-8pm).

Venezia Terminal Passeggeri

Cruise ships dock at Venice's main passenger terminal, **Venezia Terminal Passeggeri** (☎041 240 3000; www.vtp.it; Marittima Fabbricato 248), which is located at the western end of Santa Croce between the Isola del Tronchetto and Piazzale Roma.

The terminal is accessible by road but cars must be parked on the nearby Isola del Tronchetto. When in port, most big cruise ships provide their passengers with a complimentary shuttle bus or boat service into Venice.

Alilaguna Boat Shuttle

The blue line operated by **Alilaguna** (☎041 240 17 01; www.alilaguna.it) connects the cruise terminal with San Marco (one-way €8), the Lido and points in-between. The service also continues on to the airport (one-way €15, two hours).

Land & Water Taxis

Land taxis to the airport cost around €30 to €40. Or, they can ferry you and your luggage the brief 900m distance to Piazzale Roma (about €5) where you can pick up airport buses.

A water taxi direct to your hotel in Venice will set you back around €90.

Bus

A frequent, free shuttle bus connects the cruise terminal to Piazzale Roma. It runs every 15 to 20 minutes from Monday to Saturday during cruise season and whenever a big ship is in port.

Monorail

The **People Mover Monorail** (APM; www.avmspa.it; Piazzale Roma; per ride €1.50; ⏱7.10am-10.50pm Mon-Sat, 8.10am-9.50pm Sun) connects the cruise ship terminal with Piazzale Roma. It takes less than two minutes and runs until 11pm at night.

San Basilio Terminal

San Basilio Terminal (Old Stazione Marittime; Map p276; Fondamenta Zattere Al Ponte; 🚢San Basilio) is a small ferry terminal on the southern side of Dorsoduro which serves high-speed **Venezia Lines** (☎041 847 09 03; www.venezialines.com) boats from Croatia and Slovenia during the summer months.

Vaporetto

Vaporetto line 2 links San Basilio Terminal with Tronchetto, Piazzale Roma and San Zaccaria.

Fusina Terminal

Fusina Terminal (☎041 547 01 60; www.terminalfusina.it; Via Moranzani 79, Fusina) on the mainland, 12km south of Mestre, handles small ferries from Greece. Run by **Anek Lines Italia** (☎041 528 65 22; www.anekitalia.com; Via Dell'Elettronica, Fusina) there are four services a week with boats docking at Igoumenitsa (25½ hours) and Patras (dorm bed €172; 32 hours).

Vaporetto

To reach Fusina from Venice take the Circolare LineafusinA *vaporetto* from Zattere (€8, 25 minutes, hourly) or Alberoni (€7, 35 minutes, every two hours) at the southern end of the Lido.

Car & Motorcycle

To get to Venice by car or motorcycle, take the often-congested Trieste–Turin A4, which passes through Mestre. From Mestre, take the 'Venezia' exit. Once over Ponte della Libertà from Mestre, cars must be left at a car park in Piazzale Roma or on the Isola del Tronchetto. Be warned: you'll pay a hefty price in parking

---

CHEAP THRILLS ON THE GRAND CANAL

A *traghetto* is the gondola service locals use to cross the Grand Canal between its widely spaced bridges. *Traghetti* rides cost just €2 for non-residents and typically operate from 9am to 6pm, although some routes finish by noon. You'll find *traghetto* crossings at Campo San Marcuola, the Rialto Market, Riva del Vin, San Tomà, Ca' Rezzonico and beside the Gritti Palace, though note that service can be spotty at times at all crossings.

fees, and traffic backs up at weekends.

Isola del Tronchetto

Isola del Tronchetto is an artificial island located at the westernmost tip of Santa Croce that now acts as the city's main car park. To reach Tronchetto from the causeway stay in the right-hand lane and follow the signs for 'Tronchetto' and car parks.

Parking

Prices in Venice start at €3.50 per hour and rise to €32 for five to 24 hours. At peak times, many car parks become completely full. However, you can book a parking place ahead of time at www.veneziaunica.it.

To avoid hassles (and to make the most of the cheaper car parks) consider parking in Mestre, and take the bus or train into Venice instead. Remember to take valuables out of your car.

For a range of parking options in Venice and Mestre, including prices and directions, head to www.avmspa.it.

Garage Europa Mestre (☑041 95 92 02; www.garageeuropamestre.com; Corso del Popolo 55, Mestre; per day €15; ☺8am-10pm) Has 300 spaces; ACTV bus 4 to/from Venice stops right outside the garage, or it's a 10-minute walk to the Mestre train station. It has the cheapest hourly rates.

ASM Autoremissa Comunale (☑041 272 73 07; www.asmvenezia.it; Piazzale Roma 496; cars over/under 185cm per day €29/26; ☺24hr) Has 2152 spaces; the largest lot in Piazzale Roma. Discounts available with online reservations; free parking for people with disabilities for up to 12 hours.

Garage San Marco (☑041 523 22 13; www.garagesanmarco.it; Piazzale Roma 467f; per 24hr €32, overnight 5pm-4am

€15; ☺24hr) Has 900 spaces; guests of certain hotels get discounts.

Parking Sant'Andrea (☑041 272 7304; www.avmspa.it; Piazzale Roma; per 2hr or less €7; ☺24hr) Has 100 spaces; best for short-term parking.

Interparking (Tronchetto Car Park; ☑041 520 75 55; www.veniceparking.it; Isola del Tronchetto; per 2/3-5/5-24hr €3/5/21; ☺24hr; [P]Tronchetto) Has 3957 spaces; the largest lot with the cheapest 24-hour rate. Vaporetti connect directly with Piazza San Marco, while the People Mover monorail provides connections to Piazzale Roma and the cruise terminal.

Car Ferry

Car ferry 17 transports vehicles from Tronchetto to the Lido (vehicles up to 4m and motorcycles €13).

Monorail

Venice's **monorail** (APM; www.avmspa.it; Piazzale Roma; per ride €1.50; ☺7.10am-10.50pm Mon-Sat, 8.10am-9.50pm Sun), also known as the People Mover, connects the parking lots and cruise terminal at Isola del Tronchetto to Piazzale Roma (€1.50 per person).

WAITING FOR YOUR SHIP TO COME IN

Vaporetto (small passenger ferry) stops can be confusing, so check the signs at the landing dock to make sure you're at the right stop for the direction you want. At major stops like Ferrovia, Piazzale Roma, San Marco and Zattere, there are often two separate docks for the same vaporetto line, heading in opposite directions. The cluster of stops near Piazza San Marco is especially tricky. If your boat doesn't stop right in front of Piazza San Marco, don't panic: it will probably stop at San Zaccaria, just past the Palazzo Ducale.

GETTING AROUND VENICE

The city's main mode of public transport is the vaporetto (small passenger ferry). They are frequent and convenient, but can get very full in peak season. Often, it is quicker to just walk to your destination. Cars and bikes are allowed on the Lido and Pellestrina. If you have more cash to splash, private water taxis are the most glamorous way to travel.

Vaporetto

ACTV (Azienda del Consorzio Trasporti Veneziano; ☑041 272 21 11; www.actv.it) runs all public transport in Venice, including the waterborne. Although the service is efficient and punctual, boats on main lines get full fast and can be overcrowded during Carnevale and in peak season. One-way tickets cost €7.50.

Inter-island ferry services to Murano, Torcello, the Lido and other lagoon islands are usually provided on larger motonave.

Tickets

Vènezia Unica (☑041 24 24; www.veneziaunica.it) is the main seller of public transport tickets, and you can purchase vaporetti tickets at booths at most landing stations. Free timetables and route maps are also available. Tickets and multiday passes can also be pre-purchased online.

If you're going to be using the *vaporetto* frequently (more than three trips), instead of spending €7.50 for every one-way ticket, it is advisable to consider a Travel Card (p242) – a pass for unlimited travel within a set period beginning when you first validate your ticket at the yellow machine located at *vaporetto* stops. Swipe your card every time you board, even if you have already validated it upon your initial ride. If you're caught without a valid ticket, you'll be required to pay an on-the-spot fine of €59 (plus the €7.50 fare). No exceptions.

People aged 14 to 29 holding a Rolling Venice card (p244) can get a three-day ticket for €20 at tourist offices.

Routes

From Piazzale Roma or the train station, *vaporetto* 1 zigzags up the Grand Canal to San Marco and onward to the Lido. If you're not in a rush, it's a great introduction to Venice. *Vaporetto* 17 carries vehicles from Tronchetto, near Piazzale Roma, to the Lido.

Frequency varies greatly according to line and time of day. *Vaporetto* 1 runs every 10 minutes throughout most of the day, while lines such as the 4.1 and 4.2 only

TOURIST TRAVEL CARD

The ACTV Tourist Travel Cards allow for unlimited travel on *vaporetti* (small passenger ferries) and Lido buses within the following time blocks:

24 hours €20
48 hours €30
72 hours €40
One week €60

run every 20 minutes. Night services can be as much as one hour apart. Some lines stop running by around 9pm, so check timetables.

The key *vaporetto* lines and major stops are as follows:

No 1 Runs Piazzale Roma–Ferrovia–Grand Canal (all stops)–Lido and back (5am to 11.30pm, every 10 minutes from 7am to 10pm).

No 2 Circular line: runs San Zaccaria–Redentore–Zattere–Trochetto–Ferrovia–Rialto–Accademia–San Marco.

No 3/DM 'Diretto Murano' connects Piazzale Roma and the railway station to all five stops on Murano.

No 4.1 Circular line: runs Murano–Fondamente Nove–Ferrovia–Piazzale Roma–Redentore–San Zaccaria–Fondamente Nove–San Michele–Murano (6am to 10pm, every 20 minutes).

No 4.2 Circular line in reverse direction to No 4.1 (6.30am to 8.30pm, every 20 minutes).

No 5.1 & 5.2 Runs the same route, Lido–Fondamente Nove–Riva de Biasio–Ferrovia–Piazzale Roma–Zattere–San Zaccaria–Giardini–Lido, in opposite directions.

No 6 Circular line, limited stops, weekdays only: runs Piazzale Roma–Santa Marta–San Basilio–Zattere–Giardini–Sant'Elena–Lido.

No 8 Runs Giudecca–Zattere–Redentore–Giardini–Lido (May to early September only).

No 9 Runs Torcello–Burano and back (7am to 8.45pm, every 30 minutes).

No 11 A coordinated, hourly bus+*vaporetto* service from Lido to Pellestrina and Chioggia.

No 12 Runs Fondamente Nove–Murano–Mazzorbo–Burano–Torcello and back.

No 13 Runs Fondamente

Nove–Murano–Vignole–Sant'Erasmo–Treporti and back.

No 16 Connects Fusina Terminal with Zattere.

No 17 Car ferry: runs Tronchetto–Lido and back.

No 18 Runs Murano–Sant'Erasmo–Lido and back (infrequent and summer only).

No 20 Runs San Zaccaria–San Servolo–San Lazzaro degli Armeni and back. In summer it also connects with the Lido.

N All-stops night circuit, including Giudecca, Grand Canal, San Marco, Piazzale Roma and the train station (11.30pm to 4am, every 40 minutes).

NMU (Notturno Murano) Night service from Fondamente Nove to Murano (all stops).

NLN (Notturno Laguna Nord) Infrequent night service between Fondamente Nove, Murano, Burano, Torcello and Treporti.

Gondola

A gondola ride offers a view of Venice that is anything but pedestrian. Official daytime rates are €80 for 40 minutes (it's €100 for 35 minutes from 7pm to 8am), not including songs or tips. Additional time is charged in 20-minute increments (day/night €40/50). You may negotiate a price break in overcast weather or around noon. Agree on a price, time limit and singing in advance to avoid unexpected surcharges.

Gondolas cluster at *stazi* (stops) along the Grand Canal and near major monuments and tourist hot spots, but you can also book a pickup by calling **Ente Gondola** (☑041 528 50 75; www.gondola venezia.it).

Gondolas 4 All (Map p273; ☑328 2431382; www.gondolas4all.com; Fondamente Cossetti, Santa Croce), supported by the Gondoliers

Association, offers gondola rides to wheelchair users in a specially adapted gondola. Embarkation is from a wheelchair-accessible pier at Piazzale Roma.

Water Taxi

Licensed water taxis are a costly way to get around Venice, though they may prove handy when you're late for the opera or have lots of luggage. Fares can be metered or negotiated in advance. Official rates start at €15 plus €2 per minute, €5 extra if they're called to your hotel. There's a €10 surcharge for night trips (10pm to 6am), a €5 surcharge for additional luggage (above five pieces) and a €10 surcharge for each extra passenger above the first four. Note: if you order a water taxi through your hotel or a travel agent, you will be subject to a surcharge. Tipping isn't required.

Make sure your water taxi has the yellow strip with the licence number displayed. There are official water-taxi ranks at the airport, outside the train station, in front of **Piazzale Roma** (Map p273; Fondamente Cossetti) and at Tronchetto.

Even if you're in a hurry, don't encourage your taxi driver to speed through Venice – this kicks up *motoschiaffi* (motorboat wakes) that expose Venice's ancient foundations to degradation and rot.

Boat

Aspiring sea captains can take on the lagoon (not the Grand Canal or canals in the historic centre) in a rented boat from **Brussa** (Map p274; ☑041 71 57 87; www.brussaisboat.it; Fondamenta Labia 331; ☺7.30am-5.30pm Mon-Fri, to 12.30pm Sat & Sun; 🚊Ferrovia). You can hire a 7m boat (including fuel) that can carry up to six people for an hour (€43) or a day (€196), or make arrangements for longer periods. You don't need a licence, but you will be taken on a test run to see if you can manoeuvre and park; be sure to ask them to point out the four boat-petrol stations around Venice on a map.

Bicycle

Cycling is banned in central Venice. On the larger islands of Lido and Pellestrina, cycling is a pleasant way to get around and to reach distant beaches. **Lido on Bike** (☑041 526 80 19; www.lidoonbike.it; Gran Viale Santa Maria Elisabetta 21b, Lido; bicycle rental per 90min/day €5/9; ☺9am-7pm summer; 🚊Lido SME) is located near the *vaporetto* stop; ID is required for rental.

To sort out a set of wheels for a Veneto day trip contact **Veloce** (☑346 8471141; www.rentalbikeitaly.com; touring/mountain/racing bicycle per day €20/25/35; ☺8am-8pm), which offers a handy drop-

off and pick-up service from train stations and hotels.

Car

Obviously you can't drive in Venice proper, but the Lido and Pellestrina allow cars, and they can be the most efficient way of seeing far-flung sites across the Veneto. The car-rental companies **Avis** (☑041 523 73 77; www.avis.co.uk; Piazzale Roma 496g; ☺8.30am-3.30pm Mon-Sat; 🚊Piazzale Roma), **Europcar** (☑041 523 86 16; www.europcar.co.uk; Piazzale Roma 496h; ☺8.20am-12.30pm & 2-6pm Mon-Fri, 8.30am-12.30pm Sat, 9am-noon Sun; 🚊Piazzale Roma) and **Hertz** (☑041 528 40 91; www.hertz.co.uk; Piazzale Roma 496; ☺8.30am-12.30pm & 2.30-5.30pm Mon-Fri, 8.30am-12.30pm Sat; 🚊Piazzale Roma) all have offices both on Piazzale Roma and at Marco Polo Airport. Several companies operate in or near Mestre train station as well.

Monorail

Venice's wheelchair-accessible **People Mover monorail** (APM; www.avmspa.it; Piazzale Roma; per ride €1.50; ☺7.10am-10.50pm Mon-Sat, 8.10am-9.50pm Sun) connects the car parks on Tronchetto with the cruise-ship terminal and Piazzale Roma. Purchase tickets from the vending machines near the station.

Directory A–Z

Discount Cards

The tourist information portal, **Vènezia Unica** (📞041 24 24; www.veneziaunica.it), brings together a range of discount passes and services and enables you to tailor them to your needs and pre-purchase online. Services and passes on offer include the following:

➡ land and water transfers to the airport and cruise terminal;

➡ ACTV Tourist Travel Cards;

➡ museum and church passes;

➡ select parking;

➡ citywide wi-fi;

➡ prepaid access to public toilets.

If purchasing online you need to print out your voucher displaying your reservation number (PNR) and carry it with you, then simply present it at the various attractions for admission/access.

To use public transport, however, you will need to obtain a free card (you will need your PNR code to do this), which is then 'loaded' with the credit you have purchased. You can do this at the ACTV ticket machines at Marco Polo Airport, ticket desks at *vaporetto* (small passenger ferry) stops and Vènezia Unica offices.

Chorus Pass

The association of Venice churches offers a **Chorus Pass** (adult/student under 29 years €12/8) for single entry to 16 historic Venice churches any time within one year (excluding I Frari). Otherwise, admission to these individual churches costs €3. Passes are for sale at church ticket booths; proceeds support restoration and maintenance of churches throughout Venice.

City Passes

Silver, Gold and Platinum city passes are available from Vènezia Unica, covering a bewildering array of sights, tours and facilities in varying combinations. For keen sightseers with at least four to seven days on their hands these are the most useful:

City Pass (adult/junior €39.90/29.90) Valid for seven days, offering entrance to 11 civic museums, 16 Chorus churches, the Querini Stampalia Foundation and the Jewish Museum. It also includes free admission to the casino. The junior card applies to those aged between six and 29 years.

St Mark's City Pass (€27.90) A reduced version of the City Pass allowing entry to the three civic museums on Piazza San Marco, plus three churches on the Chorus Circuit and the Querini Stampalia Foundation.

Civic Museum Passes

The **Civic Museum Pass** (adult/reduced €24/18) is valid for six months and covers single entry to 11 civic museums, including Palazzo Ducale, Ca' Rezzonico, Ca' Pesaro, Palazzo Mocenigo, Museo Correr, the Museo del Vetro (Glass Museum) on Murano and the Museo del Merletto (Lace Museum) on Burano. Short-term visitors may prefer the **San Marco Pack** (adult/reduced €20/13), which covers four museums around Piazza San Marco (Palazzo Ducale, Museo Correr, Museo Archeologico Nazionale and Biblioteca Nazionale Marciana). Available from any civic museum and the tourist office.

Other Combined Tickets

For art aficionados planning to visit Ca' d'Oro and Palazzo Grimani, consider the **combined ticket** (adult/student/senior €10/8/free), which is good for three months.

A combined ticket to the Palazzo Grassi and Punta della Dogana costs adult/reduced €18/15.

Rolling Venice Card

Visitors aged 6 to 29 years should pick up the €6 Rolling Venice card (from tourist offices and most ACTV public transport ticket points), entitling purchase of a 72-hour public transport pass (€22) and discounts on airport transfers, museums, monuments and cultural events.

ISIC

An **International Student Identity Card** (www.isic. org) can get you discounted admission prices at some sights (such as the Scuola Grande di San Rocco) and help with cheap flights out of Italy, but ISIC benefits are limited in Venice.

Electricity

Type F
230V/50Hz

Type L
220V/50Hz

Emergency

For an ambulance, call ☑118, and for an emergency police call-out, ring ☑112.

Police Headquarters (☑041 271 55 11; http://questure.poli-ziadistato.it/it/venezia; Santa Croce 500; ☺8am-8pm Mon-Sat, to 2pm Sun; ☒Piazzale Roma Santa Chiara) Venice's main police station is off the beaten track in the ex-convent of Santa Chiara, just beyond Piazzale Roma.

Gay & Lesbian Travellers

Homosexuality is legal in Italy and generally accepted in Venice and the Veneto. ArciGay (www.arcigay.it), the national gay, lesbian, bisex-ual and transgender organi-sation, has information on the GLBT scene in Italy. The useful website www.gay.it (in Italian) lists gay and lesbian events across the country, but options in Venice are slim. Head to Padua for a wider range of gay-friendly nightlife and the nearest GLBT organisation, **ArciGay Tralaltro** (☑049 876 24 58; www.tralaltro.it; Corso Garibaldi 41; ☺5-7pm Mon, 10am-noon & 5-7pm Tue, Wed & Fri, 10am-noon Thu & Sat).

Internet Access

Wi-fi access is widely avail-able in hotels, B&Bs and rental apartments, and increasingly even in cafes. If for some reason you don't have access to wi-fi in your accommodation you can purchase a connection through **Vènezia Unica** (☑041 24 24; www.veneziauni-ca.it). The cost of connection is €5/15/20 per 24 hours/72 hours/one week.

Medical Services

The standard of health care in Venice is generally good, although the public system can be a little creaky at times. Some planning can save you trouble later. Bring medications in their original, clearly labelled containers. A signed and dated letter from your physician describing your medical conditions and medication, including gener-ic names, is a good idea.

For emergency treatment, head straight to the *pronto soccorso* (casualty) section of a public hospital, where you can also get emergency dental treatment (carry your ID/passport and any relevant insurance card). Pharmacists can give you valuable advice and sell over-the-counter medication for minor illnesses.

Opening hours of medical services vary, though most are open 8am to 12.30pm Monday to Friday, and some open for a couple of hours on weekday afternoons and Saturday mornings.

Emergency Clinics

Guardia Medica (☑041 238 5648) This service of night-time call-out doctors in Venice operates from 8pm to 8am on weekdays and from 10am the day before a holiday (includ-ing Sunday) until 8am the day after.

First Aid Point (Piazzale Roma; ☺8am-8pm; ☒Piazzale Roma) Dedicated to serving out-of-town visitors, this first-aid point performs diagnostics and minor surgery, issues drug prescriptions and referrals for further hospital treatment.

Ospedale SS. Giovanni e Paolo (☑041 529 41 11; www. ulss12.ve.it; Campo Zanipolo 6777, Castello; ☒Ospedale) Venice's main hospital; for emergency care and dental

PRACTICALITIES

Weights & Measures

The metric system is used for weights and measures.

Smoking

Since 2005 smoking in all closed public spaces (from bars to elevators, offices to trains and hotel rooms) has been banned.

Media

➜ *La Nuova Venezia* (www.nuovavenezia.it) is Venice's own city paper and is a good source of information on local events. *Il Gazzettino* (www.gazzettino.it) is the Veneto's major newspaper.

➜ State-owned RAI-1, RAI-2 and RAI-3 (www.rai.it) radio stations broadcast all over the country. Venice Classic Radio (www.veniceclassicradio.eu) mines the city's rich archive of classical, baroque and chamber music, while Teatro La Fenice has its own dedicated channel (www.lafenicechannel.it).

➜ Turn on the box to watch the state-run RAI-1, RAI-2 and RAI-3 and the main commercial channels – Canale 5, Italia 1 and Rete 4 – mostly run by Silvio Berlusconi's Mediaset company (www.mediaset.it).

---

treatment. The entrance is on the water near the Ospedale *vaporetto* stop.

Ospedale dell'Angelo (☑041 965 71 11; www.ulss12.ve.it; Via Paccagnella 11, Mestre) Vast modern hospital on the mainland.

Pharmacies

Most pharmacies in Venice are open from 9am to 12.30pm and 3.30pm to 7.30pm, and are closed on Saturday afternoons and Sundays. Information on rotating late-night pharmacies is posted in pharmacy windows and listed online and in the free magazine *Un Ospite di Venezia* (www.unospitedivenezia.it).

Money

There are ATMs (*bancomats*) that accept international cards throughout the city, with many near Piazza San Marco, the Rialto Bridge and the train station. There's a daily limit on withdrawals of €250.

Changing Money

You can exchange money in banks, at post offices or in bureaux de change. The latter charge commission, which sometimes exceeds 10% on travellers cheques. Travelex has branches at the airport, Piazza San Marco and beside the Rialto Bridge on Riva del Fero.

Credit Cards

Visa and MasterCard are among the most widely recognised, but others such as Cirrus and Maestro are also accepted. American Express and Diners Club are not universally accepted, so check in advance.

Tipping

Cafes and bars Most Italians just leave small change (€0.10 to €0.20 is fine).

Hotels At least €2 per bag or night, for porter, maid or room service.

Restaurants Tips of 10% are standard – though check to see that a tip hasn't already been added to your bill, or included in the flat *coperto* (cover) charge.

Transport Tips may be given for gondolas and water-taxi service graciously provided, especially if singing is involved.

Opening Hours

The hours listed here are a general guide; individual establishments can vary. Also note that hours at shops, bars and restaurants can be somewhat flexible in Venice, as they are in the rest of Italy.

Banks 8.30am to 1.30pm and 3.30pm to 5.30pm Monday to Friday, though hours vary; some open Saturday mornings.

Restaurants Noon to 2.30pm and 7pm to 10pm.

Shops 10am to 1pm and 3.30pm to 7pm (or 4pm to 7.30pm) Monday to Saturday.

Supermarkets 9am to 7.30pm Monday to Saturday.

Post

There are a couple of post offices in every Venetian *sestiere* (district), with addresses and hours online at www.poste.it.

Post Office (www.poste.it; Calle Larga de l'Ascension 1241; ☺8.20am-1.35pm Mon-Sat; ⊠San Marco) A convenient regional branch located behind Piazza San Marco.

Public Holidays

For Venetians, as for most Italians, the main holiday periods are summer (July and especially August), the Christmas–New Year period and Easter. Restaurants, shops and most other activity also grind to a halt around Ferragosto (Feast of the Assumption; 15 August).

Capodanno/Anno Nuovo (New Year's Day) 1 January

Epifania/Befana (Epiphany) 6 January

Lunedì dell'Angelo (Good Friday) March/April

Pasquetta/Lunedì dell'Angelo (Easter Monday) March/April

Giorno della Liberazione (Liberation Day) 25 April

Festa del Lavoro (Labour Day) 1 May

Festa della Repubblica (Republic Day) 2 June

Ferragosto (Feast of the Assumption) 15 August

Ognissanti (All Saints' Day) 1 November

Immaculata Concezione (Feast of the Immaculate Conception) 8 December

Natale (Christmas Day) 25 December

Festa di Santo Stefano (Boxing Day) 26 December

Taxes & Refunds

If you're staying overnight within Venice, expect to pay €3.50 to €5 in tourist tax per person for up to five nights (additional nights are free). Children aged 10 to 15 receive a 50% discount. Children under 10 and hostels are exempt from the tax.

Value-added tax (VAT) of around 22% is added to purchases over €155 in Italy.

Telephone

The dialling code for Italy is ☑39. The city code for Venice is ☑041. The city code is an integral part of the number and must always be dialled. Toll-free (freephone) numbers are known as *numeri verdi* and usually start with ☑800.

International Calls

The cheapest options for calling internationally are free or low-cost computer programs such as Skype, FaceTime and Viber, cut-rate call centres or international dialling cards, which are sold at news-stands and tobacconists. All of these offer cheaper calls than the Telecom payphones.

If you're calling an international number from an Italian phone, you must dial ☑00 to get an international line, then the relevant country and city codes, followed by the telephone number.

To call Venice from abroad, call the international access number for Italy (☑011 in the United States, ☑00 from most other countries), Italy's country code ☑39, then the Venice area code ☑041, followed by the telephone number.

Mobile Phones

➡ Italy uses GSM 900/1800, which is compatible with the rest of Europe and Australia but not with North America GSM 1900 or the Japanese system.

➡ Of the main mobile-phone companies, TIM and Vodafone have the best coverage in Venice.

➡ To buy a SIM card you'll need to supply your passport and the address of your accommodation.

➡ Prepaid SIM cards are readily available at telephone and electronics stores. Purchase recharge cards at tobacconists and news-stands.

➡ As of June 2017 roaming charges have been abolished within the EU.

Time

Italy is one hour ahead of GMT/UTC during winter and two hours ahead during the daylight-saving period, which runs from the last Sunday in March to the last Sunday in October. Note that times are often listed using a 24-hour clock (ie 2pm is written as 14.00).

Toilets

Most bars and cafes reserve the restroom for paying customers only. Look before you sit: even in women's bathrooms, some toilets don't have seats, and sometimes there is no toilet at all – just a hole with footrests.

Nineteen public toilets (€1.50) are scattered around Venice near tourist attractions (look for the 'WC Toilette' signs), and are usually open from 7am to 7pm (sometimes closing earlier in winter). All of them have facilities for people with disabilities.

Tourist Information

Vènezia Unica (☑041 24 24; www.veneziaunica.it) runs all tourist information services and offices in Venice. It provides information on sights, itineraries, day trips, transport, special events, shows and temporary exhibitions. Discount passes can be prebooked on its website.

Tourist Offices

Airport Tourist Office (Arrivals Hall, Marco Polo Airport; ☺8.30am-7pm)

Piazzale Roma Tourist Office
(⊠lost & found 041 272 2179; ground fl ASM car park, Piazzale Roma; ⊘7.30am-7.30pm; ⊠Piazzale Roma)

San Marco Tourist Office
(Piazza San Marco 71f; ⊘9am-7pm; ⊠San Marco)

Stazione Santa Lucia Tourist Office (⊘7am-9pm; ⊠Ferrovia)

Travellers with Disabilities

With nearly 400 footbridges and endless stairs, Venice is not an easy place to visit for travellers with disabilities. But the city has made an effort to provide access to key monuments.

In its favour, Venice is a compact city. Water ferries are the most effective way to access sites and avoid bridges. Planning ahead is the key. The most accessible tourist office is the one off Piazza San Marco.

Of the other islands, Murano, Burano, the Lido and Torcello are all fairly easy to access.

In addition, with the appropriate ID, most museums offer free or discounted admission to visitors with disabilities and their companion.

Download Lonely Planet's free Accessible Travel guide from http://lptravel.to/AccessibleTravel.

Maps

A printable 'Accessible Venice' map is available from the tourist office. The map delimits the area around each water-bus stop that can be accessed without crossing a bridge. In addition, the website provides information on accessible attractions, including 12 'barrier-free' itineraries, which can also be downloaded from the website. The maps are also available from the tourist offices.

Public Transport

Vaporetti (small passenger ferries) have access for wheelchairs, offering an easy way to get around town. Passengers in wheelchairs travel for just €1.50, while their companion travels free.

Virtually all local buses, including those on the Lido, as well as those connecting Venice with mainland, are also wheelchair accessible. The monorail is wheelchair-accessible and for wheelchair users who are keen to experience a gondola ride, **Gondolas 4 All** (Map p273; ⊠328 2431382; www.gondolas-4all.com; Fondamenta Cossetti, Santa Croce) offer specially adapted boats.

Disabled Assistance Office
(Sala Blu;⊠800 906 060; Stazione Venezia Santa Lucia; ⊘7am-9.30pm) This is located at platform 4 in Venice's Santa Lucia train station.

Organisations

Accessible Italy (www.accessibleitaly.com) A San Marino–based company that specialises in holiday services for people with disabilities. This is the best port of call.

L'Altra Venezia (www.laltra-venezia.it; walking tours €70, thematic tours from €200, boat tours from €480) Offers lagoon tours in specially adapted boats that can accommodate multiple wheelchairs and up to 10 people.

Visas

Citizens of EU countries, Iceland, Norway and Switzerland do not need a visa to visit Italy. Nationals of some other countries, including Australia, Brazil, Canada, Israel, Japan, New Zealand and the USA, do not require visas for tourist visits of up to 90 days. For more information and a list of countries whose citizens require a visa, check the website of the Italian foreign ministry (www.esteri.it).

The standard tourist visa issued by Italian consulates is the Schengen visa, valid for up to 90 days. This visa is valid for travel in Italy and in several other European countries with which Italy has a reciprocal visa agreement (see www.eurovisa.info for the full list). These visas are not renewable inside Italy.

Women Travellers

Of the major travel destinations in Italy, Venice is among the safest for women, given the low rate of violent crime of any kind in Venice proper. Chief annoyances would be getting chatted up by other travellers in Piazza San Marco or on the more popular Lido beaches, usually easily quashed with a *'Non mi interessa'* (I'm not interested), or that universally crushing response, the exasperated eye roll.

Language

Standard Italian is spoken throughout Italy, but regional dialects are an important part of identity in many areas, and this also goes for Venice. You'll no doubt hear some Venetian (also known as Venet) spoken or pick up on the local lilt that standard Italian is often spoken with. This said, you'll have no trouble being understood – and your efforts will be much appreciated – if you stick to standard Italian, which we've also used in this chapter.

Italian pronunciation is straightforward as most sounds are also found in English.

Note that ai is pronounced as in 'aisle', ay as in 'say', ow as in 'how', dz as the 'ds' in 'lids', and that r is a strong, rolled sound. Keep in mind that Italian consonants can have a stronger, emphatic pronunciation – if the consonant is written as a double letter, it should be pronounced a little stronger, eg *sonno son*·no (sleep) and *sono so*·no (I am). If you read our coloured pronunciation guides as if they were English (with the stressed syllables in italics), you'll be understood.

BASICS

Italian has two words for 'you' – use the polite form *Lei* lay if you're talking to strangers, officials or people older than you. With people familiar to you or younger than you, you can use the informal form *tu* too.

In Italian, all nouns and adjectives are either masculine or feminine, and so are the articles *il/la* eel/la (the) and *un/una* oon/oo·na (a) that go with the nouns.

WANT MORE?

For in-depth language information and handy phrases, check out Lonely Planet's *Italian phrasebook*. You'll find it at **shop. lonelyplanet.com**, or you can buy Lonely Planet's iPhone phrasebooks at the Apple App Store.

In this chapter the polite/informal and masculine/feminine options are included where necessary, separated with a slash and indicated with 'pol/inf' and 'm/f'.

Hello.	*Buongiorno.*	bwon·*jor*·no
Goodbye.	*Arrivederci.*	a·ree·ve·*der*·chee
Yes./No.	*Sì./No.*	see/no
Excuse me.	*Mi scusi.* (pol)	mee *skoo*·zee
	Scusami. (inf)	*skoo*·za·mee
Sorry.	*Mi dispiace.*	mee dees·*pya*·che
Please.	*Per favore.*	per fa·*vo*·re
Thank you.	*Grazie.*	*gra*·tsye
You're welcome.	*Prego.*	*pre*·go

How are you?
Come sta/stai? (pol/inf) ko·me sta/stai

Fine. And you?
Bene. E Lei/tu? (pol/inf) be·ne e lay/too

What's your name?
Come si chiama? pol ko·me see *kya*·ma
Come ti chiami? inf ko·me tee *kya*·mee

My name is ...
Mi chiamo ... mee *kya*·mo ...

Do you speak English?
Parla/Parli *par*·la/*par*·lee
inglese? (pol/inf) een·*gle*·ze

I don't understand.
Non capisco. non ka·*pee*·sko

ACCOMMODATION

I'd like to book a room, please.
Vorrei prenotare una vo·*ray* pre·no·*ta*·re *oo*·na
camera, per favore. *ka*·me·ra per fa·*vo*·re

Is breakfast included?
La colazione è la ko·la·*tsyo*·ne e
compresa? kom·*pre*·sa

How much is it per ...?	*Quanto costa per ...?*	*kwan*·to *kos*·ta per ...
night	*una notte*	*oo*·na *no*·te
person	*persona*	per·*so*·na

KEY PATTERNS

To get by in Italian, mix and match these simple patterns with words of your choice:

When's (the next flight)?
A che ora è   a ke o·ra e
(il prossimo volo)? (eel pro·see·mo vo·lo)

Where's (the station)?
Dov'è (la stazione)? do·ve (la sta·tsyo·ne)

I'm looking for (a hotel).
Sto cercando   sto cher·kan·do
(un albergo).   (oon al·ber·go)

Do you have (a map)?
Ha (una pianta)?   a (oo·na pyan·ta)

Is there (a toilet)?
C'è (un gabinetto)? che (oon ga·bee·ne·to)

I'd like (a coffee).
Vorrei (un caffè). vo·ray (oon ka·fe)

I'd like to (hire a car).
Vorrei (noleggiare vo·ray (no·le·ja·re
una macchina).   oo·na ma·kee·na)

Can I (enter)?
Posso (entrare)?   po·so (en·tra·re)

Could you please (help me)?
Può (aiutarmi),   pwo (a·yoo·tar·mee)
per favore?   per fa·vo·re

Do I have to (book a seat)?
Devo (prenotare   de·vo (pre·no·ta·re
un posto)?   oon po·sto)

air-con	*aria condizionata*	a·rya kon·dee·tsyo·na·ta
bathroom	*bagno*	ba·nyo
campsite	*campeggio*	kam·pe·jo
double room	*camera doppia con letto matrimoniale*	ka·me·ra do·pya kon le·to ma·tree·mo·nya·le
guesthouse	*pensione*	pen·syo·ne
hotel	*albergo*	al·ber·go
single room	*camera singola*	ka·me·ra seen·go·la
youth hostel	*ostello della gioventù*	os·te·lo de·la jo·ven·too
window	*finestra*	fee·nes·tra

DIRECTIONS

Where's ...?
Dov'è ...?   do·ve ...

What's the address?
Qual'è l'indirizzo? kwa·le leen·dee·ree·tso

Could you please write it down?
Può scriverlo,   pwo skree·ver·lo
per favore?   per fa·vo·re

Can you show me (on the map)?
Può mostrarmi   pwo mos·trar·mee
(sulla pianta)?   (soo·la pyan·ta)

at the corner	*all'angolo*	a·lan·go·lo
behind	*dietro*	dye·tro
far	*lontano*	lon·ta·no
in front of	*davanti a*	da·van·tee a
left	*a sinistra*	a see·nee·stra
near	*vicino*	vee·chee·no
next to	*accanto a*	a·kan·to a
opposite	*di fronte a*	dee fron·te a
right	*a destra*	a de·stra
straight ahead	*sempre diritto*	sem·pre dee·ree·to

EATING & DRINKING

I'd like to reserve a table.
Vorrei prenotare   vo·ray pre·no·ta·re
un tavolo.   oon ta·vo·lo

What would you recommend?
Cosa mi consiglia? ko·za mee kon·see·lya

What's in that dish?
Quali ingredienti kwa·li een·gre·dyen·tee
ci sono in   chee so·no een
questo piatto?   kwe·sto pya·to

What's the local speciality?
Qual'è la specialità kwa·le la spe·cha·lee·ta
di questa regione?   dee kwe·sta re·jo·ne

That was delicious!
Era squisito!   e·ra skwee·zee·to

Cheers!
Salute!   sa·loo·te

Please bring the bill.
Mi porta il conto, mee por·ta eel kon·to
per favore?   per fa·vo·re

I don't eat ...	*Non mangio ...*	non man·jo ...
eggs	*uova*	wo·va
fish	*pesce*	pe·she
nuts	*noci*	no·chee
(red) meat	*carne (rossa)*	kar·ne (ro·sa)

Key Words

bar	*locale*	lo·ka·le
bottle	*bottiglia*	bo·tee·lya
breakfast	*prima colazione*	pree·ma ko·la·tsyo·ne
cafe	*bar*	bar
cold	*freddo*	fre·do
dinner	*cena*	che·na

drink list	lista delle bevande	lee·sta de·le be·van·de
fork	forchetta	for·ke·ta
glass	bicchiere	bee·kye·re
grocery store	alimentari	a·lee·men·ta·ree
hot	caldo	kal·do
knife	coltello	kol·te·lo
lunch	pranzo	pran·dzo
market	mercato	mer·ka·to
menu	menù	me·noo
plate	piatto	pya·to
restaurant	ristorante	ree·sto·ran·te
spicy	piccante	pee·kan·te
spoon	cucchiaio	koo·kya·yo
vegetarian (food)	vegetariano	ve·je·ta·rya·no
with	con	kon
without	senza	sen·tsa

Meat & Fish

beef	manzo	man·dzo
chicken	pollo	po·lo
duck	anatra	a·na·tra
fish	pesce	pe·she
herring	aringa	a·reen·ga
lamb	agnello	a·nye·lo
lobster	aragosta	a·ra·gos·ta
meat	carne	kar·ne
mussels	cozze	ko·tse
oysters	ostriche	o·stree·ke
pork	maiale	ma·ya·le
prawn	gambero	gam·be·ro
salmon	salmone	sal·mo·ne
scallops	capasante	ka·pa·san·te
seafood	frutti di mare	froo·tee dee ma·re
shrimp	gambero	gam·be·ro
squid	calamari	ka·la·ma·ree
trout	trota	tro·ta
tuna	tonno	to·no
turkey	tacchino	ta·kee·no
veal	vitello	vee·te·lo

Fruit & Vegetables

| apple | mela | me·la |
| beans | fagioli | fa·jo·lee |

Signs

Entrata/Ingresso	Entrance
Uscità	Exit
Aperto	Open
Chiuso	Closed
Informazioni	Information
Proibito/Vietato	Prohibited
Gabinetti/Servizi	Toilets
Uomini	Men
Donne	Women

cabbage	cavolo	ka·vo·lo
capsicum	peperone	pe·pe·ro·ne
carrot	carota	ka·ro·ta
cauliflower	cavolfiore	ka·vol·fyo·re
cucumber	cetriolo	che·tree·o·lo
fruit	frutta	froo·ta
grapes	uva	oo·va
lemon	limone	lee·mo·ne
lentils	lenticchie	len·tee·kye
mushroom	funghi	foon·gee
nuts	noci	no·chee
onions	cipolle	chee·po·le
orange	arancia	a·ran·cha
peach	pesca	pe·ska
peas	piselli	pee·ze·lee
pineapple	ananas	a·na·nas
plum	prugna	proo·nya
potatoes	patate	pa·ta·te
spinach	spinaci	spee·na·chee
tomatoes	pomodori	po·mo·do·ree
vegetables	verdura	ver·doo·ra

Other

bread	pane	pa·ne
butter	burro	boo·ro
cheese	formaggio	for·ma·jo
eggs	uova	wo·va
honey	miele	mye·le
ice	ghiaccio	gya·cho
jam	marmellata	mar·me·la·ta
noodles	pasta	pas·ta
oil	olio	o·lyo
pepper	pepe	pe·pe
rice	riso	ree·zo
salt	sale	sa·le

Numbers

1	uno	oo·no
2	due	doo·e
3	tre	tre
4	quattro	kwa·tro
5	cinque	cheen·kwe
6	sei	say
7	sette	se·te
8	otto	o·to
9	nove	no·ve
10	dieci	dye·chee
20	venti	ven·tee
30	trenta	tren·ta
40	quaranta	kwa·ran·ta
50	cinquanta	cheen·kwan·ta
60	sessanta	se·san·ta
70	settanta	se·tan·ta
80	ottanta	o·tan·ta
90	novanta	no·van·ta
100	cento	chen·to
1000	mille	mee·le

soup	minestra	mee·nes·tra
soy sauce	salsa di soia	sal·sa dee so·ya
sugar	zucchero	tsoo·ke·ro
vinegar	aceto	a·che·to

Drinks

beer	birra	bee·ra
coffee	caffè	ka·fe
(orange) juice	succo (d'arancia)	soo·ko (da·ran·cha)
milk	latte	la·te
red wine	vino rosso	vee·no ro·so
soft drink	bibita	bee·bee·ta
tea	tè	te
(mineral) water	acqua (minerale)	a·kwa (mee·ne·ra·le)
white wine	vino bianco	vee·no byan·ko

EMERGENCIES

Help!
Aiuto! — a·yoo·to

Leave me alone!
Lasciami in pace! — la·sha·mee een pa·che

I'm lost.
Mi sono perso/a. (m/f) — mee so·no per·so/a

Call the police!
Chiami la polizia! — kya·mee la po·lee·tsee·a

Call a doctor!
Chiami un medico! — kya·mee oon me·dee·ko

Where are the toilets?
Dove sono i gabinetti? — do·ve so·no ee ga·bee·ne·tee

I'm sick.
Mi sento male. — mee sen·to ma·le

SHOPPING & SERVICES

I'd like to buy ...
Vorrei comprare ... — vo·ray kom·pra·re ...

I'm just looking.
Sto solo guardando. — sto so·lo gwar·dan·do

Can I look at it?
Posso dare un'occhiata? — po·so da·re oo·no·kya·ta

How much is this?
Quanto costa questo? — kwan·to kos·ta kwe·sto

It's too expensive.
È troppo caro/a. (m/f) — e tro·po ka·ro/a

Can you lower the price?
Può farmi lo sconto? — pwo far·mee lo skon·to

There's a mistake in the bill.
C'è un errore nel conto. — che oo·ne·ro·re nel kon·to

ATM	bancomat	ban·ko·mat
post office	ufficio postale	oo·fee·cho pos·ta·le
tourist office	ufficio del turismo	oo·fee·cho del too·reez·mo

TIME & DATES

What time is it?	Che ora è?	ke o·ra e
It's one o'clock.	È l'una.	e loo·na
It's (two) o'clock.	Sono le (due).	so·no le (doo·e)
Half past (one).	(L'una) e mezza.	(loo·na) e me·dza

in the morning	di mattina	dee ma·tee·na
in the afternoon	di pomeriggio	dee po·me·ree·jo
in the evening	di sera	dee se·ra

yesterday	ieri	ye·ree
today	oggi	o·jee
tomorrow	domani	do·ma·nee

Monday	lunedì	loo·ne·dee
Tuesday	martedì	mar·te·dee
Wednesday	mercoledì	mer·ko·le·dee
Thursday	giovedì	jo·ve·dee
Friday	venerdì	ve·ner·dee
Saturday	sabato	sa·ba·to

Sunday	domenica	do·me·nee·ka
January	gennaio	je·na·yo
February	febbraio	fe·bra·yo
March	marzo	mar·tso
April	aprile	a·pree·le
May	maggio	ma·jo
June	giugno	joo·nyo
July	luglio	loo·lyo
August	agosto	a·gos·to
September	settembre	se·tem·bre
October	ottobre	o·to·bre
November	novembre	no·vem·bre
December	dicembre	dee·chem·bre

TRANSPORT

At what time does the ... leave/arrive?	A che ora parte/ arriva ...?	a ke o·ra par·te/ a·ree·va ...
boat	la nave	la na·ve
bus	l'autobus	low·to·boos
city ferry	il vaporetto	eel va·po·re·to
ferry	il traghetto	eel tra·ge·to
plane	l'aereo	la·e·re·o
train	il treno	eel tre·no
bus stop	fermata dell'autobus	fer·ma·ta del ow·to·boos
one-way	di sola andata	dee so·la an·da·ta
platform	binario	bee·na·ryo
return	di andata e ritorno	dee an·da·ta e ree·tor·no
ticket	biglietto	bee·lye·to
ticket office	biglietteria	bee·lye·te·ree·a
timetable	orario	o·ra·ryo
train station	stazione ferroviaria	sta·tsyo·ne fe·ro·vyar·ya

Does it stop at ...?
Si ferma a ...? — see fer·ma a ...

Please tell me when we get to ...
Mi dica per favore quando arriviamo a ... — mee dee·ka per fa·vo·re kwan·do a·ree·vya·mo a ...

I want to get off here.
Voglio scendere qui. — vo·lyo shen·de·re kwee

I'd like	Vorrei	vo·ray
to hire	noleggiare	no·le·ja·re
a/an ...	un/una ... (m/f)	oon/oo·na ...

bicycle	bicicletta (f)	bee·chee·kle·ta
car	macchina (f)	ma·kee·na
motorbike	moto (f)	mo·to
bicycle pump	pompa della bicicletta	pom·pa de·la bee·chee·kle·ta
helmet	casco	kas·ko
mechanic	meccanico	me·ka·nee·ko
petrol/gas	benzina	ben·dzee·na
service station	stazione di servizio	sta·tsyo·ne dee ser·vee·tsyo

Is this the road to ...?
Questa strada porta a ...? — kwe·sta stra·da por·ta a ...

(How long) Can I park here?
(Per quanto tempo) Posso parcheggiare qui? — (per kwan·to tem·po) po·so par·ke·ja·re kwee

I have a flat tyre.
Ho una gomma bucata. — o oo·na go·ma boo·ka·ta

I've run out of petrol.
Ho esaurito la benzina. — o e·zow·ree·to la ben·dzee·na

VENETIAN BASICS

A few choice words in Venetian (or Venet, as it is also known) will endear you to your hosts, especially at happy hour. To keep up with the *bacaro* banter, try mixing them with your Italian:

Yes, sir!	Siorsi!
Oh, no!	Simènteve!
You bet!	Figuràrse!
How lucky!	Bénpo!
Perfect.	In bròca.
Welcome!	Benvegnù!
Cheers!	Sanacapàna!
Watch out!	Òcio!

cheap wine	brunbrùn
glass of wine	ombra (lit: a shade)
happy hour	giro di ombra (lit: round of shade)
to become Venetian	Venexianàrse
Venetian	venexiano/a (m/f)
you guys	voàltri

FOOD GLOSSARY

alla busara Venetian prawn sauce

anatra wild lagoon duck

baccala mantecato creamed cod

bigoli Venetian whole-wheat pasta

branzino sea bass

bruscandoli wild hop buds

canoce mantis prawn

capasanta/canastrelo large/small scallops

carpaccio finely sliced raw beef

castraure baby artichokes from St Erasmo Island

cicheti Venetian tapas

contorni vegetable dishes

crostini open-faced sandwiches

crudi Venetian sushi

curasan croissant

dolci sweets

dolci tipici venexiani typical Venetian sweets

fatto in casa house-made

fegato alla veneziana liver lightly pan-roasted in strips with browned onion and a splash of red wine

filetto di San Pietro fish with artichokes or *radicchio trevisano*

fritole sweet fritters

fritto misto e pattatine lightly fried lagoon seafood and potatoes

frittura seafood fry

gnochetti mini-gnocchi

granseola spider crab

krapfen doughnuts

latte di soia soy milk

lingue di suocere biscuit; 'mother-in-law's tongues'

macchiatone espresso liberally 'stained' with milk

margherite ripiene all'astice com sugo di pesce ravioli stuffed with lobster in fish sauce

moeche soft-shell crabs

moscardini baby octopus

mozzarella di bufala fresh buffalo-milk mozzarella

orecchiette 'little ear' pasta

pan dei dogi 'doges' bread'; hazelnut-studded biscuits

panino sandwich

pastine pastry

peoci mussels

pizza margherita pizza with basil, mozzarella and tomato

pizzette mini-pizzas

polpette meatballs

radicchio trevisano feathery red radicchio

risotto di pesce fish risotto

saor Venice's tangy marinade

sarde sardines

sarde in saor sardines fried in tangy onion marinade with pine nuts and sultanas

senza limone without lemon

seppie squid

seppie in nero squid in its own ink

sfogio sole

sopressa Venetian soft salami

sopressa crostini soft salami on toast

sorbetto sorbet

spaghetti alla búsera spaghetti with shrimp sauce

surgelati frozen

tramezzini sandwiches on soft bread often with mayo-based condiments

verdure vegetables

zaletti cornmeal biscuits with sultanas

zuppa di pesce thick seafood soup

Behind the Scenes

SEND US YOUR FEEDBACK

We love to hear from travellers – your comments keep us on our toes and help make our books better. Our well-travelled team reads every word on what you loved or loathed about this book. Although we cannot reply individually to your submissions, we always guarantee that your feedback goes straight to the appropriate authors, in time for the next edition. Each person who sends us information is thanked in the next edition – the most useful submissions are rewarded with a selection of digital PDF chapters.

Visit **lonelyplanet.com/contact** to submit your updates and suggestions or to ask for help. Our award-winning website also features inspirational travel stories, news and discussions.

Note: We may edit, reproduce and incorporate your comments in Lonely Planet products such as guidebooks, websites and digital products, so let us know if you don't want your comments reproduced or your name acknowledged. For a copy of our privacy policy visit lonelyplanet.com/privacy.

OUR READERS

Many thanks to Lisa Bradshaw, Dawn Jonas and Sheila Penfold who used the last edition and wrote to us with helpful hints, useful advice and interesting anecdotes.

WRITER THANKS

Paula Hardy

Grazie mille to all the fun and fashionable Venetians who spilled the beans on their remarkable city: Paola dalla Valentina, Costanza Cecchini, Sara Porro, Lucia Cattaneo, Monica Cesarato, Francesca Giubilei, Luca Berta, Marco Secchi and Nan McElroy. Thanks, too, to co-authors Peter and Marc for their contributions, and to Anna Tyler for all the support. Finally, much love to Rob for sharing the beauty of the *bel paese*.

Peter Dragicevich

It turns out that it's not hard to find willing volunteers to keep you company on an extended research assignment in Venice, especially when it coincides with Carnevale. Many thanks to my Venice crew of Christine Henderson, Hamish Blennerhassett and Sarah Welch for much masked fun and many good meals. Special thanks to Christine for the unpaid but much appreciated translation services.

ACKNOWLEDGEMENTS

Illustration pp60-61 by Javier Martinez Zarracina.

Cover photograph: Gondolas and the Bridge of Sighs at dusk. Matteo Colombo / AWL ©

256

THIS BOOK

This 10th edition of Lonely Planet's *Venice & the Veneto* guidebook was researched and written by Paula Hardy, Peter Dragicevich and Marc Di Duca. The previous two editions were written by Cristian Bonetto and Paula Hardy. This guidebook was produced by the following:

Destination Editor
Anna Tyler
Product Editors Ross Taylor, Catherine Naghten
Senior Cartographer
Anthony Phelan
Book Designer Clara Monitto
Assisting Editors Michelle Coxall, Grace Dobell, Shona Gray, Victoria Harrison, Gabrielle Innes, Monique Perrin, Martine Power, Sarah

Reid, Gabrielle Stefanos, Fionnuala Twomey
Cartographer Valentina Kremenchutskaya
Assisting Book Designer Virginia Moreno
Cover Researcher Naomi Parker
Thanks to Hannah Cartmel, Kate Mathews, Anne Mason, Tony Wheeler, Amanda Williamson

See also separate subindexes for:

🍴 **EATING P259**

🍷 **DRINKING & NIGHTLIFE P260**

☆ **ENTERTAINMENT P261**

🔒 **SHOPPING P261**

🏃 **SPORTS & ACTIVITIES P262**

🛏 **SLEEPING P262**

Index

Sights 000
Map Pages **000**
Photo Pages **000**

✗ EATING

⭐ **ENTERTAINMENT**

🛍 **SHOPPING**

Venice & the Veneto Maps

Sights

- 🏖 Beach
- 🐦 Bird Sanctuary
- ⛩ Buddhist
- 🏰 Castle/Palace
- ✝ Christian
- ☯ Confucian
- 🕉 Hindu
- ☪ Islamic
- Jain
- ✡ Jewish
- ❗ Monument
- 🏛 Museum/Gallery/Historic Building
- Ruin
- Shinto
- Sikh
- Taoist
- Winery/Vineyard
- Zoo/Wildlife Sanctuary
- Other Sight

Activities, Courses & Tours

- Bodysurfing
- Diving
- Canoeing/Kayaking
- Course/Tour
- Sento Hot Baths/Onsen
- Skiing
- Snorkelling
- Surfing
- Swimming/Pool
- Walking
- Windsurfing
- Other Activity

Sleeping

- Sleeping
- Camping
- Hut/Shelter

Eating

- Eating

Drinking & Nightlife

- Drinking & Nightlife
- Cafe

Entertainment

- Entertainment

Shopping

- Shopping

Information

- 💲 Bank
- Embassy/Consulate
- Hospital/Medical
- @ Internet
- Police
- Post Office
- Telephone
- Toilet
- Tourist Information
- Other Information

Geographic

- Beach
- Gate
- Hut/Shelter
- Lighthouse
- Lookout
- ▲ Mountain/Volcano
- Oasis
- Park
-)(Pass
- Picnic Area
- Waterfall

Population

- Capital (National)
- Capital (State/Province)
- City/Large Town
- Town/Village

Transport

- Airport
- Border crossing
- Bus
- Cable car/Funicular
- Cycling
- Ferry
- Metro station
- Monorail
- Parking
- Petrol station
- S-Bahn/Subway station
- Taxi
- T-bane/Tunnelbana station
- Train station/Railway
- Tram
- Tube station
- U-Bahn/Underground station
- Other Transport

Routes

- Tollway
- Freeway
- Primary
- Secondary
- Tertiary
- Lane
- Unsealed road
- Road under construction
- Plaza/Mall
- Steps
- Tunnel
- Pedestrian overpass
- Walking Tour
- Walking Tour detour
- Path/Walking Trail

Boundaries

- International
- State/Province
- Disputed
- Regional/Suburb
- Marine Park
- Cliff
- Wall

Hydrography

- River, Creek
- Intermittent River
- Canal
- Water
- Dry/Salt/Intermittent Lake
- Reef

Areas

- Airport/Runway
- Beach/Desert
- Cemetery (Christian)
- Cemetery (Other)
- Glacier
- Mudflat
- Park/Forest
- Sight (Building)
- Sportsground
- Swamp/Mangrove

Note: Not all symbols displayed above appear on the maps in this book

MAP INDEX

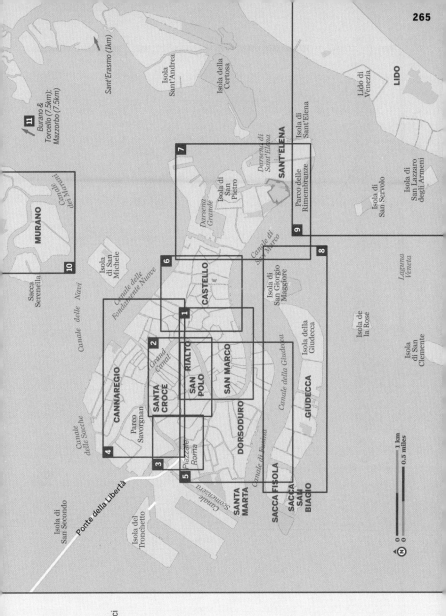

Key on p268

SAN MARCO

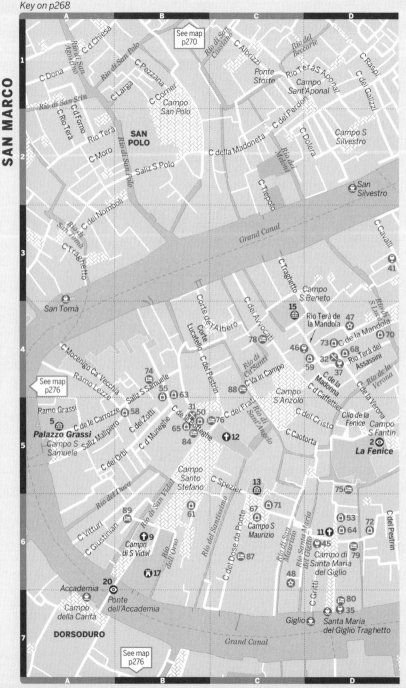

See map
p270

See map
p276

See map
p276

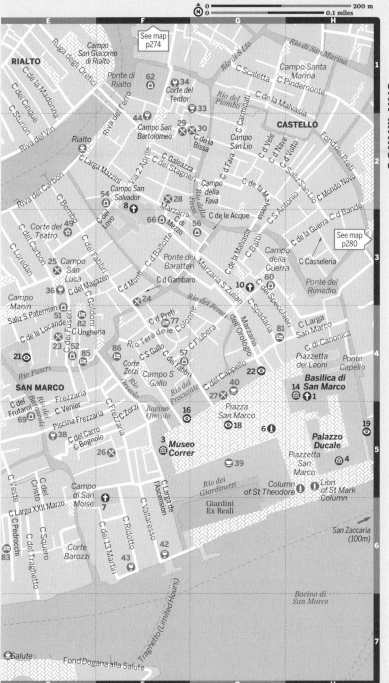

SAN MARCO *Map on p266*

SAN MARCO

SAN POLO

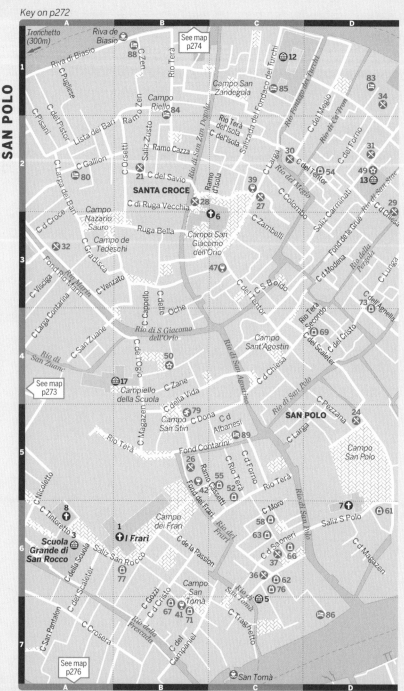

Tronchetto
(300m)
Riva de Biasio
Riva di Biasio
C Zen
88
C. Pugliese
See map
p274
Rio Terà
C dei Pistor
Campo
Riello
84
Rio Terà
del Fondaco dei Turchi
12
Campo San
Zandegola
85
C Pisani
C Gallion
Lista dei Bari
Ramo Zen
Saliz Zusto
C Orsetti
Ramo Cazza
Rio Terà
del'Isola
C del'Isola
Salizzada del Fondaco dei Turchi
83
34
C dei Megio
31
C del Forno
C Larga dei Bari
80
21
C del Savio
C di Stin Zen Degolà
Ramo
d'Isola
30
C del Tentor
54
C Larga
Rio del Megio
49
13
SANTA CROCE
39
C Colombo
Saliz Carminati
29
C d'Chiesa
C di Ruga Vecchia
28
6
27
C Zambelli
Rio di San Stae
Campo
Nazario
Sauro
Campo de
Tedeschi
Ruga Bella
Campo San
Giacomo
dell'Orio
Fond de la Grue
Rio della
Pergola
32
C Gradisca
47
C del C S Boldo
C Lunga
C d Croce
C Venzato
C del Tentor
C dell'Agnella
73
Fond Rio Marin
Rio Marin
C Cappello
C delle
Oche
Rio Terà
secondo
69
C del Cristo
C Visciga
C Larga Contarina
Rio di S Giacomo
dell'Orio
Campo
Sant'Agostin
C del Scaleter
C San Zuane
50
C de l'Ogio
C d Chiesa
See map
p273
17
C Zane
Campiello
della Scuola
C della Vida
79
Rio di San Polo
C Pezzana
24
Campo
San Stin
C Dona
C d
Albanesi
89
SAN POLO
Rio Terà
C Magazen
Fond Contarini
C Larga
Campo
San Polo
26
Rama Cassetti
55
C d Forno
C Rio Terà
52
Rio Terà
C Nicoletto
42
Fond dei Frari
8
C Tintoretto
C Moro
58
7
61
3
Scuola
Grande di
San Rocco
1
I Frari
Campo
dei Frari
63
Saliz S Polo
C d Magazen
Rio dei Frari
C d Saoneri
66
77
Saliz San Rocco
C de la Passion
37
C della Scuola
36
62
C del Scaleter
Campo
San
Tomà
5
76
86
C San Pantalon
C Gozzi
C d Cristo
67
41
71
C Traghetto
C Crosera
Rio della Frescada
C del Campaniel
See map
p276
San Tomà

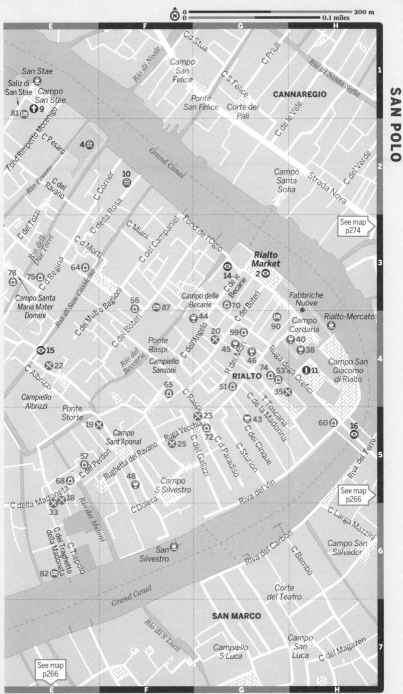

SAN POLO & SANTA CROCE *Map on p270*

SAN POLO

SANTA CROCE WEST

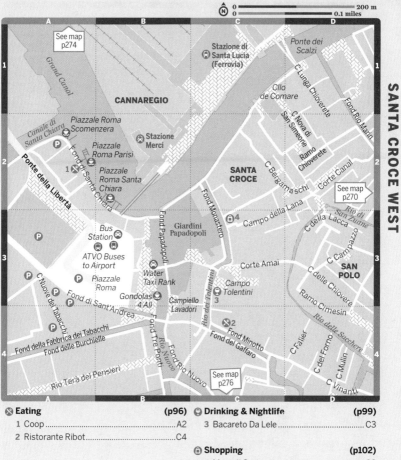

CANNAREGIO

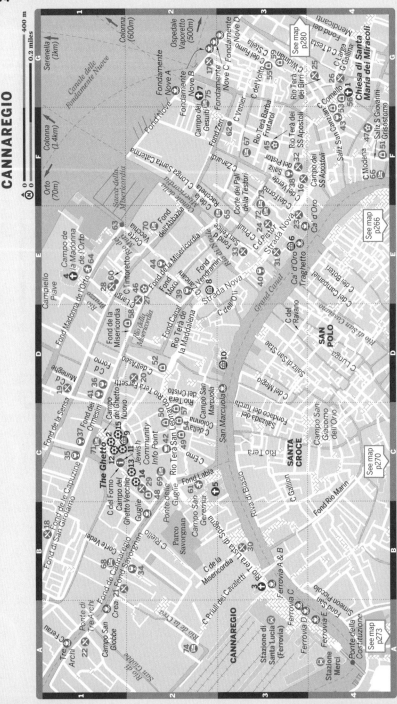

CANNAREGIO

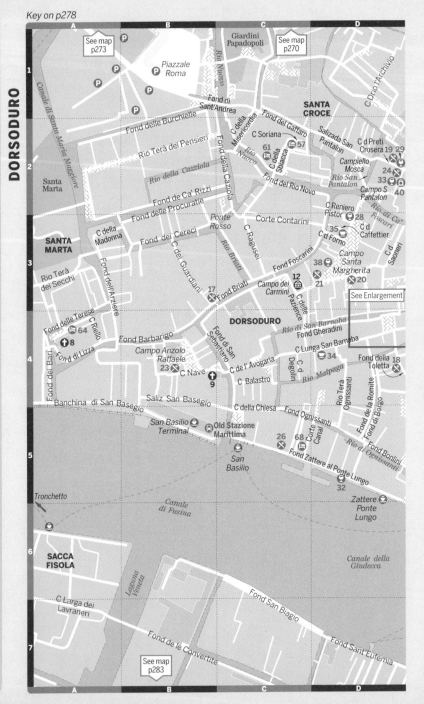

DORSODURO

SANTA CROCE

SANTA MARTA

Santa Marta

DORSODURO

SACCA FISOLA

Piazzale Roma

Giardini Papadopoli

See map p273

See map p270

See map p283

See Enlargement

Tronchetto

San Basilio

Zattere Ponte Lungo

Canale di Santa Marta Maggiore

Canale di Fusina

Canale della Giudecca

Laguna Veneta

Fond delle Burchielle
Rio Terà dei Pensieri
Rio della Cazziola
Fond de Ca' Rizzi
Fond delle Procuratie
Fond di Sant'Andrea
Fond della Misericordia
C Soriana
Fond del Gaffaro
C della Sbiacca
Fond Nuovo
Fond del Rio Novo
Salizada San Pantalon
Campiello Mosca
Rio San Pantalon
Campo S Pantalon
C d Preti Crosera
C Reniero Pistor
C d Caffettier
C d Forno
Corte Contarini
Ponte Rosso
Fond dei Cereci
C della Madonna
C dei Guardiani
Rio Terà dei Secchi
Fond dell'Arziere
Fond delle Terese
C Rielo
Fond dei Bari
Fond di Lizza
Fond Barbarigo
Campo Anzolo Raffaele
C Nave
C de l' Avogaria
C della Chiesa
Saliz San Basegio
Banchina di San Basegio
San Basilio Terminal
Old Stazione Marittima
Fond Zattere al Ponte Lungo
Fond di San Sebastiano
C Balastro
Fond Ognissanti
Corte Canal
C d Degolin
Rio Malpaga
Rio Terà Ognissanti
Fond de la Romite
Fond di Borgo
Fond Bonlini
Rio di Ognissanti
C Larga dei Lavraneri
Fond San Biagio
Fond de le Convertite
Fond Sant'Eufemia
Campo dei Carmini
Campo Santa Margherita
C delle Pazience
C Lunga San Barnaba
Rio di San Barnaba
Fond Gheradini
Fond Foscarini
Fond Briati
Rio Briati
Rio Rauseu
Rio Nuovo
Fond della Cazziola
Rio San Pantalon
Rio di Ca' Foscari
C d Saoneri
Fond della Toletta
Fond del Rio Nuovo
C Drio l'Archivio

DORSODURO

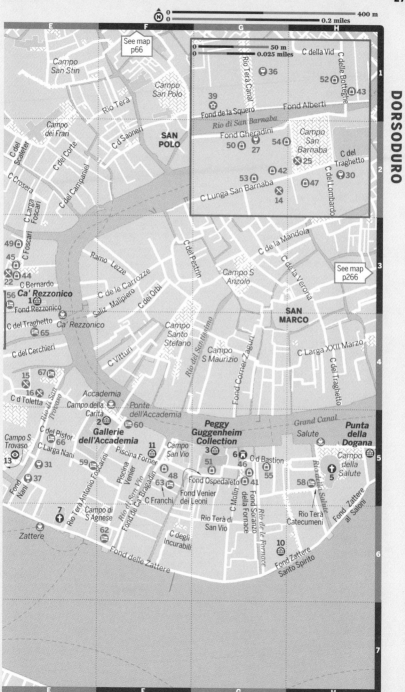

N
0 — 400 m
0 — 0.2 miles

See map
p66

Campo
San Stin

Campo
San Polo

SAN
POLO

0 — 50 m
0 — 0.025 miles

C della Vid

52 🔵 C delle Botteghe
🔵 36   43 🔵

39 ⭐

Fond de la Squero   Fond Alberti

Rio di San Barnaba

Rio Terà Canal

Fond Gheradini   Campo
San
Barnaba

50 🔵   54 🔵
27   ❌ 25   C del
Traghetto

Campo
dei Frari

C del
Scaleter

C Larga
Corte

C del Campaniel

C C Saoneri

53 🔵   42 🔵   47 🔵   30 🔵

C Lunga San Barnaba   ❌ 14   C del Lombardo

C Crosera
C Larga
Foscari

49 🔵
45
🔵 44
22 C Bernardo

56 🔵 **Ca' Rezzonico**
1 🏛
Fond Rezzonico

C del Traghetto
🔵 65

Ramo Lezze

C de le Carrozze

Saliz Malipiero

C dei Orbi

Campo S
Anzolo

C del Pestrin

C de la Mandola

C de la Verona

See map
p266

SAN
MARCO

C del Cerchieri

C Vitturi

Campo
Santo
Stefano

Campo
S Maurizio

C Larga XXII Marzo

C del Traghetto

15 🔵 67 🔵
16 ❌
C d Toletta

Accademia

Campo della
Carità

Ponte
dell'Accademia

2 🏛 🔵 60

**Gallerie
dell'Accademia**

Campo S
Trovaso

C del Pistor
C Larga Nani

13 🔵

🔵 31   59 🔵

37 🔵

Piscina Forner

Piscina
Venier

11 🔵
Campo
San Vio

48 🔵
63 🔵

C Franchi

Fond Ospedaleto

Fond Venier
dei Leoni

**Peggy
Guggenheim
Collection**

3 🏛   6 🏛
51   46 🔵
55
41 🔵

C d Bastion

Grand Canal

Salute 🔵   **Punta
della
Dogana**

Campo
della
Salute

58 🔵   5 🔵

7 🔵

Campo di
S Agnese

62 🔵

C degli
Incurabili

C Molin

Rio Terà di
San Vio

Fond Soranzo
della Fornace

Rio de le Fornace

Rio della Salute

Fond Zattere
al Saloni

Rio Terà
Catecumeni

Zattere

Fond Nani

Fond delle Zattere

10 🔵
Fond Zattere
Santo Spirito

DORSODURO *Map on p276*

CASTELLO *Map on p280*

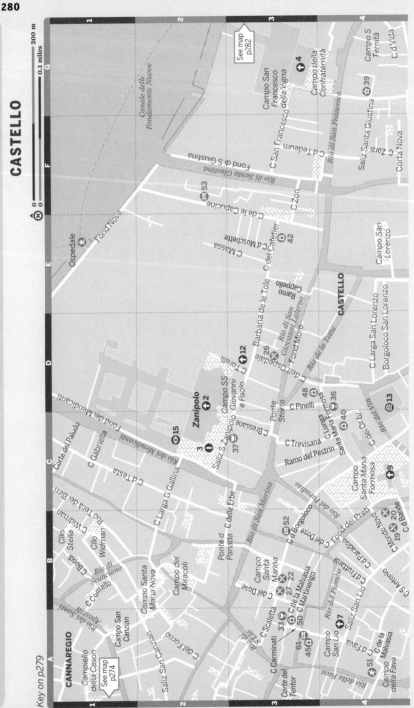

CASTELLO

Key on p279

0   0.1 miles
0   200 m

CANNAREGIO

See map p274

See map p282

CASTELLO

Zanipolo

Campo San Francesco della Vigna

Campo della Confraternità

Campo S Ternità

Ospedale

Fond Nove

Canale delle Fondamente Nuove

Rio di Santa Giustina

Fond di S Giustina

C San Francesco

C d Tedeum

Rio di San Francesco

Saliz Santa Giustina

Campo San Lorenzo

C de le Capucine

C del Cafetier

C d Moschette

C Massa

Campo SS Giovanni e Paolo

C Torelli

Barbaria de le Tole

Ramo Cappello

Rio di San Giovanni Laterano

Fond Moro

Rio de la Tetta

C Larga San Lorenzo

Borgoloco San Lorenzo

C d Vida

Corta Nova

C Zorzi

C Zon

Fond dell'Ospedale

Ponte Storto

C Pinelli

C Trevisana

Ramo del Pestrin

C Lunga Santa Maria Formosa

C de' Or bi

Rio del Vin

Campo Santa Maria Formosa

Corte del Paludo

Fond del Mendicanti

Rio dei Mendicanti

C Gabriella

C d Testa

C Larga G Gallina

Saliz S Zanipolo

C Bressana

C delle Erbe

Ponte d Panada

C d Paludo

Cllo Bordi

Cllo Stella

Cllo Widman

C Widman

Rio Tera dei Biri

Rio di Scanciano

C Cornello

Campo Santa Maria Nova

Campo dei Mirácoli

Campo San Canzian

Saliz San Canzian

C del Forno

Rio dei Santi

Rio dei Apóstoli

Rio di San Marina

C del Dose

C d Borgoloco

Fond dei Preti

C Mondo Novo

C d Paradiso

C Fruttaiol

Rio del Piombo

C S Antonio

Campo Santa Marina

C de la Malvasia

C Martinengo

C del Dose

C Scaletta

C Carminati

Corte del Tentor

Rio S Lio

Campo San Lio

Saliz San Lio

C de Fava

C de la Malvasia

Campo della Fava

Rio della Fava

Rio del Paradiso

C d Bande

C Trevisana

15

2

3

12

53

42

26

48

36

40

13

9

52

27 22

33

50

61

45

7

51

19

20

39

4

CASTELLO

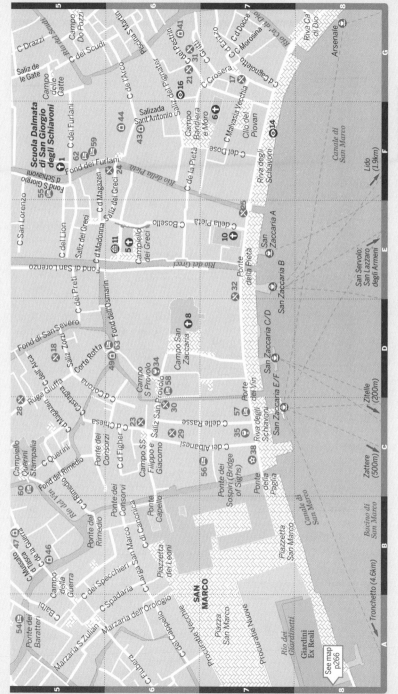

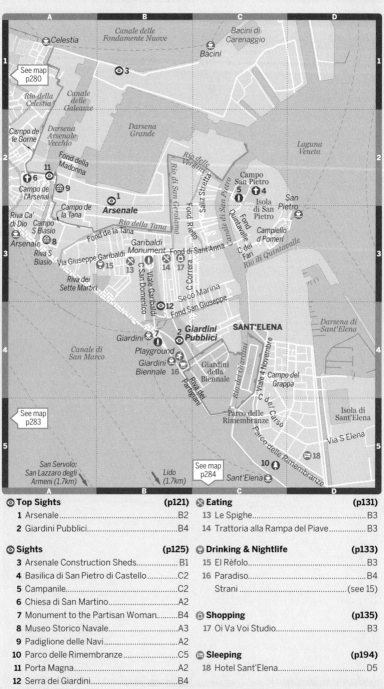

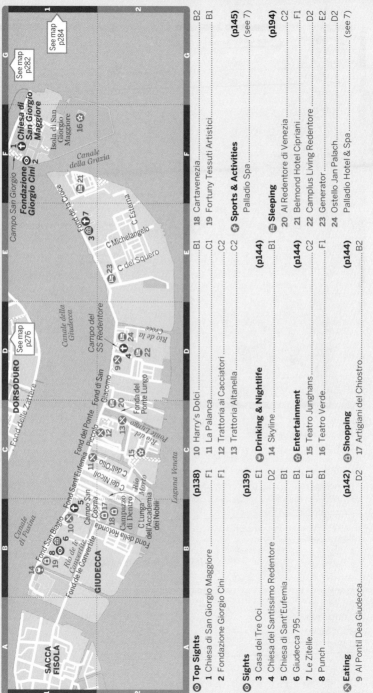

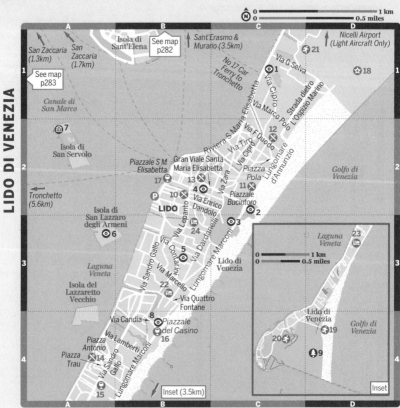

⊙ **Sights** (p141)

1 Antico Cimitero Israelitico.......................C1
2 Blue Moon...C2
3 Grand Hotel des Bains C3
4 Grande Albergo Ausonia &
Hungaria B2
5 Lido di Venezia.......................................B3
6 Monastero di San Lazzaro degli
Armeni...A3
7 Museo del Manicomio.............................A2
8 Palazzo della Mostra del Cinema B4
9 Pineta degli Alberoni..............................D4

🍽 **Eating** (p143)

10 al Mercà...B2
11 El Pecador...C2
12 La Favorita..C2
13 Magiche Voglie.......................................B2
14 Mercato Settimanale del Lido................A4

🍷 **Drinking & Nightlife** (p144)

15 Da Cri Cri e Tendina...............................A4
16 Lion's Bar..B4
17 Villa Laguna..B2

🎭 **Entertainment** (p144)

18 Pachuka...D1

🏆 **Sports & Activities** (p145)

Acquolina Cooking School.............(see 24)
19 Bagni Alberoni..D4
20 Circolo Golf Venezia...............................C4
21 Heliair.it..D1

🛏 **Sleeping** (p194)

22 Albergo Quattro Fontane.......................B3
23 Le Garzette...D3
24 Villa Ines..B3

MURANO

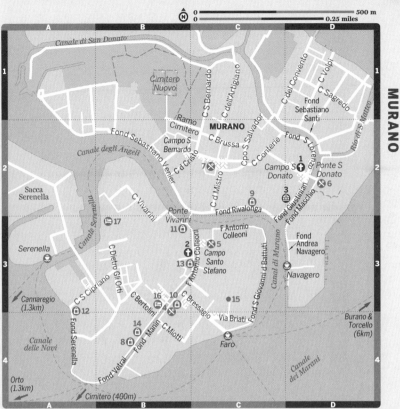

BURANO & TORCELLO

Our Story

A beat-up old car, a few dollars in the pocket and a sense of adventure. In 1972 that's all Tony and Maureen Wheeler needed for the trip of a lifetime – across Europe and Asia overland to Australia. It took several months, and at the end – broke but inspired – they sat at their kitchen table writing and stapling together their first travel guide, *Across Asia on the Cheap*. Within a week they'd sold 1500 copies. Lonely Planet was born.

Today, Lonely Planet has offices in Franklin, London, Melbourne, Oakland, Dublin, Beijing and Delhi, with more than 600 staff and writers. We share Tony's belief that 'a great guidebook should do three things: inform, educate and amuse'.

Our Writers

Paula Hardy

Dorsoduro, San Polo & Santa Croce Paula Hardy is an independent travel writer and editorial consultant, whose work for Lonely Planet and other flagship publications has taken her from nomadic camps in the Danakil Depression to Seychellois beach huts and the jewel-like bar at the Gritti Palace on the Grand Canal. Over two decades, she has authored more than 30 Lonely Planet guidebooks and spent five years as commissioning editor of Lonely Planet's bestselling Italian list. These days you'll find her hunting down new hotels, hip bars and up-and-coming artisans primarily in Milan, Venice and Marrakesh. Get in touch at www.paulahardy.com. Paula also wrote the Venice Today and The Fragile Lagoon chapters, along with the Plan Your Trip and Survival Guide sections.

Peter Dragicevich

San Marco; Cannaregio; Castello; Giudecca, Lido & the Southern Islands; Murano, Burano & the Northern Islands After a successful career in niche newspaper and magazine publishing, both in his native New Zealand and in Australia, Peter finally gave into Kiwi wanderlust, giving up staff jobs to chase his diverse roots around much of Europe. Over the last decade he's written literally dozens of guidebooks for Lonely Planet on an oddly disparate collection of countries, all of which he's come to love. He once again calls Auckland, New Zealand his home – although his current nomadic existence means he's often elsewhere. Peter also wrote the History, Architecture and The Arts chapters.

Marc Di Duca

Day Trips from Venice A travel author for the last decade, Marc has worked for Lonely Planet in Siberia, Slovakia, Bavaria, England, Ukraine, Austria, Poland, Croatia, Portugal, Madeira and on the Trans-Siberian Railway, as well as writing and updating tens of other guides for other publishers. When not on the road, Marc lives between Sandwich, Kent and Mariánské Lázně in the Czech Republic with his wife and two sons.

Published by Lonely Planet Global Limited
CRN 554153
10th edition – January 2018
ISBN 978 1 78657 260 8
© Lonely Planet 2018   Photographs © as indicated 2018
10 9 8 7 6 5 4 3 2 1
Printed in China